D1555158

THE CENTER FOR CHINESE STUDIES
at the University of California, Berkeley,
supported by the East Asian Institute
(University of California, Berkeley) and the
State of California, is the unifying
organization for social science and inter-
disciplinary research on modern China.

MARXIST LITERARY THOUGHT IN CHINA:
THE INFLUENCE OF CH'Ü CH'IU-PAI

This volume is sponsored by
the Center for Chinese Studies
University of California, Berkeley

Marxist Literary Thought in China

The Influence of Ch'ü Ch'iu-pai

Paul G. Pickowicz

UNIVERSITY OF
CALIFORNIA PRESS

Berkeley • Los Angeles • London

University of California Press
Berkeley and Los Angeles, California

University of California Press, Ltd.
London, England

© 1981 by The Regents of the University of California

Printed in the United States of America

1 2 3 4 5 6 7 8 9

Library of Congress Cataloging in Publication Data

Pickowicz, Paul G.
  Marxist literary thought in China. The Influence
of Ch'ü Ch'iu-pai
  Bibliography: p.
  Includes index.
  1. Ch'ü, Ch'iu-pai, 1899-1935—Criticism and interpretation. 2. Communism and literature. 3. Chinese
literature—20th century—History and criticism.
4. Criticism—China. I. Title.
PL2755.C5Z77   895.1'5'09   80-19054
ISBN 0-520-04030-9

To Maurice Meisner and Gene Rich

Contents

Preface

For many years now I have been fascinated by the intellectual history of modern China. Many important intellectual developments have taken place in China during the past century, but nothing has attracted my attention more than the spectacular modern literary movement that commenced with the iconoclastic "New Culture" whirlwind of 1915. The modern literary movement was explosive and controversial because it developed during a period of extraordinary cultural cosmopolitanism in China, and was, therefore, profoundly influenced by a variety of previously unknown Western literary ideas. The first phase of that movement, when romanticism, realism, and other liberal Western schools were making a revolutionary impact on Chinese literary life, is beginning to receive a significant amount of scholarly attention. By the late 1920s, however, liberal influence began to give way to Marxism, another prominent Western tradition of literary thought. But despite the fact that Marxism dominated the Chinese literary scene in the 1930s, and continues to do so to the present day, little is known about the manner in which Chinese Marxist literary thought developed in the early days.

The Marxist phase of China's modern literary movement is of interest to the historian because leftist writers in China were concerned with social and political problems and thus were drawn to literary theories that seemed to define the all-important relationship between literature and society. Socially conscious writers in China disagreed on many issues, but as a group they were more active politically than writers who participated in other twentieth-century social reform movements. Indeed, many of the important questions that need to be asked about the modern literary movement, and the Marxist trend in particular, are related to its essentially political orientation. What, for example, are the obligations of socially conscious writers who find themselves in a revolutionary environment? What moral and political dilemmas do they face when they feel compelled to integrate politics and art? In what ways do literary revolutions (and revolutionary literary works) contribute to mass political movements that aim at a radical transformation of society? To what extent is cultural revolution a prerequisite for fundamental socio-economic change? The Chinese case is important to scholars interested in the general subject of writers and revolution—for the simple reason that these questions were debated with unusual intensity in the intellectual centers of Peking and Shanghai during the 1920s and 1930s.

The study of the development of Chinese Marxist literary thought can, of course, be approached in a number of ways. But in view of the fact that virtually all revolutionary writers in China regarded themselves as Marxists of one sort or another and used Marxist analytical categories to discuss China's cultural problems, it is both logical and necessary to understand and explain their literary thought in terms of Marxist theory itself. It would be extremely difficult to evaluate the various Chinese Marxist literary schools without referring to the diverse and often contradictory Western Marxist literary tradition with which they consciously identified. To understand Chinese Marxist writers it is necessary to take them seriously not only as Marxists, but as thinkers who deliberately looked abroad for answers to China's modern problems. Bonnie McDougall is correct when she writes: "In their aspirations and also in their achievements, the writers of the May Fourth movement brought China into *world literature* and underlined the necessity for the new literary movement to be studied in the *world context*, not as an isolated phenomenon unique to China."[1]

The purpose of this study, therefore, is to look at Chinese Marxist literary thought in relation to the Western tradition of Marxist literary thought. Why were Chinese writers attracted to Marxist theory, and how did they interpret it? When one examines the Western Marxist writings on literature known in China in the 1920s and 1930s, it becomes evident that the most esteemed authorities were Marx, Engels, Georg Plekhanov, Lenin, Trotsky, Anatoly Lunacharsky, and a number of critics associated with the intriguing Russian "proletarian cultural" school. It is sometimes difficult to determine why an individual Chinese writer was attracted by the literary thought of any single Western Marxist figure; but if the fragmentary writings of the men mentioned above are viewed as a whole, several basic problems

1. Bonnie S. McDougall, "The Impact of Western Literary Trends," in Merle Goldman, ed., *Modern Chinese Literature in the May Fourth Era* (Cambridge: Harvard University Press, 1977), p. 61. Emphasis added.

appear to be addressed time and again in their work, problems that were obviously important to Chinese readers. From Marx to Lunacharsky, complex questions are raised concerning the nature of art, the social role of the artist, the impact of capitalism on artistic culture, the manner in which the artistic heritage of the past should be perceived, and the function of art in distinctively socialist revolutionary movements.

As social revolutionaries, Chinese Marxists approached the problem of the "nature" of art in a rather narrow way. While they were concerned about purely aesthetic matters, they tended to be preoccupied with the problem of defining the relationship between art and society. What factors were responsible for the appearance of artistic culture in a given historical era? A second issue, the "role" of the individual artist, is a closely related problem. What role, they asked, does the artist play in society, or, more to the point, during a radical transformation of society?

As students of capitalism who were congregated in industrialized cities like Shanghai, they also wanted to know more about Western Marxist perspectives on the impact of capitalist socio-economic development on artistic life. As sophisticated young intellectuals who had been trained abroad and influenced by the masterpieces of Western bourgeois literature, they were understandably curious about the manner in which Western Marxist thinkers regarded the "treasures" of the past. Should they be rejected or embraced enthusiastically? Finally, they were concerned about the direction in which the revolutionary literary movement in China was headed. What, they asked, is the role of art during the "transition to socialism"? What is "proletarian" art? Indeed, what would constitute artistic life in the utopian society of the future?

Chinese Marxist literary intellectuals were interested in these questions in the 1920s and 1930s because they seemed relevant to China's contemporary cultural problems, but it is important to recognize that the amorphous Western Marxist texts they studied provided no "orthodox" answers. On the contrary, Western Marxist literary thinkers differed sharply on these matters. It is necessary, therefore, to explore the relationship between the patterns of intellectual contention present in Western Marxist literary thought and the intellectual disputes that divided leftist writers in China. Western Marxist ideas about literature and society are thus referred to in appropriate places throughout this study. But since I have already written on the Western Marxist literary ideas known in China in the May Fourth era, it seems unnecessary to open this book with yet another lengthy introduction to theory. Those who want to read a more systematic discussion of the Marxist intellectual context, or at least that portion of it familiar to Chinese writers, may wish to consult my monograph entitled *Marxist Literary Thought and China: A Conceptual Framework.*[2]

When I began this study, one of my first tasks was to determine what means I would use to reach conclusions about the evolution of Chinese Marxist literary thought. From the outset it seemed that one way to approach the subject of revolution and writers in China would be to study the intellectual development of Ch'ü Ch'iu-pai, China's first important Marxist literary thinker. Thanks to the pioneering scholarship of Benjamin Schwartz, Ch'ü's role as a major leader of the Chinese Communist Party has been carefully researched, but his prominence as a political leader has obscured the fact that his most creative and enduring contribution to the Chinese revolution was in the field of Marxist literary thought. This study is essentially an intellectual biography, but one that seeks to analyze the general development of China's modern literary movement, in both its liberal and Marxist phases, from the point of view of a literary specialist who was a youthful participant in the May Fourth Movement and a key figure in most of the early Marxist debates on the nature of the relationship between literature and revolution.

Initially, I was attracted to Ch'ü Ch'iu-pai because he was the dominant Marxist literary thinker of the period and because no major study of his literary thought had been done in the West. It was not until I read the introduction to the Peking edition of his selected works prepared in the early 1950s that I began to suspect that I was dealing with an unusual figure. In an essay that made a number of predictable attempts to glorify and celebrate his contributions to the development of Chinese Marxist literary thought, several unexpected notes of caution were included. Ch'ü's "evaluation" of the "accomplishments and significance of the May Fourth literary revolution," it was said, was not entirely correct. This remark intrigued me, and I soon discovered what the editors meant. In their estimation, Ch'ü had been excessively critical of the celebrated (and sacred) May Fourth generation of revolutionary writers! Although it was some time before I was able to piece together the details of Ch'ü's critique, I was delighted to know that I was doing research on a man who was viewed by his Marxist colleagues as a critic of the highly regarded leftist literary movement. And in making such criticisms he spoke for neither the Communist Party nor any of the feuding leftist literary factions. I realized that a study of Chü Ch'iu-pai's literary thought would not only shed light on his own interpretation of Marxist theory, but would also focus attention on his critical review of the history of the modern literary movement.

2. Paul G. Pickowicz, *Marxist Literary Thought and China: A Conceptual Framework* (Berkeley: The Center for Chinese Studies, University of California, Berkeley, 1980).

At an earlier stage of my research, when I tended to view Ch'ü as merely a vehicle for discussing the exciting literary issues of the 1930s, I was anxious to plunge directly into the period when Ch'ü led the well-known Shanghai League of Left-wing Writers. But the more I read about his early years, the more I appreciated the fact that Ch'ü was an exceptionally interesting and sensitive person. More important, it became clear that Ch'ü's literary thought of the early 1930s and his critical evaluation of the promethean May Fourth generation could be understood only when they were seen in the light of his early intellectual growth. He was in a position to criticize the failings of his colleagues because he had experienced similar problems in earlier phases of his own development. On the other hand, many of the intellectual concerns he expressed in his final years had been nagging him since his youth. To appreciate the significance of Ch'ü's literary thought of the 1930s it thus is necessary to be familiar with his pre-Marxist intellectual predispositions and the circumstances under which he developed an interest in Marxist literary thought.

Most of this book is devoted to a discussion of Chinese Marxist literary thought in the period from 1931 to 1935. During this time Ch'ü Ch'iu-pai wrote voluminously and was widely regarded as the intellectual leader of the leftist literary movement, but when one first reads his works their significance is not immediately apparent. He wrote on a variety of topics, but never systematically. His works sometimes appear to be unrelated fragments. Upon closer inspection, however, a number of patterns of thought can be discerned. Ch'ü left behind no single *magnum opus*, but he had a great deal to say about the history of the modern literary movement, the various ways in which Western Marxist literary thought had been interpreted in China, and the failings of leftist writers who were struggling with the problem of the relationship between art and society.

Ch'ü's writings on revolution and literary intellectuals are of theoretical interest because they raise issues not treated in the Western Marxist texts that were known in China, issues related to problems that arise in distinctively non-European modern historical environments. Above all, Ch'ü was concerned with one overriding problem, the phenomenon of Europeanization. In his view, the question of cultural Europeanization was at the very heart of the issues confronting politically conscious Chinese writers. He believed that patterns of Europeanization were responsible for factionalism within the leftist literary movement, and served to widen the already enormous gap that separated revolutionary writers from the masses whose interests they professed to be serving. Ch'ü suggested that before Chinese writers could determine the nature of their role in the revolution, they would have to reevaluate their attitude toward European culture, including the Marxist tradition. The theme that runs through almost all of Ch'ü's writing is the tension between the elements of cultural iconoclasm and political nationalism in the literary thought of most leftist writers. In what ways, he asked, might revolutionaries approach problems related to cultural continuity in an age of great cultural discontinuity?

Ch'ü Ch'iu-pai was the first serious Marxist literary thinker to appear in China or any other non-European precapitalist society. Despite their failings, his writings tell us a good deal about the condition of the leftist literary movement, the school that has dominated modern literary life in China from the mid-1920s to the present day. Ch'ü's writings force us to reconsider a number of assumptions about the early impact of Marxist literary thought on China. For example, this study will show that Marxist literary thought did not have a monolithic or one-dimensional intellectual impact on the Chinese literary scene. Not only did the Communist Party have no coherent policy toward the arts in the period before 1935, but leftist literary groups disagreed profoundly on many of the major intellectual problems posed by Marxist literary theory. It is also necessary to question the assumption that the acceptance of Marxist literary thought in China in the late 1920s represented a radical departure from the liberal literary traditions of the early May Fourth period. This book will suggest that Chinese interpretations of Western Marxist literary thought were shaped, in large part, by Western ideas about literature and society that had won favor in China during the high tide of May Fourth liberalism. In short, the Marxist literary trend should be viewed in the context of the entire May Fourth literary tradition.

Ch'ü Ch'iu-pai's writings are important because he was the first major figure to raise critical questions about the transition from liberal to Marxist literary thought in China, and to analyze the failings of the leftist literary movement. His writings are of contemporary relevance because the issues he raised were not resolved in his lifetime. On the contrary, they continue to be debated today.

Acknowledgments

Now that this study of post-May Fourth literary developments is finished, it seems appropriate to begin by acknowledging the early encouragement and assistance I received at the University of Wisconsin, where the problems posed by the May Fourth intellectual revolution are taken very seriously. It would have been impossible to begin this study without the advice of Chow Tse-tsung, Edward Friedman, Lin Yü-sheng, and, above all, Maurice Meisner. Their friendship and guidance made my years at Wisconsin extremely pleasant and intellectually rewarding.

The research and writing of this book were facilitated by the patience and cooperation of individuals at several academic institutions. I especially wish to thank the staff members and administrators of the history department of the University of Wisconsin, the Universities Service Centre in Hong Kong, the John King Fairbank Center for East Asian Research at Harvard University, the Chinese University of Hong Kong, and the history department of the University of California, San Diego. I am also grateful for the financial support I received from the history department and East Asian Area Studies Committee of the University of Wisconsin, the history department and the Academic Senate of the University of California, San Diego, the Regents of the University of California, and particularly the Joint Committee on Contemporary China of the Social Science Research Council and the American Council of Learned Societies, whose generosity permitted me to devote full time to this book during the 1976-1977 academic year.

I should also like to thank the following friends and colleagues who read part or all of the manuscript and offered me their valuable advice: Stanley Chodorow, Donald Gibbs, Merle Goldman, Fredric Jameson, Leo Ou-fan Lee, Philip Lilienthal, Herbert Marcuse, Maurice Meisner,

Allan Mitchell, Earl Pomeroy, Harry Scheiber, Benjamin Schwartz, Jack Service, and Frederic Wakeman. Thanks are also due to my two former graduate assistants, Leslie Bolinger, who typed the manuscript, and George Alexandrov, who provided me with English translations of all the Russian-language sources used in this work.

My book is dedicated to Professors Maurice Meisner and Gene Rich. I will always be indebted to them for their inspirational teaching, enduring friendship, and unselfish humanity.

Without the help of the individuals and organizations mentioned here, this book could never have been completed. Needless to say, any errors of fact or interpretation are entirely my own responsibility.

Abbreviations

CCPWC *Ch'ü Ch'iu-pai wen-chi* [Selected literary works of Ch'ü Ch'iu-pai], Peking: Jen-min wen-hsueh ch'u-pan-she, 1953-1954. 4 vols.

CPSL Chang Ching-lu, ed., *Chung-kuo hsien-tai ch'u-pan shih-liao* [Documentary sources on publications of contemporary China], Peking: Chung-hua shu-chü, 1954-1957.

HSSL Ch'ü Ch'iu-pai, trans., Lu Hsün, ed., *Hai-shang shu-lin* [Shanghai miscellany], Hong Kong: San-lien shu-tien, 1950. 2 vols.

SWLH Lu Hsün, Selected Works of Lu Hsün, Peking: Foreign Languages Press, 1964. 4 vols.

TKTL *Chung-kuo hsien-tai wen-hsueh shih ts'an-k'ao tzu-liao* [Research materials on the history of modern Chinese literature], Peking: Kao-teng chiao-yü ch'u-pan-she, 1959-1960. 3 vols.

TYTH Ch'ü Ch'iu-pai, "To-yü te hua" [Superfluous words], in Ssu-ma Lu, *Chü Ch'iu-pai chuan* [A biography of Ch'ü Ch'iu-pai], Hong Kong: Tzu-lien ch'u-pan-she, 1962, pp. 125-161.

1 Youth in Changchow

K'u Mu

In poverty, I can no longer regard kin as kin
I acquire nothing but new traces of tears on my blue gown.
Now who will show concern for the hunger and cold
Of the departed parent's beloved child?

CH'Ü CH'IU-PAI, 1915[1]

Ch'ü Ch'iu-pai, the man who was to become China's most significant Marxist literary thinker, was less than a year old when Georg Plekhanov, the "father" of Western Marxist literary thought, published his famous study entitled *Unaddressed Letters*. Ch'ü was born on January 29, 1899, in a small room in the family residence in the southern portion of Changchow, a relatively small city in Kiangsu province. The Ch'ü's were a prosperous family who for centuries had belonged to the scholar-gentry class, China's traditional ruling elite, and this was the first child born to a new branch of the clan.[2]

Despite the apparent tranquility of the setting, Ch'ü, like others who were to become the early leaders of the Chinese communist movement, was born at a time when traditional Chinese society and culture were entering an advanced and unprecedented stage of disintegration. For a century the rulers of the Ch'ing dynasty (1644-1911) had been unable to deal successfully with the related problems of popular rebellion and foreign invasion. Beginning with the Opium

1. Ts'ao Tzu-hsi, *Ch'ü Ch'iu-pai te wen-hsueh huo-tung* [Ch'ü Ch'iu-pai's literary activity] (Shanghai: Hsin wen-i ch'u-pan-she, 1958), p. 6. This translation is found in Bernadette Yu-ning Li, "A Biography of Ch'ü Ch'iu-pai: From Youth to Party Leadership (1899-1928)" (Ph.D. dissertation, Columbia University, 1967), p. 15. Minor changes have been made in some of the Li translations of Ch'ü's writings used in this study.

2. Wen Chi-che, "Ch'ü Ch'iu-pai t'ung-chih chan-tou te i-sheng" [Comrade Ch'ü Ch'iu-pai's battling life], *Hung-ch'i p'iao-p'iao*, 5:79; Bernadette Li, p. 1.

War of 1839, China had lost every significant contest with the industrialized Western nations during the nineteenth century. The treaties
imposed by the West after each defeat steadily eroded China's national sovereignty. Internally, the massive Taiping peasant revolution, with its anti-Confucian ideology and its program for social reform, came exceedingly close to overthrowing the faltering *ancien ré-
gime* in the 1850s and early 1860s. China's humiliating military defeat
in the Sino-Japanese War of 1894 symbolized the failure of the much
acclaimed Self-Strengthening Movement of the 1870s and 1880s, a
conservative attempt to restore Ch'ing authority and China's sovereignty by means of reaffirming the universal validity of traditional
Confucian values and borrowing Western technology to modernize
China's military forces.

January 1899, the month in which Ch'ü Ch'iu-pai was born, was a
fateful time in late Ch'ing history. On one hand, China was still
recovering from the bloody aftermath of the abortive Reform Movement of 1898. Shocked by China's defeat in the Sino-Japanese War,
young reform-minded Confucian intellectuals had begun questioning
the traditionalistic "restoration" approach to China's problems embodied in the Self-Strengthening strategy. Attracted more by Western social and political institutions than by Western technology, they
had begun advocating fundamental institutional reforms. For a brief
period the reformers influenced the thinking of the young emperor,
Kuang-hsü; but in the months before Ch'ü Ch'iu-pai's birth, the
movement was crushed by conservative forces, and its leaders either
were executed or fled China.

On the other hand, yet another popular uprising, the Boxer Rebellion, was gaining momentum in neighboring Shantung province,
north of Ch'ü's home. The Boxer Movement, and its suppression by
the foreign powers, demonstrated two facts with great clarity: popular discontent was still very much alive, and China was as vulnerable
as ever to foreign expeditionary forces. Internally, rebellion was
spreading and traditional values were losing their hold on intellectuals; externally, powerful foreign interests were on the verge of
reducing the nation to a colony.

THE YOUNG GENTLEMAN

The tale of Ch'ü Ch'iu-pai's early childhood environment and activities is more like a description of the early lives of legendary Confucian scholars than an account of the early days of a socialist revolutionary. The Changchow setting was splendid, and conformed in
every important detail to the Confucian ideal of the "good society."
Situated midway between Shanghai and Nanking, Changchow had a

proud history of some twenty-three centuries. The Temple of Celestial Peace (T'ien-ning ssu) and the Red Plum Pavilion (Hung-mei t'ang), constructed over a thousand years before during the T'ang dynasty (618-917), were familiar sights to residents of the city. The renowned natural splendor of the area, highlighted by the beautiful Lake T'ai to the southeast and the Yangtze River to the north, had been an inspiration to poets, musicians, and artists for centuries. The magnificent Grand Canal, which lapped against the walls of Changchow, enhanced the physical beauty of the city, but it was also responsible for the unusual prosperity of a region in which a thriving agriculture was balanced by important commercial activity.[3]

Academically, Changchow scholars had compiled a notable record of excellence. During the Ming dynasty (1368-1644) Changchow ranked fifth in the nation, producing 666 men who had earned the *chin-shih* degree by passing the prestigious metropolitan examination (*hui-shih*) in Peking. During the Ch'ing dynasty Changchow ranked even higher, fourth, by producing 618 *chin-shih*.[4]

Ch'ü Ch'iu-pai's memories of Changchow remained vivid throughout his life. "My soul," he later wrote, "was nourished by the landscape south of the Yangtze, the delicate hills and lovely waters; my body was nourished by the *lu* fish of Sung-chiang and the cabbage of Hsi-hsiang. My heart was delighted by the natural tunes of the insects chirping under the sheds laden with beans or melons; I was refreshed by the poetic ideas flowing in with early morning breezes against a fading moon, and warmed by subtle, innocent love affairs, the gentle brushing of a curl of hair, and the hushed, sweet small talk."[5]

Ch'ü recalled that, as typical members of the educated elite, his family had lived on taxes and land rentals, and had "produced scholars

3. Mark E. Shneider, *Tvorcheskii Put' Tsiui Tsiu-bo, 1899-1935* (Moscow: Izdatel'stvo Nauka, 1964), p. 10; Bernadette Li, p. 2. Changchow was also known by the name Wu-chin. See Lü Chien, *Li Ta-chao ho Ch'ü Ch'iu-pai* (Shanghai: Shang-wu yin-shu-kuan, 1951), p. 16. I want to acknowledge the assistance of my former graduate student, George Alexandrov, who made available to me his complete English translation of the Shneider book.

4. Ho Ping-ti, *The Ladder of Success in Imperial China* (New York: Columbia University Press, 1964), pp. 246-247. During the Ch'ing period, eminent Changchow intellectuals included Liu Feng-lu, an early figure in the Modern Text, or *chin-wen*, movement, and the founders of the Yang-hu School of literary style, Chang Hui-yen and Yun Ching. See Bernadette Li, pp. 2-3.

5. Ch'ü Ch'iu-pai, *O-hsiang chi-ch'eng* [A journey to the land of hunger], in Ch'ü Ch'iu-pai wen-chi [Selected literary works of Ch'ü Ch'iu-pai] (Peking: Jen-min wen-hsueh ch'u-pan-she, 1953-1954) 4 vols., hereafter CCPWC; 1:121. This passage is quoted in T.A. Hsia, *The Gate of Darkness: Studies on the Leftist Literary Movement in China* (Seattle: University of Washington Press, 1968), pp. 11-12. Minor changes have been made in some of the Hsia translations of Ch'ü's writings used in this study.

and officials in abundance" during the Ming and Ch'ing periods.[6] A granduncle, Ch'ü Keng-shao, whose wealth supported much of the extended family, served first as lieutenant-governor and later as acting governor of Hupeh province toward the end of the Ch'ing dynasty. An uncle was a county magistrate (*hsien chih-shih*) in Chekiang province.[7] In a home so "permeated with the scent of books," it was simply assumed that Ch'ü, the first son, would carry on the family tradition.[8]

Ch'ü's father, Ch'ü Shih-wei, was capable and well educated, but had done little to contribute to the family's wealth or scholarly reputation. Content to live on the family fortune, he had never earned an academic degree and had no job. Although he had been assigned the responsibility of looking after his widowed mother, in whose home the family lived, the land and property once owned by his father had been gradually sold off decades before, leaving the new family dependent on wealthy relatives.[9] Ch'ü Shih-wei's somewhat bizarre interest in the occult, his opium addiction, and his general irresponsibility embarrassed and annoyed his relatives, but Ch'ü Ch'iu-pai clearly had an affectionate childhood relationship with his father. Leaving to others the problem of providing the young Ch'ü with a formal classical education, Ch'ü's father and uncles took great delight in introducing him to other, less practical pursuits. On occasions when a book was an appropriate gift, his father was more likely to present him with a popular historical romance, like *Dream of the Red Chamber* [*Hung lou meng*] or *Romance of the Three Kingdoms* [*San kuo yen-i*], than to burden him with yet another scholarly text.[10]

Ch'ü's most meaningful childhood relationship was, however, with his mother, Chin Heng-yü, an extraordinary woman by any standard. Like his father, Ch'ü's mother came from a scholarly family. Her father, for example, had once held the important post of salt-intendant of Kwangtung province. As a rule, the young women in gentry

6. Ch'ü Ch'iu-pai, "To-yü te hua" [Superfluous words], hereafter referred to as TYTH, in Ssu-ma Lu, *Ch'ü Ch'iu-pai chuan* [A biography of Ch'ü Ch'iu-pai] (Hong Kong: Tzu-lien ch'u-pan-she, 1962), p. 135. A translation of this important autobiographical document can be found in D.J. Li, ed., *The Chinese Revolution: 1911-1949* (New York: Van Nostrand, 1970), pp. 159-176. All remaining quotations from TYTH will be based on the D.J. Li translation and will refer to the original text contained in Ssu-ma Lu's book.

7. Ssu-ma Lu, *Ch'ü Ch'iu-pai chuan*, p. 4; TYTH, p. 135; Li K'e-ch'ang, "Ch'ü Ch'iu-pai fang-wen chi" [An interview with Ch'ü Ch'iu-pai], *Kuo-wen chou-pao* [National news weekly], 8 July 1935, p. 2.

8. Shang-kuan Ai-ming, *Ch'ü Ch'iu-pai yü wen-hsueh* [Ch'ü Ch'iu-pai and literature] (Nan-ching: Chiang-su wen-i ch'u-pan-she, 1959), p. 1; Li K'e-ch'ang, "Fang-wen chi," p. 2.

9. TYTH, p. 135.

10. Ts'ao Tzu-hsi, *Wen-hsueh huo-tung*, p. 3; Shneider, *Tvorcheskii Put'*, pp. 10-11.

families did not receive a formal classical education because, among other things, they were prohibited from taking degree examinations or holding public office. Chin's father was, however, exceedingly fond of his only daughter, and hired private tutors to instruct her in poetry, history, and literature. Convinced that her first son had great intellectual potential, it was Chin Heng-yü, rather than her husband, who guided Ch'ü Ch'iu-pai in his formal preschool education. Aside from introducing him to standard topics in Chinese history and selections from the Confucian classics, she placed considerable emphasis on literature and poetry, fields in which she had great expertise. At the age of four, Ch'ü could recite from memory many of the great poems written during the T'ang dynasty.[11] For the remainder of his life, Ch'ü spoke of his mother with great affection, never failing to recognize that it was she who had introduced him to the splendors of Chinese artistic culture and thereby started him on the road to a literary life. Despite his involvement in political activities in later years, he continued throughout his life to write elegant classical poetry and to regard himself as a "literary personality" (*wen-jen*).[12]

Ch'ü's formal education began in 1905 when he enrolled in an exclusive private school called Chü-hsing Hall to continue his study of the Confucian classics.[13] Like other gentry students, Ch'ü recalled in later years that he had "lived the life of a young gentleman" (*shao-yeh*). This meant that he never engaged in physical labor and was expected only to concentrate on his studies in order to establish a favorable scholastic record. "As members of a gentry family," he noted, "we never washed our own clothes or cooked our own food; and, of course, we always wore long gowns."[14] Before long Ch'ü transferred from the Chü-hsing Hall preschool, where the traditional pedagogical method of rote learning was employed, to the Changchow Ssu-li Kuan-ying Elementary School, a more progressive private institution.[15]

Although the Ch'ing dynasty remained in power, the traditional examination system that had brought his family so much wealth and power had been abolished in 1905. Consequently, when Ch'ü enrolled in the Kiangsu Fifth Middle School in Changchow in 1909 at the age of ten, some important changes had been made in the curriculum. Until he left school in 1914, Ch'ü received what he later characterized

---

11. Yang Chih-hua, "I Ch'iu-pai" [Recollections of Ch'iu-pai], *Hung-ch'i p'iao-p'iao*, 8:26; Shneider, *Tvorcheskii Put'*, p. 11; Ssu-ma Lu, *Ch'ü Ch'iu-pai chuan*, p. 5; Ts'ao Tzu-hsi, *Wen-hsüeh huo-tung*, p. 3.

12. TYTH, p. 148.

13. Shang-kuan Ai-ming, *Ch'ü Ch'iu-pai yü wen-hsüeh*, p. 1.

14. TYTH, p. 135; D.J. Li, p. 164.

15. Wen Chi-che, "Ch'ü Ch'iu-pai t'ung-chih," p. 80.

as a "Europeanized" (*Ou-hua*) high school education, which meant that it stressed science, a subject for which he showed little enthusiasm.[16] Although Ch'ü was a model student, his personality and behavior reflected the fact that he found little intellectual stimulation in the new curriculum. He belonged to a small group of bookish students whose friendship he valued, but he was seen as an introvert by his peers. His decision to help organize a small poetry club in the school suggests that his real interests continued to reside in the familiar field of traditional cultural studies.[17]

Reforms in education and the civil service did little to prepare Ch'ü for the dramatic changes that were transforming the lives of the gentry families throughout China. On the contrary, the relative tranquility of life in Changchow during the first decade of Ch'ü's life permitted his family to enjoy the illusory security of refined gentry ways. It was only later that he realized he had been born in a "new era" of Chinese history. Reflecting on his childhood years, Ch'ü observed: "China had slowly awakened from her sweet and pleasant dream to find the sun already high in the sky. But she lazily stretched herself with eyes half open, still reluctant to rise. By the time I was seven or eight years old, Chinese society had undergone a tremendous upheaval and showed an uncontrollable and very apparent tendency toward drastic change."[18]

Even during the idyllic years of Ch'ü's childhood, unusual developments were taking place in Changchow itself. The most important of these was the construction in 1908 of a portion of the Nanking-Shanghai Railway passing through Ch'ü's hometown. His family was simply not prepared for the arrival of the industrial age and the inevitable transformation of the traditional economic system and its age-old culture. To make matters worse, at about the time the Ch'ing dynasty collapsed in January 1912, the financial pillars of Ch'ü's family, his granduncle and his uncle, had died, leaving their totally unprepared dependents to fend for themselves. Thus the death of the monarchial system in China coincided almost exactly with the collapse of the Ch'ü family of Changchow.

CONFUCIAN MASKS

Ch'ü Ch'iu-pai, like so many other revolutionary Chinese intellectuals of gentry background, saw the affluence and privilege of his childhood vanish rather suddenly. From 1912 to 1915 his family experienced a slow but irreversible economic decline. For a time the family was able to survive by selling much of its household property.

16. CCPWC, 1:21.   17. Bernadette Li, p. 10.
18. CCPWC, 1:20; Bernadette Li, pp. 3-4.

Because Ch'ü was the oldest child, it was often his responsibility to make periodic and humiliating trips to the local pawnshop to sell antique furniture, calligraphy, paintings, books from his father's library, and other family heirlooms. As debts mounted, it eventually became necessary for Ch'ü's father to sell the house and arrange for his family to move into the clan temple nearby.[19] Although at times there was scarcely enough food to eat, Ch'ü's parents continued to retain a servant and ordered at least some of their clothing from a tailor. "The general idea," Ch'ü recalled bitterly in 1935, "was that the prestige of a gentry family must be maintained."[20]

Ch'ü was confused and embarrassed by the plight of the family, and the introspective tendencies already present in his personality became more pronounced. His resolve to "escape from the finite world" (*pi shih*) was pursued in a thoroughly traditional and culturalistic manner. In brief, it was the familiar world of classical literary and philosophical studies that determined the form of escapism practiced by Ch'ü Ch'iu-pai. Although we do not know what texts they studied, Ch'ü indicated several years later that the goal of his small circle of high school companions was to become "unconventional scholars" (*ming-shih*) who, instead of preparing for the mundane world of bureaucratic service, would strive to realize "spiritual transcendence" (*hsing-ling*).[21]

The young Ch'ü did not understand modern politics, and he made no systematic attempt to educate himself in these matters. Nevertheless, he was exposed, perhaps superficially, to several basic trends in contemporary political thought. It is known, for example, that Ch'ü and his classmates studied the Taiping peasant revolution in school and read some of the writings of Liang Ch'i-ch'ao and other exiled leaders of the abortive Reform Movement of 1898. One of his favorite texts was T'an Ssu-t'ung's *A Study of Benevolence* [*Jen-hsüeh*], probably the most radical philosophical treatise of the late nineteenth-century reform movement.[22] More important, there was considerable anti-Ch'ing sentiment at the Kiangsu Fifth Middle School. In fact, the principal and many of the faculty members belonged to the subversive Chinese Revolutionary Alliance (Chung-kuo ko-ming t'ung-meng-hui), organized by Sun Yat-sen in 1905.[23] But Ch'ü was probably too

19. Ts'ao Tzu-hsi, *Wen-hsueh huo-tung*, pp. 4-5; Shneider, *Tvorcheskii Put'*, p. 11. After 1949 the clan temple was converted into a memorial to Ch'ü Ch'iu-pai.

20. TYTH, p. 135; D.J. Li, p. 164.

21. CCPWC, 1:21. By "unconventional scholarship" Ch'ü probably meant Buddhism. It is likely that he associated the study of Confucianism with preparation for routine public service.

22. Shneider, *Tvorcheskii Put'*, p. 12.

23. Wen Chi-che, "Ch'ü Ch'iu-pai: Revolutionary and Man of Letters," *People's China*, 1 July 1955, p. 18; Ts'ao Tzu-hsi, *Wen-hsueh huo-tung*, p. 4; Shang-kuan Ai-ming, *Ch'ü Ch'iu-pai yü wen-hsueh*, p. 2.

young and too preoccupied with personal problems to have been swept up by the republican cause. If the Wuchang Uprising gave him any hopes for China, they were soon dashed in the disillusioning months that followed the 1911 Revolution.

Around 1914, just after the family's home had been sold, it became apparent that there was hardly a trace of affection left in the relationship between Ch'ü's father and mother. One day, his father simply abandoned his family and wandered north to Tsinan, Shantung province, where he accepted a minor teaching position and lived with an old friend.[24] Ch'ü was hardly exaggerating when he recalled, late in life, that "my family was poor by the time I reached thirteen or fourteen."[25] The family financial crisis had become so grave by 1914 that Ch'ü was forced to withdraw from high school at the age of fifteen. Graduation was only six months away, but Ch'ü's mother could not afford the school's fees. It came as a terrible psychological blow to Chin Heng-yü that such an outstanding student was unable to graduate. Instead it became necessary for the young Ch'ü to find a job. On the strength of a relative's recommendation, he was appointed headmaster of a remote village elementary school in nearby Wu-hsi district, east of Changchow. Ch'ü was extremely miserable at his new job, and revealed in later years that he viewed it as "a spiritual life imprisonment."[26] It was hoped that his modest income of six yuan per month would ease the financial pressures on his mother, sister, four brothers, and ailing grandmother, and permit the schooling of at least some of the children to proceed. Ch'ü was willing to sacrifice himself in this way, but he desperately missed his small circle of friends in Changchow.

Ch'ü's "life imprisonment" in rural China was short-lived. In the months following his departure from Changchow, the responsibilities and pressures of providing for the family fell with increasing force on the shoulders of Ch'ü's mother. Ordinarily she would have gained status and authority within the family by developing a warm relationship with her husband, bearing and raising successful sons, and eventually supervising her own daughters-in-law.[27] In Chin's case, however, her children had been forced out of school, and her husband, who could have protected her from critical relatives, had abandoned the family. Before long, Chin's in-laws began to circulate malicious rumors blaming her for the family's problems.

Tensions within the family reached a climax just before the celebra-

24. Ssu-ma Lu, *Ch'ü Ch'iu-pai chuan*, p. 5.   25. TYTH, p. 135; D.J. Li, p. 164.
26. CCPWC, 1:21; Bernadette Li, p. 12.
27. Kay Ann Johnson, "Women in China: Problems of Sex Inequality and Socioeconomic Change," in Joan I. Roberts, ed., *Beyond Intellectual Sexism* (New York: David McKay, 1976), pp. 287-288.

tion of the lunar new year in February 1915. Traditionally, this was a time when creditors called at the homes of their customers to settle accounts. The pressure on Chin Heng-yü was unbearable. Hounded by bill collectors and cruel charges that she had failed miserably as a wife and mother, she became desperate. On February 15, 1915, shortly after Ch'ü's sixteenth birthday, he was overcome by the news relayed to him in Wu-hsi that his mother had attempted suicide by swallowing a deadly solution of phosphorous match heads dissolved in wine. By the time he reached his mother's side, she was dead.[28] This traumatic experience was one from which Ch'ü never fully recovered.

For several bewildering months following the suicide, Ch'ü's emotions were dominated by grief and anger. As a filial son, he responded to the event in the manner of a traditional Confucian scholar by resigning his post in Wu-hsi and officially observing a six-month period of mourning at his mother's side.[29] Yet in his poem "K'u Mu" [Crying for Mother], the most eloquent and moving of his early years, Ch'ü struck an untraditional chord by suggesting in vivid language that he was deeply suspicious of the role played by the extended family in the events leading to the suicide. Furthermore, the disintegration of his own nuclear family was now complete.

It was humiliating for Ch'u to realize that a proper funeral for his mother could not be arranged. He had been able to scrape together enough money to purchase a coffin, but his affluent relatives were apparently unwilling to pay for a funeral. Consequently, for the remainder of Ch'ü's life his mother's body remained in the coffin inside the clan temple, awaiting burial.[30] Ch'ü knew that the charges against his mother were false, and became convinced that the Confucian family system was partly responsible for her death. Even at the end of his own life he still insisted that "my mother chose to commit suicide so that we brothers would be able to pursue an academic career."[31] "Her love has a permanent place in my heart," he wrote a few years after the suicide. "It is the only legacy she bequeathed me."[32]

After receiving some funds from an aunt in late summer 1915, Ch'ü finally left Changchow in search of his cousin, Ch'ü Ch'un-pai, a stable and brotherly figure who worked for the government in Wuchang, Hupeh province. While residing with his cousin, Ch'ü decided to resume his studies in order to satisfy what he later described as his insatiable hunger for knowledge.[33] He was enrolled, for a time,

28. Ssu-ma Lu, *Ch'ü Ch'iu-pai chuan*, p. 8; Ts'ao Tzu-hsi, *Wen-hsueh huo-tung*, p. 5.

29. Yang Chih-hua, "I Ch'iu-pai," p. 26.

30. Wen Chi-che, "Ch'ü Ch'iu-pai t'ung-chih," p. 81; Ts'ao Tzu-hsi, *Wen-hsueh huo-tung*, p. 5. In 1939, well after his own death, a group of Ch'ü's friends raised the funds to bury his mother in a public cemetery in Changchow.

31. TYTH, p. 135; D.J. Li, p. 164.

32. CCPWC, 1:164; Bernadette Li, p. 8.   33. CCPWC, 1:21.

as a student of English in the Foreign Language College of Wuchang, but he soon lost interest in this new subject and dropped out of school. Discouraged, he wandered just north of Wuchang to Huang-p'o in yet another attempt to borrow funds from an aunt whose husband was a prosperous landlord. Ch'ü failed to get the money, but he experienced the unexpected pleasure of developing an immediate intellectual companionship with his cousin Chou Chün-liang. During the visit, which lasted three or four months, Chou influenced Ch'ü by suggesting that he might find comfort in a return to the solitary world of esoteric traditional studies. This, of course, was a form of escapism already familiar to Ch'ü. Discouraging Ch'ü "from finding political solutions to social problems,"[34] his cousin diverted their attention to the composition of classical poetry and revived in Ch'ü "an old interest in Buddhism."

It is impossible to know precisely what attracted Ch'ü to Buddhism in this period because he wrote nothing about his early Buddhist beliefs. But, as Marián Gálik has speculated, it is likely that Ch'ü was interested in the Consciousness-Only School (wei-shih) of Buddhist thought, an extremely idealistic system that had declined in the ninth century, but was revived in the early twentieth century.[35] In certain respects, the Consciousness-Only School was well suited to Ch'ü's psychological needs because, among other things, it assumed that the objective world was totally illusory: it existed only in the mind of the perceiver.

In later years he remembered this brief period as a relatively happy time in his life. Indeed, removed from the agonies of Changchow and immersed in Buddhist texts, Ch'ü genuinely seems to have achieved some form of transcendental inner tranquility. When he learned that his cousin and guardian, Ch'ü Ch'un-pai, had been transferred from Wuchang to Peking sometime in early 1916, Ch'ü confidently announced his intention to join him and begin a more formal study of traditional philosophy and literature at a major university.[36]

As Ch'ü prepared for his fateful journey to Peking and what would be an entirely new phase of his life, there was little indication that he was likely to become involved in the radical May Fourth Movement. He had virtually no interest in politics and little knowledge of the sort of national and international affairs that would lead to the eruption of May 4, 1919. Arriving with a heavy Changchow accent and provincial manners, Ch'ü was a country bumpkin by sophisticated Peking stan-

34. CCPWC, 1:21-22.
35. Marián Gálik, "Studies in Modern Chinese Intellectual History: II. Young Ch'ü Ch'iu-pai (1915-1922)," Asian and African Studies, 12 (1976): 90-95.
36. CCPWC, 1:22; Hsia, Gate of Darkness, pp. 13-14; Bernadette Li, p. 18. Ssu-ma Lu, Ch'ü Ch'iu-pai chuan, p. 11; Ts'ao Tzu-hsi, Wen-hsueh huo-tung, p. 7.

dards. And, at a time when many students were defiantly rejecting the classics, Ch'ü was preparing to begin a systematic study of several traditional schools of thought. Unlike the young intellectuals of Peking, he had little interest in Western culture.

Nevertheless, in other important respects, Ch'ü and others like him were prime candidates for recruitment into the spectacular early twentieth-century youth rebellion. Although Ch'ü was not fully conscious of it at the time, his class status was in flux. Writing in the early 1920s when his political consciousness was considerably higher, Ch'ü acknowledged that "social life during my childhood" was strongly influenced by new political and economic developments occurring throughout the nation. The abolition of the old examination system and the introduction of modern and foreign subjects in school curricula effectively undermined the road to fame and fortune traditionally followed by the Ch'ü family. "By then," Ch'ü recalled, "I was already not a pure product of Chinese culture. The upheavals in economic life had brought about myriad changes. I was only one of them."[37] In fact, the final economic collapse of his family left him without a class. Several years later he observed:

> Poverty was not accidental. Although there was assistance from relatives because of the maintenance of the family system, in reality everyone was in the same sinking boat adrift in a stormy sea. Except for weeping together, none could really help the other. My mother had already been driven from this world by poverty, and my father was only a relic of this poverty. In a social status almost like that of the lumpen-proletariat (*yu-min wu-ch'an chieh-chi*), I do not even know what had become of my state of mind.[38]

In this sense, Ch'ü's early life closely parallels the lives of numerous gentry intellectuals who abandoned their social class to play a leading role in the revolutionary movement. Ch'ü, like others, had experienced the luxury of gentry affluence as well as the miseries of poverty. He had experienced gentry life and studied Confucianism as an "insider," but he no longer had reason to remain loyal to his class origins.

More important, his analysis of the circumstances leading to his mother's tragic suicide eventually forced the young Ch'ü Ch'iu-pai to reach some startling conclusions about the Confucian family system. In the early 1920s he recalled bitterly:

> My childhood environment was a complete reflection of the bankruptcy of the extended family system. At first it tottered;

37. CCPWC, 1:20; Bernadette Li, p. 4.   38. CCPWC, 1:13; Bernadette Li, p. 14.

then it gradually vanished. I shall speak of the dying Chinese family system as a social phenomenon only according to what I have heard and witnessed, and according to my personal experience. I see only that this process is accelerating day by day. In the good families, people lead a monotonous and dull life. In difficult ones, every member of the extended family . . . , because of economic conflicts and the disintegration of family bonds such as love between husband and wife, wears a Confucian mask (*k'ung-chiao te chia mien-chü*) when they meet, while secretly doing everything to hurt one another.[39]

He added: "Only pains of ephemeral revivals of the dying family system penetrated my heart and influenced my life."[40]

In later years Ch'ü would be attracted to the scientism and materialism of Marxist theory, but the harsh experience of his youth instilled in him an emotional and humanistic concern for the sufferings of real people. After witnessing the malicious feuding that destroyed his family, Ch'ü noted: "The relationship between man and man has become a big question in my mind. Although I have harmonious strings in my heart, the meaning of life appears so vague to me that I am unable to strike a harmonious tune."[41]

Ch'ü had not yet abandoned hope of finding personal salvation and, indirectly, a humanistic solution to contemporary problems by reexamining portions of China's intellectual heritage. He responded to his private crisis in the only way he knew, and it gave him some comfort. But it is also clear that the seeds of iconoclasm had been sown the moment he began expressing reservations about the Confucian family system. In Peking he would learn of new approaches to the question of the meaning of life.

39. Ibid.   40. Ibid.   41. Ibid.

2 The May Fourth Movement

*I have now understood that though it seems to people that they live
by care for themselves, in truth it is love alone by which they live.*
LEO TOLSTOY, 1882[1]

Ch'ü Ch'iu-pai's years in Peking began uneventfully. He arrived sometime in 1916 to settle in with his cousin's family in the eastern portion
of the city. "My ambition was to become a school teacher," he recalled
in later years, "and such grand designs as 'bringing peace and order to
the nation and the world' were far from my mind."[2] Ch'ü was disappointed, however, in his first attempts to establish a new life for
himself. His first desire was to enter Peking University, the nation's
leading institution of higher learning. Although he had not completed
his high school education, Chü apparently had no trouble passing
the difficult entrance examination given by the department of Chinese literature. But he was unable to enroll because he had no funds
for tuition, and his cousin, who had financial problems of his own,
was unable to provide assistance. Ch'ü Ch'un-pai undoubtedly hoped
that his young cousin would now forget his vague intellectual ambi-
tions and turn his attention to the more pedestrian task of finding a
secure job. Thus Ch'ü was urged to follow his cousin's footsteps and
take the civil service examination. Ch'ü accepted the advice, but failed
the examination.[3]

Like so many other eager students who had found their way to the
center of intellectual life in Peking, Ch'ü Ch'iu-pai—similar to the

1. For Ch'ü's 1920 translation of Tolstoy's famous short story see "Jen i ho-wei
sheng" [What men live by], CCPWC, 3:1328-1350. The English translation used in this
chapter is based on Ernest J. Simmons, ed., *Leo Tolstoy Short Stories* (New York: Modern
Library, 1965), 2:49-72.

2. TYTH, p. 127; D.J. Li, p. 160.   3. TYTH, p. 128.

young Mao Tse-tung a little later—was allowed to audit courses at Peking University for six months beginning in early 1917. It is unknown what lectures Ch'ü attended, but he had at least some exposure to the new and sometimes radical currents of thought that had been sweeping through the university during the administration of the liberal-minded chancellor Ts'ai Yuan-p'ei. If Ch'ü learned anything from the students and faculty of Peking University it was that the Peking government was politically bankrupt, and that the Chinese nation was in the midst of a desperate struggle for survival.

Ironically, Ch'ü's fateful decision to enter the National Institute of Russian Language (Kuo-li O-wen chuan-hsiu-kuan) in the summer of 1917 was not based on an interest in the literature or history of Russia; Ch'ü clearly had no knowledge of either subject. Instead, his decision was prompted by guilt and nagging doubts about human relationships, specifically his relationship with his well-intentioned cousin. While auditing courses at Peking University he had become troubled by what he later characterized as his "parasitic existence." "The rice I then ate," he lamented, "was not mine, but my cousin's."[4] Thus it was only as "a last resort" in his search for independence and security that Ch'ü entered the Institute of Russian Language operated by the Ministry of Foreign Affairs. He frankly admitted that he was attracted to the Institute because, unlike every other college-level institution in Peking, it did not charge tuition fees, and promised its graduates a "great future" as officers of Chinese consulates in Tsarist Russia or as staff members of the Chinese Eastern Railway. Moreover, the students were given a modest monthly stipend. "At the time I did not know that Russia had already had a revolution," Ch'ü later proclaimed, "nor was I aware of the great significance of Russian literature. As far as I was concerned, Russian language was merely a convenient means of earning a livelihood."[5]

THE BODHISATTVA

Ch'ü's carefully conceived plan of action demonstrates that he had no intention whatever of abandoning his original goal of becoming immersed in the study of various traditional modes of thought. But, more important, his statements about the ultimate purpose of his study indicate that he was also being influenced by the increasingly

4. CCPWC, 1:22; Bernadette Yu-ning Li, "A Biography of Ch'ü Ch'iu-pai: From Youth to Party Leadership (1899-1928)" (Ph.D. dissertation, Columbia University, 1967), p. 22.

5. TYTH, p. 128; D.J. Li, p. 160. Ch'ü was probably referring to the 1917 February Revolution. Also see Li K'e-ch'ang, "Ch'ü Ch'iu-pai fang-wen chi," *Kuo-wen chou-pao* [National news weekly], 8 July 1935, p. 2: Mark E. Shneider, *Tvorcheskii Put' Tsiui Tsiu-bo, 1899-1935* (Moscow: Izdatel'stvo Nauka, 1964), pp. 14-15.

radical intellectual climate of Peking. His day-to-day study activities reflected what he characterized as his "dualistic view of life" (*erh-yuan te jen-sheng-kuan*). "I allotted a part of my time," he explained, "to discharge my 'worldly' [*shih-chien-te*] duties—preparation for a career which would enable me to make a living. I used another part of my time to prepare myself diligently for the 'unworldly' [*ch'ü-shih-chien*] service of saving China by cultural means."[6] Ch'ü's mundane worldly duties consisted of making steady progress in the Institute's five-year program. Ch'ü expected to do well, but the daily routine at the Institute was supposed to provide him with security, rather than intellectual stimulation.[7] Although Ch'ü was regarded as a brilliant student by his teachers and classmates, his real interests were elsewhere. Of much greater significance in Ch'ü's scheme was his unworldly obligation to save China.

Ch'ü proposed to do this by pursuing traditional studies in the evening when his Institute work was finished. Unfortunately for us, Ch'ü never made any organized attempt to explain the goals he hoped to achieve by studying traditional thought; nor did he leave any record of the conclusions he reached, if in fact he reached any. Although this was a brief phase in Ch'ü's early intellectual development, it is one that should be noted, because it is clear that his traditional studies were not random in nature. Brief remarks contained in his autobiographical writings provide at least some details about the texts he studied and the ultimate purpose of his research in what might be called the Buddhist phase of his early intellectual development. In the early 1920s, for example, Ch'ü noted that after his arrival in Peking his "attempts to solve life's problems through Buddhist studies kindled the hope to humanize Buddhism by practicing Bodhisattvahood."[8] In another passage, written in 1935, he recalled that at the age of sixteen or seventeen he began studying texts "such as *Fo ching* [The Buddhist classics], *Ta-chi ch'i* [Teachings of Mahayana Buddhism] and *Hsin lun* [On Buddhist faith]."[9]

Under the influence of his cousin, Chou Chün-liang, Ch'ü had already embraced the extremely idealistic Consciousness-Only School of Mahayana Buddhism, but in the Peking environment he began to modify his views. For example, he gradually came to accept the objective existence of the finite world and the subjective existence of the ego. He now believed they had an independent existence and, therefore, were not merely products of human consciousness.[10] Although Ch'ü may have continued to believe that it was possible for the indi-

6. CCPWC, 1:22; Bernadette Li, p. 22.   7. Bernadette Li, p. 20.
8. CCPWC, 1:22; Bernadette Li, p. 22.   9. TYTH, p. 137.
10. Marián Gálik, "Studies in Modern Chinese Intellectual History: II. Young Ch'ü Ch'iu-pai (1915-1922)," *Asian and African Studies*, 12 (1976): 92-93. Gálik argues that this transformation occurred somewhat later.

vidual mind to transcend the finite world (illusory or not), merge with the Mind of the Universe, and enjoy a perpetual life of bliss, he no longer sought to escape from the world, but rather to "save China." Ch'ü proposed to accomplish this task by becoming a bodhisattva, or Buddhist saint. The tradition of Mahayana Buddhism that Ch'ü studied in Peking was alluring precisely because it did not ignore the sufferings of people in the material world. Instead it stressed the unity of the spiritual and finite worlds. It was the duty of the bodhisattva, as one who had achieved spiritual enlightenment, to renounce a life of bliss and return to free the world from suffering. When Ch'ü spoke of "humanizing Buddhism" by practicing bodhisattvahood he was referring to the Mahayana ideal of creating a utopian spiritual world in the world of material existence.[11]

It would be misleading to suggest that Ch'ü Ch'iu-pai's early scholarly activities in Peking were simply a continuation of a pattern of behavior established in Changchow or during his lengthy visit with Chou Chün-liang. To be sure, Ch'ü still looked to traditional texts for answers to difficult problems, but in several important respects he was being influenced, perhaps unconsciously, by new social and intellectual concerns sweeping the capital. For instance, Ch'ü's desire to "save China" showed an obvious shift from a preoccupation with individual salvation to a new and almost patriotic concern for the "nation." Even his continued pattern of social isolation had a new meaning in Peking. Contrasting the "escapism" of his youth to his "cynical" state of mind in the 1916-1918 period, Ch'ü explained: "The 'republican' way of living of the new bureaucrats in Peking greatly distressed me. I became increasingly cynical during these three years of philosophical studies. But my cynicism at that time was different from my earlier escapism. There had been a gradual change in my way of thinking."[12] Ch'ü's views about the plight of the nation and the ineffectiveness of government were not only new; they also coincided almost exactly with current opinion at Peking University, where Ch'ü had audited courses. Of course, the central difference between Ch'ü's approach and the one adopted by other students was that while he looked to the past for answers, they began looking abroad. Nevertheless, in one important respect, Ch'ü's early intellectual orientation was compatible with the rising tide of "New Culture" thought. He was an idealist: hence, like "New Culture" advocates, he assumed that China could only be saved "by cultural means," which required, among

11. The role of the bodhisattva is discussed in Richard C. Howard, "K'ang Yu-wei (1858-1927): His Intellectual Background and Early Thought," in Arthur F. Wright and Denis Twitchett, eds., *Confucian Personalities* (Stanford: Stanford University Press, 1962), p. 107.
12. CCPWC, 1:22; Bernadette Li, p. 22.

other things, a new generation of moral leaders. And despite his interest in traditional thought, his loyalty to Confucian society (the central target of the New Culture Movement) was exceedingly tenuous.

THE NEW CULTURE AND MAY FOURTH "WHIRLPOOL"

It was in 1918, Ch'ü Ch'iu-pai recalled, that he began to read "many new magazines" that tended to instill in him "a new outlook on life."[13] Ch'ü was, of course, referring to the publications of the celebrated New Culture Movement of 1915-1919, one of the crucial turning points in the history of the Chinese revolution. Ch'ü had arrived in Peking just after the New Culture Movement was launched at Peking University in 1915. Like others, Ch'ü learned about the movement by talking with other students and reading the enormously influential magazine, *Hsin Ch'ing-nien* [*New Youth*]. Ch'ü learned that although the leaders of the New Culture Movement were, like himself, intellectuals from elite gentry families, they had become thoroughly alienated from traditional Chinese culture and values. Unlike K'ang Yu-wei and Liang Ch'i-ch'ao, who believed that China's transition to the modern world could and should be carried out within what they understood to be the Confucian intellectual framework, New Culture thinkers held that the Confucian tradition itself had been the problem all along. Disgusted with contemporary Chinese politics and the deterioration of the republican movement after 1911, New Culture intellectuals asserted that in China a radical cultural revolution would have to precede meaningful political revolution.

Convinced of the superiority of the bourgeois Western cultural model, they promoted iconoclastic assaults on all aspects of traditional Chinese society. The tyranny of the traditional family system, the subjugation of women, and the hypocrisy of Confucian ideology were among the subjects treated with merciless ridicule. They assumed that China could be saved only if its traditional Confucian culture was completely scrapped and replaced by a Western-style "democratic" and "scientific" culture. Cultural revolution was, in their view, a precondition for political, social, and economic revolution. It was, in brief, a struggle between a young, new culture and an old, corrupt culture. And, as Ch'ü soon learned, an elite corps of young gentry intellectuals was assigned the vanguard task of leading the cultural revolution.

The effect of New Culture thought on Ch'ü Ch'iu-pai was gradual and cumulative; although its ideas fascinated him and caused him to reexamine the merits of his own plan to "save China" by reexamining

13. TYTH, p. 128.

modes of traditional thought, there was no single moment at which he suddenly converted to New Culture beliefs. He preferred to observe the progress of the movement from a safe distance. The same cannot be said of his dramatic involvement in the May Fourth Movement, which, he acknowledged in later years, he joined "with an unbelievable fury."

The New Culture Movement, still gaining in momentum, underwent a drastic and unforeseen shift on the eve of the May Fourth Incident in 1919. Until that time, radical Chinese thinkers favorably disposed toward the bourgeois democracies of the West had viewed World War I in the most idealistic terms. To many, the Allied victory of November 1918 meant that democracy and progress had triumphed over despotism. The Chinese, as participants on the Allied side, looked forward to the return of territories in Shantung province formerly controlled by Germany. Shock and disbelief swept through New Culture intellectual circles in the early days of May 1919 when it was announced that the Treaty of Versailles did not provide for Chinese control over former German territories, but rather turned them over to Japan. Beginning with the massive student demonstration of May 4, 1919, there occurred a wave of strikes and protests against the major Western powers and officials in the Peking warlord government of Tuan Ch'i-jui who protected Japanese interests in China. In a few weeks, the May Fourth Incident had become the May Fourth Movement. Its leadership was composed of the same iconoclastic intellectuals who were active in the New Culture Movement, yet the character of the movement had changed significantly. Continued assaults were made on all aspects of traditional Chinese society and values, yet a new commitment to direct political action supplemented notions about the primacy of "cultural revolution." The united participation of students, merchants, and workers broadened the base of the movement and guaranteed the effectiveness of strikes and demonstrations. Interest in Western culture as an alternative to traditional Chinese culture continued to increase during the May Fourth Movement; but there was profound disillusionment with Western political systems and methods of conducting international diplomacy. Rather suddenly, Chinese radicals became more interested in the significance of the Russian October Revolution and Marxism in general. Thus the ideology of the May Fourth Movement, which Ch'ü Ch'iu-pai and thousands of others found so compelling, had two essential components: a militant nationalism directed at foreign aggression, and a radical cultural iconoclasm that rejected the Confucian past.

The impact of the early May Fourth furor was so great that, almost overnight, it transformed apolitical students like Ch'ü Ch'iu-pai, who were known for their caution and restraint, into angry social activists.

Just as suddenly Ch'ü suspended his study of traditional thought. "I believed that the world was to be saved through the practice of bodhisattvahood [*p'u-sa-hsing*], and that everything was impermanent, including the social system. But such a philosophy could not hold for long when the May Fourth Movement sucked me in like a whirlpool. My solitude was finally broken."[14] Ch'ü's rise from obscurity to prominence during the early months of the May Fourth Movement followed a typical pattern of student activism. Respected by his fellow students, and regarded as a competent writer and persuasive speaker, Ch'ü was elected by his classmates to represent the Institute of Russian Language at the important meetings of Peking student leaders prior to the May Fourth Incident.[15] On the day of May 4 itself, Ch'ü actually led the Institute delegation on the famous May Fourth march from the Gate of Heavenly Peace in central Peking, through the Foreign Legation Quarter and into the house of Ts'ao Ju-lin, Minister of Communications and an important member of the pro-Japanese group in the government. Following a clash between students and police in which Ch'ü participated, Ts'ao's house was stormed and set ablaze.[16]

Ch'ü was unprepared physically for this sort of initiation into the world of direct political action. When he returned from the demonstration coughing blood, it became apparent that poor dietary habits and years of exhausting study had damaged his health. The symptoms of tuberculosis were unmistakable, and the disease would haunt Ch'ü Ch'iu-pai for the remainder of his life.[17] Nevertheless, Ch'ü continued to involve himself in the May Fourth Movement with characteristic intensity. Almost immediately Ch'ü helped organize a small circle of students who collaborated on several projects. The group consisted of Keng Chi-chih, a fellow student at the Institute of Russian Language, Ch'ü Shih-ying and Hsu Ti-shan of Hui-wen University in Peking, and Cheng Chen-to, a student at the government's Railway Administration School, all of whom became prominent literary figures in later years.[18]

Ch'ü remained politically active throughout May 1919. After weeks

14. CCPWC, 1:23; T. A. Hsia, *The Gate of Darkness* (Seattle: University of Washington Press, 1968), p. 15.

15. Li An-pao, "'Wu-ssu' shih-ch'i te Ch'ü Ch'iu-pai" [Ch'ü Ch'iu-pai during the May Fourth period], *Chiao-hsueh yü yen-chiu* [Pedagogy and research], May 1959, pp. 67-68.

16. Shneider, *Tvorcheskii Put'*, p. 16; Li An-pao, "'Wu-ssu' shih-ch'i," p. 68.

17. Ting Ching-t'ang, "'Wu-ssu' ch'u-ch'i te Ch'ü Ch'iu-pai t'ung-chih" [Ch'ü Ch'iu-pai in the early phase of the May Fourth Movement], in Ting Ching-t'ang, ed., *Hsueh-hsi Lu Hsün ho Ch'ü Ch'iu-pai tso-p'in te cha-chi* [Learn from the message of Lu Hsün's and Ch'ü Ch'iu-pai's works] (Shanghai: Shanghai wen-i ch'u-pan-she, 1961), p. 124.

18. Cheng Chen-to, "Chi Ch'ü Ch'iu-pai t'ung-chih tsao-nien erh-san shih" [A few anecdotes in Comrade Ch'ü Ch'iu-pai's early life], *Hsin kuan-ch'a* [New observer], 12:26.

of protest and demonstration organized by the Student Union, Ch'ü Ch'iu-pai was apprehended by the police on June 5, 1919, during a prolonged series of mass arrests, and jailed, first in police head-quarters, and later, with hundreds of other students, in the Peking University Law School Building. When they realized the popularity of the students' patriotic protest and the gravity of the political situation following the strike of merchants and workers in Shanghai, an embarrassed government and police force made a public apology to the students. On June 8, 1919, a jubilant Ch'ü Ch'iu-pai was among imprisoned students who marched, triumphant and free, from the Law School Building amidst the cheers of hundreds of their supporters.[19]

The strikes and student demonstrations subsided in the following months, but the New Culture and May Fourth Movements continued to influence intellectual and political life in China for decades. At twenty years of age Ch'ü had been intoxicated by the dazzling successes of the radical student movement, and like many others he remained active for the remainder of his life. His was the May Fourth generation, and it would provide China with its primary source of revolutionary leadership for the next half-century. Ch'ü was excited by the spontaneity of the student movement, but readily conceded that the thinking of his group "was as vague as watching the morning mist through a screen window."[20] "We were all aware of the deep-seated maladies of the society to which we belonged, yet ignorant of their cure. Feelings alone, however, ran so strong that restlessness could no longer be contained. That was, so far as I can see, the real significance of the student movement. There was a demand for 'change,' and that demand came in an outburst. It had then at least its shocking and rousing effects, for as Kropotkin said, one riot does more than thousands of books and pamphlets."[21]

Ch'ü also realized that knowledge is important; thus, when the highly emotional phase of the movement abated, he resumed his studies at the Institute. He was no more enthusiastic about preparing for a career than he had been when he entered the Institute, but in the wake of the May Fourth upheaval it had become clear that his knowledge of the Russian language could now be put to unexpected and immediate social and political use. May Fourth disillusionment with the Western liberal democracies had given rise to a new interest in the significance of the October Revolution in Russia. In December 1919 Ch'ü joined the Society for the Study of Socialism organized by Li Ta-chao, professor of history at Peking University and co-founder of the Chinese Communist Party in 1921. Its members included several peo-

19. Ting Ching-t'ang, *Hsueh-hsi Lu Hsün*, 125; Shneider, *Tvorcheskii Put'*, p. 16.
20. CCPWC, 1:24; Bernadette Li, p. 37.
21. CCPWC, 1:23; Hsia, *Gate of Darkness*, p. 16.

ple who later became prominent leaders of the Chinese Communist Party, such as Ch'en Tu-hsiu, Mao Tse-tung, Teng Chung-hsia, Chang Kuo-t'ao, and Chou En-lai. Ch'ü's circle of friends and associates had obviously widened.[22]

SOCIAL AND POLITICAL VIEWS

Beginning in the summer of 1919, Ch'ü Ch'iu-pai's May Fourth role shifted from student organizer and political activist to writer and publisher. From July 1919 to October 1920, the "May Fourth" phase of Ch'ü's literary career, he published thirty-three articles. These included original essays on contemporary social and political topics, translations of foreign social theory, original literary works, and translations of foreign literature.[23] Most of them appeared in a single journal, *Hsin She-hui* [*New Society*], an influential magazine founded in November 1919 by Ch'ü and his trusted friends Cheng Chen-to, Hsu Ti-shan, Ch'ü Shih-ying, and Keng Chi-chih. Financial support for the journal, one of over seven hundred new periodicals to appear between 1915 and 1923, came from the Association for the Advancement of Society (She-hui shih-chin hui), an affiliate of the Peking YMCA. Published "to disclose the evils of the old society and to establish a democratic new society by peaceful and practical methods,"[24] *New Society* was distributed as far away as Manchuria and the distant provinces of Szechwan, Kwangtung, and Kwangsi. Concerned about the radical implications of its content, the police ordered *New Society* to cease publication in April 1920, just as the nineteenth issue was about to be printed. Determined to regroup, Ch'ü and his four friends published the first issue of a new magazine entitled *L'Humanité* (*Jen-tao*) on August 5, 1920, but the French title did not confuse its critics for long. Before the second issue appeared the financial support of the Association for the Advancement of Society was withdrawn, and the disappointed young editors found it impossible to continue.[25]

22. Wen Chi-che, "Ch'ü Ch'iu-pai t'ung-chih chan-tou te i-sheng" [Comrade Ch'ü Ch'iu-pai's battling life], *Hung-ch'i p'iao-p'iao*, 5:85; TYTH, p. 129. Ch'ü may have participated in Li's Marxist Research Society (Ma-k'e-shih-chu-i yen-chiu-hui) founded in late 1918. See Maurice Meisner, *Li Ta-chao and the Origins of Chinese Marxism* (Cambridge: Harvard University Press, 1967), p. 72-73.

23. For the publication details of Ch'ü's May Fourth writings discussed in this chapter see Ting Ching-t'ang and Wen Ts'ao, eds., *Ch'ü Ch'iu-pai chu i hsi-nien mu-lu* [A chronological bibliography of Ch'ü Ch'iu-pai's writings and translations] (Shanghai: Jen-min ch'u-pan-she, 1959), pp. 1-4.

24. Chow Tse-tsung, *Research Guide to the May Fourth Movement* (Cambridge: Harvard University Press, 1963), p. 148. Ting Ching-t'ang, *Hsueh-hsi Lu Hsün*, pp. 125-127.

25. Cheng Chen-to, "Chi Ch'ü Ch'iu-pai," p. 27; Ting Ching-t'ang, *Hsueh-hsi Lu Hsün*, p. 127. Ch'ü also published in other journals, including *Reconstruction* [Kai-tsao], *Morning Post* [Ch'en pao], *New China* [Hsin Chung-kuo], *Emancipation and Reconstruction*

In general, the articles Ch'ü wrote for *New Society* and other journals express many of the basic political beliefs held by May Fourth students. Ch'ü was well aware that the convergence of the New Culture intellectual revolution and the May Fourth nationalist movement had "raised cataclysmic waves that shook through all China." Like thousands of others, he had become an unwavering anti-imperialist. "The patriotic movement had actually a deeper meaning than mere patriotism," he observed. "The taste of colonialism, in its full bitterness, had never come home to the Chinese until then, even though we had already had the experience of several decades of foreign exploitation behind us. The sharp pain of imperialist oppression then reached the marrow of our bones and it awakened us from the nightmares of impractical democratic reforms."[26] At the same time, Ch'ü's iconoclastic articles ridiculing traditional Confucian society and values show that he had finally become enthusiastic about participating in the assault on Chinese culture. Aside from expressing compassion for poor people in general and all those who were the "victims" of Confucian society, his writings showed a special concern for the plight of Chinese women, all of whom he felt suffered from "spiritual imprisonment."[27] Ch'ü now understood the tragic fate of his mother in a broader social context.

Shortly after the May Fourth Movement, however, Ch'ü Ch'iu-pai revealed that the social and political thought of his small group was confused. In a sense, Ch'ü recalled, the social thought of Peking youth was similar to the thought of Russian youth in the 1840s; they were aware that Chinese society was afflicted with a serious illness, but its cure was still unknown.[28] Ch'ü's own beliefs are difficult to analyze because, despite his iconoclastic attacks on Confucian society, he was probably still influenced by Buddhism, and, despite his hostility toward the Western powers, he was also attracted to liberal ideology. It is reasonable to characterize Ch'ü as a fledgling socialist in this period. Ch'ü was not by any means a sophisticated socialist thinker, but one cannot dismiss the importance of his participation in Li Ta-chao's various socialist study groups. It is clear, however, that Ch'ü was not yet a Marxist. He had read *The Communist Manifesto* and other Marxist writings, but he admitted at the time and later in life that he did not understand Marxism, and that, among his close friends, "no one understood the materialist conception of history."[29]

There is no reason to doubt Ch'ü's statement that "we were con-

---

[Chieh-fang yü kai-tsao], and *Dawn* [Shu-kuang], which were all based in Peking, and *Women's Review* [Fu-nü p'ing-lun] a Soochow publication.

26. CCPWC, 1:23; Hsia, *Gate of Darkness*, p. 16.
27. Ting Ching-t'ang, *Hsueh-hsi Lu Hsün*, p. 130.
28. CCPWC, 1:23-24.   29. TYTH, p. 137; CCPWC, 1:24.

fused by the different socialist schools, and were not quite clear about the definition of socialism" during the early May Fourth period, but his writings and his assumptions about history and revolution confirm the view, expressed by Ch'ü in 1935, that in his Peking years he was a utopian socialist, or more precisely, a "Tolstoyan anarchist."[30] Like utopian socialists elsewhere, it was the promise of somehow skipping directly from precapitalist society to the socialist utopia of the future, thus bypassing the odious capitalist stage, that attracted Ch'ü Ch'iu-pai to utopian anarchist thought. And by his own admission, Ch'ü had less interest in the objective laws of history, which in the Marxist view required a capitalist stage of development in order to achieve socialism, than he had in the "ultimate ideals" (*chung-chi li-hsiang*) of society.[31] He was interested in the Russian revolution because, as he understood it, the Russians had been able "to leap [*yueh*] from a monarchial system of state to a socialist nation."[32]

In several places in his writings Ch'ü discussed in the most general terms his vision of a utopian society. In the foreword to the first issue of *New Society*, Ch'ü and his friends proclaimed that their aim was to help create "a happy new society in which there exists freedom and equality; a peaceful society in which there is no class distinction and warfare."[33] Late in life, Ch'ü recalled that he had believed utopian society to be one in which "peace and love dominate the world and permeate all humankind."[34] Ch'ü's view of capitalism was shaped by May Fourth nationalist concerns. Capitalism was perceived not as an inevitable stage of internal development that produced antagonistic social classes, but as an aggressive and unnatural external force that took the form of imperialism, a phenomenon that would be resisted by the Chinese people as a whole. In Ch'ü's opinion, the Chinese student movement "leaned toward socialism" precisely because it identified "capitalism" with imperialism.[35]

It is also apparent that Ch'ü's beliefs about the means by which the socialist utopia would be realized in China stand in sharp contrast to Marxist assumptions. Although Ch'ü did not rule out the possibility that violence might be necessary, the theme of class struggle did not have an important place in his early writings. On the contrary, he hoped that socialism would arrive in China because the various social classes and groups had finally united to restructure Chinese society, remove the national traitors from power, and stand up to imperialism. If force was necessary, it would be the Chinese people as a whole who would exert it on their enemies, foreign and domestic. But, like utopian

30. CCPWC, 1:24–25; TYTH, p. 128, 136. The young Mao Tse-tung expressed an interest in anarchism at about the same time.

31. TYTH, p. 138.   32. CCPWC, 2:544.   33. Bernadette Li, p. 30.

34. TYTH, p. 138; D.J. Li, p. 165.   35. CCPWC, 1:23.

socialists elsewhere, he tended to assume that the transition to social-ism could be carried out by "peaceful methods." In articles such as "The Time for Reform Has Arrived," and "The Labor Question in China? The Labor Question in the World?" that appeared in *New Society* in November and December 1919, Ch'ü suggested that violence could be avoided if sufficient attention was given to mass education, the development of science, and the "promulgation of knowledge."[36] In an effort to convince others of the revolutionary potential of edu-cation, Ch'ü translated an essay by Tolstoy entitled "On Education," one of many articles in which Tolstoy expressed a hostility toward lifeless formal education and encouraged a more popular and natural "living and learning" educational environment.[37]

Furthermore, Ch'ü made it clear in another *New Society* article "Vic-tims of the Social Movement," that the responsibility of leading such a revolutionary movement would naturally be assumed by a small group of enlightened intellectuals who shared the socialist vision of the good society. Ch'ü acknowledged later in life that ever since his childhood he had been interested in the question of "why Chinese intellectuals always want to 'bring peace and order to the nation and the world.'"[38] During his Peking days, Ch'ü clearly believed that subjective forces played a more decisive role than objective forces in transforming so-ciety, and that intellectuals had a moral obligation to impose their socialist consciousness on objective reality and lead the downtrodden masses into the future.

The utopian socialist or Tolstoyan elements present in Ch'ü's thought were expressed philosophically in a remarkable essay entitled "She-hui yü tsui-o" [Society and evil] that appeared in *New Society* in March 1920. This essay is interesting because, while it deals with the problem of the existence of evil in society, and the means by which evil is to be eradicated, it makes no use whatever of Marxist analytical cate-gories such as mode of production or dialectical materialism. As Ber-nadette Yu-ning Li has pointed out, Ch'ü's simple philosophical scheme recognizes only two basic moral precepts in human society, "love" (*ai*) and "non-love" (*pu-ai*). Human deeds based on the absolute principle of love are meritorious and will inevitably benefit society; actions moti-vated by the false principle of non-love are evil and, therefore, harm-ful to society. Since society is composed of the individuals who inhabit it, society can be evil if a significant portion of individuals act contrary

36. Shneider, *Tvorcheskii Put'*, p. 19. In fact, Ch'ü believed that the "new faith" itself would serve as the foundation of a "new life." See Bernadette Li, p. 37.

37. Ting Ching-t'ang and Wen Ts'ao, *Hsi-nien mu-lu*, p. 4. See Leo Tolstoy, *Tolstoy on Education* (Chicago: University of Chicago Press, 1967) for a collection of Tolstoy's "proto-Summerhillian" essays.

38. Shneider, *Tvorcheskii Put'*, p. 19; TYTH, p. 137; D.J. Li, p. 165.

to the absolute principle of love and create evil social institutions and ideologies that constitute a barrier to the development of love.[39] In this article Ch'ü failed to express any faith in the existence of objective laws of history, laws that insured the eventual arrival of socialism. In no sense should morally evil phenomena such as capitalism and imperialism be regarded as historical prerequisites for the achievement of socialism. Instead, the "good" society of the future would be brought about by highly motivated human beings who acted on the basis of their utopian vision and the principle of universal love. Society may appear to mold individuals, but ultimately the human will is decisive.

Even though Ch'ü had rejected the important notion of passive resistance to evil, the influence of Tolstoy is quite apparent in this essay. Indeed, Ch'ü is known to have been reading and translating Tolstoy when he was writing this essay. But Ch'ü's enthusiasm for Tolstoyan socialism does not mean that he had succeeded in making a clean break from the influence of traditional Chinese schools of thought. On the contrary, there are obvious affinities between Ch'ü's May Fourth social and political views and the notions about ultimate principles, good and evil, and moral conduct that are contained in the schools of Buddhism discussed earlier. As Derk Bodde has argued, Tolstoy was himself profoundly influenced by Buddhist thought.[40] Nevertheless, the manner in which Ch'ü now perceived the utopian society of the future was definitely socialist.

It is true that Ch'ü's interest in Tolstoy began to waver in early 1920 as he began to explore Marxism more thoroughly. What is interesting, however, was Ch'ü's choice of Marxist reading material. It was not Marx or Lenin themselves that he studied, but the German Marxist August Bebel. In April 1920 Ch'ü used a Russian text to translate Bebel's long essay "Socialization of Society" and wrote an article of his own, entitled "The Pan-labor Theory of Bebel," that appeared in *New Society*. Bebel was by no means a utopian socialist; but, in the works known to the young Ch'ü Ch'iu-pai, Bebel was primarily concerned with offering his readers an unusually elaborate glimpse at the utopian society of the future. What Marxists in Russia saw as weakness in Bebel's work (that is, his assertion that a fully developed socialist society would emerge immediately following the revolutionary victory, and his tendency to ignore the need to develop the material prerequisites for such a society), Ch'ü Ch'iu-pai perceived as strength. There is, therefore, no reason to doubt Ch'ü's own statement that his

39. For a sound analysis of this essay see Bernadette Li, pp. 39-41.
40. Derk Bodde, *Tolstoy and China* (Princeton: Princeton University Press, 1950), pp. 75-89.

early interest in socialism and Marxism was based primarily upon the appeal of their "ultimate ideals."[41]

LITERARY THOUGHT

A unique feature of the intellectual and political revolutions of the New Culture and May Fourth periods is that they were led by people who were essentially literary figures. As Chow Tse-tsung has observed: "Literature was the major profession of the traditional Chinese intellectuals."[42] It is hardly surprising, therefore, that although the gentry intellectuals who led the New Culture Movement had defected from their social class and rejected its ideology, they retained a keen interest in literature and its role in society. As a result, the modern literary revolution, which had been under way for some time, became symbolic of the overall movement for cultural revolution during the May Fourth period, and was actually thrust into a vanguard role in the youth rebellion. The young Ch'ü Ch'iu-pai was typical of many young intellectuals who participated in the May Fourth Movement first as patriotic political activists, but whose fundamental concern came eventually to center upon the literary revolution. Like many others, when Ch'ü turned his attention to advancing the all important cultural revolution, he was naturally inclined to specialize in the literary field, an area that had fascinated him since childhood.

The literary revolution was characterized primarily by its iconoclastic rejection of both the form and the content of classical literature (*wen-yen*). The leaders of the movement viewed the difficult classical language as an aristocratic code that permitted the traditional elite to monopolize literary life. They opposed the archaic and stereotyped style of classical literature, and objected to the view that only poetry and nonfictional prose could be considered serious literary forms. More important, the literary revolutionaries rejected the role played by classical literature as a vehicle for Confucian ideology. It was said that the obscure forms and Confucian content of classical literature constituted obstacles to modern progress and, hence, the salvation of the nation.[43]

As Ch'en Tu-hsiu stated in an article entitled "On the Literary Revolution" that appeared in *New Youth* on February 1, 1917, one of the central objectives of the movement was to create a "plain-speaking and popular literature of society in general."[44] Ch'en and others

41. Ting Ching-t'ang, *Hsueh-hsi Lu Hsün*, p. 136. See August Bebel, *Society of the Future* (Moscow: Progress Publishers, 1971).
42. Chow Tse-tsung, *The May Fourth Movement* (Stanford: Stanford University Press, 1967), p. 269. See chapter 11 of Chow's book for a summary of the literary revolution.
43. Ibid., p. 276.   44. Ibid.

urged young writers to use the vernacular language (*pai-hua*) in order to facilitate communication with a large audience, and to experiment with new literary forms, especially fiction. On the assumption that there were no viable sources of literary inspiration to be found in the Chinese tradition, the advocates of literary revolution eagerly turned to models imported primarily from Western Europe, America, and Tsarist Russia. The anti-imperialist movement had resulted in widespread disillusionment with liberal Western political thought, but had not dampened the enthusiasm of cosmopolitan intellectuals for the great nineteenth-century Western literary and cultural heritage. It was not the avant-garde or futurist writers of Europe and Russia, but rather the nineteenth-century masters who were translated and discussed in the pages of *New Youth*, *New Tide* [Hsin ch'ao] and other iconoclastic publications. Chinese writers were, on the whole, concerned more with the progressive social content of foreign literature than with purely formal experiments. The thrust of the movement was reflected quite clearly in Ch'en Tu-hsiu's urgent request of February 1917 for those who were "willing to become a Chinese Hugo, Zola, Goethe, Hauptmann, Dickens, or Wilde" to step forward at once.[45]

One of the most radical positions adopted by young writers was their insistence upon autonomy and independence for the literary world. Because Chinese society was so highly integrated, they argued, literature had served for centuries as an important cog in the Confucian state; thus, by definition, it tended to play a conservative political role by promoting ideological orthodoxy. The leaders of the literary revolution did not object to the notion that literature should play an active social role; what they objected to was the role literature played in China as a defender of state ideology. Literature, in their view, should play a progressive role in society by criticizing outmoded thought and promoting social change; but to do so required its independence from the state. There was, of course, debate among early May Fourth writers about what constituted "progressive" writing. Some believed writers should concentrate on "exposing" the evils of traditional society, some wanted to propose alternatives, and still others concentrated on the liberation of the individual, an ego-expanding process that sometimes required transcendental flights from society.

In many respects Ch'ü Ch'iu-pai was a typical standard-bearer of the literary revolution. Like others, he focused his attention on the literature of a single foreign country, Russia. He knew nothing about Russian literature when he enrolled in the Institute of Russian Lan-

45. Ibid.

guage, but some of his lessons involved reading Russian short stories. By 1919 he was able to read Russian with the aid of a dictionary, and thus was able to carry on independent research. Before long he concluded that his model, nineteenth-century Russian literature, was more relevant to China than any of the other foreign models.

It must be assumed that Ch'ü accepted most of the arguments made by those who attacked classical Chinese literature, but Ch'ü's own writings did not dwell upon these familiar themes. Instead, he preferred the more positive approach of introducing foreign literature. Ch'ü's early rudimentary views of Russian literature were expressed in three short essays written in February and March 1920. Two of these, "Preface to *A Collection of Short Stories by Famous Russian Writers*" and "On Pushkin's *Belkin's Tales*," appeared in a book published by *New China* magazine in July 1920; the third essay was appended to Ch'ü's translation of Gogol's "The Servant's Quarters," which appeared in the literary journal *Dawn* [Shu-kuang] in early 1920. Ch'ü conceded in these writings that he was among those who once believed that little could be learned by studying foreign literature because the languages, cultures, and social problems of countries were vastly different.[46] But once he grasped what he understood to be the peculiarities of the Bolshevik revolution—that is, Russia's leap from a traditional (and essentially precapitalist) monarchial society to a socialist society—his thinking about the relevance of foreign literature changed.[47] Although politically Ch'ü was beginning to acquaint himself with Marxist theory, he seems to have known nothing about Marxist literary thought or postrevolutionary Soviet literature. The October Revolution was important in Ch'ü's literary thought only because it suggested to him that China, like prerevolutionary Russia, was a traditional precapitalist society that, in his view, was addressing the sort of social and political problems discussed, not in Russian Marxist literature, but rather in nineteenth-century Russian fiction. Thus for Ch'ü, prerevolutionary Russian literature was more relevant to China than Western European literature, because nineteenth-century Russia was more like early twentieth-century China. The new Chinese literature should model itself on the great Russian tradition, and Ch'ü specifically recommended the works of Pushkin, Gogol, Turgenev, Dostoyevsky, and Tolstoy.[48]

Ch'ü deeply appreciated the descriptive quality of Russian fiction. A

46. See Ch'ü's postscript to Gogol's "The Servant's Quarters" [P'u yu shih], CCPWC, 3:1305.

47. Ch'ü Ch'iu-pai, "*O-lo-ssu ming-chia tuan-p'ien hsiao-shuo chi* hsü" [Preface to *A Collection of Famous Russian Short Stories*], CCPWC, 2:543–544.

48. Ch'ü Ch'iu-pai, "Lun P'u-hsi-chin te *Pien-erh-chin hsiao-shuo chi*" [On Pushkin's *Belkin's Tales*], CCPWC, 2:542.

great deal could be learned about society by studying the techniques of Gogol and other "realists" (*hsien-shih p'ai*) who were willing to describe the condition of the "lower class" (*hsia-liu*), as he did in "The Servant's Quarters," or expose "social evil" (*she-hui te o*) and official corruption, as he did in *The Inspector General*. On the other hand, Ch'ü was deeply moved by the romantic or spiritual qualities of Russian literature. The vivid works of Gogol, Pushkin, and especially Tolstoy touched the hearts of Chinese readers, stimulated their emotions and aroused their "moral" (*tao-te*) feelings.[49] Although he held what might be considered a materialist view of art, Ch'ü's remarks suggest that he viewed the relationship between literature and society and the question of the social role of the writer in two ways. In certain passages he stressed the "reflective" nature of literature.[50] It is the duty of writers to investigate society and report their findings to the public. In other passages Ch'ü assigned a more active role to literature and the writer in the actual transformation of society. "Prior to revolutionary movements in all nations," he pointed out, "social thought is transformed." The Russian revolution proceeded rapidly in a very backward nation precisely because in Russia the writer did more than describe and reflect society; he served as the "mouthpiece" (*hou-she*) of society by advocating progressive social reform. What is needed in China, Ch'ü observed, is a literature that can "transform human consciousness and break down social conventions."[51]

Ch'ü was also impressed by two other features of Russian literature. Pushkin, for one, had captured the "national spirit" of the Russian people: if China needed anything, it was a modern national literature that reflected the spiritual essence of the Chinese people.[52] Ch'ü, the May Fourth patriot, expressed no interest in class-oriented literature. Finally, it is clear that Ch'ü appreciated the magnificent artistry of the Russian masters. Indeed, he believed that Pushkin and Gogol resolved the difficult problem of attempting to reach a broad audience without sacrificing artistic quality. Their stories were simple, and therefore understood by most readers, yet they were written so skillfully and beautifully that they had an emotional impact.[53] China's literary problems could also be solved if writers would create a "national literature" (*min-tsu te wen-hsueh*), which he defined as well-written, comprehensible, and moral.[54]

Nowhere are Ch'ü's utopian political beliefs and voluntarist assumptions about art combined more forcefully than in his translations of Russian literature, which include "The Servant's Quarters" and "Women" by Gogol, and three tales by Tolstoy, "Idle Talk," "The

49. CCPWC, 3:1304.   50. CCPWC, 2:544.   51. CCPWC, 3:1304.
52. CCPWC, 2:542, 543, 545.   53. CCPWC, 2:542.   54. CCPWC, 2:543, 545.

Prayer," and "What Men Live By."[55] Ch'ü admired the straightforward investigative realism of Gogol and Turgenev, but he seems to
have had a slight preference for overtly moralistic parables. For example, Tolstoy's "What Men Live By" is, in his translation, a fictional
version of the moral philosophy worked out by Ch'ü in his own essay
"Society and Evil."

Ch'ü's earliest writings on literature were rather unpolished, but it
is quite clear that he was not expressing Marxist ideas. On the contrary, one is struck by the general consistency between his "Tolstoyan," or utopian socialist, political opinions and his May Fourth literary
thought. It is sometimes forgotten that Tolstoy was the last of the
great nineteenth-century utopian socialist or populist literary thinkers. The young Ch'ü Ch'iu-pai had not yet undertaken a serious study
of the works of Herzen, Belinsky, Chernyshevsky, Dobrolyubov, and
others who developed the Russian school of utopian socialist literary
thought, but by immersing himself in Tolstoy he came to share many
of their basic assumptions about art.

One is inclined for several reasons to characterize the young Ch'ü
as a utopian socialist literary thinker. First, like Belinsky and the
others, Ch'ü espoused a materialist view of the relationship between
art and society. The Russian populist school preached that a work of
art could only be understood in the context of the society from which
it emerged. That is, artistic culture is not an autonomous realm: there
is an organic relationship between art and society. Literary works
were to be viewed foremost as social documents, as reflections of
material reality.[56]

This materialist predisposition of the Russian populists also shaped
their view of seemingly nonpolitical literature. The social values of
writers who appear to have little to say about society are expressed
indirectly or unconsciously in their work.[57] The materialism of the
populists, therefore, could be quite deterministic. As a "product" of
society, all art is social, and hence political; and all artists, whether
they recognize the fact or not, reflect social life.

Another element of utopian socialist literary theory present in the
literary thought of the young Ch'ü Ch'iu-pai is the strong tendency to
assign to both literature and literary criticism a utilitarian role in

55. See Ting Ching-t'ang and Wen Ts'ao, *Hsi-nien mu-lu*, pp. 103–105; and Ting
Ching-t'ang, *Hsueh-hsi Lu Hsün*, p. 141. Ch'ü also translated a portion of the French novel
Fromont the Younger, Risler the Elder by A. Daudet. His reading in Russian literature in-
cluded *Belkin's Tales* by Pushkin, *The Inspector General* by Gogol, and "Three Deaths,"
"Elias," "Esarhaddon," "Three Questions," "Snow Storm," and *The Resurrection* (which he
had hoped to translate) by Tolstoy.

56. Ralph E. Matlaw, ed., *Belinsky, Chernyshevsky, and Dobrolyubov: Selected Criticism* (New
York: E.P. Dutton and Co., 1962), p. 18.

57. Ibid., p. 7.

society. The artist and the critic should serve the public interest by attacking retrogressive efforts to preserve the old order, and by promoting progressive historical change. "All human activity must serve mankind if it is not to remain a useless and idle occupation," Chernyshevsky had proclaimed. "Art, too, must serve some useful purpose and not fruitless pleasure."[58] Underscoring the moral responsibilities of the writer, Chernyshevsky insisted, "the artist must pronounce judgment on the phenomenon he depicts."[59]

What one finds here, and in the May Fourth literary thought of Ch'ü, is a tension between deterministic and voluntaristic elements. But the contradiction between the idea that art merely "reflects" reality, and the notion that artists might play an active role in effecting a radical transformation of society, is more apparent than real. The utopian socialist perspective was materialist only to the extent that it viewed social development as having been shaped by objective, impersonal (and sometimes unhealthy) historical forces in the past. But the problem of explaining the past was one thing: when the utopian socialists moved to the more urgent matter of the social problems of the present, they abandoned the materialist method of analysis. In the past, human beings had been the passive and manipulated objects of material forces precisely because they were not yet conscious of the socialist vision of a rational and perfectly natural social order. But as soon as the truth of the socialist idea is firmly in mind, human beings cease to be merely the victims of objective forces; they can begin to impose their rational will on the world, and consciously move toward social ends consistent with the universal principle of natural socialist order.

For those, like Ch'ü Ch'iu-pai, who were active in the literary realm, this notion tended to mean that so long as artists were unaware of the ultimate truths about human nature and history, they were capable, at best, of "merely" reflecting or reproducing reality. But once natural law is understood, artists can at once transcend the imperfect reality of the present and consciously promote the realization of a rationally established plan designed to propel society toward the socialist utopia.

The idealist and activist strains in utopian socialist literary thought were, therefore, more important than the materialist elements. The Russian populist literary theorists, like New Culture activists in China, placed an extraordinary faith in the revolution in ideas, and viewed revolution in the cultural superstructure of society as a precondition for revolution in the material base of society. As part of the "enlight-

58. Georg Plekhanov, *Unaddressed Letters and Art and Social Life* (Moscow: Foreign Languages Publishing House, 1957), p. 150.

59. N.G. Chernyshevsky, *Selected Philosophical Essays* (Moscow: Foreign Languages Publishing House, 1953), p. 374.

ened" intelligentsia, artists were believed to be capable of playing a vanguard role. Artistic activity was thus not seen as a mechanical and passive reflection of society but, as Chernyshevsky put it, as one of the great "moral activities" of humankind. These are, of course, precisely the sort of ideas advanced by Ch'ü in 1919.

Finally, it is important to mention the iconoclastic themes so characteristic of utopian socialist literary thought and so pronounced in Ch'ü's May Fourth cultural views. The utilitarianism of the populists caused them to be ambivalent or even hostile toward the belief that there must be cultural continuity between the past and the present. The perspective on the "classics" of thinkers like Pisarev was that they were filled with incorrect and unscientific ideas about social evolution, and thus were largely irrelevant politically, socially, and aesthetically. Furthermore, these men were hostile toward bourgeois culture and skeptical about the "bourgeois cultural stage" because they identified the "unnatural" division of labor and the steady deterioration of human artistic sensibilities with the growth of capitalism in Western Europe. But more important, the emphasis they placed on consciousness as the motor of history permitted them to assert that the capitalist stage of cultural development might be skipped in relatively backward precapitalist societies like Tsarist Russia and that revolutionary and utopian goals, such as the cultural awakening and liberation of the masses, might be achieved directly. They were unwilling to accept the view that the laws of history required all societies to pass through a capitalist stage on the road to socialism. Socialism was produced by people who had the will to construct a socialist society.

When viewed in the perspective of nineteenth-century utopian socialist literary thought, Ch'ü's random remarks on literature and his scattered translations become comprehensible. Ch'ü was stating literary views that were entirely consistent with his Tolstoyan social and political opinions. The writings of Belinsky and Chernyshevsky did not come to his attention at this time, but his ideas—the moral obligations of art, the significance of "cultural revolution," the desirability of bypassing the capitalist cultural stage, and the need to build a "national" people's culture—were compatible with the populist outlook and based upon populist assumptions about history and revolution. There was, accordingly, not the slightest trace of Marxism in the first set of modern literary ideas expressed by the man who was to become China's foremost Marxist literary thinker. On the contrary, Ch'ü began as a utopian.

The May Fourth episode in Ch'ü Ch'iu-pai's life ended before he could develop these basic literary views. Just after the collapse of *L'Humanité*, he received a startling offer from the Peking newspaper *Ch'en pao* [*Morning Post*]. Ch'ü and two others, Yu Sung-hua and Li

Tsung-wu, were asked to serve as news correspondents for the *Morn-ing Post* in Moscow at an annual salary of 2,000 yuan.[60] Ch'ü had difficulty in making a decision, but ultimately he decided to accept because the student movement was losing momentum, and an oppor-tunity to visit the world's first socialist society could not be allowed to slip away.

60. Li K'e-ch'ang, "Fang-wen chi," p. 2.

3 A Journey to the Land of Hunger

Some "inner demand" is driving me onward—me, who only by a narrow chance has escaped turning into a callous, misanthropic "recluse" under miserable circumstances. I have steeled my heart to part with my aged father, my brothers, cousins, and all relatives and friends and set out on my journey westward.

CH'Ü CH'IU-PAI, 1920[1]

Among those who eventually became leaders of the Chinese Communist Party and the League of Left-wing Writers, Ch'ü Ch'iu-pai was the first to visit the Soviet Union, and thus the first to be regarded as an expert on Soviet affairs.[2] His writings were remarkably popular among urban youth in Shanghai and Peking because for many young progressives they were the only reliable and stimulating source of information on post revolutionary Russia.[3] Yet it is also apparent that

1. CCPWC, 1:14; T. A. Hsia, *The Gate of Darkness* (Seattle: University of Washington Press, 1968), p. 12.

2. Most Western scholarship on Ch'ü focuses on this period of his life. For example, see Hsia, *Gate of Darkness*, pp. 3-42; Marián Gálik, "Studies in Modern Chinese Intellectual History: II. Young Ch'ü Ch'iu-pai (1915-1922)," *Asian and African Studies*, 12 (1976): 85-117; Li Yu-ning and Michael Gasster, "Ch'ü Ch'iu-pai's Journey to Russia, 1920-1922," *Monumenta Serica: Journal of Oriental Studies*, 29 (1970-71): 537-556; and Ellen Widmer, "Qu Qiubai and Russian Literature," in Merle Goldman, ed., *Modern Chinese Literature in the May Fourth Era* (Cambridge: Harvard University Press, 1977), pp. 103-125.

3. See Li Po-chao, "Ch'ü Ch'iu-pai t'ung-chih te *Ch'ih-tu hsin shih*" [Comrade Ch'ü Ch'iu-pai's *Impressions of the Red Capital Seen Through the Mind*], *Lu-hsing-chia* [The traveller], 6 (June 1956): 34; and Liu Chih-ling and Chang Po-hai, "Ch'ü Ch'iu-pai t'ung-chih te O-hsiang chi-ch'eng ho Ch'ih-tu hsin-shih" [Comrade Ch'ü Ch'iu-pai's *A Journey to the Land of*

Ch'ü's writings were captivating because they were autobiographical and romantic. Young intellectuals had no difficulty identifying with Ch'ü because the emotions and personal dilemmas he discussed were common to the troubled May Fourth generation. It was easy for Ch'ü's peers to think of his distant pilgrimage as their own.[4] Thus, aside from providing information about the homeland of socialism, Ch'ü's extraordinary writings told the unusual story of his own intellectual odyssey in the more than two years between October 1920 and January 1923. When Ch'ü left China his thinking, vague and incomplete, reflected the condition of early May Fourth intellectual life. Still searching, he had almost no idea of the role he would play in the salvation of China. By the time he returned, he was a dedicated and enthusiastic member of the new Chinese Communist Party. Ch'ü's observations about his own intellectual transformation were alluring because they were honest and, at the same time, melodramatic. Ch'ü confessed to his readers that he knew very little about the Russian revolution or Marxist ideology, and had no idea what he would find in the Soviet Union. Nevertheless, he believed it was in his own interest and in the interest of China that he embark upon this journey into the unknown.

The *Morning Post* offer of September 1920 reached Ch'ü at just the right moment. *L'Humanité* had suddenly collapsed and Ch'ü sensed that the potential for intellectual growth in Peking was now limited. It was time for a new adventure. Still, the decision was difficult and many factors had to be taken into consideration. The promise of a salary of 2,000 yuan was very attractive; but to accept, Ch'ü would have to drop out of the Russian Language Institute after three years of hard work and forfeit his right to a routine but secure diplomatic or administrative position in the future. It is unlikely that he saw the offer as an opportunity to launch a career in journalism, because he readily admitted that he was not qualified and should not accept the position.[5] Having failed to understand his motives, several friends and relatives attempted to discourage Ch'ü from taking such a hazardous trip. Not only was Russia strange and unknown, they insisted, but its people were suffering miserably from a variety of catastrophes stemming from the violent revolutionary upheaval. Many friends were concerned for his personal safety. But Ch'ü explained that he could no

---

Hunger and *Impressions of the Red Capital Seen Through the Mind*], *Wen shih che* [Literature, history, philosophy], June 1958, pp. 8-13.

4. For a superb discussion of the appeal of romantic writings during the early May Fourth period, see Leo Ou-fan Lee, *The Romantic Generation of Modern Chinese Writers* (Cambridge: Harvard University Press, 1973).

5. CCPWC, 1:27.

longer "sit in the prison of the past." "At first, cousin Ch'un absolutely opposed my going to Russia, believing that I was deliberately going toward my doom."[6] Ch'ü refused to give in, sensing that a break with his family and China itself might be a precondition for his personal development.

Actually, Ch'ü Ch'iu-pai sought much more than his own liberation when he decided to go to Russia. He believed that in the course of striving for his personal freedom he might find the solution to China's problems. Someone, he thought, had to rise above the "ideological confusion" of the May Fourth era and seek answers to questions about socialism and the Soviet Union if Chinese social thought was to continue to develop. Ch'ü's announced goals were bold and egotistic. He hoped he would be able "to fulfill part of the responsibility of leading Chinese society to the path of a new life," and saw no conflict between his desire to develop his "individuality" (*ko-hsing*) and his determination to find a solution to the "China problem."[7] And he had no intention of apologizing for his heroic ambition to accept the responsibility for putting Chinese thinking on the right course. As a May Fourth patriot it was his duty to accept the challenge and report his findings: "I believe there is no 'private possession of thought,' and that is why I have made up my mind to go." Ch'ü obviously took some delight in the knowledge that his journey might be unpleasant and perhaps dangerous. To the skeptics he said: "Let us ignore the facts of hunger and cold, that one will have nothing to eat there, nothing to wear, and so forth; the significant fact is that this is the first country that has realized social revolution; it is the center of world revolution where Western and Eastern cultures meet. I shall not be troubled by the means I take to make the trip possible."[8]

In an allegorical sense, Ch'ü conceived of the trip as a fantastic voyage to what he called the "Land of Hunger." He pointed out that, according to the eighteenth-century Ch'ing scholar Kuan T'ung, the Land of Hunger was a distant place where one engaged in self-sacrifice and endured material deprivation in order to achieve high ideals. Po-i and Shu-ch'i, he recalled, retreated to their Land of Hunger on Mount Shou-yang rather than betray the rulers of the Shang dynasty by accepting the "dishonorable rice" of the new Chou dynasty during the twelfth century B.C. Although they starved to death in the Land of Hunger, they achieved their goals, which were, according to Ch'ü, "psychological" and not material. The lesson was clear: "We should,

6. CCPWC, 1:15; Bernadette Yu-ning Li, "A Biography of Ch'ü Ch'iu-pai: From Youth to Party Leadership (1899-1928)" (Ph.D. dissertation, Columbia University, 1967), p. 45.

7. CCPWC, 1:8; Li and Gasster, "Ch'ü Ch'iu-pai's Journey," p. 543.

8. CCPWC, 1:27; Hsia, *Gate of Darkness*, p. 20.

within the limits of our capacity, do the utmost to meet the demands of our hearts and, at whatever cost, endeavor to realize our private wishes."[9] For Ch'ü, the Land of Hunger was not a dreadful place. It was the promised land of the future that could only be reached by transcending the familiar Chinese world. The journey would be arduous and perhaps painful, but, he proclaimed, "I shall find in Soviet Russia my Land of Hunger."[10]

To heighten the drama of his heroic departure, Ch'ü employed powerful Buddhist symbols pertaining to the cycle of death and rebirth. His journey to the Land of Hunger was, in his view, nothing less than a departure from the world. In some passages Ch'ü suggested that his absence would be temporary; he would return to the world (*hui-hsiang*) when he learned the truth about the coming world order.[11] Elsewhere he hinted that his absence from China might be permanent, that his decision to go was "tantamount to a 'renunciation of the world'" (*ch'u-shih*).[12] Ch'ü's language was exaggerated, but it conveyed his deep feelings of emotional anxiety to his youthful readers. When he finally made the decision to renounce the Chinese world, he felt obligated to prepare his admirers for the possibility that he might not return. He noted, with some nostalgia, that his last-minute farewell letters to childhood friends were written with the intent that "they should carry a farewell forever."[13] Ch'ü's need to say "farewell forever" and his remark that "I did not care about the loss of my life"[14] can be interpreted in two ways, however. On one hand, he realized the journey would be perilous and that he might actually die. On the other hand, he was telling his readers that his pilgrimage would necessarily involve a spiritual death and a simultaneous rebirth as a child of the new world order.

PASSAGE TO THE LAND OF HUNGER

Ch'ü Ch'iu-pai's first well-known book, *A Journey to the Land of Hunger* [*O-hsiang chi-ch'eng*], focused almost exclusively on his arduous three-month trip from Tientsin to Moscow. The trip was important in his intellectual development because he experienced a variety of unanticipated difficulties that forced him to reassess the ultimate purpose of his pilgrimage.

Ch'ü's initial comments dwelled upon his unhappy reaction to the widespread material poverty he observed in China itself as his train

9. CCPWC, 1:27; Hsia, *Gate of Darkness*, p. 19.
10. CCPWC, 1:27; Hsia, *Gate of Darkness*, p. 20.   11. CCPWC, 1:8, 44.
12. CCPWC, 1:15; Hsia, *Gate of Darkness*, p. 21.
13. CCPWC, 1:16; Hsia, *Gate of Darkness*, p. 21.   14. Ibid.

passed through Manchuria on its way to the Soviet frontier. The backwardness of Harbin's social and economic life raised a number of questions in Ch'ü's mind about the methods the Soviets were using to transform similar regions in Russia. If there was to be hope for China, he would have to discover precisely how the Soviets had been able to realize the "ideal society of scientific socialism" in their own backward areas, like Siberia.[15] "Since I assume that social reconstruction has been realized in Russia," he reasoned, "it—the Russian Communist Party—must have appropriate methods for dealing with the practical aspects of life."[16] Ch'ü believed he could learn about such matters by studying Russian literature, which he believed to be "the starting point for the development of the new culture from the old culture."[17]

But Ch'ü's arrival in Irkutsk on January 7, 1921, marked the beginning of his unforgettable and highly disillusioning "Siberian experience." Siberia's "medieval society" and "semifeudal economic organization" caught Ch'ü by surprise.[18] Somehow he had expected to see some evidence of a society in the throes of a transition to socialism. The stark reality of life in Irkutsk, Omsk, and other Siberian towns through which the train passed was, however, one of widespread starvation, deprivation, and general human misery. Ch'ü was deeply moved by the ghastly sight of the ragged, seemingly faceless masses who straggled along the railway tracks in subfreezing temperatures. Commenting on his first piece of "Soviet black bread," Ch'ü remarked: "Its bitterness and sourness, with an odor of rotten grass mixed with mud, was something that no Chinese has ever tasted or can imagine."[19]

Ch'ü's Siberian experience, as Marián Gálik has suggested, caused him to question some of his assumptions about the importance of the role played by new thought (*ssu-hsiang*) in the transformation of society. He had, of course, stated repeatedly that the purpose of his trip was to study communist ideology in order to promote the reform of Chinese social thought. But in Siberia he learned that the power of ideology alone was not as great as he once believed. In Siberia people were selling books to buy food.[20] Ch'ü stated flatly: "Before coming to Russia, I thought that contemporary Russia was a 'laboratory of communism,' and that the Bosheviks were like chemists who were experimenting with 'the formulas of socialist theory' and using the 'nations of Russia' as 'Soviet test tubes' in which 'socialist compounds' were being produced. It was only my journey across Siberia that showed me I was wrong."[21] Ch'ü now began looking elsewhere for explanations of the

15. CCPWC, 1:43; Li and Gasster, "Ch'ü Ch'iu-pai's Journey," p. 546.
16. CCPWC, 1:44; Bernadette Li, p. 80.
17. CCPWC, 1:71; Gálik, "Young Ch'ü Ch'iu-pai," p. 99.   18. CCPWC, 1:79.
19. CCPWC, 1:76; Hsia, *Gate of Darkness*, p. 31.
20. CCPWC, 1:78.   21. CCPWC, 1:79; Gálik, "Young Ch'ü Ch'iu-pai," p. 99.

meaning of the Russian revolution. Its significance certainly was not apparent in the material conditions of Soviet life.

On January 25, 1921, four days before his twenty-second birthday, Ch'ü finally arrived at Moscow's Yaroslavsky Station around eleven o'clock at night. "Under the chilly moon, and amidst the hubbub of the crowd in the railway station," Ch'ü noted, "I knew I was in the Land of Hunger." He added, "My first glance at the 'Red Capital' left a deep impression on me. The Child of the East was now gradually feeling his inner strength."[22]

INTERPRETING THE RUSSIAN REVOLUTION

Ch'ü Ch'iu-pai's two-year stay in Moscow can be divided into two distinct parts. In the period from January 1921 to January 1922 he concerned himself almost exclusively with the task of interpreting the Russian revolution. Beginning in February 1922, after he had been "awakened" by what he understood to be the truth of the October Revolution, Ch'ü devoted himself to practical political matters until he departed from Moscow in December 1922. Of the two periods, Ch'ü's first year is more fascinating intellectually because his Siberian experience had convinced him to look beyond Marxist ideology to explain the mysteries of the Russian revolution. The thoughts and emotions recorded in his second book, *Impressions of the Red Capital Seen Through the Mind* [*Ch'ih-tu hsin-shih*], show that, although he never questioned the belief that some unprecedented historical development of universal significance was unfolding in Russia, he felt that its true source was being obscured by superficial manifestations of reality.[23] Throughout his first year he groped about in what he called a misty, dreamy realm as he searched for a satisfactory explanation of the revolution.

When Ch'ü began to reach some conclusions about the origins and meaning of the Russian revolution, he did not make much use of Marxist analytical categories. On the contrary, the extremely complex philosophical reflections contained in *Impressions of the Red Capital Seen Through the Mind* indicate that Ch'ü's new interpretation of the Russian revolution was built upon the conceptual language of the Consciousness-Only School of Mahayana Buddhism and stressed the role of powerful but mysterious subjective forces. However, in view of the fact that Ch'ü accepted the existence of the material world and was already a socialist, it would be wrong to suggest that he had reverted to Consciousness-Only beliefs. Ch'ü's renewed interest in Buddhist thought was limited specifically to an interest in Consciousness-Only notions about the structure and function of the individual human

22. CCPWC, 1:84; Hsia, *Gate of Darkness*, p. 33.
23. The full text of this book is in CCPWC, 1:94-196.

mind and the role of the cosmic Mind of the Universe. And, as Marián Gálik has observed, Ch'ü radically redefined and perhaps misused such concepts when explaining what he believed to be the appearance of a new and universal proletarian world order.[24]

The best method of illustrating Ch'ü's unusual use of Buddhist concepts is to analyze some of his observations about the Russian revolution. For instance, in several passages in his second book Ch'ü stated emphatically that it had been changes in what he called "mass psychology" (*ch'ün-chung hsin-li*) or "social psychology" (*she-hui hsin-li*) or "the mind of real life" (*shih-chi sheng-huo hsin*), rather than changes in material forces of production or social thought, that were fundamentally responsible for the arrival of the new proletarian age.[25] "The history of social evolution," Ch'ü wrote, "is the record of psychological changes in society. It is a 'shadow' indicating the fluctuations of emotions and feelings. It is not a learned record of social ideology and social teachings. It is not a general formula or a chart that, with the aid of reason, it would be possible to trace and discuss."[26]

In Ch'ü's opinion, there were several important things to know about "mass psychology." First, it was a collective force that had sprung forth spontaneously from the individual minds of the Russian people, and it accounted for the strength and creativity of the revolution. But, because it was a subconscious force, it was hidden from view. Second, "mass psychology" was more significant than social thought or material forces in the socialist transformation of society because it was nothing less than a worldly manifestation of a totally new proletarian Mind of the Universe. Although it is clear that by "Mind of the Universe" Ch'ü meant the ultimate principles of truth and perfection underlying the new proletarian age, he said very little about how this new Mind of the Universe had evolved or why it had acted first upon the minds of the Russian people. Ch'ü simply assumed that the Russian people and Russian culture had special qualities that made Russian minds subconsciously receptive to the force of these ultimate principles.

When dealing with the question of why the role of "mass psychology" was not more apparent, Ch'ü once again employed Buddhist concepts. According to Consciousness-Only doctrine, the human mind is capable of eight types of sensory activity. The first six record and coordinate the information gathered by the five senses. The seventh function of the mind is to interpret objective reality and thereby produce social thought. But, the most important and creative sensory activity, the eighth function of the mind, is capable of comprehending the Mind of the Universe and therefore the truth and order underlying

24. Gálik, "Young Ch'ü Ch'iu-pai," p. 117.   25. CCPWC, 1:79, 84.
26. CCPWC, 1:85; Gálik, "Young Ch'ü Ch'iu-pai," pp. 95-96.

the superficialities of objective reality. And in contrast to the first seven functions of the mind, the eighth function is carried on in a subconscious realm of the mind, and therefore human beings are scarcely aware of its role and power. As Gálik has suggested, when Ch'ü spoke of the "mind of real life" he was referring specifically to the subconscious powers of perception and motivation that are ordinarily associated with the eighth type of sensory activity.[27] The presence of the Mind of the Universe and the role of "mass psychology" in the revolution are obscured simply because the first seven types of mental activity are limited to conscious perception. It was for this reason that Ch'ü de-emphasized the role of ideology: the ego's interpretation of reality was superficial and unreliable.[28]

Having identified the relationship between the new Mind of the Universe and the "mass psychology" of the Russian people, Ch'ü utilized the Buddhist terms "Mind's sea" (*hsin-hai*) and "Mind's waves" (*hsin-p'o*) to articulate the manner in which the principles and energy of the new universe were converted into material forces and changes in Russian society. Ch'ü consistently used the term "Mind's sea" as a metaphor for the new proletarian Mind of the Universe, while "Mind's waves" referred to the constant movement and flow of "mass psychology." Although the "Mind's waves" (or mass psychology) were linked to the underlying "Mind's sea," they were blown about, like waves in a stormy sea, by the violent winds of a sometimes hostile material world. Thus Moscow, the symbol of the October Revolution, was seen by Ch'ü as an "island" floating on the crests of the "Mind's waves" that rose up powerfully from the proletarian "Mind's sea," but was "tossed and shaken by capitalist winds and typhoons" among other hostile external elements.[29] Progress in the revolutionary transformation of Russian society resulted from an interplay between "mass psychology" and the material world, or, as Ch'ü put it, between "social psychology—one of the aspects of the 'mind' of real life—and economic life—one of the aspects of the material resources of real life."[30] The "rising and falling of the Mind's waves," therefore, was seen by Ch'ü as a dynamic and creative phenomenon. The hidden strength (*han-liang*) of the Russian revolution resided in the force of "mass psychology" that was derived from the "Mind's sea." When this intangible force was harnessed, as Ch'ü believed it had been in the

---

27. Gálik, "Young Ch'ü Ch'iu-pai," p. 94.

28. Ch'ü's lack of faith in the powers of "reason" was not new. As he was leaving Peking in late 1920 he said that because "realistic theories" had been the foundation of human life for millennia his friends expected a "reasonable" explanation of the purpose of his trip when there was no reasonable explanation.

29. CCPWC, 1:84.   30. CCPWC, 1:79; Gálik, "Young Ch'ü Ch'iu-pai," p. 95.

"method of social organization of new Russia," it could be used to effect revolutionary material and social change.[31]

As we shall see, Buddhist terminology was by no means the only language used by Ch'ü in 1921, but a knowledge of these concepts helps to shed light on his understanding of the nature of the Russian revolution and the ultimate purpose of his trip. His sentiments were expressed rather eloquently in the last few lines of *A Journey to the Land of Hunger*:

> I looked [in China] for my own "shadow." But, as the rays mu-
> tually destroyed one another in the dark valley, I groped blindly
> for twenty years and was at a loss. My long sleeves flapped in a
> chaotic dance, but this only made my confused situation more
> difficult. Now I am happy for I have seen the lighthouse of the
> Mind's sea. Even though it is but a single red ray weak and
> indistinct, it is possible to see in it the approaching infinite pro-
> gress. I left my distant native village and came lonely and aban-
> doned into this country cut off from the world where rough
> food sticks in my throat. My soft muscles have been tempered
> into steel in this "hungry" Land of Hunger. In addition, my
> parents, brothers, sister, and all human relations have remained
> in the "land" outside this Land of Hunger. It seems that thus
> abandoned and lonely, I have come far away from the "realm of
> reality" and turned my back on my own principles. But there is
> yet the "realm of reali of the Land of Hunger, and the magnetic
> needle of my boat is set toward it. One day it will circumnavi-
> gate the Mind's sea of the universe and return to its true "native
> land."[32]

Until one had a proper understanding of the nature of the "Mind's sea" and the role of the "Mind's waves," Ch'ü was saying, one neces-
sarily lived in a dream world and had a distorted view of reality. Ch'ü's goal was to be reborn by "awakening" from both the dream world of China and the distorted images of material hardship surrounding him in the Land of Hunger.

Although Ch'ü made extensive use of Buddhist terminology to explain the October Revolution to Chinese intellectuals, he continued to employ language and concepts familiar to New Culture radicals in China. For example, young iconoclasts like Ch'ü were especially fond of using metaphors taken from the natural world when they discussed China's cultural crisis. It was stated repeatedly that Confucian culture and society were like a rotting carcass—stinking, dead, useless, and dangerously toxic. If China was to be saved, this stagnant culture

31. CCPWC, 1:84.
32. CCPWC, 1:91-92; Gálik, "Young Ch'ü Ch'iu-pai," pp. 102-103.

would have to be completely discarded. The "New Culture," on the other hand, was always identified with spring and everything that is youthful and vibrant. Inevitably winter and death yielded to spring and rebirth.

It is no surprise, therefore, that traditional Russian society was characterized by Ch'ü as a "proud and independent old tree," "a remnant of ice and snow," whose tired roots were unable to hold during the tumultuous October storm. Following its collapse, the "inner strength of spring" (*ch'un-i chih nei-li*) contained within the decaying colossus was finally able to burst forward. "Suddenly, a fresh, tender, green bud emerged from the old and rotten root."[33]

Neither is it surprising that Ch'ü believed that the first signs of "spring" in Russia could be detected in the culture and spirit of the revolutionary Soviet people. He assumed, like many intellectuals in China, that the development of a new culture was a precondition for future social and economic revolution. His personal encounter with the Russian people, for whom he had a profound admiration, had convinced him that they possessed revolutionary spiritual strength precisely because they had suffered countless hardships and difficulties throughout their history, and not because the mode of production had reached a stage that engendered socialist revolution. On the contrary, Ch'ü was telling his Chinese readers that the Russian case was significant because it demonstrated that material factors such as poverty and economic backwardness were less important in waging revolution than cultural and spiritual factors. Consequently, the material hardships he observed in the Soviet Union never caused him to question the revolution or criticize its leaders; instead, he accepted the argument that evils such as natural disaster, imperialism, counterrevolution, and "bourgeois psychology" were responsible for these problems. Thus he predicted that although "the radiance of the cultural star is being obscured by material sufferings in the Red Capital, such as cold, hunger, war, and epidemic," a "bright future" could be anticipated nevertheless.[34]

Finally, it is clear that Ch'ü's views about the significance of the Russian revolution for China continued to be shaped by his May Fourth assertion that China should follow the example of the Russian revolution because China and Russia shared certain national characteristics and historical experiences. Elaborating on this conviction in his writings, Ch'ü emphasized that the new universal culture he saw in

33. CCPWC, 1:89-90; Bernadette Li, p. 80.

34. CCPWC, 1:99-100; Bernadette Li, p. 81. According to Mark E. Schneider, *Tvorcheskii Put' Tsiui Tsiu-bo, 1899-1935* (Moscow: Izdatel'stvo Nauka, 1964), p. 33, Ch'ü made a symbolic attempt to ease the material suffering of the people by contributing his gold pocket watch to the government during a campaign to build up gold reserves.

Moscow had arisen from "the combination of two cultures, the Western and the Eastern, which have been opposed in the past and which now, since the beginning of the new era, can begin to complement each other."[35] Thus, in Ch'ü's view, the Russian revolution was unique and important to Chinese because Russia was neither a purely European nor a purely "Eastern" society. Although the Russian revolution had definite "roots" in the cultures of East and West, it also represented a sharp break with what Ch'ü understood to be the burdensome traditions of both cultures. When Ch'ü spoke of "Western" society, he was referring to capitalism; it contributed materialism and modern notions about progress and development to the new universal culture, but its tradition of spiritual bankruptcy would be repudiated. By "Eastern," Ch'ü meant the precapitalist societies of Asia; the East would contribute Asian spirituality to the cultural merger, but its legacy of stagnation and "slumber" would be rejected. Of the two elements, matter and spirit, Ch'ü clearly stressed the decisiveness of the latter, or Asian, element.[36] The spiritual strength of the Russian people, about which he had so much to say, was derived from the Asian roots of the Russian revolution. Material progress was essential, but it must be guided by spiritual imperatives. It is ironic that Lenin, who recognized the existence of similar forces in Russia, believed that the "Oriental" element made little contribution and was largely responsible for Russia's "Asiatic backwardness."

In any event, Ch'ü asserted time and again that China's cultural situation was similar to that of Russia in the 1840s. If China, like Russia, could successfully combine Eastern and Western elements in its revolution, a "shortcut" (*chieh-ching*) to socialism might be taken. China would be able to awaken from its Eastern slumber and modernize, but at the same time avoid the dreadful and alien capitalist stage of development, which Ch'ü associated with Western imperialism. The utopian element still present in Ch'ü's thinking about Russia and China is reflected quite clearly in a remark he made in October 1921. "Alas," he wrote, "the nightmare of capitalism shook the nerves of Russia and caused her to seek a 'shortcut' for an early awakening. It is a pity that the span of time can only be contracted a little, it is impossible to skip the necessary steps. Those controversial issues between Westernizers and Slavophiles have now been solved by time. *The direc-*

35. CCPWC, 1:165; Widmer, "Qu Qiubai and Russian Literature," p. 114.

36. Ch'ü's treatment of "East" and "West" can be regarded as a variant of the *t'i-yung* (Chinese learning as the substance, Western learning for practical application) formula popularized in nineteenth- and twentieth-century intellectual circles in China. In Ch'ü's dichotomy, however, "t'i" did not refer to Confucianism. See Joseph R. Levenson, *Confucian China and Its Modern Fate: A Trilogy* (Berkeley: University of California Press, 1968), pp. 59-78; and Stuart Schram, ed., *Chairman Mao Talks to the People* (New York: Pantheon Books, 1974), pp. 34-36.

tion of China's cultural movement is even more direct and its speed greater. It is about to take the step which Russia has already taken. It is the same dream; the merging of Eastern and Western cultures in China is after all the same as in Russia."[37] What is remarkable about this passage and virtually all of Ch'ü's writings in Russia is the absence of any serious discussion of revolutionary political strategy. Ch'ü simply assumed that revolutionary victory could be achieved eventually if a sufficient number of people awakened to the truth of the new world culture. Relying once again upon New Culture metaphors, Ch'ü proclaimed: "I sincerely hope that I can be an embryo of the new culture of humankind."[38]

SOCIETY AND SELF: HEAD AND HEART

Ch'ü Ch'iu-pai's writings on Russia were interesting to Chinese readers not only because he provided them with a meaningful analysis of the revolution, but also because Ch'ü went one step further and raised serious questions about the strength of his own character. To strive for an understanding of the October Revolution and its significance for China was one thing, but was he strong enough to serve Chinese society in a revolutionary manner?

Self-doubt seems to have plagued Ch'ü when his body was weak, and there were many such occasions during his first year in Moscow. Throughout July 1921 Ch'ü suffered attacks of tuberculosis, and, according to Ts'ao Ching-hua, one of his students, Soviet physicians informed Ch'ü that he would probably die in two or three years.[39] In early August a deeply depressed Ch'ü wrote: "A few days ago, the doctor found a lesion in my left lung and advised me to go home. Did I not spit blood again yesterday? I was laid up for one month in July, and felt that I had become lifeless and that my soul was wearing away. Return to me my character, give me back the energy I need for service to society!"[40] In September, as the attacks continued, he noted: "I am a sick man. Because of my limitations in energy, ability, and knowledge, I have accomplished little in eight months!"[41] At one point he decided to return to China, but changed his mind when his health improved temporarily. Finally, on December 15, Ch'ü was admitted to Moscow's High Hill Sanatorium (Vysokie gory) where he remained until mid-January 1922. It was at times like these that Ch'ü worked out the personal psychological problems that others of his generation continued to postpone.[42]

37. CCPWC, 1:91; Bernadette Li, p. 87. Emphasis added.   38. CCPWC, 1:165.
39. Ts'ao Ching-hua, *Hua* [Flowers] (Peking: Tso-chia ch'u-pan-she, 1962), p. 38.
40. CCPWC, 1:130; Hsia, *Gate of Darkness*, p. 36.
41. CCPWC, 1:139; Bernadette Li, p. 72.
42. CCPWC, 1:140; Bernadette Li, p. 73.

In certain respects Ch'ü analyzed the tensions present in his own psychological makeup in much the same way he analyzed the nineteenth-century cultural crisis of Russia and the twentieth-century cultural crisis of China. Once again Ch'ü presented his readers with two seemingly incompatible elements or "currents" that had to be reconciled if progress was to be made. On the one hand, he declared, "I was born a romantic (*lang-man p'ai*), who always wanted to transcend the environment and accomplish some miraculous deed, which would amaze and move the people. Acts of impulse know no limit, no limit." Of course, Ch'ü's dramatic journey to the Land of Hunger and his break with the "Chinese world" were precisely acts of this sort. But, he continued: "Since my childhood, I have had a strong bent for the inner strength of realism (*hsien-shih p'ai*). I must carefully study reality and do things one by one. The power of reason imposes its dictatorship over me."[43] Like "East" and "West" in his cultural scheme, romanticism and realism were treated by Ch'ü as opposing poles that had negative as well as positive qualities. If the realist element became too dominant, the ego might become bound by the constraints imposed by society, thus stifling the development of individuality. On the other hand, Ch'ü realized that excessive romanticism might isolate the individual from society. The "convergence of these two streams," Ch'ü observed, caused conflicts and tensions in his mind and in society itself. Consequently, not only did Ch'ü see himself as "a victim of the conflict between European and Chinese culture," he was torn by an "inner incongruity" between romanticism and realism. If he could reconcile these two elements, China might benefit.

Ch'ü was at times during his illness haunted by the fear that, failing to resolve the tensions in his personality, he ran the risk of becoming an intellectually ineffective and politically paralyzed "superfluous person" (*to-yü te jen*). As Ch'ü lay awake in the sanatorium he began to think of himself as another Rudin, the well-intentioned hero of Turgenev's famous novel who attempted but failed to serve society. In a remorseful moment Ch'ü wrote: "I have become a superfluous person! I am repentful, sad, and morbid. I thought that I was different from ordinary people. But looking back, can I find any uniqueness in myself? How ludicrous! I must conform like ordinary people. 'What after all can you do? It would be better to be just one of the ordinary people!'"[44] When Ch'ü asked, "What should I do with this conflict between head and heart?" he undoubtedly had the sympathy of many of his readers. The temptation to "escape" to a sanctuary was strong; but he concluded: "I would rather shed my blood for society than let society kill my feeling."

43. CCPWC, 1:170; Bernadette Li, p. 90.
44. CCPWC, 1:171; Bernadette Li, p. 91.

It is clear that, as Ch'ü attempted to resolve these "inner" problems, he continued to be influenced by the kind of moral philosophy expressed in his May Fourth article "Society and Evil." To avoid becoming superfluous, Chinese youth would have to resolve these tensions by balancing the elements of realism and romanticism, and society and self. It was essential, in Ch'ü's view, that these problems be worked out in a social context.[45] "When ego and non-ego are united," he said, "there is harmony. When ego and non-ego are placed in opposition there is an awareness of the uniqueness of individuality. There must be a way to unite the two, and that is love."[46] By "love" Ch'ü meant the kind of human compassion and selflessness to which he constantly referred in his Tolstoyan phase. "Our prideful nature," he warned, "if not improved by love, will become likewise our curse."

Ch'ü's decision to join the Chinese Communist Party was undoubtedly related to his private struggle to resolve these psychological tensions and "reenter" Chinese society. His writings of January 1922 show that he had "awakened" to the truth of the October Revolution and discovered the strength of his own character at approximately the same time. No longer were there any obstacles blocking the road to practical social service. Recovering in the sanatorium, Ch'ü was delighted to learn that the Comintern had invited him to participate in the upcoming First Congress of the Toilers of the East, not as a journalist but as a member of the Chinese delegation. On his twenty-third birthday, January 29, 1922, Ch'ü wrote a short essay entitled "Sunrise" that expresses the exuberance of "rebirth." "Moscow suddenly moved closer to East Asia," he wrote; "the convening of the Congress of the Toilers of the East needed me—the Child from the East. Thus I left the High Hills and suddenly I felt refreshed, as if I had climbed atop a high mountain looking at the glory of early dawn during a long summer."[47] The primary objectives of his journey to the Land of Hunger had now been achieved: he understood the true nature and significance of the revolution, and he knew he possessed the strength to serve Chinese society. It was time to turn to other matters.

In early February Ch'ü and Chang T'ai-lei, a former Changchow schoolmate who had arrived from China, traveled to Petrograd to attend the final meetings of the Congress. Returning to the hotel in the freezing cold one night, Ch'ü collapsed in the street. Delirious and coughing blood, he was returned to Moscow and readmitted to the High Hills Sanatorium on February 7. It is unknown precisely when, but just before or just after this new attack, Ch'ü Ch'iu-pai joined the Chinese Communist Party through the sponsorship of Chang T'ai-lei.

45. CCPWC, 1:164.
46. CCPWC, 1:173; Bernadette Li, p. 91. By "non-ego" (*pu-wo*), Ch'ü meant society.
47. CCPWC, 1:178; Gálik, "Young Ch'ü Ch'iu-pai," p. 117.

Although it was now evident that he would not be free of tuberculosis in his "new life," Ch'ü was not discouraged. On March 20, 1922, the final day of his hospitalization, he wrote an optimistic final essay, entitled "Life," for his second book. "Since activities for the new culture are in the real world," he reflected, "those who work in the real world are also in the midst of life. They are all living."[48]

LITERARY STUDIES

Before Ch'ü Ch'iu-pai entered Russia he stated that one of his primary goals in the Soviet Union would be to study Russian literature, which he believed to be the "starting point" for the rise of the new culture from the old. But once he became preoccupied with philosophical and personal problems, he postponed his literary studies. Very little is said about literature in either *A Journey to the Land of Hunger* or *Impressions of the Red Capital Seen Through the Mind*. It was not until late 1921, at about the time of his "awakening," and especially in 1922, that Ch'ü completed any significant research on Russian literature.

Ch'ü's most interesting work on literature was a short and rather curious book-length study entitled *A History of Russian Literature* [*O-kuo wen-hsueh shih*].[49] Ch'ü finished the volume in 1922, but it was not published until 1927. When it finally appeared, it had been edited, not by Ch'ü, but by his former student Chiang Kuang-tz'u, and the original manuscript was lost. In sharp contrast to Ch'ü's other writings of the period, it contains no romantic or introspective material, and China is never mentioned. It is likely that Ch'ü merely compiled the book by reading and then paraphrasing one or more Soviet texts. Nevertheless, it is significant that Ch'ü chose to do so, and it must be assumed that the book reflects his interest in Russian literature during this important transitional period. In many ways its thrust is compatible with Ch'ü's general interpretation of the crisis of Russian culture in the nineteenth century.

In general, the ideas contained in the book are an elaboration of the views on Russian literature expressed by Ch'ü in the May Fourth period. For example, Ch'ü chose not to discuss Marxist or proletarian trends in art, but rather what he characterized as the "great" nineteenth-century tradition. Among the critics, the populists Herzen, Belinsky, Chernyshevsky, and Dobrolyubov were referred to frequently, but Plekhanov, the Marxist, was not even mentioned. Among

48. CCPWC, 1:195; Hsia, *Gate of Darkness*, p. 42. See Shneider, *Tvorcheskii Put'*, p. 33.

49. The revised text of this book is in CCPWC, 2:461–539. The history of this manuscript is discussed in Ting Ching-t'ang and Wen Ts'ao, eds., *Ch'ü Ch'iu-pai chu i hsi-nien mu-lu* [A Chronological bibliography of Ch'ü Ch'iu-pai's writings and translations] (Shanghai: Jen-min ch'u-pan-she, 1959), pp. 15 and 107–108.

the great writers, it was Ch'ü's May Fourth favorites—Pushkin, Gogol, Turgenev, Tolstoy, Dostoyevsky, and Chekov—who were featured. And although Ch'ü's views were stated in greater depth in *A History of Russian Literature*, it is clear that he admired these writers for essentially the same reasons he had given in Peking. Their writings "reflected" Russian social life; they aroused the moral indignation of the reader and thus tended to promote progressive social reform; they embodied the national spirit of the Russian "people" (*p'ing-min*); and they were written beautifully and in a relatively colloquial language. Ch'ü recognized differences among the writers mentioned above, but in general these were the qualities he stressed.[50]

Other remarks made by Ch'ü in *A History of Russian Literature* seem out of character. For example, his criticism of the romantic and individualist strains in Pushkin, Lermontov, and Dostoyevsky seem to contradict statements made in other writings about the importance of romantic and heroic elements in his own personality. Similarly, his criticism of the utopianism and idealism of Tolstoy—who, according to Ch'ü, failed to understand that Russian capitalism was sowing the seeds of socialism—sounds strange coming from a young idealist who hoped the capitalist stage could be skipped in China.[51] In fact, Ch'ü's book was permeated with an element of determinism that appears nowhere else in his writings on Russia. It is true, of course, that since the May Fourth period, Ch'ü had a materialist view of the relationship between literature and society. In his opinion, literature simply could not be understood outside its social context. But in his study of Russian literature Ch'ü said much more than this. He injected Marxist notions of social evolution in a rather deterministic manner, and began to stress the role of impersonal historical laws more than he had in other writings. The great Russian writers were presented more as outstanding products of their time than as independent historical actors; and the reflective value of their literature was stressed more than its vanguard revolutionary role. Ch'ü now believed that great writers, like Chekov, could not become great social activists unless they lived in potentially revolutionary times. As Ellen Widmer has pointed out, Ch'ü believed that literature and the artist can play a catalytic role when social change is already imminent, but not before.[52] And even then writers are only capable of heightening the level of consciousness of those who really do make history by "saying what the ordinary people want to say but cannot, by revealing the emotions of contemporary society."[53]

50. CCPWC, 2:481-482, 485, 493 496, 513, and 514-516.
51. CCPWC, 2:479, 486, 506-507, and 510-511.
52. Widmer, "Qu Qiubai and Russian Literature," pp. 106-116.
53. CCPWC, 2:473.

There is no formal discussion of Marxist thought in the book, but his remarks show that Ch'ü was beginning to familiarize himself with some features of Marxist literary thought following his own conversion to Marxism. Portions of Ch'ü's study indicate that his stay in the Soviet Union was a transitional period in the evolution of his literary views. It is not known how Ch'ü acquired his knowledge of Marxist literary thought, but *A History of Russian Literature* represents an attempt on his part to bring his literary views into harmony with what he now perceived to be orthodox Marxist political ideas. Ch'ü did this by stressing the degree to which artistic activity is determined by movements in the economic and social spheres. Ch'ü now began to emphasize the role played by objective laws of history that propelled human society through various clearly defined stages of socio-economic development. As a result of this shift in his thinking, Ch'ü began to qualify the degree to which the cultural superstructure of society is independent from the economic base. Likewise, Ch'ü began to place restraints on the ability of artists to generate historical change by bringing about a revolution in human consciousness. Ch'ü was, for the first time, making deterministic remarks about the relationship between art and society.

This phase of Ch'ü's development must be regarded as transitional, however, because in the same book he continued to express views and write about themes that had attracted him in his utopian socialist period in Peking. Ch'ü gave no clues in his book as to the message he wanted Chinese readers to derive from his study, but it is hard to believe that his only purpose was to demonstrate Marxist methods of conducting research in literary history or to promote deterministic ideas on art and society that Ch'ü himself barely grasped. On the contrary, his May Fourth utopian socialist literary beliefs continued to be the decisive element in his cultural thought. Any Chinese reader familiar with the analysis of Russia's nineteenth-century cultural crisis contained in Ch'ü's first two books would be able to detect the underlying significance of Ch'ü's study of Russian literature. Ch'ü wrote about nineteenth-century Russian writers because he continued to believe that they were the first to confront the problems created by the collision of Eastern and Western values. Chinese writers, who were confronting the same problems in the twentieth century, would do well to study the Russian experience.

It is hardly a coincidence, therefore, that throughout his book Ch'ü expressed an utter contempt for what he understood to be "bourgeois culture" (*tzu-ch'an wen-hua*) or the bourgeois cultural stage, a theme that was present in his May Fourth writings and became even more important in Ch'ü's literary thought in later years. Ch'ü was attracted to nineteenth-century Russian literature for many reasons, but especially because it was not bourgeois. His definition of bourgeois culture and literature stressed two characteristics: it was one of the by-products of Western European capitalism and, above all, it was "philistine" (*shih-k'uai*).[54] Therefore bourgeois literature was, in Ch'ü's estimation, entirely devoid of any redeeming qualities; and thus the bourgeoisie had made no enduring contributions to human culture. Ch'ü implied in his study that Russian literature was different from and superior to European literature in precisely the same way that Russian society was different from European society. Russian literature was superior precisely because it had not been contaminated by bourgeois values but, rather, was based upon the spiritual or "Asian" element in Russian society. Invariably, Ch'ü's study highlighted those Russian writers who had been least influenced by the philistine spirit of Western European literature.

The anti-bourgeois strain that runs through *A History of Russian Literature* was also expressed in *Impressions of the Red Capital Seen Through the Mind* when Ch'ü stated flatly that "the bourgeoisie did not contribute anything to Russian culture."[55] Ch'ü could make such statements because his definition of bourgeois culture was so narrow. He found nothing progressive in bourgeois culture because, unlike other Marxists, he was unwilling to distinguish between the progressive literature of the early bourgeois period and the commercialized or decadent literature of the late bourgeois period. In the Russian case, Ch'ü refused to characterize the reformist literature written either before or after the liberation of the serfs as bourgeois. He celebrated the politically progressive nature of works by Pushkin, Gogol, Turgenev, and others, but he did not regard them as having played a role in advancing the bourgeois cause. In *A History of Russian Literature* bourgeois culture was treated exclusively as an alien, money-minded, cultureless force that had intruded into Russian society in the late nineteenth century, and thus caused the decline of Russian literature.

If it was not the bourgeoisie, then who had been responsible for producing the magnificent and progressive literature of nineteenth-century Russia? For Ch'ü, a gentry aristocrat turned revolutionary, the answer was simple: the Russian gentry and intelligentsia had been responsible. Ch'ü had already stated in his autobiographical writings that "historically speaking almost all the literary figures and social thinkers have been gentry" in Russia, and that "the intellectuals among the Russian gentry really detested bourgeois culture."[56] Imbued with the "Eastern" spiritual quality, these writers were close to the people and highly sensitive to the penetration of "Western" materialism. The writers who appeared most prominently in Ch'ü's book were the

54. CCPWC, 2:506 and 512. Also see CCPWC, 1:165.
56. CCPWC, 1:126.   55. CCPWC, 1:126.

gentry writers who opposed serfdom before the liberation, "con-science-striken nobles" who joined the populist movement after the liberation, and late-century intellectuals who were repulsed by the advance of bourgeois philistinism.[57] Thus, in contrast to Plekhanov, who treated Russia as part of Europe and Pushkin as an early bour-geois progressive, Ch'ü consistently stressed the distinctiveness of Russian literary history. Ch'ü may have come to believe that a brief capitalist stage was inevitable in the Russian case, but his writings on Russian literature assumed that great writers would do everything possible to confine the spread of bourgeois culture.

Ch'ü's study of Russian literature, like his autobiographical works, stressed the theme of the "superfluous person" in the writings of Turgenev and Dostoyevsky.[58] Ch'ü seemed to be warning gentry writ-ers in China, on whom the revolution would depend for leadership, that there were two alternatives open to them. Like some of their Russian counterparts they might fail in their mission to serve society and become superfluous and "pitiful, backward members of the bour-geoisie," or they might effectively transform themselves and identify with the newly rising class, the proletariat. In his autobiographical works he stressed that among the Bolsheviks "there are many who were gentry at an earlier time."[59] Thus, just as progressive gentry in-tellectuals might avoid the contamination of bourgeois culture and help the nation to skip or cut short the bourgeois cultural stage, so too could the gentry avoid identifying with the bourgeoisie and identify directly with the proletariat. Toward the end of his second autobiographical volume, Ch'ü referred to the situation in China: "There will be a day when the entire 'scholar' class will be proletarianized. Then we shall do what we are capable of doing. There will be such a day."[60]

In light of Ch'ü's criticism of European bourgeois culture, one is tempted to say that his early writings on literature were highly un-usual and tended to separate him from his May Fourth contemporaries who were still primarily interested in the literature of Western Eu-rope.[61] Nevertheless, if one rejects Ch'ü's narrow definition of bour-geois literature and views the work of Pushkin, Turgenev, and Tol-stoy along with the work of Balzac, Dickens, and Zola as part of the nineteenth-century Western literary heritage, Ch'ü's interest in for-eign literature appears somewhat less unusual. Ch'ü was not immune

57. CCPWC, 2:492-493, 500, and 516-517. For Ch'ü, Turgenev was a typical pre-liberation progressive, the populist writers were the "conscience-striken nobles," and Gorky was a leader of those who opposed "philistinism."

58. CCPWC, 2:479, 494-495.   59. CCPWC, 1:126.

60. CCPWC, 1:164; Hsia, *Gate of Darkness*, p. 39.

61. The domination of Western European literature is carefully documented in Bonnie S. McDougall, *The Introduction of Western Literary Theories Into Modern China, 1919-1925* (Tokyo: The Centre for East Asian Cultural Studies, 1971).

to the influence of Western bourgeois culture, broadly defined, and was, in many respects, typical of young Chinese intellectuals who studied abroad in the 1920s and insisted that their own foreign literary model was the most appropriate one for China.

Despite his aversion to bourgeois culture, Ch'ü, like other members of his generation, failed to show much interest or understanding of the proletarian cultural experiments that were being conducted around him. His writings contain only a few random and vague remarks on the subject. For example, his statements of February 1921, shortly after his arrival, show that futurism (*chiang-lai-chu-i*) surprised and confused him. Unable to decide whether the futurist art he encountered was bourgeois or proletarian, he stated that it represented the last dark moment of bourgeois culture and, at the same time, the dawning of proletarian culture.[62] Somewhat later, Ch'ü acknowledged that he had been deeply impressed with Mayakovsky, with whom he discussed Chinese literature during a brief meeting; but he frankly admitted that he "did not understand" Mayakovsky's poetry.[63] Finally, Ch'ü's translations of Russian literature were confined almost exclusively to nineteenth-century works: poems by Lermontov, Tiutchev (a Slavophile), and Gorky; and short stories by Zlatovratsky (a populist), and Albov (a disciple of Dostoyevsky).

And despite his objections to bourgeois culture, Ch'ü, like all the other writers of the May Fourth generation, had not been able to do very much about the language problem. It is significant that he began to develop a system for romanizing Chinese ideographs while he was in the Soviet Union. He believed that a language reform of this sort would facilitate mass literacy in China. Nevertheless, Ch'ü's own writings, like the works of the nineteenth-century Russian masters and the works of his Europeanized May Fourth contemporaries, were not intended for and could not be understood by the preliterate masses. Ch'ü firmly believed that one of the functions of great literature was to arouse the people, but his own works, written in an extremely difficult semiclassical, semi-Europeanized language, were incomprehensible to the masses in China.

BEYOND HIGH HILLS

Relatively little is known about Ch'ü Ch'iu-pai's activities in the period from early April, when he left the sanatorium for the last time, to late December 1922, when he left Moscow. It is clear, however, that he began to move in several new directions after he joined the Communist Party. No longer did his social and political writings raise

62. CCPWC, 1:98. 63. CCPWC, 1:99.

fundamental questions about his own character of the nature and significance of the Russian revolution. Furthermore, Ch'ü finally abandoned any remaining interest in traditional Chinese thought. He no longer used Buddhist concepts, or any other traditional categories of thought, to analyze the phenomenon of modern socialist revolution. Instead, he became involved in the sort of activities he had originally intended to pursue before his Siberian experience. Specifically, he engaged in political affairs, an activity he had avoided in his first year, and he began to focus more of his attention on a number of practical questions raised in Marxist ideology. Ch'ü had once again become preoccupied with the task of helping to lead China out of the ideological confusion of the May Fourth period.

The circumstances that led to Ch'ü's decision to return to China began to unfold in November 1922 when the Fourth Comintern Congress was convened in Moscow. During the conference Ch'ü served as an interpreter for the small Chinese Communist delegation, and became very well acquainted with Ch'en Tu-hsiu, one of his May Fourth heroes who was now serving as the first secretary general of the Communist Party. As a participant in the conference Ch'ü was forced for the first time to concern himself with the tensions and complexities necessarily associated with any attempt to devise a political strategy for revolution in China. Who was in the best position to formulate such a strategy, the wise leaders of the Comintern who resided at the very center of world revolution, or those local communists like Ch'en Tu-hsiu who lived on Chinese soil but whose political party claimed only three hundred members, most of whom were intellectuals and students? Ch'ü Ch'iu-pai's disastrous political career was only beginning in November 1922, and political pressures were not yet great. In this early period Ch'ü was reluctant to question the wisdom and authority of the Comintern.

Ch'en Tu-hsiu's personal reservations about the advisory role of the Comintern seem to have had no bearing on his early relationship with Ch'ü. He was so impressed by Ch'ü's talents that he urged him to return to China to become active in party affairs. Ch'ü was flattered. On December 21, 1922, he joined Ch'en and other party luminaries on their return trip to China. This time Ch'ü's passage was smooth, and he arrived in Peking on January 13, 1923, just before his twenty-fourth birthday.

Ch'ü was still unclear about the political role he would play in China, but there is little doubt that he continued to regard himself as a literary personality, even after he joined the Communist Party. In later years he recalled that at first he hesitated to join the party because he was under the mistaken impression that if he joined he "would not be able to concentrate on studying literature." He added,

"The notion that studying literature was unrevolutionary was already quite prevalent at the time."[64] Apparently he became convinced that his party membership would not interfere with his desire to participate in the cultural and literary revolutions. "I have enrolled myself in the ranks of the vanguard of the world's cultural movement which will open new avenues for the whole of human culture. Through this action, the glories of Chinese culture with a history of four thousand years will be restored."[65] In other words, he was still a nationalist and he still dreamed of "saving China by cultural means."

64. TYTH, pp. 129-130; Bernadette Li, p. 61.
65. CCPWC, 1:166; Bernadette Li, p. 89.

4 The Introduction of Marxist Literary Thought

No matter by what means, the growth of the bourgeoisie cannot be stopped. It is impossible to skip the bourgeois [stage] and realize utopia immediately. . . . Russia has gone through it, so China must do so now. Marxists differ from unscientific narodniks and anarchists in that they entertain no illusion at all of bypassing capitalism and arriving directly at socialism. There is only one way [to socialism], that is, to carry out class struggle on the very basis of and within the sphere of capitalism.

CH'Ü CH'IU-PAI, 1923[1]

The period from January 1923 to mid-1924 was a brief but interesting phase in the literary career of Ch'ü Ch'iu-pai. By the end of this period Ch'ü was devoting all his time to revolutionary political activities, but upon his return to China he instinctively sought to make a contribution to the cultural world by asserting his influence in leading literary circles. Ch'ü was aware that although many Chinese intellectuals were familiar with the basic tenets of Marxist social and political thought, virtually nothing was known about Marxist literary thought. Full of enthusiasm, Ch'ü accepted the challenge and made what can be regarded as the first relatively systematic attempt to introduce Marxist literary thought into China. As a result, Ch'ü no longer had much to

1. Ch'ü made this remark in his most important political essay of the early 1920s, "Ts'ung min-chih-chu-i chih she-hui-chu-i" [From democracy to socialism], *Hsin ch'ing-nien* [New Youth], 2 December 1923; quoted in Bernadette Yu-ning Li, "A Biography of Ch'ü Ch'iu-pai: From Youth to Party Leadership (1899-1928)" (Ph.D. dissertation, Columbia University, 1967), pp. 154-155.

say about the magnificent nineteenth-century Russian literary tradition that had served as his model for China during his Peking and Moscow years. Instead, he began to stress the importance of Marxist literary theory and Soviet proletarian literature, subjects he had all but ignored in previous years. It is apparent, however, that Ch'ü failed in his mission. Modern Chinese writers did not express a serious interest in Marxist literary thought or proletarian literature until the late 1920s. Ch'ü's failure was undoubtedly the low point of his literary career, but it is an interesting episode nonetheless. To understand why Ch'ü made the attempt and why he failed is to understand the condition of modern literary movement in the immediate post-May Fourth period and the serious deficiencies of Ch'ü's early understanding of Marxist literary thought.

Ch'ü assumed that he would have little difficulty convincing his old associates to embrace Marxist literary thought; but he failed to appreciate the degree to which the modern literary movement had been transformed during his two-year absence. Several tightly-knit professional literary societies emerged and contended vigorously for leadership of the literary world. The effect was to erode the spontaneity and unity of the early May Fourth literary revolution. The Literary Research Association (Wen-hsueh yen-chiu hui) and the Creation Society (Ch'uang-tsao she) were the dominant organizations. In a sense, the rise of the literary societies put an end to the general May Fourth search for relevant foreign literary models; individual writers and critics now began to cluster in groups that emphasized the "special" significance of a particular nineteenth- or early twentieth-century Western bourgeois literary school, such as realism or romanticism. Many writers, therefore, continued to show interest in Ch'ü's old model, nineteenth-century Russian literature, which they perceived as belonging to the larger Western tradition, but postrevolutionary proletarian art and Marxist literary thought were largely ignored. The political implications of the trend toward professionalism were rather far-reaching. Most modern writers remained at least vaguely sympathetic to the idea of a "national" revolution, but clearly the tenuous links they had forged with workers and merchants during the strikes and demonstrations of the early May Fourth period had been all but broken in the early 1920s as these elite and exclusive literary societies appeared one after another. In other words, many writers who got their start in 1919 were now a few years older and less inclined to become involved in political affairs. Absent from the literary scene was that intangible May Fourth sense of political urgency. The new trends were nowhere more apparent than in the early history of the Literary Research Association and the Creation Society.

Organized at the end of 1920, just after Ch'ü departed for Russia, the Literary Research Association was one of the most prestigious and powerful literary groups to emerge from the May Fourth literary revolution. Among its twelve founding members were Mao Tun and Chou Tso-jen, two of China's most distinguished twentieth-century writers, and Hsu Ti-shan, Ch'ü Shih-ying, Cheng Chen-to, Keng Chi-chih, and Chiang Pai-li, all of whom, it will be recalled, belonged to Ch'ü Ch'iu-pai's inner circle of political and literary companions in 1919 and 1920. Had Ch'ü not traveled to Russia he probably would have continued to work with this group and been among the founders of the Literary Research Association. By 1923 the Association had over seventy members, and in later years its ranks swelled to over one hundred and seventy.[2]

The members of the Literary Research Association were primarily interested in questions that dealt with the relationship between literature and society, and the social responsibilities of the writer. Mao Tun expressed the opinion of many in 1921 when he asserted: "Literature at present has become a kind of science whose subject matter for study is humanity—contemporary humanity—and whose tools of study are poetry, drama, and fiction. With artistic skill, the writer's revelation of humanity must be the life of all mankind, without an iota of selfishness or the least particle of subjectivity."[3] As Chow Tse-tsung has pointed out, the social-science orientation of many Association writers tended to make them especially receptive to Western realism and naturalism.[4] It is important to recognize, however, that much of the literary theory written by young Chinese who belonged to the Literary Research Association and other groups was imitative and superficial. Explanations of Western literary theory often amounted to little more than brief summaries of foreign textbooks. Articles of this sort were frequently written by Chinese students who, having recently completed their studies at a European or an American university, were determined to "introduce" their favorite authors and critics.

The leading rival of the Literary Research Association was the Creation Society, the only other major literary group to emerge in the early 1920s. It was founded in Japan in July 1921, and its early leaders were Kuo Mo-jo, Ch'eng Fang-wu, Yü Ta-fu, Chang Tzu-p'ing, and

2. A number of studies discuss the origins of the Literary Research Association. See Bonnie S. McDougall, *The Introduction of Western Literary Theories Into Modern China, 1919-1925* (Tokyo: The Centre for East Asian Cultural Studies, 1971), pp. 23-37; Marián Gálik, *Mao Tun and Modern Chinese Literary Criticism* (Wiesbaden: Franz Steiner Verlag Gmblt, 1969), pp. 42-53; and Chow Tse-tsung, *The May Fourth Movement* (Stanford: Stanford University Press, 1967), pp. 283-286.

3. Chow Tse-tung, *May Fourth*, p. 284.   4. Ibid., p. 285.

T'ien Han. Although the followers of the Creation Society were also members of the May Fourth generation, their assumptions about literature and criticism contrasted sharply with those held by the leaders of the Literary Research Association. They were not inspired by humanist conceptions such as "art for life's sake" (*wei jen-sheng erh i-shu*), the slogan of the Literary Research Association, nor were they interested in undertaking sober, objective investigations of society. Creation Society members advanced the cause of "art for art's sake" (*wei i-shu erh i-shu*) and insisted on the absolute autonomy of the artist from society. It was not realism or naturalism that attracted the Creationists, but romanticism and the liberation of the individual. Their study of Western models was less organized than the efforts of the Literary Research Association, but they emulated figures like Byron, Shelley, and Goethe. And, in contrast to their rivals, the Creationists were more concerned with mastering certain *forms* of literature, such as poetry, than they were with providing their readers with socially relevant content.[5] As Ch'eng Fang-wu put it, "To seek perfection and beauty in literature is the work of our lives. A beautiful piece of literature may not have anything to teach us, but it gives us the feeling of comfort and we cannot ignore it."[6]

Although prominent members of the Creation Society and Literary Research Association would join hands eventually to play leading roles in the left-wing literary movement of the early 1930s, their relationship during the 1920s can be characterized only as one of mutual hostility. The first of two serious clashes between the rival literary societies occurred in the early 1920s. The friction was not caused by major political differences, since both organizations were composed of May Fourth patriots and anti-traditionalists. Initially the tension was related to differences in their views about the role of literature. As Bonnie McDougall has shown, the formation of the two organizations actually polarized the literary world into two major groups of writers: "sober, studious, and realistic," on one hand; "inspirational, individualistic, and romantic," on the other.[7] Each organization became concerned that the other might monopolize the literary scene, and thus each used its publications to exchange literary polemics with the other. Before long their legitimate literary rivalry degenerated into bitter and counterproductive personal confronta-

5. For discussions of the early history of the Creation Society see David Roy, *Kuo Mo-jo: The Early Years* (Cambridge: Harvard University Press, 1971), pp. 108-133; and C.T. Hsia, *A History of Modern Chinese Fiction* (New Haven: Yale University Press, 1971), pp. 93-102.

6. Amitendranath Tagore, *Literary Debates in Modern China, 1918-1937* (Tokyo: Centre for East Asian Cultural Studies, 1967), p. 54. For Kuo Mo-jo's early romantic view see Roy, *Kuo Mo-jo*, pp. 87-88.

7. McDougall, *Western Literary Theories*, p. 40.

tions. By 1923, following Ch'ü Ch'iu-pai's return to China, there was an open split in the modern literary movement, one that symbolized the breakdown of unity among May Fourth literary intellectuals. Consolidating early triumphs had cost the modern literary movement much of its vitality.

THE LITERARY SCENE

One of the first things Ch'ü Ch'iu-pai learned upon his return to China in January 1923 was that Peking was no longer the intellectual center of the Chinese revolution. The excitement generated by the New Culture and May Fourth Movements had subsided and the political and intellectual atmosphere had become increasingly repressive. Ch'ü had no trouble securing suitable living accommodations with his generous cousin Ch'ü Ch'un-pai, but he had considerable difficulty reestablishing himself in what remained of the Peking literary world.[8] At the suggestion of his May Fourth mentor, Li Ta-chao, Ch'ü applied for a position in the Russian language department at Peking University. An institutional affiliation of this sort would put Ch'ü in touch with many leading intellectuals. But despite his expertise in Russian language and literature and the enthusiastic support of Li Ta-chao, a leading professor at Peking University, his application for a teaching post was rejected.[9]

Ch'ü's personal disappointment was insignificant compared with the disaster that struck the Communist Party shortly thereafter. On February 7, 1923, Wu P'ei-fu, the local warlord who controlled much of North China, ordered the violent suppression of a strike by the communist-dominated Peking-Hankow Railway Workers' Union. Forty-five workers were massacred, and communist leaders in Peking were forced to flee as the proletarian base for revolutionary activities in North China was demolished in one blow. Ch'ü's membership in the Communist Party was still unknown, but because of the worsening political climate in Peking he followed other revolutionary leaders to Shanghai, the new focal point of the Chinese revolution.

The atmosphere in Shanghai was, of course, much better. Following the conclusion of a January 1923 agreement between the Comintern and its new ally in China, Sun Yat-sen's Kuomintang, there was considerable talk in Shanghai and Canton, where Sun's revolutionary government held power, about the advantages of cooperation between the Communist Party and the Kuomintang. Many, including Ch'ü, believed that such an alliance would hasten a revolution that would overthrow the warlords, unify the nation, and reclaim China's

8. Wen Chi-che, "Ch'ü Ch'iu-pai t'ung-chih," p. 91.
9. Ts'ao Ching-hua, *Hua* [Flowers] (Peking: Tso-chia ch'u-pan-she, 1962), p. 40.

national sovereignty. Although Shanghai was ruled by foreign powers, it was a haven for intellectuals who wanted to live in a cosmopolitan cultural environment and for revolutionaries who hoped to organize its large working-class population.

Everything that Ch'ü felt was missing in Peking he found in Shanghai. For one thing, his arrival in Shanghai in late February 1923 marked his triumphant return to Kiangsu, his home province, after an eight-year absence. Despite his youth, Ch'ü was already something of a celebrity in Shanghai. Many of his former Peking friends who had relocated in Shanghai admired Ch'ü's writings about Russia and were eager to renew their acquaintance with him. Chang Kuo-t'ao, one of the founding members of the Communist Party, noted in his memoirs that Ch'ü was, for a time, the only ranking member of the party who could function in public, because he had not yet engaged in revolutionary activities and his party membership was unknown to the police. As plans to build a united front with the Kuomintang and other progressives became more definite, Ch'ü was encouraged by his revolutionary companions to widen his contacts in the world of letters. Before long he converted his residence in the Chapei district of Shanghai into an "author's studio," and became active in Shanghai intellectual circles.[10]

It is not surprising that the Literary Research Association was the first literary group Ch'ü joined following his arrival in Shanghai.[11] Several of his former friends were founding members, and the Association had already published one of Ch'ü's autobiographical volumes and two of his translations of nineteenth-century Russian literature, and would soon publish the second autobiographical work.[12] Ch'ü's friendship with several leading romantics, such as Kuo Mo-jo, T'ien Han, and Chiang Kuang-tz'u, suggests that it was not his intention to take sides in the dispute between the Literary Research Association and the Creation Society; but clearly Ch'ü was more attracted to the social orientation of the Association's literary credo, and believed that its members were, therefore, more likely to be receptive to the "social-scientific" thrust of Marxist literary thought. Ch'ü was by no means a central figure in the organization, but his role was unique. In contrast to the other members, who were primarily interested in Western bourgeois realist and naturalist literature, Ch'ü, the only Communist Party member who was active in the Association in the early 1920s,

10. Chang Kuo-t'ao, *The Rise of the Chinese Communist Party, 1921-1927* (Lawrence: University of Kansas Press, 1971), 1:297.

11. Gálik, *Mao Tun and Modern Chinese Literary Criticism*, p. 43.

12. The Literary Research Association's press also agreed to publish Ch'ü's book *On the Russian Revolution* [O-lo-ssu ko-ming lun], but government censorship policies blocked its appearance.

was the organization's spokesman on proletarian literary trends in the Soviet Union. Although Ch'ü represented a side current in the Literary Research Association, he was a popular and highly regarded figure.[13]

In addition to his participation in the Literary Research Association, Ch'ü was also involved in the founding of Shanghai University. The university was cosponsored by the Communist Party and the left wing of the Kuomintang, and its purpose was to recruit and train potential cadres for the forthcoming national revolutionary movement. Classes began in the fall of 1923 and continued until June 4, 1925, when the university was closed temporarily by the authorities of the International Settlement because of faculty and student activity in the strikes and demonstrations following the May Thirtieth Incident.[14]

Unlike most of Ch'ü's colleagues in the Literary Research Association, those who flocked to Shanghai University were politically active. When the university opened, Yü Yu-jen, a prominent Kuomintang writer, was its president, and Ch'ü served concurrently as dean of studies and chairman of the department of social studies.[15] Communist faculty members, many of whom were recruited by Ch'ü, included Chang T'ai-lei, Ts'ai Ho-sen, Li Ta, and two of Ch'ü's former students in Moscow, Jen Pi-shih and the novelist Chiang Kuang-t'zu. Ch'ü also associated quite closely with Yun Tai-ying, Teng Chung-hsia, and Hsiao Ch'u-nü, three young communist faculty members who shared Ch'ü's interest in Marxist literary thought. Kuomintang members of the staff included such well-known personalities as Hu Han-min, Wang Ching-wei, and Tai Chi-t'ao, with all of whom Ch'ü worked to build the United Front and reorganize the Kuomintang prior to the long-awaited First Kuomintang Congress in January 1924. Among the non-communist, but politically active, literary talents who lectured in the department of Chinese literature were Kuo Mo-jo and T'ien Han of the Creation Society and Mao Tun of the Literary Research Association.[16]

Ch'ü taught two courses at the university, "Introduction to the Social Sciences" and "Social Philosophy." The students' grasp of Marxist theory being quite superficial, Ch'ü was regarded as an expert on

13. See Mao Tun, "Ch'ü Ch'iu-pai tsai wen-hsueh shang te kung-hsien" [Ch'ü Ch'iu-pai's contribution to literature], *Jen-min jih-pao*, 18 June 1949; Mao Tun, "Chi-nien Ch'iu-pai t'ung-chih, hsueh-hsi Ch'iu-pai t'ung-chih" [Commemorate Comrade Ch'iu-pai, Learn from Comrade Ch'iu-pai], *Jen-min jih-pao*, 18 June 1955; and Ts'ao Ching-hua, *Hua*, pp. 39-41.

14. Chang Kuo-t'ao, *The Chinese Communist Party*, 1:297; TYTH, p. 130; T.A. Hsia, *The Gate of Darkness* (Seattle: University of Washington Press, 1968), 72.

15. The most detailed account of Ch'ü's Shanghai University activities is contained in Yang Chih-hua, "I Ch'iu-pai" [Recollections of Ch'iu-pai], *Hung-ch'i p'iao-p'iao*, 8:24-33.

16. Bernadette Li, p. 135.

the subject, and his books *Outline of the Social Sciences* and *Lectures on Social Science* were printed in numerous editions.[17] According to K'ang Sheng, who later became an influential communist leader, Ch'ü's lectures were extremely popular.[18] Some of Ch'ü's appeal was undoubtedly his youth. Despite his notoriety, Ch'ü was, at twenty-four years of age, not much older than most of his students. The bohemian and revolutionary youth cultures that attracted rootless Chinese youths to cosmopolitan Shanghai probably helped to rekindle for Ch'ü some of the personal excitement he had experienced during his Peking years. As Leo Lee has observed, hundreds of self-styled "literary youths" arrived in Shanghai in the 1920s. Some studied, some brooded about life, some hoped to make contact with famous literary intellectuals, and others became politically active.[19]

Ch'ü's third base of operation in the early 1920s was in the Communist Party itself. With a membership of less than a thousand, the party was still relatively small in 1923, but it had a fairly wide following among Shanghai's students and intellectuals. There were two reasons for Ch'ü's personal power and influence within the party. First, he was well known to the leaders of the Comintern during a period when its representatives were extremely active in China. Ch'ü supported Comintern policies without hesitation and was constantly at the side of Maring, Borodin, and other Comintern advisors as they attempted to assist the Kuomintang and help launch the so-called "national" revolution. Ch'ü served as a trusted interpreter for Comintern representatives visiting China, and was responsible for producing the Chinese translations of many important policy directives.[20] Second, Ch'ü was viewed by his Chinese colleagues within the party as a man who was particularly skillful in literary and journalistic pursuits. These factors explain why Ch'ü was elected, at age twenty-four, to membership in the Central Committee of the Chinese Communist Party at its Third Congress, held in Canton in June 1923. Ch'ü had been a member of the party for only a year when he became the youngest member of its Central Committee. Ch'ü was immediately assigned to work in the party's propaganda department, headed by Ts'ai Ho-sen. One of his primary duties was to serve as editor of the famous New Culture publication *New Youth*, which had been revived by the party in 1923 as a communist journal devoted to ideological and

17. Ting Ching-t'ang and Wen Ts'ao, eds., *Ch'ü Ch'iu-pai chu i hsi-nien mu-lu* [A chronological bibliography of Ch'ü Ch'iu-pai's writings and translations] (Shanghai: Jen-min ch'u-pan-she, 1959), pp. 73-76; TYTH, p. 139.

18. Yang Chih-hua, "I Ch'iu-pai," p. 25.

19. For an excellent summary of the "literary scene" (*wen-t'an*) see Leo Ou-fan Lee, *The Romantic Generation of Modern Chinese Writers* (Cambridge: Harvard University Press, 1973), pp. 30-35.

20. Chang Kuo-t'ao, *The Chinese Communist Party*, 1:300, 329; TYTH, p. 130.

theoretical issues. Ch'ü was also appointed to the editorial boards of two leading communist current-events periodicals, *Guide Weekly* [*Hsiang-tao chou-pao*] and *Vanguard* [*Ch'ien-feng*].21

Finally, Ch'ü was active in the party's Socialist Youth Corps when several of its members launched a new communist periodical called *Chinese Youth* [*Chung-kuo ch'ing-nien*] which was to be the official publication of the two-thousand-member organization. *Chinese Youth* carried a variety of articles on the role of youth in the revolutionary movement; of special interest is a series of articles on literature and revolution written between November 1923 and May 1924 by Ch'ü and others.22

MARXIST LITERARY THEORY

Ch'ü's most concise discussion of the basic theoretical aspects of Marxist literary thought is contained in a chapter on art in his popular book *Outline of the Social Sciences*. Among other things, Ch'ü's discussion reveals that his ideas about literature and society had changed in a number of important respects. In marked contrast to the beliefs he had held in his May Fourth and Russian periods, Ch'ü presented a highly deterministic interpretation of Marxist literary theory to his students at Shanghai University. In doing so, he did not advance ideas he had developed on his own, as he had in his autobiographical writings, but instead mechanically summarized the analysis of the relationship between art and society contained in Nikolai Bukharin's *Historical Materialism*, a book he had read in the Soviet Union.

The central thesis of Bukharin's original argument and Ch'ü's adaptation was the familiar assertion that "directly or indirectly, art is ultimately determined in various ways by the economic structure and the stage of the social technology."23 Elaborating on this theme, Ch'ü explained that an economic substructure (composed of the mode of production and corresponding social relations of production) existed

21. Wen Chi-che, "Ch'ü Ch'iu-pai t'ung-chih," pp. 91-92.

22. Chang Pi-lai, "I-chiu-erh-san nien *Chung-kuo ch'ing-nien* chi-ko tso-che te wen-hsueh chu-chang" [The literary views of several writers associated with *Chinese Youth* magazine in 1923], in Li Ho-lin, ed., *Chung-kuo hsin wen-hsueh shih yen-chiu* [Research on the history of modern Chinese literature] (Peking: Hsin-hua shu-tien, 1951), pp. 36-37. At about the same time several romantics, led by Kuo Mo-jo, Yü Ta-fu, Ch'eng Fang-wu, and Chiang Kuang-tz'u, abandoned the "art for art's sake" approach of the early Creation Society and began to write on the theme of literature and revolution. For a concise discussion of their efforts, see Li Ho-lin, ed., *Chin erh-shih nien Chung-kuo wen-i ssu-ch'ao lun* [Chinese literary thought of the past twenty years] (Shanghai: Sheng-huo shu-tien, 1939), pp. 105-114.

23. Nikolai Bukharin, *Historical Materialism: A System of Sociology* (Ann Arbor: University of Michigan Press, 1969), p. 196. Bukharin's remarks on art and the superstructure are found on pp. 187-203, 224-230.

as the foundation of society in any historical era. Built upon this base, and related to it, is a superstructure composed of social institutions and organizations, cultural patterns, and a variety of religious, philosophic, artistic, and ideological beliefs. Consequently, Ch'ü reasoned, the art of all historical periods can only be understood as a reflection of various aspects of economic relations in a given society. Art is "organically" rooted in the material conditions of society; it is not an independent, free-floating force that transcends society. Ch'ü, like Bukharin, conceded that under certain circumstances the superstructure, in its turn, might influence the economic base, but he qualified this statement by asserting that ultimately the development of the superstructure was dependent upon the evolution of productive forces.[24]

However, Ch'ü wanted to do much more than affirm the materialistic conception of art, a notion that had already been accepted by many writers in groups such as the Literary Research Association. He was now saying that not only was art a "product" of society, but, more important, society itself passed through specific, Marxist-defined "stages" of growth. Thus the nature of art in a given period was determined by the *particular stage of development* at which society had arrived. By implication Ch'ü was saying that the most politically progressive art of a given period is the art that closely corresponds to and reflects the inexorable flow of history.

For Ch'ü the study of history confirmed the existence of this relationship between art and society. In "primitive societies" where the economic base and forms of art are quite simple, the relationship is rather direct. "In primitive society," he pointed out, "singing, dancing, and drawing all had a close relationship to the mode of production at the time."[25] As modes of production and societies become more complex, and as the division of labor increases, the interrelationship between art and the economic base becomes more complex, especially in bourgeois society. Nevertheless, artistic development is ultimately determined by developments at the economic base.

In complex class societies, the prevailing aesthetic standards are always the standards of the ruling class, but ruling-class art was not always the most progressive politically. Indeed, the development of art reflects the inevitable class struggle that occurs in society. Revolutionary bourgeois art, for example, becomes increasingly important in the late feudal period as class struggle intensifies.

Perhaps the most interesting portion of Ch'ü's discussion was a section entitled "Art and Social Reform." There he discussed the de-

24. Ch'ü Ch'iu-pai, *She-hui k'o-hsueh kai-lun* [Outline of the social sciences] (Shanghai: Ch'un-i ch'u-pan-she, 1949), p. 47.

25. Ibid.

velopment and function of art in bourgeois society by identifying four major trends: early anti-feudal literature and art in support of the modern bourgeois revolution; reformist literature exposing the evils of bourgeois society; decadent literature of despair in the period of bourgeois decline; and, finally, emerging proletarian literature.[26] This categorization of the literature of the bourgeois period shows that Ch'ü's conception of bourgeois art had undergone a radical change. Not only is the bourgeois cultural stage accepted in this formulation, but three of its phases are shown to be politically progressive. And each phase is presented as the inevitable result of changes in the economic bedrock. Furthermore, Ch'ü now identified romanticism with early revolutionary bourgeois quests for individual freedom, and realism with the social reform literature of the mature capitalist period.

In mentioning early "proletarian-oriented" literature, Ch'ü added a new element not discussed in Bukharin's original work.[27] He seems to have viewed proletarian-type literature as the most politically progressive of the four general categories of art in bourgeois society; but it is clear that by "proletarian" Ch'ü did not mean the "futurist" proletarian literature produced in post-revolutionary Russia by avantgarde intellectuals, or "pure" proletarian literature produced by workers themselves. Rather, he meant a realistic literature that was not merely reformist but recognized, instead, the inevitability of the rise of the proletariat and the end of capitalism. Such "new realist" literature was different from the reformist literature of the second category primarily because its content was more progressive politically. Moreover, the proletarian-oriented literature of which Ch'ü spoke was clearly a prerevolutionary trend that arose within bourgeois society itself. This meant that difficulties would confront such literary movements in the period before bourgeois rule was completely overthrown. First, bourgeois standards would continue to exert a strong influence in the period of bourgeois decline, thus causing many writers otherwise sympathetic to the working-class movement to dismiss the proletarian-inspired art. Second, because of its cultural deprivation, the proletariat, unlike the bourgeoisie during its own rise, could not develop "its own thoroughly independent art." Thus a small group of radical intellectuals had to take the lead in expressing and representing the views of the working class in the world of letters.[28]

Ch'ü's book shows that his grasp of Marxist theory had improved

26. Ibid., pp. 48-49.
27. Although Bukharin did not discuss proletarian art in his book, it is known that he was less hostile to postrevolutionary proletarian art than Lenin or Trotsky. Herman Ermolaev, *Soviet Literary Theory: 1917-1934* (Berkeley: University of California Press, 1963), pp. 2, 13, and 44-47.
28. Ch'ü Ch'iu-pai, *She-hui k'o-hsueh kai-lun*, p. 49.

somewhat following his return from the Soviet Union. He seems to have realized that few problems are more central to Marxist literary theory than the question of the relationship between society and art, or, as it is characterized in Marxist vocabulary, the relationship between the productive forces of society and the cultural superstructure. Without question, Ch'ü's ideas were consistent with the *general* Marxist notion that there is an "organic" relationship between society and artistic culture, that artistic culture does not enjoy an autonomous existence. But clearly Ch'ü was not aware of, or chose to ignore, questions raised in Marxist theory about the *extent* to which components of the superstructure are determined by the substructure. If artistic activity is not totally autonomous, does it follow that it has no autonomy at all, that it is completely shaped by material forces?

Ch'ü did not realize that the writings of Marx and Engels—works with which he was not yet familiar—are open to a variety of interpretations on this question. In 1857, while drafting an outline of *A Contribution to the Critique of Political Economy*, Marx was willing to assign considerable autonomy to the superstructure in his attempt to account for the appearance of a magnificent Greek art in a society where the economic base was backward. He conceded that there might be an "unequal relationship of development of material production . . . to artistic production."[29] "In the case of art," he explained, "it is well known that certain flourishing periods by no means stand in direct relationship to the general development of society, that is, to the material foundation."[30] Yet, two years later when he wrote the foreword to *A Contribution to the Critique of Political Economy*, Marx made what was undoubtedly his most deterministic statement about the connection between base and superstructure. In describing the relationship between the components of society Marx asserted: "Men enter into definite [social] relations of production which correspond to a definite state of the development of their material productive forces." Speaking of the superstructure, he added: "The mode of production of material life conditions the social, political and intellectual life process in general." In the same passage, Marx accounted for the *sequence* in which these elements were transformed in periods of social change: "At a certain stage of their development, the material productive forces of society come into conflict with existing relations of production . . . then begins an epoch of social revolution. With the change of the economic foundation the entire immense superstructure is more or less rapidly transformed."[31] Clearly, this formulation represents a

29. Peter Demetz, *Marx, Engels and the Poets: Origins of Marxist Literary Criticism* (Chicago: University of Chicago Press, 1967), p. 68.

30. Ibid.

31. Lee Baxandall and Stefan Morawski, eds., *Marx and Engels on Literature and Art: A Selection of Writings* (St. Louis: Telos Press, 1973), p. 85.

theory of causality in which artistic expression is thoroughly sub-ordinated to material variables.

But in the 1890s, Engels made several statements that apportioned considerably more independence to the superstructure. In a letter to Hans Starkenburg, Engels explained that political, legal, philosophical, religious, and literary activities are based upon economic develop-ment. "But," he added, "they all react upon one another and upon the economic base. It is not so that the economic situation is *cause, active by itself alone,* and all the rest only passive effect. Rather it is mutual interaction based upon economic necessity that always realizes itself ultimately."[32]

No less ambiguous are the views of Marx and Engels on the closely related matter of the social role of the individual writer. Their less deterministic statements about the relationship between substructure and superstructure imply that there is a strategic role to be played by the creative intellect of the individual artist, among others, in pro-pelling history forward. Indeed, in their early years Marx and Engels were literary activists themselves. In 1839 Engels believed that the social function of the writer was to arouse the working person—"to make him conscious of his power, his rights, his freedom, to awaken his courage and his patriotism."[33] But in works like his foreword to *A Contribution to the Critique of Political Economy*, Marx placed the superstruc-ture, and thus the individual literary personality, entirely at the mercy of impersonal and inexorable historical forces. As Peter Demetz has pointed out, under these circumstances the social role of the individ-ual artist has been reduced to passively taking note of "the distant tremors of the economic bedrock" from the sidelines of history.[34]

Ch'ü's acceptance of the deterministic interpretation of the rela-tionship between art and society and the social role of the writer altered his outlook on the "capitalist stage" of cultural evolution. Ch'ü now subscribed to a more orthodox Marxist belief in objective laws of history that move human history through clearly defined stages of socio-economic development. Ch'ü was certainly no champion of bourgeois culture, but he now accepted the inevitability and historical necessity of the capitalist stage. In brief, capitalism created social and economic conditions that would insure the ultimate arrival of the socialist revolution.

It is obvious that in treating the fundamental questions of the relationship between literature and society, the evolution of art, and the role of the artist, Ch'ü deliberately emphasized several of the most deterministic strains in Marxist literary thought. As such, Ch'ü's essay represents a radical departure from the idealist and voluntarist

32. Demetz, *Marx, Engels and the Poets*, p. 147.   33. Ibid., p. 19.   34. Ibid., p. 73.

views on culture and art that he had expressed so clearly in his Peking, and even his Moscow, writings. Utopian socialist notions about the relative autonomy of the cultural sphere, the vanguard role of the revolutionary intellectual, and the possibility of skipping undesirable cultural stages were nowhere in evidence in Ch'ü's first discussion of Marxist literary theory. On the contrary, artistic development was now seen by Ch'ü as being thoroughly shaped by impersonal and objective historical forces. Writers do not make history: they reflect its movement.

It is difficult to know why Ch'ü changed his views on art, but it is clear that in doing so he brought his literary thought into harmony with his new political beliefs.[35] It will be recalled that Ch'ü was originally attracted to Marxism because he thought it held out the hope that the capitalist stage might be bypassed or at least abbreviated on the road to socialism. But the Comintern's decision to emphasize the leading role of the Kuomintang, a "bourgeois" revolutionary party, forced Ch'ü to revise his views about capitalism and history itself. In fact, Ch'ü was one of the first Chinese communists to express the orthodox view that a capitalist stage was necessary for China, and that all communists, while keeping in mind the special nature of their own objectives, should cooperate with the Kuomintang to achieve desirable bourgeois-democratic goals, such as the destruction of "feudalism" and the expulsion of the imperialist powers. Accordingly, Ch'ü's essay on Marxist literary theory stressed the inevitability and historical necessity for a bourgeois cultural stage. Ch'ü now emphasized that the bourgeois period in fact produced great literature, such as early romantic literature that celebrated human individuality and creativity, and reform-minded realist literature that criticized the social evils of advanced capitalist society.

The central weakness of Ch'ü's simplistic introduction of Marxist literary thought was, of course, his total failure to relate this new framework to the Chinese context. Was the present bourgeois literary movement in China in the anti-feudal, the reformist, or the declining-decadent stage? Were his warnings about the pitfalls of the "art for art's sake" and "art for life's sake" approaches meant to be oblique references to the powerful Creation Society and Literary Research Association, respectively? Were his remarks to be understood as a call for a prerevolutionary Chinese "proletarian" literary movement? It is impossible to answer these questions definitively, for nowhere in this early discussion of theory is China mentioned. Like so many post-May Fourth volumes on literary theory, Ch'ü's was little more than a summary of a foreign original.

35. These new political views are expressed with great clarity in his December 1923 article, "Ts'ung min-chih-chu-i chih she-hui-chu-i."

SOVIET PROLETARIAN LITERATURE

"Russia" was still Ch'ü's foreign literary model, but beginning in 1923 he no longer stressed the prerevolutionary nineteenth-century tradition. On the contrary, as an active member of the Literary Research Association, Ch'ü did as much as he could to direct the attention of his old May Fourth friends away from bourgeois Western literary models and toward the new proletarian trends evident in postrevolutionary Soviet society. Although six years had passed since the Bolshevik victory, Chinese intellectuals knew almost nothing of the dynamic literary developments taking place in the Soviet Union. Although they were fragmentary and unoriginal, Ch'ü's *Fiction Monthly* articles, such as "New Writers of Workers' and Peasants' Russia" and "The First Swallows of Red Russia's New Literary and Artistic Period," should be viewed as pioneering attempts to bring modern Chinese writers up to date.

But to reach conclusions about the ideas Ch'ü tried to convey in these articles, it is necessary to know something about the origins of the "proletarian" cultural movement, a movement that carried on the rich nineteenth-century Russian utopian socialist literary tradition. Although this school was unknown in China, Russian Marxists such as Anatoly Lunacharsky an Alexander Bogdanov began formulating theories about "proletarian culture" as early as 1910. Influenced by utopian socialist assumptions, they asserted that the proletariat should move toward socialism not only by economic and political means, but by cultural means as well. Since they believed that the realm of the superstructure had been badly neglected, they argued that revolutionaries could and should begin at once, even in a period when bourgeois rule still prevailed, to develop distinctively proletarian cultural modes. Contrary to the logic of Marxism, they argued that bourgeois culture, indeed all cultures of the past, were generally unsuited to the task of organizing and promoting the proletarian revolution. The working class was to have its own culture and art. Since proletarian cultural theorists did not require a proletarian inheritance of bourgeois culture, they tended, like the utopians, not to be particularly troubled by the low cultural and educational level of the masses. Implicit in their thinking was the notion that the absence of this and all other burdensome and irrelevant traditions might actually facilitate a speedy breakthrough in developing proletarian culture.[36]

In early 1917 Bogdanov founded the Proletarian Cultural Organization (Proletkult), an independent association committed to the sort of ideas about proletarian culture he had sketched out some years

36. For a summary of the assumptions held by early advocates of proletarian culture, see Ermolaev, *Soviet Literary Theory*, pp. 1-26.

before. Yet, from the beginning, those who accepted the basic assumptions of the movement quarreled about the precise nature of proletarian artistic culture and the means by which it might be created. There were many shades of opinion, but it is useful to distinguish between two contrasting views expressed by members of Proletkult both before and after the demise of the organization in 1920.

One tendency, "futurist" proletarianism, was evident in the thought of figures like Vladimir Mayakovsky and V. E. Meyerhold, who greatly influenced Proletkult in its early years and who were instrumental later in the founding of futurist proletarian literary groups such as LEF (Left Front of the Arts) in 1923.[37] Three points about the futurist proletarian orientation deserve mention: their ranks were filled with "proletarianized" intellectuals who had defected from the old order in prerevolutionary days; they advocated a radical break with most traditional and bourgeois artistic conventions; and they placed great emphasis on daring experiments in new artistic forms and language.

A secondary tendency, "pure" proletarianism, arose, in part, in reaction to the influence of the futurists in Proletkult. Led by Mikhail Gerasimov, Vasily Kazin, and others, the "pure" proletarians withdrew from Proletkult in early 1920 to organize a group known as Kuznitsa (The Smithy). As Herman Ermolaev has pointed out, one of the most unusual features of Kuznitsa was in fact its "pure" social composition: 80 percent came from a working-class background.[38] The social makeup of Kuznitsa was not coincidental. They believed that the proletariat and proletarian life were the only appropriate subjects for proletarian art, and only those who knew proletarian life from the inside could hope to treat it artistically. Consequently, a strain of anti-intellectualism ran rather deep in groups like Kuznitsa. Their opposition to the futurist proletarians was also reflected in their skepticism of avant-garde experiments in artistic form and language, which, in the "pure" view, amounted to little more than decadent, bourgeois posturing. To be sure, Kuznitsa writers treated the proletariat in a highly romantic and heroic manner, but they tended to employ familiar forms of poetry and fiction when doing so. Finally, while the "pure" proletarians showed a lack of reverence for the artistic heritage of the past, they were not as militantly iconoclastic as the futurists.

Ch'ü Ch'iu-pai's articles on these trends were sketchy, but he had a more detailed knowledge of Soviet proletarian artistic life than anyone else in China. In "New Writers" Ch'ü pointed out that, while there may have been agreement in Soviet literary circles on the necessity and possibility of building a uniquely proletarian artistic culture, there

37. Ibid., pp. 72-80.   38. Ibid., pp. 19-20.

was significant disagreement about the nature of that culture and the means by which it might be achieved. On the one hand, Ch'ü recognized the influence that "futurist" proletarians like Mayakovsky had exerted in the early Proletkult movement. He correctly pointed out that the futurist writings of Mayakovsky and other intellectuals were revolutionary because their iconoclastic rejection of traditional literary forms and language had the effect of undermining the old order. On the other hand, Ch'ü specifically mentioned the Kuznitsa or "pure" proletarians led by Gerasimov, Kazin, and others who withdrew from Proletkult in early 1920. In contrast to the futurists, the pure proletarians placed a greater emphasis on recruiting workers from among the ranks of the working class itself, placed more stress on proletarian subject matter, and were less concerned about avant-garde experiments in form.[39]

Ch'ü's second *Fiction Monthly* article, "The First Swallows of Red Russia's New Literary and Artistic Period," featured the literary careers of Pavel Bessalko and Feodor Kalinin, two "pure" proletarian and anti-intellectual figures active in the early proletarian cultural movement. A student of Alexander Bogdanov and head of Proletkult in Petrograd, Bessalko was as iconoclastic as the futurist proletarians, but he ridiculed their approach to proletarian culture. As a former factory worker, Bessalko insisted on genuine proletarian leadership in cultural affairs and wrote in simple Russian for mass consumption. Kalinin, also a former worker and co-founder of Proletkult with Bogdanov, was presented by Ch'ü in much the same way.[40]

But Ch'ü did not reach any startling conclusions about the meaning of postrevolutionary Russian literature for a distinctively prerevolutionary China. In fact, China is mentioned nowhere in the reports. Ch'ü, like many others in the early 1920s, was content to merely describe developments in what he believed to be the most progressive foreign nation. Nowhere is the relevance of these trends spelled out. Furthermore, it is clear that, in typical May Fourth style, at least one of these reports, "First Swallows," was adapted from two commemorative editorials that had appeared in *Proletarskaya Kultura* in 1920.[41]

Ch'ü must have realized that some of the views he attributed to Soviet proletarian literary groups, such as the anti-intellectual and

39. Ch'ü Ch'iu-pai, "Lao-nung O-kuo te hsin tso-chia" [New writers of workers' and peasants' Russia], *Hsiao-shuo yueh-pao* [Fiction monthly] 14:9 (September 1923); in CCPWC, 2:545-550. For a discussion of the "futurist" and "proletarian" groups, see Ermolaev, *Soviet Literary Theory*, pp. 32-33.

40. Ch'ü Ch'iu-pai, "Ch'ih-O hsin wen-i shih-tai te ti-i yen" [The first swallows of Red Russia's new literary and artistic period], *Hsiao-shuo yueh-pao* 15,6 (June 1924); in CCPWC, 2:550-558.

41. Mark E. Shneider, *Tvorcheskii Put' Tsiui Tsiu-bo, 1899-1935* (Moscow: Izdatel'stvo Nauka, 1964), pp. 83-84.

anti-bourgeois thrusts of proletarian cultural iconoclasm, would be controversial in Chinese literary circles, where the leading role of bourgeois art and intellectuals was taken for granted; but he chose not to confront these problems. Nor was he inclined to side with either the "futurist" or "pure" proletarian cultural camps. Ch'ü also seems to have been unaware that Lenin and Trotsky were highly skeptical of both the "futurist" and "pure" proletarian trends in the postrevolutionary cultural movement.[42]

Although they did little to prohibit or promote the flourishing proletarian cultural movement, they had made their views known in no uncertain terms. The principal thesis of Trotsky's eloquent *Literature and Revolution* was that, historically speaking, proletarian culture could not exist, and that all efforts to create such a culture were misguided and bound to fail. Feudal and bourgeois culture arose because the feudal and capitalist periods were long, and the ruling class in each period had sufficient time to develop an elaborate superstructure. A distinctively proletarian culture "will never exist" in a proletarian state "because the proletarian regime is temporary and transient."[43] It is the historical mission of the proletarian revolution, not to create yet another imperfect class culture, but to pave the way for the advent of the truly human and classless society of the communist future.

In contrast to Trotsky, Lenin stressed the exceptional cultural backwardness of the masses and the deformed historical development of Russia itself as the primary obstacles blocking proletarian cultural development. He did not rule out the possibility of achieving a proletarian culture at some future date, but the first order of business was to develop modern industry and assault backward precapitalist cultural modes. Furthermore, the various proletarian cultural experiments offended the personal and highly conventional aesthetic tastes of Trotsky and Lenin. "Very often," Lenin wrote, "the most absurd ideas were hailed as something new, and the supernatural and incongruous were offered as purely proletarian art."[44] Ch'ü Ch'iu-pai's articles left the impression that the proletarian cultural movement was endorsed by the state. His readers certainly would have received a different picture of the movement if he had presented some of the views of Marxists who opposed it.

Even more curious is the fact that Ch'ü seems not to have been aware that early Soviet proletarian cultural activists held assumptions on the relationship between culture and society that conflicted with

42. According to Shneider, *Tvorcheskii Put'*, p. 83, Lenin specifically criticized Bessalko and Kalinin.

43. Leon Trotsky, *Literature and Revolution* (Ann Arbor: University of Michigan Press, 1966), p. 14.

44. V.I. Lenin, *On Literature and Art* (Moscow: Progress Publishers, 1970), p. 129.

the rather deterministic Marxist literary ideas he presented in his Shanghai University lectures. Like Plekhanov before him, Ch'ü had argued that cultural change always follows a fundamental transformation of the economic base. The early Soviet proletarian cultural groups discussed above may have disagreed on several questions, but they, like their utopian socialist forerunners, shared the assumption that certain basic changes in the superstructure could be achieved before, and presumably independently of, the transformation of the economic base. Ch'ü's early reports on the Soviet scene failed to treat these controversies and their implications for China.

FROM LITERARY REVOLUTION TO REVOLUTIONARY LITERATURE

More relevant to the Chinese literary scene was Ch'ü's work with Yun Tai-ying, Teng Chung-hsia, Shen Tse-min, and Hsiao Ch'u-nü in well-known communist publications such as *Chinese Youth* and *New Youth*.[45] Only in short articles, such as "In a Wasteland—Chinese Literature in 1923," and "To Young People Who Study Literature," did Ch'ü discuss China and point to the direction he felt the modern literary movement should take. In doing so, he made some perceptive, if fragmentary, observations about the problems of the literary revolution.

It is clear, for example, that Ch'ü was beginning to reassess the impact of the May Fourth literary revolution. Ch'ü and his colleagues conceded that the literary revolution to undermine the classical tradition by introducing modern Western literature and using a more vernacular literary language had been quite successful. But unless further progress was made, they warned, there was a danger that the trends of forming elite groups and "conserving" early victories of the literary revolution might intensify. As cultural revolutionaries, they were afraid that the modern cultural movement might fall behind contemporary political developments and stagnate. Ch'ü appreciated the fact that very few modern Chinese writers had shown much interest in formalism, symbolism, and other avant-garde, "late bourgeois" literary forms, but he was increasingly aware that the language used in conventional realist and romantic literature could not be considered entirely vernacular, and thus the common people could not understand even those bourgeois writings that were politically progressive.[46]

45. For a good general summary of the significance of the activities of this group, see Chang Pi-lai, "Wen-hsueh chu-chang," pp. 36-49.

46. Ch'ü Ch'iu-pai, "Huang-mo li—I-chiu-erh-san nien chih Chung-kuo wen-hsueh" [In a wasteland—Chinese literature in 1923], *Hsin ch'ing-nien* [New youth], 20 December 1923; in CCPWC, 1:232-233.

He was even more concerned with the political problem of literary content, and criticized what he believed to be the overly sentimental, narcissistic, or escapist content of works by Hsu Chih-mo, Yü P'ing-po, Hsu Yü-no, Chu Tzu-ch'ing, and others.

It is difficult to know precisely what sort of content Ch'ü wanted to see. In none of his articles did he explicitly call for the launching of a "proletarian" literary movement. But, impatient for the next stage of the modern literary movement to begin, Ch'ü and his young Marxist colleagues advocated a shift from the "literary revolution" of the May Fourth period to a movement for "revolutionary literature." Ch'ü hoped that by this means the modern literary movement might be placed once again in the mainstream of the Chinese revolution and that the organic link between literature and society, so pronounced at the time of the May Fourth Incident, might be reestablished. Ch'ü tried to persuade writers to embrace the political goals of the proletarian contingent in the United Front and to reflect this ideology in their writing. In 1923, this meant attention to the labor movement, support for anti-imperialist nationalism, and condemnation of the feudal power of landlords and warlords.

To get the content of the new literature out of the clouds and onto the streets, essays in *Chinese Youth* urged writers to make direct contact with the urban masses, and to participate in the revolutionary struggle. In "To Young People Who Study Literature," Ch'ü proclaimed: "Friend, you need not know in detail how to become a writer. You must put into effect what you know. Like Tolstoy you must go among the people *(tao min-chien ch'ü),* like Buddha you must descend into hell, you must follow where people have gone. You must taste every human bitterness, endure every human ignominy."[47] In Ch'ü's view it was a "disgrace" that there were no Chinese writers going into the coal mines to learn about the lives of workers. To encourage contact between revolutionary intellectuals and factory workers, Ch'ü, Yun Tai-ying, and Teng Chung-hsia personally organized the Workers' Part-Time School, the West Shanghai Workers' Club, and the Workers' Association for the Promotion of Virtue.[48]

The question of whether the Communist Party might take an ac-

47. Ch'ü Ch'iu-pai, "Kao yen-chiu wen-hsueh te ch'ing-nien" [To young people who study literature], *Chung-kuo ch'ing-nien,* 17 November 1923; in *Chung-kuo hsien-tai wen-hsueh shih ts'an-k'ao tzu-liao* [Research materials on the history of modern Chinese literature] (Peking: Kao-teng chiao-yü ch'u-pan-she, 1959-60) (hereafter TKTL), 1:196; Gálik, *Mao Tun and Modern Chinese Literary Criticism,* p. 84. This article was signed "Ch'iu-shih." Its author, as Chang Pi-lai has speculated, was probably Ch'ü. Chang Pi-lai, "Wen-hsueh chu-chang," p. 38. Gálik *(Mao Tun and Modern Chinese Literary Criticism,* p. 84) has suggested that Teng Chung-hsia wrote the article.

48. Bernadette Li, p. 162; Jean Chesneaux, *The Chinese Labor Movement, 1919-1927* (Stanford: Stanford University Press, 1968), p. 255.

tive role in supervising or directing the movement for "revolutionary literature" once it was under way was not raised by Ch'ü. He simply wanted to point out to individual writers that they could not ignore society, nor avoid deciding whether to play a bourgeois role, a "proletarian" role, or no role in the current bourgeois stage of the revolution. Of course, a bourgeois role would be progressive, but he hoped they would participate as heralds of the proletariat. In Ch'ü's estimation the issues that faced the modern literary world were essentially political and not literary.

Ch'ü acknowledged the existence of distinctively literary problems, such as the tendency of modern writers to imitate stylish Western bourgeois literary models and language; but he assumed in 1923 that if the *political* consciousness of modern writers underwent the appropriate transformation, the literary movement would automatically shift from the "literary revolution" characteristic of early bourgeois movements to the "revolutionary literature" of a more mature national, but presocialist, revolutionary movement. In later years Ch'ü would realize he had been wrong: the *political* radicalization of writers would not result in the resolution of literary problems associated with the early bourgeois cultural stage.

RETREAT FROM IDEALISM

Ch'ü Ch'iu-pai's cultural writings were quite fragmentary in 1923 and 1924, but they reveal that some significant changes had occurred in his political and literary thought, changes that began to take shape in his final months in Moscow after he joined the Chinese Communist Party. In general, these changes involved a reinterpretation of socialist theory, that is, a shift from Ch'ü's former interest in employing revolutionary cultural means to achieve an early realization of the utopian ends of socialist revolution to a new and more Marxian respect for the limitations imposed on human revolutionary activities by objective historical laws and material forces. This shift in Ch'ü's ideological orientation can be detected in his enthusiastic support for a political alliance between the Communist Party and the Kuomintang to achieve the bourgeois-democratic goals of the revolution, and in his uncharacteristically deterministic statements about the relationship between art and social change, which implied an acceptance, if not a celebration, of the bourgeois cultural stage.

The change in Ch'ü's intellectual disposition was reflected quite clearly in his vigorous attacks on those who sought to denounce "Western materialism" by proclaiming the superiority of traditional "Asian spirituality." For example, Ch'ü played a leading role in the movement to discredit the Indian poet Rabindranath Tagore who, during his lecture tour of China, asserted that the peoples of the East should reject Western notions of material culture and revive traditional Asian spiritual culture. Ch'ü objected to Tagore's ideas not simply because they were "anachronistic," but because they were based on what he called "idealist" intellectual assumptions that disregarded objective historical laws. In sharp contrast to the views he expressed in his Moscow writings, Ch'ü no longer believed that "East" and "West" were meaningful analytical categories, and he no longer saw the revolution as a blending of the two cultures. "As there is no so-called East and no so-called West, therefore there is no such problem as harmonizing them!"[49] For Ch'ü in 1923 there were only classes, class struggle, and the objective laws of dialectical materialism.

Ch'ü was equally critical of those in China, like Liang Shu-ming and Chang Chün-mai, who admired Tagore and attempted in the early 1920s to lead a movement to revive Confucian culture.[50] In ridiculing those who hoped to reverse the iconoclastic trends that had been set in motion during the New Culture Movement, Ch'ü made it clear that the salvation of China would depend not upon the revival of abstract metaphysical systems, but rather upon the organization of a powerful mass political movement appropriate for China's particular "stage" of historical development.[51]

Even more startling were Ch'ü's attacks on the sort of radical utopian socialist and populist views he had espoused in earlier years. A good example was Ch'ü's lengthy discussion of the social and political significance of Boris Savinkov's autobiographical novel, *The Pale Horse*, published in 1909 and translated into Chinese in 1924. Ch'ü applauded the book because it was the story of a former member of the populist Russian Social Revolutionary Party who had "repented." The Social Revolutionaries, like the "narodniks" (*min-ts'ui-p'ai*), were bound to fail, Ch'ü insisted, because, among other things, they overemphasized the role of intellectuals, human will, and the acts of "heroic individuals," and because they believed the capitalist stage could be bypassed.[52] Ch'ü's readers could hardly have mistaken his message: the

49. Stephen N. Hay, *Asian Ideas on East and West: Tagore and His Critics in Japan, China, and India* (Cambridge: Harvard University Press, 1970), p. 230.

50. For an excellent discussion of this short-lived reaction to the New Culture movement, see Jerome B. Grieder, *Hu Shih and the Chinese Renaissance: Liberalism in the Chinese Revolution, 1917-1937* (Cambridge: Harvard University Press, 1970), pp. 135-150. Also see Guy S. Alitto, *The Last Confucian: Liang Shu-ming and the Chinese Dilemma of Modernity* (Berkeley and Los Angeles: University of California Press, 1979).

51. See Ch'ü Ch'iu-pai, "Chu Pa-chieh: Tung Hsi wen-hua yü Liang Shu-ming Wu Chih-hui" [Chu Pa-chieh: Eastern and Western cultures and Liang Shu-ming and Wu Chih-hui], *Chung-kuo ch'ing-nien*, 17 November 1923; in CCPWC, 1:226-228.

52. Ch'ü Ch'iu-pai, "Hui-se ma yü O-kuo she-hui yun-tung" [*The Pale Horse* and Russia's social movement], *Hsiao-shuo yueh-pao* 14,11 (November 1923): 1-10. See Shneider, *Tvorcheskii Put'*, p. 41.

revolutionary youth of China should update their political ideology by rejecting idealistic and romantic solutions to China's problems, and by joining a mass political movement organized and led by a political party that knew precisely what revolutionary goals could be achieved at a given moment in history.

Although Ch'ü Ch'iu-pai had a good deal of success recruiting young, politically charged intellectuals for the revolution, he clearly had much less success in transforming the literary movement itself. Despite his efforts to introduce Marxist literary theory and Soviet proletarian literature, and to promote a shift from "literary revolution" to "revolutionary literature," the Shanghai literary world was, on the whole, rather unreceptive to these new ideas in 1923. For one thing, the dynamic modern literary movement that had been a by-product of the social and political turmoil of the New Culture and May Fourth Movements had become increasingly elitist, professional, and politically detached during the rise of the major literary societies in the early 1920s. Ch'ü sought to encourage proletarian "tendentiousness," but the bourgeois literary schools to which many writers still subscribed stressed the apolitical theme of "art for art's sake," or the humanistic theme of "art for life's sake." Even some who saw a social role for literature believed that writers could be objective observers of society only if they avoided partisanship and political involvement. Some of Ch'ü's observations about the problems of the literary movement were perceptive, but by no means can his analysis be considered comprehensive. He simply felt that the literary movement was lagging behind political developments, and he was disappointed that so many of his old May Fourth literary colleagues did not share his enthusiasm.

The major reason for Ch'ü's lack of success lies in his failure to demonstrate the relevance of Marxist literary theory or Soviet proletarian literature to the Chinese literary scene. He summarized Bukharin's deterministic theoretical statements; but he never made explicit use of them to analyze the Chinese case. Similarly, he was the first to introduce Chinese writers to Soviet proletarian literature; but he failed to explain the significance of the theoretical differences that separated early proletarian cultural thinkers from Bukharin and others who represented a more conservative tradition of Marxist literary thought. It is likely that some of his readers were impressed by the role played by proletarian cultural activists in Russia; but Ch'ü never took a stand on the issues that separated the various proletarian factions. Some of Ch'ü's colleagues were probably alarmed about the hostility of "futurist" proletarians toward the masterpieces of bourgeois culture and the anti-intellectualism of "pure" proletarians; but he did little to explain these developments. Introducing Marxism into

Chinese political life had been much easier because Western liberalism had been discredited long before 1923; but despite the appeal of Marxist politics, the influence of Western bourgeois culture and literature had increased steadily after the May Fourth Incident.

Ch'ü simply did not present a very coherent picture of Marxist literary thought. To be sure, the Western tradition of Marxist literary thought is exceedingly diverse, but Ch'ü had grasped only fragments of this amorphous body of theory. In view of the contradictions and gaps that appeared in Ch'ü's writings, it is somewhat ironic that he seems to have been unaware that the Western tradition of Marxist literary thought contained elements decidedly less hostile to the bourgeois tradition and to bourgeois literary experts themselves, elements that might have appeared, and later did appear, more attractive to May Fourth writers.

Ch'ü's early efforts may have failed, but his attempts to introduce Marxist theory and proletarian trends were solidly within the familiar May Fourth pattern of introducing foreign literary schools. Although his model had changed by 1923 from "nineteenth-century Russia" to "Soviet Russia," Ch'ü's lifelong commitment to Marxist literary thought grew out of his early study of the Russian language, his reading of the nineteenth-century Russian masters, and his travel in that most "advanced" foreign nation. And, in typical May Fourth fashion, his grasp of the Marxist and Soviet literary model was both imitative and superficial. Ironically, in essays such as "In a Wasteland" and "To Young People Who Study Literature," which show touches of originality, it is fairly difficult to trace his indebtedness to either Marxist theory or Soviet proletarian models. In later years, he would criticize—with considerable justification—the failure of May Fourth writers to relate their foreign literary models to distinctively Chinese conditions. But Ch'ü himself was guilty of that offense in 1923.

It is important, therefore, to see the introduction of Marxist literary thought not as an exotic and alien trend in early May Fourth literary and intellectual history, but as a trend that falls squarely *within* the May Fourth tradition. There were many shortcomings in Ch'ü's pioneering writings, but, in a sense, he was only one step ahead of his companions. Under more favorable circumstances a few years later, Marxist literary thought would hold considerable interest for many of those May Fourth writers who were ambivalent about it in 1923.[53] Under new conditions, Chinese writers would begin to see Marxist literary thought as a legitimate part of the Western cultural

53. There were, of course, several notable exceptions. By 1923 the political thought of both Mao Tun and Kuo Mo-jo had undergone a radical transformation and they began to advocate revolutionary literature. See Roy, *Kuo Mo-jo*, pp. 134-161; and Gálik, *Mao Tun and Modern Chinese Literary Criticism*, pp. 83-97.

heritage and, thus, as a legitimate offspring of the May Fourth tradition.

By mid-1924, Ch'ü's interest in the literary movement and in saving China by "cultural means" had all but vanished. His difficulties made it easier for him to accept a more deterministic view of the role of the superstructure during a revolutionary transformation of society. It was easy to conclude that the literary movement was indeed less important than he once believed. By late 1924, Ch'ü was completely absorbed in revolutionary political activities. The early success of the United Front excited Ch'ü and made him extremely optimistic about the immediate future of the political revolution. And in late 1924 there was every reason for Ch'ü to predict that he would be a principal actor in the forthcoming national revolution to unite China and expel the imperialists. Who needed the lethargic literary movement?[54]

54. Ch'ü's creative efforts were rather meager in this period. He wrote one short story, one song, five poems, and translated four Russian stories. "Ch'ih ch'ao ch'ü" [Song of the red wave] is important because Ch'ü hoped it would become the national anthem of the revolution. For a translation, see Rewi Alley, ed., *Poems of Revolt* (Peking: New World Press, 1962), pp. 147-148. The Chinese text is in CCPWC, 1:211-212.

5 The Leftist Literary Scene

The upsurge of revolutionary literature here looks different on the face of it from that in other countries, being due not to a high tide of revolution but to a setback.

LU HSÜN, 1931[1]

Ch'ü Ch'iu-pai had been unable to generate much enthusiasm for Marxist literary thought or "revolutionary literature" in 1923, but not long after his departure from the cultural world members of the Literary Research Association and the Creation Society began to show considerable interest in both subjects. In part, it was the progress of the revolution that helped to change the attitudes of many young writers. In 1923, people like Ch'ü could only offer promises about the bright future of the United Front and the national revolution. But two years later it was apparent to most intellectuals, including some whom Ch'ü later characterized as "bohemians" (*po-hai-min*),[2] that the revolution had actually arrived. Many were swept up first by the impressive labor movement of the mid-1920s and later by the Northern Expedition. Ch'ü had failed in the early 1920s, but by 1926 the slogan "from literary revolution to revolutionary literature" was widely accepted, and, for the first time, serious attention was given to Marxist literary thought.

1. Lu Hsün, "A Glance at Shanghai Literature," in *Selected Works of Lu Hsün* (hereafter referred to as SWLH) (Peking: Foreign Languages Press, 1964), 3:120.
2. Ch'ü Ch'iu-pai, *"Lu Hsün tsa-kan ch'uan-chi hsu-yen"* [Preface to *The Miscellaneous Writings of Lu Hsün*], April 8, 1933, in *Lu Hsün tsa-kan ch'uan-chi* [The miscellaneous writings of Lu Hsün] (Shanghai: Ch'ing-kuang shu-tien, 1933), in CCPWC, 2:995.

THE INTELLECTUAL ORIGINS OF THE
LEFTIST LITERARY MOVEMENT

The first and perhaps most dramatic transformation occurred in the ranks of the Creation Society, the organization that had advocated the "art for art's sake" approach in the immediate post-May Fourth period. Abandoning the apolitical and transcendental romanticism of their early history, writers like Kuo Mo-jo and Ch'eng Fang-wu began proclaiming in articles entitled "Revolution and Literature" and "From Literary Revolution to Revolutionary Literature" that the existence of the Creation Society could be justified only to the extent that it contributed to the progress of the revolution. Kuo Mo-jo's assertion that "literature is a forerunner of the revolution" was appealing to many young writers in 1926.[3] By 1928 the membership of the Creation Society was comprised of young Marxists, like P'an Han-nien, Li Ch'u-li, Feng Nai-ch'ao, P'eng K'eng, Chu Ching-wo, and others, who had returned to China in the mid-1920s after a period of study at leftist universities in Japan. Although the revolution suffered a serious defeat in 1927, the revolutionary fervor of the "new" Creation Society was not dampened. Indeed, their writings show that after 1927 they advocated a shift from the United Front movement for revolutionary literature to a distinctively socialist movement for "proletarian literature."[4]

Another leftist literary group to emerge from the May Fourth romantic tradition was the Sun Society (T'ai-yang she), which was formed in January 1928. Led by Chiang Kuang-tz'u (Ch'ü's former colleague at Shanghai University), Ch'ien Hsing-ts'un, Hua Han, and others, the Sun Society was also primarily concerned with promoting a proletarian literary movement that would help pave the way for the forthcoming socialist revolution.[5] In the early months of 1928 there was some factional strife between members of the Creation and Sun groups over which would lead the revolutionary literary movement,

---

3. These two essays by Kuo and Ch'eng are found in TKTL, 1:210-225. Translations of the two essays appear in *Bulletin of Concerned Asian Scholars*, 8,1 (January-March 1976): 28-37. Kuo's article was written immediately after his Spring 1926 meeting with Ch'ü in Shanghai. It is believed that it was Ch'ü's recommendation that got Kuo a position as head of the Department of Literature at Chung-shan University in Canton. See Bernadette Yu-ning Li, "A Bibliography of Ch'ü Ch'iu-pai: From Youth to Party Leadership (1899-1928)" (Ph.D. dissertation, Columbia University, 1967), pp. 174-175.

4. For a survey of this transformation, see Li Ho-lin, ed., *Chin erh-shih nien Chung-kuo wen-i ssu-ch'ao lun* [Chinese literary thought of the past twenty years] (Shanghai: Sheng-huo shu-tien, 1939), pp. 115-168.

5. On Chiang Kuang-tz'u and the origins of the Sun Society, see Fu-tan ta-hsueh Chung-wen hsi, ed., *Chung-kuo hsien-tai wen-hsueh shih: 1919-1942* [A History of modern Chinese literature: 1919-1942] (Shanghai: Shanghai wen-i ch'u-pan-she, 1959?), pp. 166-188.

but an alliance was finally forged because, among other things, their views about literature and society were essentially the same.

The revolutionary upheavals of the 1925-1927 period also had a significant impact on non-romantic writers who belonged to the Literary Research Association or those who simply subscribed to the realist and naturalist schools of literature. Mao Tun, the leader of the Literary Research Association, became a Marxist, participated enthusiastically in the revolution, and endorsed the revolutionary literary movement. In doing so, he discarded some of his earlier humanist and "scientist" convictions about the role of literature. Lu Hsün, another major May Fourth figure who had long believed that literature should play a role in social reform, was one of the first among the sober realists to be attracted by the literary thought of Plekhanov and Lunacharsky. The Unnamed Society (Wei-ming she), a Peking literary group organized by Lu Hsün in 1925, published a number of translations of nineteenth- and twentieth-century Russian literature and criticism, and several works on Marxist literary thought, including Trotsky's *Literature and Revolution*.[6]

Considering Ch'ü Ch'iu-pai's pessimistic appraisal of the literary scene in 1924, it was gratifying to him that interest in revolutionary literature and Marxist literary thought had become widespread in China by 1928. But by no means had all modern Chinese writers submerged themselves in the revolutionary tide. Indeed, one of the most highly regarded literary groups of the mid-1920s was the Crescent Moon Society (Hsin yueh she). Organized by the poet Hsu Chih-mo in 1923, the Society represented precisely the trend in the modern literary movement that had driven Ch'ü into the political arena. The Crescent group was dominated by American-trained writers, like Hsu Chih-mo, Liang Shih-ch'iu, Hu Shih, and others, who continued to hold a favorable view of Western liberalism at a time when many intellectuals were taking a firm anti-imperialist stand. In 1923 the intellectual distance between the Crescent, Creation, and Literary Research organizations had not been particularly great; but by 1928 the situation had changed drastically. Veterans of the Creation Society and Literary Research Association now openly supported the United Front and were willing to permit their art to serve revolutionary political ends. The Crescent Moon group continued to assert that

6. Another group that seems to have emerged from the realist tradition was the Tatler Society (Yü-ssu she) to which Lu Hsün belonged throughout the 1920s. See Amitendranath Tagore, *Literary Debates in Modern China, 1918-1937* (Tokyo: Centre for East Asian Studies, 1967), pp. 59-64. On the transformation of Lu Hsün and Mao Tun, see Li Ho-lin, ed., *Chin erh-shih nien Chung-kuo wen-i ssu-ch'ao lun*, pp. 169-195; and Huang Sung-kang, *Lu Hsün and the New Culture Movement of Modern China* (Amsterdam: Djambatan, 1957).

writers should not become involved in partisan politics (an old Literary Research Association view) and that there was no material relationship between literature and society (an old Creation Society view).[7]

Nothing better reflected the condition of the modern literary movement than the fierce debate on the nature of revolutionary literature that was waged in Shanghai's literary journals from 1928 to the beginning of 1930. By 1928, just after the failure of the revolution, most of China's influential modern writers had moved to Shanghai, now the undisputed center of the modern cultural scene. Each of the three groupings mentioned above participated in the debate: the Crescent Moon Society, the Creation and Sun coalition, and a group that looked to Lu Hsün and Mao Tun to represent its views.

The most conspicuous clash, but by no means the most important, pitted the Creation and Sun romantics, who advocated "proletarian" literature, against the Crescent Moon Society, which opposed revolutionary literature of any sort. Liang Shih-ch'iu, the leader of Crescent Moon opposition, denied repeatedly that literature has a class character and disputed the notion that artists have any particular social or political obligations other than to represent all that is universal in human society.[8] Although talented intellectuals participated on both sides of the exchange, the defenders of the Crescent Moon viewpoint stood little chance of gaining the sympathy of those outside their organization. The national political and social crisis had widened, and few writers could refrain from speaking out on the issues of the day or avoid becoming politically engaged. Certainly the Crescent group could expect no help from Lu Hsün, Mao Tun, and others who participated in the debate. In fact, Lu Hsün is known to have intensely disliked Liang Shih-ch'iu.[9]

The really significant encounter, and the one that had the greatest bearing on the literary problems Ch'ü Ch'iu-pai would confront in 1931, was between the romantic coalition and the writers who clustered around Lu Hsün and Mao Tun.[10] Both groups accepted the notion that China must have a revolutionary literary movement; both professed a sincere interest in Marxist literary thought. But, like European and Russian Marxists before them, they disagreed violently on

7. Ibid., pp. 221-242; Tagore, *Literary Debates*, 67-70. Ch'ü had begun criticizing the views of writers in this group as early as 1923.

8. The best collection of documents on the debate is Li Ho-lin, ed., *Chung-kuo wen-i lun-chan* [Chinese literary polemics] (Peking: Hua-hsia ch'u-pan-she, 1930). The Crescent Moon position is spelled out on pp. 417-444. Also see Tagore, *Literary Debates*, pp. 106-111.

9. Lu Hsün sniped at Liang Shih-ch'iu and Hsu Chih-mo throughout the late 1920s. For example, see "Some Thoughts on Our New Literature," SWLH, 3:45.

10. See Li Ho-lin, ed., *Chung-kuo wen-i lun-chan*, pp. 11-415, for the relevant documents.

the related problems of the *nature* of revolutionary literature and the role of the left-wing writers. The debates of 1928 and 1929 were the first serious discussion of Marxist literary thought held in China, and they influenced the course of leftist literary thought for many years thereafter.

One way to distinguish between the two groupings is to place their literary views in the context of Western Marxist literary thought. It is quite apparent, for example, that the views of the Creation Society and Sun Society romantics, as articulated by Ch'eng Fang-wu, Cheng Po-ch'i, Feng Nai-ch'ao, Ch'ien Hsing-ts'un, Chiang Kuang-tz'u, and others, are thoroughly consistent with the idealist tradition of Western Marxist literary thought.[11] Most of the romantics had, in fact, been influenced by the proletarian literary movement in Japan, and thus, indirectly, by the assumptions held by the various proletarian literary groups of pre- and postrevolutionary Russia.[12] In brief, the romantic or idealist Marxists in China tended to believe that not only was the superstructure of society relatively independent from the economic base, but that elements of the cultural superstructure, including artistic culture, could be transformed in advance of the economic base and play a vanguard role in the revolution. Thus the Creation and Sun coalition called for an explicitly "proletarian" literary movement in China, despite the fact that most Chinese Marxists understood the defeat of the revolution in 1927 to be a setback for the manifestly presocialist and bourgeois-democratic phase of the cultural movement. Presumably the romantics believed that a "proletarian" cultural movement would hasten the arrival of a proletarian political and social revolution. Bursting with optimism, they argued that the new proletarian literary movement should concentrate almost exclusively on the condition of the working class and should agitate on its behalf. Furthermore, in keeping with many Russian proletarian cultural assumptions, the romantics harbored no illusion that the working class could produce such proletarian literature. Instead, they advocated that proletarian literature be written by intellectuals who possessed a "genuine" proletarian consciousness.[13]

It is equally apparent that the more amorphous coalition of leftist writers who emerged from the realist tradition of the Literary Re-

11. See Paul G. Pickowicz, *Marxist Literary Thought and China: A Conceptual Framework* (Berkeley: The Center for Chinese Studies, University of California, Berkeley, 1980), pp. 19-26, 36-39, 55-62.

12. Chiang Kuang-tz'u had direct experience in the Soviet Union. For a discussion of the Japanese proletarian literary movement, see Tatsuo Arima, *The Failure of Freedom: A Portrait of Modern Japanese Intellectuals* (Cambridge: Harvard University Press, 1969), pp. 173-213.

13. In this respect the romantic view was closer to the "futurist" proletarian than to the "pure" proletarian Soviet position.

search Association and its various splinter groups represented a second Marxian tradition. Led by Mao Tun and Lu Hsün, and some of their principal supporters, including Feng Hsueh-feng, Jou Shih, and Pai Mang, these writers were revolutionaries who had a genuine interest in Marxist literary thought; but the tradition they upheld was the decidedly materialist literary school of Plekhanov and Trotsky.[14] It would be misleading, therefore, to suggest that they were not revolutionaries or that their views represented a categorical rejection of proletarian literature. Rather, they objected to the idealist approach to proletarian literature taken by the Marxist romantics.[15] Like Plekhanov and Trotsky, this group was quite reluctant to place the literary movement in the vanguard of the revolution, a conviction that implies that they understood changes in the superstructure of society to be quite dependent upon a transformation of the economic base. Thus it was the duty of revolutionary writers to "reflect," accurately and honestly, the condition of society from a revolutionary perspective rather than to glorify a single class, the proletariat, about whom the romantics knew exceedingly little. In short, the Lu Hsün-Mao Tun group believed that the proletarian cultural movement promoted by Cheng Po-ch'i, Ch'ien Hsing-ts'un, and others was premature and therefore ran the risk of attributing to the proletariat a level of political and social development that it had not yet achieved. Such a picture would be heroic but inaccurate.

Another way to explain the difference between these two leftist literary trends is to refer to the particular May Fourth tradition from which each group emerged. Although as early as 1926 Kuo Mo-jo insisted that the shift to revolutionary literature constituted an abandonment of romanticism, it is clear that Kuo's transformation and the transformation of his younger colleagues in the Creation Society had taken place well within the framework of romanticism.[16] If "romanticism" is treated as both a literary and a political concept, then it is evident that the proletarian romantics of 1928 merely replaced the individualistic, transcendental, and "bourgeois" romanticism of their early history with a more explicitly political and socially directed romanticism. Their fundamentally idealist view of the relationship between literature and society (that is, the independence of culture from

14. See Pickowicz, *Marxist Literary Thought and China: A Conceptual Framework*, pp. 26-47.

15. Mao Tun stated explicitly in his famous article "Ts'ung Ku-ling tao Tung-ching" [From Kuling to Tokyo] that although the romantics claimed to be realists, they were in fact "idealists." Mao Tun also identified the romantics with postrevolutionary Soviet proletarian artists. For a translation of this essay, see *Bulletin of Concerned Asian Scholars*, 8,1 (January-March 1976): 38-44.

16. Ibid., p. 33. As Marián Gálik has pointed out ["Ch'ien Hsing-ts'un and the Theory of Proletarian Realism," *Asian and African Studies*, 5 (1969): 55-58] Ch'ien Hsing-ts'un, another leading Marxist romantic, insisted that he advocated "realist" literature.

the economic bedrock), and their hostility toward materialist conceptions of art (however implicitly it was expressed), remained unchanged. Their attraction to the idealist tradition in Western Marxist literary thought and their lack of enthusiasm for Plekhanov and Trotsky was, therefore, quite consistent with the romantic and idealist strain that ran throughout the history of the Creation Society.

Similarly, the non-romantics like Lu Hsün and Mao Tun who showed an early interest in Marxist literary thought did so, in part, on the basis of their May Fourth literary experience. Although many writers who identified with the Literary Research Association converted to Marxism in the mid-1920s, they retained a healthy respect for the role played by "objective laws of history" in shaping human society. Their humanistic concern for society as an undifferentiated whole and their faith in the ability of writers to be dispassionate observers of society were now regarded as bourgeois outlooks and rejected, but this group tended, nevertheless, to be attracted to the tradition of Western Marxist literary thought that stressed the relationship of dependence between literature and society. It is thus no coincidence that their polemical writings criticized the idealist tendency present in the "proletarian" cultural theory of their Creation and Sun rivals.

Of what significance are these observations about the 1928-1930 debate on revolutionary literature? For one thing, this debate involved a good deal more than a clash of personalities. It is true, of course, that personalities collided. There is little doubt that Ch'ien Hsing-ts'un, Feng Nai-ch'ao, and Fu K'o-hsing behaved in an exceedingly obnoxious manner throughout the exchange. In their view, Mao Tun and especially Lu Hsün were tired pessimists who were hopelessly out of touch with the revolutionary mainstream.[17] Lu Hsün and Mao Tun, for their part, saw the romantics as infantile leftists who sought to dominate the leftist literary scene.[18] This clash of personalities should not be allowed to obscure the significance of issues that were being debated. Indeed, in certain respects the debates of 1928 were quite similar in content to the confrontation between the Creation Society and the Literary Research Association in the early 1920s. In both episodes there were counterproductive personal attacks, but in both the central issue concerned substantive differences between writers who approached literature from essentially idealist and materialist points of view. A pattern of May Fourth intellectual contention was thus perpetuated.

17. Ch'ien Hsing-ts'un also included Ting Ling among the pessimists. Gálik, "Ch'ien Hsing-ts'un," p. 67.
18. Lu Hsün, "Befuddled Wooliness," SWLH, 3:11-17; *Bulletin of Concerned Asian Scholars*, 8,1 (January-March 1976): 41.

The event that had occurred in the period between these two major polemical exchanges was the national revolution itself. Both groups responded to the rising revolutionary tide by endorsing the revolutionary literary movement and embracing appropriate schools of Marxist literary thought in ways that were consistent with their May Fourth literary beliefs. More important, both groupings also responded to the *failure* of the revolution in ways that sharply divided them. Mao Tun and Lu Hsün, for example, interpreted the events of 1927 as a disastrous defeat for the revolution. In fact, both men went through a temporary but agonizing period of disillusionment and pessimism about the future of the revolution.[19] Even as late as 1930 they believed that, as a result of the failure, Chinese society was in the throes of a reactionary period in which the forces of counterrevolution were on the offensive in urban China. They further believed that revolutionary writers would be mistaken to ignore this fact. The Marxist romantics, on the other hand, were much less inclined to view the events of 1927 as the beginning of a prolonged trough between revolutionary waves, and were therefore more optimistic about the prospects of socialist revolution. In intellectual terms, the romantic response to 1927 was unwillingness to accept the constraints of what many believed to be unfavorable "objective conditions." Writers like Lu Hsün and Mao Tun responded by showing greater concern for material conditions. Had the combatants used contemporary Chinese Marxist *political* language, the romantics would have been accused of "adventurism," while the realists would have been branded "capitulationists" or "right deviationists."

It is also important to realize that this first significant debate on Marxist literary thought in China occurred in a fairly spontaneous manner. There were Communist Party members in each group, but the party, as such, played no role in the controversy. In 1928 the party had not yet formulated an official policy toward the arts, and thus no faction spoke for the party. In short, Marxist literary thought did not arrive on the literary scene in China as a monolithic ideological force. Although Chinese writers were only beginning their study of Marxist aesthetics in the mid-1920s, they seem to have realized that it was a diverse intellectual tradition. They tended to stress those portions of the heritage that corresponded most closely to their particular intellectual predispositions.

19. A stimulating discussion of Mao Tun's disillusionment is contained in John Berninghausen, "The Central Contradiction in Mao Tun's Earliest Fiction," in Merle Goldman, ed., *Modern Chinese Literature in the May Fourth Era* (Cambridge: Harvard University Press, 1977), pp. 233-259. As for Lu Hsün's response to 1927, see Paul G. Pickowicz, "Lu Xun Through the Eyes of Qu Qiu-bai," *Modern China*, July 1976, pp. 350-351.

Why had Chinese writers not shown greater interest in revolutionary literature or Marxist literary thought at an earlier date? Part
of the answer is the failure in 1923 of Ch'ü Ch'iu-pai and others to
demonstrate the richness and diversity of Western Marxist literary
thought. But more important, it was not until after 1925, and especially after 1927, that social and political developments created a sense
of urgency in the modern literary world. At first it was a feeling of
hope and excitement that led writers to support literary radicalism
during the 1925-1927 national revolution; later, after the debacle, it
was a sense of national crisis. When modern writers finally turned
their attention to Marxism, they learned that it was not as incompatible with their May Fourth literary beliefs as it seemed at first glance.
On the basic questions—the relationship between literature and society (and hence the relationship between literature and revolution),
and the role of the revolutionary writer—May Fourth romantics were
drawn to the idealist tradition in Marxist literary thought, and May
Fourth realists were attracted to the materialist tradition.

In noting the dissonant themes in May Fourth literary thought, it is
important not to overlook areas of broad agreement. Romantics and
realists looked through the same May Fourth lenses on many vital
questions.

For example, May Fourth romantics and realists both learned that,
in the main, Western Marxist literary thought was not especially
hostile to the bourgeois tradition in artistic culture. Indeed, with the
exception of the "futurist" proletarians whose beliefs never attracted
much attention in China, the Marxist tradition steadfastly opposed
the iconoclastic rejection of the Western bourgeois literary heritage.
Despite their critique of capitalism, the writings of Marx and Engels
simply did not advocate a radical break with the bourgeois cultural
past. On the contrary, they assumed that it was both desirable and
necessary for the proletariat to inherit the cultural legacy of humankind. Engels looked forward to a time when "what is really worth
preserving in historically inherited culture . . . may not only be pre-
served but converted from a monopoly of the ruling class into the
common property of the whole society."[20] Georg Lukács is certainly
correct when he insists that Marx believed that the working class was
"heir to all mankind has produced of value over the millennia."[21] It is
in this sense that Marx and Engels believed that socialist culture presupposed bourgeois culture. Just as the bourgeois cultural stage could
not be skipped, neither could it be rejected by socialist revolutionaries.

20. Lee Baxandall and Stefan Morawski, eds., *Marx and Engels on Literature and Art* (St.
Louis: Telos Press, 1973), p. 73.

21. Georg Lukács, *Writer and Critic and Other Essays* (New York: Grosset and Dunlap,
1971), p. 74.

This position was stated even more explicitly by Lenin and Trotsky. "We must take the entire culture that capitalism left behind and build socialism with it," Lenin proclaimed in 1919.[22]

Furthermore, virtually all leftist Chinese writers eagerly accepted the conviction expressed by most Western Marxist literary thinkers that the revolutionary literary movement was the responsibility of revolutionary intellectuals. As Lenin and Trotsky had pointed out with great clarity, the important task of passing along the essential ingredients of progressive bourgeois artistic culture would not be assigned to the proletariat, but, ironically, would be placed in the hands of the bourgeois experts who were the principal bearers of such culture. Lenin remarked: "We have bourgeois experts and nothing else. We have no other bricks with which to build."[23] Thus, the sort of division of labor and specialization that Marx believed was responsible for the alienation of artistic sensibility among the masses in capitalist society was sanctioned in the era of the transition to socialism. None of the Marxist groups in China suggested that revolutionary literature be written by the working class itself. The view of the Soviet postrevolutionary "pure" proletarian group was simply ignored.

Neither did revolutionary writers in China have much interest in popular mass art. They appear to have readily accepted the rather elitist Western Marxist view that capitalism had converted the masses into a "crippled monstrosity," culturally speaking.[24] With few exceptions, they never pretended to write for anything other than an intellectual audience; and, while they may have decried the cultural backwardness of the masses, they tended to believe, as Marx did, that the inclusion of the masses in the literary life of society would have to await the transformation of the economic base.

Finally, May Fourth literary Marxists welcomed the view, expressed by Engels, Lenin, and Trotsky, that creative writing requires the independence of the writer. Neither Marx nor Engels believed that direct political involvement or membership in a political party was a prerequisite for social writing. Engels endorsed literary "tendentiousness," a phenomenon defined by Georg Lukács as "the attempt of the artist to demonstrate, propagate or exemplify a political or social view," but he preferred that such writing be indirect and subtle.[25] The political tendency "must spring forth from the situation and the action itself, without explicit attention called to it; the writer is not

22. V.I. Lenin, *On Literature and Art* (Moscow: Progress Publishers, 1970), p. 123; Leon Trotsky, *Literature and Revolution* (Ann Arbor: University of Michigan Press, 1966), p. 38.

23. Lenin, *On Literature and Art*, p. 123.

24. Karl Marx and Frederick Engels, *Literature and Art: Selections from Their Writings* (New York: International Publishers, 1947), p. 24.

25. Lukács, *Writer and Critic*, pp. 81-82.

obliged to offer to the reader the future historical solution of the social conflict he depicts."[26] Trotsky continued this tradition by insisting that the state and the Communist Party should not interfere in Soviet artistic life. "The domain of art," Trotsky proclaimed, "is not one in which the Party is called upon to command."[27] Even Lenin, whose highly controversial essay "Party Organization and Party Literature" is open to a variety of interpretations, denied that he intended to "impose collective control" on all literary activities in society.[28] More important than anything Lenin said, however, is the way he acted. In the immediate postrevolutionary period, his behavior was generally consistent with the notion that the party should neither favor any particular cultural group nor attempt to control the cultural world. May Fourth leftist writers, who had fought to secure the independence of literature from the Confucian state, approved of this view. Groups like the Sun Society, it is true, probably hoped to be recognized by the party as the leading proletarian literary organization, but they certainly did not want the party directing their affairs.

THE LEAGUE OF LEFT-WING WRITERS

More important than the intellectual and personal differences that divided leftist writers was the fact that they stood united in their opposition to the Kuomintang regime and the presence of the imperialist powers in China, and that they supported a movement for revolutionary literature. Thus, despite the problems associated with the birth of the left-wing literary movement, on March 2, 1930, the League of Left-wing Writers (Tso-i tso-chia lien-meng) was established in Shanghai. The six-year history of the League is, in fact, the most interesting period in the history of China's revolutionary literary movement. Not since the May Fourth Movement had modern writers been as well organized or able to influence social thought as they were during these years. After the League was dissolved, Chinese writers would never again play such a crucial role. The League's membership included the most outstanding body of literary figures brought together in a single group during the Chinese revolution, or perhaps any other revolution.

Two factors seem to have led to the preliminary discussions that took place in the last months of 1929. Many prominent revolutionary writers had a strong desire to end the divisiveness of the post-1928 period, particularly the assaults on Lu Hsün and Mao Tun. Second, the Li Li-san leadership of the Communist Party, before its downfall,

26. Baxandall and Morawski, *Marx and Engels*, p. 113.
27. Trotsky, *Literature and Revolution*, p. 218.
28. Lenin, *On Literature and Art*, p. 25.

sought to promote intellectual opposition to the Kuomintang government. The party gave limited organizational and financial support,
but had no elaborate policy of its own toward the arts and attempted
to appeal to writers who did not belong to the party. As preliminary
steps, the Shanghai Research Association on Literature and Art was
formed in January 1930 to discuss methods of organizing sympathetic
writers, and a Preparatory Committee to Organize Left-wing Authors
of the Country was founded on February 16, 1930. Its membership of
twelve included Lu Hsün, Feng Hsueh-feng, and Jou Shih. Finally, on
March 2, 1930, the first formal meeting of the League of Left-wing
Writers was held at the Shanghai Art College with more than fifty
writers in attendance.[29]

Enough is known about the founding members to make some general remarks about the nature of the League. First, virtually all the
participants shared a common heritage—they were literary intellectuals of the May Fourth generation who had lived through the various phases of the modern literary revolution, and thus had been influenced by Western literary thought, both bourgeois and socialist.
Many of the members had studied abroad. Second, the composition of
the League included leftist writers who had participated in both sides
of the 1928-1930 debate on revolutionary literature. Of the more
than fifty who signed the inaugural resolution, thirty-two names are
known, and most seem to have belonged to one of the following
groups: Sun Society (Ch'ien Hsing-ts'un, Chiang Kuang-tz'u, Hua
Han, and Hung Ling-fei); Creation Society (Feng Nai-ch'ao, P'an Han-
nien, Chou Ch'uan-p'ing, Li Ch'u-li, P'eng K'eng, Cheng Po-ch'i, T'ien
Han, Chu Ching-wo); and the Lu Hsün group (Lu Hsün, Feng Hsueh-
feng, Yü Ta-fu, Pai Mang, Jou Shih). Other well-known writers among
the original signers included Mao Tun and Ting Ling, who shared
much in common with the Lu Hsün group, and Hsia Yen, who identified with the Creation and Sun groups.[30]

The March 2 meeting was chaired by Lu Hsün, Hsia Yen, and
Ch'ien Hsing-ts'un. A League Executive Committee composed of
Feng Nai-ch'ao, Hsia Yen, Cheng Po-ch'i, Lu Hsün, T'ien Han, Hung
Ling-fei, and Ch'ien Hsing-ts'un was selected. The program approved
at the inaugural session was exceedingly ambitious. It was agreed that
the League would have three subdivisions: the Society for the Study

29. Harriet C. Mills, "Lu Hsün, 1927-1936; The Years on the Left" (Ph.D. dissertation, Columbia University, 1963), pp. 160-161. Ting I, *Chung-kuo hsien-tai wen-hsueh shih-
lueh* [A short history of modern Chinese literature] (Peking: Tso-chia ch'u-pan-she,
1955), pp. 69-74.

30. Chang Ching-lu, ed., *Chung-kuo hsien-tai ch'u-pan shih-liao* [Documentary sources
on publications of contemporary China, hereafter referred to as CPSL] (Peking: Chung-
hua shu-chü, 1954-1957), 3:35-49.

of Popular Literature and Art, the Research Society of Marxist Literary and Art Theory, and the International Culture Research Society. These titles suggest that League members were still receptive to Western culture and intended to deepen their knowledge of Marxist literary thought. They also indicate that the organization was composed almost entirely of intellectuals. In order to establish a link between workers and intellectuals, and possibly to train working-class writers, a Committee for Worker, Peasant, and Soldier Correspondence Literature was created.[31]

Membership in the League grew steadily after the inaugural meeting, and especially after the Japanese invasion of Manchuria in September 1931 and the increasingly harsh persecution of revolutionary writers that followed. Although branches of the League were founded in other cities, the center of the leftist literary movement remained in Shanghai, where writers could reside in the foreign settlements beyond the direct jurisdiction of Chinese authorities.

Not since the May Fourth Movement had the modern literary world been so conscious of its social and political role, yet it is clear that modern Chinese historians have overemphasized the solidarity that existed in the League of Left-wing Writers.[32] The direct assaults on Lu Hsün and Mao Tun had, of course, been suspended, and League members did, in fact, stand united in their opposition to the Kuomintang and imperialism; but important differences of opinion continued to exist on the question of the nature of revolutionary literature and the precise role of revolutionary writers. For example, the text of the League's inaugural resolution reveals that the views of the former Creation and Sun Society romantics tended to dominate League thinking on many crucial issues. The resolution spoke of poets as "prophets" and "leaders of humankind" who stood "in the front line" of the proletarian struggle. It also called for a "proletarian" literary movement.[33] The ideas that the place of leftist writers was in the vanguard of the revolution, and that it was possible for proletarian literature to be produced by intellectuals on behalf of the working class, were cornerstones of Creation and Sun Society thought in 1928. Organizationally, the League was dominated by romantics: six of the seven members of the Executive Committee were sympathetic to the romantic Marxist viewpoint.

Lu Hsün, on the other hand, was unquestionably the leading personality of the League. His address, entitled "Thoughts on the League

31. Ibid., p. 48; Ting I, *Wen-hsueh shih-lueh*, p. 71; Mills, "Lu Hsün," p. 166.

32. See, for example, Ting I, *Wen-hsueh shih-lueh*, pp. 68-89; and Fu-tan ta-hsueh Chung-wen hsi, ed., *Chung-kuo hsien-tai wen-hsueh shih: 1919-1942*, pp. 292-310.

33. The complete text of the resolution can be found in Ting I, *Wen-hsueh shih-lueh*, pp. 70-71.

of Left-wing Writers," to the League's inaugural meeting expressed
the opinions of his group. He warned against the danger of becoming
divorced from concrete social realities: "Behind closed doors it is very
easy to spout radical ideas, but equally easy to turn 'rightist.'"[34] Lu
Hsün's speech was a thinly veiled criticism of the romantic position.
He noted that in China's revolutionary literature movement there
was no shortage of "romantic" dreamers who believed that "the poets
and writers who support the workers' revolution today will be richly
rewarded by the working class when the revolution is accomplished."[35]
Lu Hsün did not reject the concept of proletarian literature; rather he
denied the right of the Creation and Sun faction to act as official
representatives of the working class. Referring to the attacks made on
him two years before, Lu Hsün accused the romantic Marxists of
failing to make a careful study of Marxist theory. "I was waiting to be
attacked by someone who had mastered the Marxist method of criticism, but no such person appeared."[36] There can be no doubt that Lu
Hsün was thinking of the materialist theoretical writings of Plekhanov and Lunacharsky which Lu Hsün and his disciple Feng Hsueh-
feng were translating at the time. From the outset, therefore, the
League of Left-wing Writers was split in much the same way that the
modern literary world had been divided in 1921 and 1928.

CH'Ü CH'IU-PAI'S RETURN
TO THE CULTURAL WORLD

Between 1924 and 1930, when Marxist literary thought was taking
root in China, Ch'ü Ch'iu-pai played no role whatever in the leftist
literary movement. During this time Ch'ü was totally immersed in
Communist Party affairs, and eventually succeeded Ch'en Tu-hsiu as
secretary general of the Central Committee.[37] No purpose is served
by detailing the well-known story of Ch'ü's high-level political involvement, but it would be misleading to assume that there was no
relationship between Ch'ü's disillusioning political experiences and his
decision to reenter the cultural arena. During the May Fourth period,
his utopian socialist political beliefs influenced his selection of Tolstoy
as a literary model. His support for the United Front political strategy
in 1923 made him receptive to deterministic Marxist notions about
the relationship between substructure and superstructure. Thus there
is every reason to believe that his provocative literary thought of the

34. Lu Hsün, "Thoughts on the League of Left-wing Writers," SWLH, 3:93.

35. Ibid., pp. 94-95.

36. Ibid., p. 97.

37. Benjamin Schwartz, *Chinese Communism and the Rise of Mao* (New York: Harper
Torchbooks, 1967), pp. 46-171; Bernadette Li, pp. 108-287.

1930s was conditioned by the way he experienced the catastrophic political disasters of the 1920s.

The most characteristic feature of Ch'ü's political behavior in the 1924-1930 period was unquestionably his unwavering support of the various strategies for revolution in China mapped out by the Comintern in Moscow.[38] No Chinese communist worked more closely with Comintern representatives than Ch'ü during the United Front with the Kuomintang, the May Thirtieth Movement, the Northern Expedition, and the Wuhan period. Ch'ü's acceptance of the wisdom of Comintern theorists caused him to criticize repeatedly those in China who expressed doubts about the reliability of Comintern policies.[39]

But Ch'ü's view began to change in the spring of 1928 when he learned that Moscow intended to evade responsibility for the failure of a series of Comintern-inspired armed uprisings staged in late 1927, by placing the blame on Ch'ü. Ch'ü was labeled a "putschist" by the Comintern in February 1928 and ordered to report to Moscow, where, in June 1928, he was once again made the scapegoat for the abortive uprisings of the previous autumn.[40]

There were occasional triumphs and even some peaceful moments during Ch'ü's two-year stay, but on the whole his second visit to the Soviet Union involved a seemingly endless series of bitter personal and political struggles. During his first visit in 1921, Ch'ü was aware of the material hardships that plagued Soviet society, but he was convinced that the "spiritual strength" of the Soviet people would ultimately prevail. By 1928 the economic situation had improved, but Ch'ü would soon gain firsthand knowledge of the Stalinist political terror that now gripped the Red capital.

Ch'ü's worst experience was his attempt to prevent Pavel Mif, Stalin's leading China specialist, from installing Wang Ming and his followers as the new leaders of the Chinese Communist Party. To discredit Ch'ü, Mif accused him of encouraging the activities of "heretics" among the Chinese students in Moscow, and harboring "anti-Comintern" sentiments.[41] Mif sent Ch'ü's wife, Yang Chih-hua, to

38. The following discussion of Ch'ü's political experiences is based primarily upon three sources: Chang Kuo-t'ao's memoir, Ch'ü's final autobiographical essay (TYTH), and Ch'ü's 1928 book-length report entitled *Chung-kuo ko-ming yü kung-ch'an-tang* [The Chinese revolution and the Communist Party]. A translation of Ch'ü's report is contained in *Chinese Studies in History* 5,1 (Fall 1971): 4-72 under the title *The Past and Future of the Chinese Communist Party.*

39. Schwartz, *Chinese Communism*, p. 71.

40. Robert North, *Moscow and Chinese Communists* (Stanford: Stanford University Press, 1967), p. 128.

41. Chang Kuo-t'ao, *The Rise of the Chinese Communist Party, 1921-1927* (Lawrence: University of Kansas Press, 1971), 2:101-102; TYTH, p. 145.

do corrective labor in a factory, and later arranged to have Ch'ü dismissed from the Chinese delegation to the Comintern. According to Chang Kuo-t'ao, who was in Moscow at the time, Ch'ü "despised" Mif and the Wang Ming group.[42]

Ch'ü was determined to put an end to his "bitter life" in Moscow and finally got Comintern approval to return to China in August 1930; but his struggle with Mif and Wang Ming, both of whom were dispatched to China, was not yet over.[43] For a time, Ch'ü was able to regain control of the party, but the Comintern came to regard the activities of Ch'ü and his supporters in Shanghai as a rebellion against the Comintern.[44] With the full support of Moscow, Mif organized a high-level party meeting in January 1931 at which Ch'ü Ch'iu-pai was denounced and expelled from the Politburo. His political career in ruins, Ch'ü placed the blame on the Comintern and the new party leadership. "Being completely exhausted," he later observed, "I took long leave to recuperate. To all intents and purposes, I had left the political stage for good."[45]

Ch'ü Ch'iu-pai lived in seclusion for two or three months following his banishment from the new inner circle of communist leadership. In 1935 he revealed that there were many occasions on which he objected to the wisdom of decisions made by the Wang Ming leadership; but he no longer had the will to resist their rule, preferring instead to simply ignore them.[46] Ch'ü had been able to submerge his interest in literature for nearly seven years only because the political arena seemed so promising. When the political situation deteriorated, it was only natural that he would return to literature, especially as prospects for "cultural revolution" once again appeared favorable.

It is interesting that while Ch'ü was profoundly disillusioned with the current party leadership, he had no intention of dropping out of the revolutionary movement. Ch'ü remained a party member and never expressed any reservations about the Leninist conception of the vanguard role the party was destined to play. Nevertheless, as an individual, he now preferred, as he had in his youth, to advance the revolution by cultural means.

Ch'ü's departure from political life was bound to have an impact on his literary activities. For one thing, Ch'ü could now act independently. His estrangement from the party leadership probably made his cultural work a bit easier because no restraints were placed on his intellectual activity by political obligations. More important, Ch'ü's unhappy encounter with the Comintern made him less reluctant to question the validity of foreign "theories" about the Chinese revolu-

42. Chang Kuo-t'ao, *The Chinese Communist Party*, 2:102.
43. Ibid., 2:103-104.   44. Ibid., 2:129-130.
45. TYTH, pp. 145-147; quoted in D.J. Li, p. 169.   46. TYTH, p. 141.

tion, and more willing to criticize those in both the political and cultural realms who accepted foreign ideas uncritically. If the Wang Ming group represented anything, it was dogmatic, slavish acceptance of "superior" foreign ideas. In short, the groundwork was laid for Ch'ü's reemergence as a cultural nationalist. And when Ch'ü began to take a more careful look at Western Marxist literary thought, he was emotionally prepared to impose these new nationalist standards of criticism.

CH'Ü CH'IU-PAI AND
THE LEAGUE OF LEFT-WING WRITERS

When Ch'ü returned to China in August 1930, the League had been functioning for nearly six months. At first he merely served as an advisor to the League, since his struggle with Mif and the Wang Ming group made it impossible for him to take any more prominent role. Following his expulsion from the Politburo, Ch'ü remained out of sight for a time. However, by April 1931 he was once again active in the literary world. For more than two and a half years, until his final departure from Shanghai in January 1934, Ch'ü was the acknowledged leader of the League of Left-wing Writers. It is not known how he got the position; it seems likely that he was regarded as an impartial figure who could be trusted by all sides. Although he associated more closely with writers like Mao Tun, Ting Ling, Feng Hsüeh-feng, and Lu Hsün, he was also respected by Chiang Kuang-tz'u and other romantics, many of whom he had helped in the past.

The League had undergone several changes by the time Ch'ü assumed leadership. The internal disputes discussed above had not disappeared, nor was the League any less hostile toward the Kuomintang; but the relationship between the League and the Communist Party had been altered. Although the Li Li-san leadership had no intention of controlling or dictating the literary work of League members, it did take an active interest in supporting the League and fostering opposition to the Kuomintang. Both communist and noncommunist members of the League accepted Li as the legitimate leader of the communist movement. The same cannot be said of the Wang Ming leadership that came to power in January 1931. Indeed, there was mutual hostility and distrust between the Wang Ming group and leftist literary intellectuals. In light of Ch'ü Ch'iu-pai's own bitter encounter with the Twenty-eight Bolsheviks, it seems unlikely that he could have been chosen by them to lead the League of Left-wing Writers—or that Ch'ü did much to strengthen the bond between the party center and the League. Feng Hsüeh-feng, a well-known League member, pointed out in his colorful memoir: "It was not the decision of the party but rather his own zeal that led Comrade Ch'ü Ch'iu-pai to participate in and guide the work of the League of Left-wing Writers."[47]

The reasonable conclusion seems to be that the League of Left-wing Writers was an influential but loose coalition of revolutionary intellectuals during the period from Spring 1931 to January 1934 when Ch'ü served as its leader. The League's relationship with the Communist Party was not especially close, nor did it respond mechanically to directives issued by international communist literary organizations based in Moscow. Ch'ü's personal experience with the Comintern probably made him skeptical of such arrangements; and, in any event, League members expressed surprisingly little interest in contemporary Soviet literary affairs. Under Ch'ü's leadership, the League of Left-wing Writers resembled the various voluntary federations of leftist writers that existed in Russia just before and just after the October Revolution much more than the state- and party-sponsored literary unions that appeared under Stalin and in China after 1949.

47. Quoted in C. T. Hsia, *A History of Modern Chinese Fiction* (New Haven: Yale University Press, 1971), p. 127.

6 "Europeanization" and the Literary Left

The cadres of revolutionary literature are captives of the bourgeois May Fourth cultural movement. The majority of them are standing on the other side of a Great Wall—they do not have a common language with the Chinese working people, and to the middle and lower ranks of the people they are almost "foreigners." They live in "their own country of intellectual youth" and in the stationery stores of the Europeanized gentry.

CH'Ü CH'IU-PAI, 1931[1]

When he reentered the literary arena in the summer of 1931, Ch'ü Ch'iu-pai's first instinct was to attack those he perceived to be the opponents of the leftist literary movement. In *Luan t'an* and other collections of satirical essays, which established him as one of the outstanding *tsa-wen* stylists of the twentieth century, Ch'ü assailed the foreign powers but also various literary groups, such as the Crescent Moon Society, that refrained from criticizing the Kuomintang government.[2]

These early essays are significant not because they had anything new to say about imperialism, the Kuomintang, or the Crescent Moon

1. Ch'ü Ch'iu-pai, "Ta-chung wen-i te wen-ti—ch'u-kao p'ien-tuan" [The question of popular literature and art—draft fragments] (1931?), in Ting I, ed., *Ta-chung wen-i lun-chi* [Essays on popular literature and art] (Peking: Pei-ching shih-fan ta-hsueh ch'u-pan-pu, 1951), p. 145.

2. For a typical article praising Ch'ü's *tsa-wen* essays, see Li Yeh-chun, "Tu Ch'ü Ch'iu-pai te tsa-wen" [Read Ch'ü Ch'iu-pai's *tsa-wen* essays], *Kuang-ming jih-pao*, 17 July 1954.

group, but because they show that Ch'ü's painful political experiences of the 1924-1930 period had caused him to reconsider once again the problem of the capitalist stage of development. Beginning in 1923, it will be recalled, Ch'ü abandoned his May Fourth political beliefs, and began to defend the Comintern contention that Chinese society (and the Chinese revolution) would have to pass through a bourgeois-democratic, or capitalist, stage on the road to socialism. Ch'ü expressed various views about which political party was in the best position to lead the revolution; but he consistently characterized the movement as bourgeois-democratic in nature, and expressed a willingness to accept, among many other things, the cultural consequences of the capitalist stage. The defeat of the revolution permitted him to raise critical questions about the role of the Comintern, and also to argue that the "bourgeoisie" had failed to carry out the bourgeois-democratic revolution. Ch'ü was now in a position to assert that there would be no separate bourgeois political or cultural stage for China. If there were bourgeois tasks still to be performed, the proletariat would perform them. But more important, the goal of the revolution was now to move away from, rather than toward, the bourgeois stage. In brief, Ch'ü's old May Fourth aversion to bourgeois culture could be given full expression once again.

Ch'ü's treatment of the bourgeois stage in his *Luan t'an* collection was more, however, than a simple return to May Fourth modes of thought. In his youth he was inclined to view the bourgeois stage of historical development as unnatural and vulgar; in 1931 he began to treat it as alien and foreign as well. Indeed, Ch'ü made every effort to link all things "bourgeois" with the forces of imperialism that threatened the existence of the Chinese nation.[3] For example, the Chinese bourgeoisie and its political party, the Kuomintang, he proclaimed, had collaborated with imperialism and betrayed the bourgeois-democratic or national revolution in order to block the internal mass movement. Thus all things bourgeois were associated in the public mind, Ch'ü suggested, with the act of national betrayal. For political reasons, Ch'ü avoided the term "nationalism," but it is clear that he regarded the communist movement as the only legitimate bearer of the nationalist banner in both political and cultural fields, and that he considered himself to be a revolutionary cultural nationalist.

It is no coincidence that at precisely the moment of Ch'ü's reentry into the cultural world he began once again to discuss the theme of the "superfluous" intellectual. In his *tsa-wen* essays he argued that writers like Hsu Chih-mo were superfluous intellectuals because, like the Kuomintang, they were identified so thoroughly with foreign and

3. Ch'ü Ch'iu-pai, "Fei-chou kuei-hua" [An African ghost tale], *Pei tou*, 20 October 1931, in CCPWC, 1:262-265.

bourgeois forces.[4] "Europeanized" intellectuals were, in effect, cultural traitors and collaborators who were responsible for the failure of the bourgeois-democratic cultural revolution.

But one is left with the definite impression that Ch'ü was not primarily interested in writers like Hsu Chih-mo and Hu Shih, and did not believe they were especially influential. If he had confined himself to protesting Kuomintang failures or satirizing the reactionary or merely "superfluous" writers he associated with the Kuomintang, he would have been remembered in twentieth-century Chinese history as an unusually effective literary polemicist who played an important role in the Kuomintang's loss of intellectual and student support.

Actually, Ch'ü's reputation as China's first important Marxist literary thinker does not rest on the fact that he attacked the Kuomintang. His most noted concern was tension within the leftist literary movement. To be sure, Ch'ü's random essays on the current problems of the literary left lack unity, but they reveal that his criticism of the League was surprisingly far-reaching and deceptively elaborate. His writings are important as a critique of the leftist literary movement, and also because they relate contemporary problems to the historical experience of the May Fourth generation. Ch'ü stressed what Chinese historians in recent decades have de-emphasized or ignored: the failures of the renowned May Fourth generation of revolutionary writers. Stylistically, Ch'ü's essays on the left are interesting because, in sharp contrast to the more muted exchanges that were usual among close revolutionary allies, his approach was direct and even abrasive. Ch'ü's colleagues may have been disturbed by his observations, but they took his views seriously because he was a widely respected figure.

In order to understand Ch'ü's specific criticisms of leftist writers and his proposals for the future, it is necessary to have some idea of his general assessment of the brief history of the modern literary movement and its revolutionary offspring. The assumption that the problems of the early 1930s had their origin in the New Culture and May Fourth Movements was in fact central to Ch'ü's criticism of leftist writers. Although Ch'ü never attempted to write a formal history of the revolutionary literary movement, several works, such as his famous "Preface to *The Selected Works of Lu Hsün*," "Long Live the Literary Warlords," "Europeanized Literature and Art," and "Who are 'We'?" say a great deal about the conclusions he reached.

It is clear, for example, that Ch'ü believed that the modern literary movement had passed through three general stages. Using a dialectical analysis that placed the literary movement in a series of rapidly changing social contexts, Ch'ü attempted to identify what he believed

4. Ch'ü Ch'iu-pai, "Hsiao Chu-ko" [Little Chu-ko Liangs], *Pei tou*, 20 May 1932, in CCPWC, 1:315-317; CCPWC, 2:990.

were the primary "contradictions" or struggles in each phase. In the familiar 1915-1925 New Culture and May Fourth period of "literary revolution," the main contradiction, in his view, was between the forces of tradition and modernity. "Chinese intellectuals of the literati type," he explained, "quite clearly formed into two camps: the traditionalists and the Westernized school."[5] In his youth, Ch'ü tended not to perceive the literary revolution as a bourgeois cultural movement. To him "bourgeois" meant "philistine," and "capitalist."[6] He was interested in "foreign" thought, but not "bourgeois" foreign thought. In the early 1930s, however, he did not hesitate to characterize the early May Fourth literary revolution as the beginning of an essentially bourgeois-democratic cultural movement, despite the fact that certain "utopian" elements were contained in it.

As a bourgeois cultural movement, Ch'ü asserted, the literary revolution, as everyone knew, had achieved some remarkable victories. It was a "renaissance in literature and art led by the bourgeoisie," he wrote.[7] Traditional classical literature, for example, was dealt a blow from which it never recovered. Moreover, Chinese writers became "Europeanized" (*Ou-hua*) in their literary values and tastes. By "Europeanized" Ch'ü meant that young iconoclastic gentry intellectuals had abandoned their class and its ideology and become modern "bourgeois" thinkers.[8] Young writers rejected both the archaic forms and conservative content of traditional literature and substituted modern Western forms and content. In the context of the "contradiction" between tradition and modernity this represented a decisive step forward.

The difference between Ch'ü and many of his leftist literary companions in the 1930s was that when he looked back at the May Fourth origins of the leftist movement, he tended to dwell upon the problems and unacknowledged failures of the movement. For example, he now believed that while the literary revolution had been "bourgeois," it had not been particularly "democratic." The fruits of modern artistic culture had not really filtered down to the masses, as they had in the West, but were concentrated in the hands of a few professional literary organizations, like the Creation Society and Literary Research Association.[9] The class standing of the new writers had changed, but

5. CCPWC, 2:985.   6. See chapter 2 above, "Literary Thought."

7. Ch'ü Ch'iu-pai, "Ta-chung wen-i te wen-t'i—ch'u-kao p'ien-tuan," p. 143.

8. It is important to note that Ch'ü tended to use the terms "bourgeois" and "European" interchangeably. Typical of "first stage" mentality is the remark made in 1922 by Li Chih-ch'ang, a member of the Literary Research Association, to the effect that "the plan which will fulfill the present mission of literature" is the "Westernization of Chinese literature." Quoted in Bonnie S. McDougall, *The Introduction of Western Literary Theories into Modern China, 1919-1925* (Tokyo: The Centre for East Asian Cultural Studies, 1971), p. 161.

9. Ch'ü Ch'iu-pai, "Ta-chung wen-i te wen-t'i—ch'u-kao p'ien-tuan," p. 142.

literary life continued to be monopolized by a small group of intellectuals, as it had been in Confucian China. The language they used was not classical (*wen-yen*), but neither, he insisted, was it really vernacular (*pai-hua*), as it was in Western bourgeois literature. Thus it remained far beyond the reach of China's predominantly preliterate population.[10] Moreover, "Europeanization" also had the unexpected effect of causing divisions within the once united modern literary movement because of the tendency of writers to cluster in cliquish societies and then feud on the basis of their special interest in specific Western literary schools, such as romanticism and realism. In Ch'ü's eyes, these problems represented unnoticed secondary contradictions that had arisen in the wake of major May Fourth literary achievements.

The second stage of the literary movement, according to Ch'ü, coincided exactly with the period of the abortive national revolution of 1925-1927. "For approximately the period between the May Fourth Movement and the May Thirtieth Incident," Ch'ü explained, "thinking circles in China were gradually preparing for the second 'great split.' This was no longer a rupture between retrogression and the new culture, but a *split within the ranks of the new culture.* . . . This split, although not completed until the end of 1927, was under way between 1925 and 1926."[11] In light of Ch'ü's own revolutionary experiences during this critical period, it is not hard to determine what he meant by this statement.[12] The contradiction to which he referred was not literary or cultural in nature, but political. It involved the question of how those who had already converted to the "new culture" were going to respond to the surging mass movement generated by the Kuomintang-Communist United Front.

It will be recalled that Ch'ü and his youthful followers attempted to raise this political question in 1923, but failed. After 1925, however, there was an increasing amount of debate on the proposed transition from "literary revolution" to "revolutionary literature." Since it was generally assumed that the literary revolution had been completed, the discussion centered upon the problem of what political stance the new literature should assume.[13] The split, as Ch'ü understood it, was between bourgeois Europeanized writers who welcomed the mass movement and favored either a progressive bourgeois-democratic political and social revolution or perhaps even a socialist revolution at a later date, and Europeanized writers who feared the mass move-

10. The inaccessibility of May Fourth literature would not have been a problem if modern writers were indifferent about reaching the people, but of course they were not indifferent.

11. CCPWC, 2:988. Emphasis added.

12. See chapter 4 above, "From Literary Revolution to Revolutionary Literature."

13. In the period before 1925, Ch'ü assumed that any "literary" problems that remained would be somehow resolved after the forthcoming political transformation.

ment and thus were not enthusiastic about pressing on with the "anti-feudal" and "anti-imperialist" movements.

The outcome of this second split was, in Ch'ü's eyes, somewhat contradictory. In one important sense, Ch'ü believed, the modern literary movement had taken a significant step forward in this period. A transition from literary revolution to revolutionary literature had, in fact, been completed. Before the revolutionary defeat, most modern writers gave active support to the political goals of the United Front in their writings, and many expressed a serious interest in Marxist literary thought.[14] More important, even after the defeat, the revolutionary literary movement continued to grow and voice intellectual opposition to the new but repressive Kuomintang regime.

Nevertheless, the defeat of the bourgeois-democratic political revolution had a major impact on the manner in which Ch'ü analyzed the course of the revolutionary literary movement. The political revolution failed, in his opinion, because the bourgeoisie had betrayed the movement by compromising with the forces of reaction and with the imperialist powers. The failure caused Ch'ü to lose all confidence in the ability of any bourgeois force to lead, or even participate in, any phase or aspect of the revolution. The defeat of 1927 convinced him that there would be no independent bourgeois-democratic stage of the Chinese revolution. If there were still "bourgeois" tasks to be performed, they would be carried out under socialist or proletarian political auspices.[15]

In forming these ideas Ch'ü used Marxist class categories in a highly unusual manner. Presumably, he believed that the class status of those who belonged to the working masses was determined by objective criteria, but he seems to have believed that the class standing of intellectuals was determined by subjective criteria. When Ch'ü spoke of writers as being "feudal," "bourgeois," or "proletarian," he was referring, not to their objective class backgrounds, but to their thought. He implied, therefore, that intellectuals were capable of changing their class identity, although the process of ideological transformation, which would necessarily accompany such a shift, might be long and arduous. But, however voluntaristic Ch'ü's beliefs about

14. As early as late 1929 a significant portion of the works on artistic culture by Plekhanov, Lunacharsky, Lenin, Trotsky, and several Japanese proletarian literary thinkers, including Kurahara Korehito and Arishima Takeo, were well known among writers who had shifted from "literary revolution" to "revolutionary literature." See Marián Gálik, *Mao Tun and Modern Chinese Literary Criticism* (Wiesbaden: Franz Steiner Verlag Gmblt, 1969), pp. 58-59.

15. Ch'ü Ch'iu-pai, "Ta-chung wen-i te wen-t'i" [The question of popular literature and art], *Wen-hsüeh yüeh-pao* [Literature monthly], 15 September 1932; in CCPWC, 2:886. For my complete translation of this important article, see *Bulletin of Concerned Asian Scholars* 8,1 (January-March, 1976): 45-52.

class might have been, his ideas about what constituted a politically progressive class status at any given moment changed with his estimate of the current "objective stage" of the revolution. Thus writers who, like Ch'ü himself, came in fact from the gentry class appear as "progressive bourgeois" Europeanized intellectuals in his writings on the early May Fourth period, and as either "traitorous bourgeois" Europeanized writers or potentially "proletarian" writers in his writings on the period after 1927.

To understand this aspect of Ch'ü's thought in the early 1930s it is important to realize that he believed that as the bourgeois political revolution failed in China, the unfinished bourgeois cultural revolution also had failed. It had failed not simply because those he chose to call "bourgeois intellectuals" had defected, but because intellectuals who had participated on both sides of the political debate incorrectly assumed that the bourgeois literary revolution had been completed at a much earlier stage. The political thought of modern writers may have been revolutionized before and after 1927, but their literary thought had still not progessed beyond what he now saw as the contemptible and deformed European stage.[16] The most desirable or "democratic" features of bourgeois cultural revolution simply had not been realized in China.

The most intriguing of Ch'ü's "stages" was the last. From 1928 onward, following the political radicalization of the literary movement and the defeat of the revolution, the main contradictions, in his opinion, were no longer between old culture and new culture, or between revolutionary and nonrevolutionary political orientations. Those particular contradictions were now secondary, and largely resolved. The main contradictions now, Ch'ü implied, were, of all things, between forces within the revolutionary camp itself! In Ch'ü's view, the central problem of the literary movement in the period of the League of Left-wing Writers had two aspects: first, the contradiction between the two contending leftist factions within the League; and second, the contradiction between leftist writers as a whole and the common people.[17]

Both of these contradictions had, in his estimation, been looming in the background ever since the immediate post-May Fourth era. Each was intimately related to the phenomenon of Europeanization, which he now looked upon, as he had in his youth, as an undesirable and problem-causing trend. By the contradiction between contending

16. Ch'ü Ch'iu-pai, "Ou-hua wen-i" [Europeanized literature and art] (May 5, 1932), in CCPWC, 2:880.

17. Ch'ü alluded to the difficulties between Lu Hsün and the romantics in his long essay on Lu Hsün, CCPWC, 2:996. He mentioned the second contradiction in several places including "Ta-chung wen-i te wen-t'i—ch'u-kao p'ien-tuan," p. 141.

Europeanized factions, Ch'ü was, of course, referring to the literary polemics that had separated the romantics from the realists both before and after each group had converted to its own school of Marxism. In Ch'ü's mind this was one of the legacies of Europeanization that haunted the leftist literary movement and reduced its influence. By the contradiction between all League writers and the common people, Ch'ü was referring to an even more serious legacy of Europeanization, the tendency of all revolutionary writers, despite their rivalries and conflicting interpretations of the Western literary heritage, to remain aloof from the people, and to write in a language unknown to the people. The people, Ch'ü charged, looked upon writers with European identities and tastes as internal "foreigners" whose homeland was not China but Shanghai's Europeanized bookshops. In effect, then, Ch'ü was saying that contrary to the views of many, the League was not really unified, nor had it ever been placed squarely on a mass base. Needless to say, many writers found this message exceedingly unsettling.

EUROPEANIZATION AND CONTRADICTIONS: SOME IMPLICATIONS

Ch'ü's analysis of the "third stage" represents a significant departure from conventional leftist views about the history of the modern literary movement. By citing the dual problems of the internal feuding within the League and the isolation of League members in general from the masses, and by explicitly linking these problems to the Europeanized condition of the leftist literary movement, Ch'ü was stating with disturbing clarity that the current problems of the leftist literary movement had their origins in the celebrated New Culture and May Fourth period. He was, therefore, the first Chinese Marxist to criticize openly important aspects of the May Fourth intellectual revolution, a blasphemous act even by leftist standards in the early 1930s.[18] Equally disquieting was the unmistakable implication that at a relatively early date the May Fourth tradition not only had ceased to be revolutionary, but had become politically and culturally conservative. It was culturally conservative in the sense that May Fourth writers, including leftist writers, were content to conserve and defend their cherished May Fourth victories, which included the introduction of European literary forms, language, and life styles. It was politically conservative in the sense that, having failed to deepen the democratic cultural revolution, leftist writers who presumably desired to have close contact with the masses, lived and worked in total isolation from

18. CCPWC, 2:879-880; Ch'ü Ch'iu-pai, "Hsueh-fa wan-sui!" [Long live the literary warlords] (June 10, 1931), in CCPWC, 2:593.

the masses, and therefore learned nothing from them and had little influence upon them. The May Fourth path, he implied, led away from rather than directly toward a socialist future for China.

Furthermore, Ch'ü asserted that the bourgeois-democratic cultural revolution had developed in a distorted fashion in China. It was distorted not because it had been advanced prematurely or incorrectly, but because May Fourth cultural revolutionaries attempted to impose a European type of bourgeois cultural revolution in a country where historical and material conditions were markedly different from those in Europe at the time of its bourgeois revolution. Whether Ch'ü believed that a natural "Chinese" bourgeois revolution might have occurred in the absence of the distortions brought on by the importation of a foreign version is unclear. He did believe that no such independent bourgeois stage, foreign or domestic, was possible for China in view of the failures of 1927.[19] All that had happened, he observed, was that a relatively small group of intellectuals had successfully carried out a Western-style bourgeois cultural revolution among themselves, thus unintentionally differentiating and isolating themselves from the masses on whose behalf they hoped to speak. The age-old structure of elitism in the world of letters had not been upset. Instead, the cultural gap now separated the new Europeanized intellectuals and the non-Europeanized masses. Not surprisingly, therefore, writers were seen as "foreigners" by the people. Ch'ü was fond of saying that Europeanized writers had succeeded in constructing a "Great Wall" around the working people, which cut them off from modern revolutionary cultural life. Consequently, he charged: "All the scientific and artistic knowledge of the new period will be able to reach only ten or twenty thousand intellectual youth."[20] Ch'ü was not the first to say that the bourgeois-democratic revolution had failed, but by linking that failure to the mainstream of May Fourth thought, he was the first to conclude that, logically speaking, the May Fourth cultural revolution had to be regarded as a failure. "The May Fourth New Culture Movement," he proclaimed, "was a waste of time with regard to the people!"[21]

Furthermore, by attacking the May Fourth origins of the leftist literary movement and charging that the democratic cultural revolution had failed, Ch'ü was saying that the specifically literary revolution associated with the first stage had not been completed and that modern writers should no longer assume that it had. Particularly disturbing to Ch'ü's revolutionary colleagues was his assertion that although the language and forms employed by revolutionary writers

19. CCPWC, 2:881.
20. Ch'ü Ch'iu-pai, "Ta-chung wen-i te wen-t'i—ch'u-kao p'ien-tuan," p. 143.
21. CCPWC, 2:885.

were inadequate, relatively little had been done to solve the problem. Ch'ü obviously approved of the increasingly revolutionary political posture assumed by modern writers after 1927, but his point was that this political transformation had occurred within the framework of the abortive May Fourth bourgeois literary tradition. Thus while Ch'ü was aware that the social isolation of writers imposed limitations upon the *content* of revolutionary literature, he was more concerned with questions of language and form. His point was that the "literary revolution" had not been completed, and as a consequence, the militant message of modern writers simply was not reaching the people.[22] It was Ch'ü who coined the pejorative term "new classical" (*hsin wen-yen*) to characterize the literary language used by revolutionary writers. He conceded that it was not the "old" classical, but he could not agree that it was the vernacular language (*pai-hua*) promised by the heralds of the May Fourth Movement. The "new classical" was "neither donkey nor horse" (*fei lü fei ma*), but rather a "mule" language— the sterile offspring of classical and Europeanized language.[23] Not only did the "new classical" retain a considerable amount of old classical expressions and structure, but it also borrowed heavily from European grammar and vocabulary. New words were invented by writers, and untranslated European words were simply inserted in the Chinese text—all of which hampered the spread of the new culture.[24] In short, Ch'ü was in favor of reopening many literary questions May Fourth writers considered closed.

Perhaps the most controversial implication of Ch'ü's general critique was that the well-publicized conversion of Europeanized writers to Marxist political and aesthetic beliefs before and after the 1927 debacle had done little to resolve the contradictions discussed above. On the contrary, their conversion to Marxism was carried out entirely within the May Fourth framework and guided by their May Fourth intellectual predispositions. Bourgeois romantics became proletarian romantics, and bourgeois realists became proletarian realists, but the two factions continued to feud and continued to remain isolated from the people. In Ch'ü's opinion the phenomenon of Europeanization was responsible for this development. Indeed, for many, the conversion to Marxist literary and political thought was merely the latest and most fashionable phase of the Europeanization process. The acceptance of Marxism, therefore, was viewed by Ch'ü, not as a departure from the May Fourth literary tradition, but as an acceptance of it, an acceptance

22. CCPWC, 2:595, 887.
23. CCPWC, 2:596. By stating that the "new classical" contained elements of the "old classical," Ch'ü was saying that even the "anti-feudal" cultural revolution had not been completed.
24. CCPWC, 2:888.

that only perpetuated the problems that had been submerged in the May Fourth tidal wave for so long. In this important sense, the introduction of Marxist literary thought represented a conservative political trend in the literary world. "Early revolutionary and proletarian literature," Ch'ü remarked, "which clearly arose from this May Fourth foundation, simply provided the Europeanized gentry with yet another sumptuous banquet to satisfy their new tastes while the laboring people were still starving."[25]

In "Europeanized Literature and Art," Ch'ü stated explicitly that the transition to "proletarian literature" in 1928 had occurred within the framework of the abortive bourgeois-democratic cultural movement. "From the beginning," Ch'ü observed, "the proletarian literary movement was the recipient of this bourgeois heritage. Consequently, for a long time it has been separated from the broad masses."[26] The social stratum that had monopolized literature and reading in traditional and May Fourth times continued to monopolize it in "proletarian" times. In "Who are 'We'?" Ch'ü further pointed out that the formation of the League of Left-wing Writers had by no means solved these problems. By openly criticizing the attitudes of his colleague Cheng Po-ch'i, a prominent League member, Ch'ü hoped to focus attention on the errors of those who attempted to promote a "proletarian literary movement" within the Europeanized May Fourth framework. Ch'ü jibed: "Aside from empty talk, nothing has been accomplished in the last few years! Of course, the most significant reason is that the proletarian literary movement has not yet gone beyond the stage of 'research societies'; it is still an intellectual clique, and not a mass movement." The majority of revolutionary writers and "literary youth," he stated flatly, "stand *outside* the people, intent on positioning themselves above the people and instructing the people."[27]

Ironically, Ch'ü's assaults on the May Fourth legacy and the phenomenon of Europeanization in general are a return, on his part, to the critical standards he had adopted during his own May Fourth days. For example, the defeat of the revolution in its bourgeois-democratic phase revived in Ch'ü the hostility he had felt in his youth toward all things bourgeois. Now, more than ever before, Ch'ü saw bourgeois culture as alien culture, unsuited to China's needs. The difference between Ch'ü's view and the view of utopian socialist thinkers in the West who opposed the bourgeois stage because it was "unnatural" and "alien" was that in the Chinese case, as he under-

---

25. CCPWC, 2:885.   26. CCPWC, 2:880.

27. Ch'ü Ch'iu-pai, "'Wo-men' shih shei?" [Who are "we"?] (May 4, 1932), in CCPWC, 2:875. For my complete translation of this bluntly critical essay, see *Bulletin of Concerned Asian Scholars*, 8,1 (January–March, 1976): 46-47.

stood it, the bourgeois stage was quite literally "foreign." Further-more, the bourgeois culture imported from abroad was the culture of the imperialist nations that had been exploiting China for so long. Thus bourgeois culture not only was "foreign" to the people, but was identified with the enemy.[28] Under such circumstances the bourgeois stage was bound to be distorted and thus fail to influence the people. Ch'ü was again firmly convinced that in China there would not and could not be a long and independent cultural stage dominated by the bourgeoisie. And, as in his youth, Ch'ü feared that those, including revolutionary writers, who pursued the bourgeois dream and con-tinued on the road toward Europeanization ran the risk of becoming "superfluous" intellectuals, like Hsu Chih-mo and Hu Shih.[29]

In some ways, the nationalist element in Ch'ü's literary thought was even more pronounced than it had been in his youth. Ch'ü was skeptical about Western literary influence because it was bourgeois and because it was foreign; but one gets the impression that his skep-ticism was now based somewhat more upon the fact that it was for-eign. His suspicion of Western culture appears extreme because he spoke at a time when Western literary influence was great. But even when Ch'ü exaggerated contemporary problems he never called for the wholesale rejection of either Western bourgeois or Marxist lit-erary traditions. Ch'ü was himself an ardent student of foreign litera-ture, who recognized and appreciated the contribution of foreign lit-erature and continued to call for Chinese receptivity to foreign ideas.[30] What makes Ch'ü unique is the fact that he was not primarily inter-ested in reminding May Fourth writers of the rich legacy of foreign literature. Others were more than happy to do that. What was new in Ch'ü's perspective was that he dwelled upon the tendency of leftist writers to embrace foreign schools uncritically and sometimes dog-matically, as Ch'ü himself had accepted Marxist literary thought in 1923. It was time for writers to think more about the peculiarities and uniqueness of historical conditions in China, and rely less on foreign formulas for China's salvation.[31] Ch'ü's own literary writings were, in

28. The psychological impact of "cultural imperialism" on Westernized anti-imperi-alist intellectuals is discussed in Peter Worsley, *The Third World* (London: Weidenfeld and Nicolson, 1964), p. 24. Worsley states: "If Gatling guns and Lancashire textiles provided the technical means for establishing the dominance of Europe, it was the internalization and acceptance of the total superiority of European culture, not force alone, that was to hold the non-European in lengthy psychological subordination."

29. For more of Ch'ü's remarks on Hu Shih and Hsu Chih-mo, see CCPWC, 2:603-608.

30. Indeed, at one point Ch'ü calls for "genuine Europeanization" (*chen-cheng te Ou-hua*), by which he meant "critical" acceptance of foreign ideas. CCPWC, 2:881.

31. Of course Ch'ü welcomed Marxism-Leninism, but he insisted that it be "ap-plied" (*yun-yung*) to distinctively Chinese conditions. CCPWC, 2:883.

fact, strikingly original. He regarded himself as a Marxist, of course; but his analysis of the brief history of the modern literary movement and the problems that currently faced leftist writers was not copied from a Soviet textbook: it was born of an intimate knowledge of Chinese conditions.

Ch'ü's nationalist concerns are also evident in another area. By proclaiming that the Europeanization of the literary movement had gone too far, Ch'ü was at the same time saying that leftist writers schooled in the May Fourth period were excessively iconoclastic or nihilistic in their view of Chinese culture. Ch'ü, it is true, had been a young iconoclast in his youth, but he now believed that the repudiation of Chinese culture had widened the gap between the newly Europeanized writers and the people whom they hoped to save. Ch'ü was by no means calling for a revival of traditional Confucian culture. He was saying that during the iconoclastic days of New Culture and May Fourth radicalism, China's popular culture had been rejected along with its elite culture.[32] With no indigenous base upon which to build the modern literary movement, young intellectuals quite naturally turned to the West for inspiration. Consequently, the literary movement, even in its proletarian phase, failed to make contact with the popular tradition. Chinese national culture, including the culture of the masses, was simply viewed as backward culture that should be disposed of or at least ignored.[33]

Ch'ü Ch'iu-pai's leading position in the League of Left-wing Writers guaranteed that he would have an audience for his writings, but it seems that his views were not widely accepted. After all, in the space of only a few months he had challenged many of the basic assumptions held by leftist writers. The New Culture Movement, he proclaimed, was excessively iconoclastic; modern writers were "foreigners" in their own country; the May Fourth literary revolution had failed; leftist writers had inherited the legacy of May Fourth failures; the League of Left-wing Writers was not united; and the revolutionary literary movement had almost no mass base.

32. CCPWC, 2:890.

33. The influence Ch'ü had on Lu Hsün's thinking concerning the problems of "Europeanization" and "national" culture is reflected in a remark Lu Hsün made to Nym Wales after Ch'ü's death. "China cannot go through a period of true bourgeois literary development any more than it can go through a period of independent bourgeois political development. There is no time for it, and no privilege of choice before us. The only possible culture for China today is left revolutionary culture, the alternative being colonial acceptance of an invading imperialist culture, which means to have no independent or national culture at all." Nym Wales, "The Modern Chinese Literary Movement," in Edgar Snow, ed., *Living China: Modern Chinese Stories* (New York: John Day, 1936), p. 348.

7 Romanticism Reconsidered

*They had been infected with the fin de siècle spirit of Europe.
These "hot-headed" intellectuals often began by being caught up
in the angry tide of revolution; but they could be the first to
"drop out," "grow decadent," or "turn renegade" if they did not
resolutely overcome their romanticism. . . . Now they want to
be sole representatives of working class literature and art.*

CH'Ü CH'IU-PAI, 1933[1]

Ch'ü Ch'iu-pai must have realized that his days in Shanghai were
numbered. His writings are those of a man who wanted to accomplish
a great deal in a short period of time. He was obviously willing to play
the role of someone who raised new and provocative questions, made
some random observations of his own, and then moved on to another
subject. Ch'ü simply did not have time to reflect upon and develop
most of the themes he introduced in leftist literary circles. His writings leave one with the impression that, despite his constantly having
to keep one step ahead of the secret police, he always had three or
four literary projects in the works. Using pseudonyms, he was able to
publish some of these important exploratory pieces, but many others
had to be passed around in manuscript form and appeared in print
only after his execution. To work in this manner, something had to be
sacrificed: in Ch'ü's case it was depth.

An instance in point is his treatment of the "first" contradiction
that confronted leftist writers in the early 1930s—the contradiction
between contending factions within the League of Left-wing Writers.
Ch'ü was not at all reluctant to elaborate on what he meant by this
contradiction or to take a controversial stand on the issue, but he
failed to do so systematically. We are left, therefore, with fascinating

1. CCPWC, 2:995-996.

glimpses of what might have been the first chapter in a more comprehensive statement about leftist literary factionalism. This much is clear: Ch'ü believed the split was between romantics and realists, and he tended to side with the realists. Although Ch'ü's views were expressed in a miscellaneous fashion, their significance should not be underestimated. Ch'ü was the first major Marxist intellectual outside the Lu Hsün-Mao Tun group to criticize the romantics, and he did so at a time when they were still a majority in the leadership of the League.

What distinguishes Ch'ü from Lu Hsün and Mao Tun, and makes his views more interesting and credible, is that his evaluation of romanticism was, to a certain extent, made from the "inside." Indeed, Ch'ü had proclaimed in his youth that he was "born a romantic, who always wanted to transcend environment and accomplish some miraculous deed, which would amaze and move the people."[2] Ch'ü never belonged to the Creation Society, but he associated quite closely with its members and published some of his works in their press. Unlike Lu Hsün, Ch'ü harbored no personal hostility toward the Marxist romantics, and his reservations about their literary thought were qualified by an appreciation of their contributions. He counted Chiang Kuang-tz'u, Cheng Po-ch'i, Ch'ien Hsing-ts'un, and Hua Han, the four romantics he criticized by name in leftist journals, to be among his personal friends. In fact, some sources indicate that Ch'ü was among those who helped to launch the radical Sun Society, although Ch'ü never mentioned any role in this regard.[3]

Ch'ü treated the "first contradiction" not as an emotional and personal issue but as an intellectual and political problem that had its origin in the "Europeanization" phenomenon. For the split between romantics and realists to be resolved it would be necessary to determine which elements in contemporary romantic thought were "bourgeois" May Fourth remnants that retarded the revolution and which elements were compatible with socialist thought and therefore tended to propel the revolution. The weaknesses in contemporary Marxist romantic literary thought, he implied, could be attributed to the ongoing influence of bourgeois romanticism.

It would be erroneous, therefore, to suggest that Ch'ü condemned romanticism or advocated that leftist writers renounce the romantic tradition. Ch'ü's view of literary romanticism was relatively complex.

2. CCPWC, 1:170.

3. This is mentioned by Mark E. Shneider, *Tvorcheskii Put' Tsiui Tsiu-bo, 1899-1935* (Moscow: Izdatel'stvo Nauka, 1964), p. 164; and Fu-tan ta-hsueh Chung-wen hsi, ed., *Chung-kuo hsien-tai wen-hsueh shih: 1919-1942* [A History of modern Chinese literature: 1919-1942] (Shanghai: Shanghai wen-i ch'u-pan-she, 1959?) p. 184.

On the one hand, he distinguished between "bourgeois" and "social-ist" romanticism; on the other, he recognized that the bourgeois and socialist schools were related, inasmuch as some basic assumptions about the independence and creativity of the human "spirit" were shared by all who were attracted to romanticism. Ch'ü would have agreed with Leo Ou-fan Lee's observation that romantics, bourgeois and leftist, conceived of reality "not as a preestablished structure or schema to be grasped by systematically applying the human intellect, but rather as a fragmented flow, never static, never totally compre-hensible, only to be felt and glimpsed through intuition and intima-tion. Thus what is emphasized in this outlook is impulse, not result; motive, not objective; creative will, not retrospective analysis; feeling and sensitivity, not reason and ritualization."[4] In brief, romantics were primarily interested in the role played by subjective factors in the development of the individual and society, and tended to assume that neither self-realization nor the liberation of the creative human spirit were limited or restricted by any objective historical laws.

More important to Ch'ü was his belief that from this common point of departure literary romanticism developed in two historically pro-gressive directions. Bourgeois romantics stressed the need to rescue the individual from what they perceived to be an essentially restric-tive and confining social environment. Only by "transcending" society could poets develop their personality and begin to grasp the truth of the universe. Ch'ü undoubtedly believed that turning one's back on society, as he himself had done in his youth, was a necessary first step in any movement to transform a social system that oppressed indi-viduals. Indeed, he was keenly aware that romanticism had played this sort of role in the early European bourgeois revolution.[5] At certain moments in history, moments that history itself provided for, indi-viduals can and must consciously refuse to be molded by their social and material environment. Later, these same romantic assumptions about the ability of human beings to defy material forces permitted some romantics to move in a second and decidedly more socialist direction. The individualistic and transcendental romanticism of the May Fourth period was converted by some into a promethean social-revolutionary romanticism. The subjective elements of emotion and spirit continued to be stressed, but now added to them was a strain of anti-determinist social voluntarism that emphasized the ability of hu-man beings acting in concert to rise up against and overcome even the most unfavorable objective conditions. Indeed, Ch'ü was well aware

4. Leo Ou-fan Lee, *The Romantic Generation of Modern Chinese Writers* (Cambridge: Har-vard University Press, 1973), p. 295.

5. Ch'ü Ch'iu-pai, "Ma-k'o-ssu wen-i lun te tuan-p'ien hou-chi" [A draft postscript on Marxist aesthetics] (1933); in CCPWC, 2:1009.

that the Marxist romantics had launched the "proletarian" literary movement at just the moment of the revolution's greatest defeat.

Ch'ü was profoundly attracted to the voluntarist and social revolutionary implications of romantic thought. He appreciated that this strain was linked intellectually to earlier and more individualistic forms of romanticism, but he obviously welcomed the change that had occurred. It was Ch'ü's hope that the socially oriented variety of romanticism would supply the leftist literary movement with the spiritual strength and sense of optimism necessary to overcome seemingly overwhelming material obstacles.[6] He was more concerned, however, with other—less desirable—aspects of the fundamentally subjective, idealist, and emotional thrust of Marxist romanticism, the "leftist" and "rightist" excesses that romantic literary thinkers might potentially commit.

In Ch'ü's opinion, the romantic left had, since 1928, made serious "leftist" or "idealist" errors in their handling of two major problems in Marxist literary thought: the relationship between the superstructure of society and the economic base; and the role of writers in the transformation of society. What did Ch'ü mean by "idealist" errors? It is clear that the problem of idealism, as Ch'ü understood it, did *not* refer to the somewhat embarrassing fact that the proletariat played no role whatever in the early "proletarian" literary movement launched by the romantics. Neither did Ch'ü find anything particularly idealist about the call for a proletarian cultural movement in a society where the bourgeois cultural movement had not yet been completed. Ch'ü simply conceded that these unusual developments represented an "historical error" (*li-shih te wu-hui*). "The literary theory of the proletariat," he explained, "often begins to take shape after writers of the revolutionary petty-bourgeoisie have become awakened; then by degrees it mobilizes new forces among the laborers and workers."[7] The idealism of the romantic left was excessive, he stated, because, among other things, they never bothered to correct this "historical error" by "rallying new recruits" from the working class. As Ch'ü put it, the romantics wanted to be the permanent "proxies of the working class in cultural affairs."[8]

Thus while Ch'ü agreed that there should be a proletarian literary movement and that intellectuals should play an important role, he disagreed with the romantic definition of proletarian culture and objected to the political role they assigned to the proletarian cultural movement. The romantic left was excessively idealist, Ch'ü suggested, because it assumed that it was possible to write proletarian literature by merely adopting "proletarian consciousness." Not only was it unnecessary to recruit workers to write proletarian literature, it was

6. CCPWC, 2:1008.   7. CCPWC, 2:994.   8. CCPWC, 2:994.

also unnecessary to have any direct contact with the proletariat. The essence of the proletarian condition could be grasped intuitively. Second, the romantic left was excessively idealist because it grossly overestimated the revolutionary political role to be played by the proletarian cultural movement. The romantics misunderstood the relationship between the cultural superstructure of society and the economic and social base. They held the "infantile" (*yu-chih*) belief that changes in the superstructure paved the way for changes in the economic bedrock, and therefore placed the proletarian cultural movement, which they monopolized, alone in the vanguard of the revolution.[9] Those who had been active in the Creation and Sun groups, Ch'ü stated flatly, "think they are the only ones who understand their literary theory."[10] They tended to "act blindly" (*hsia-tung-chu-i*) and desired to establish their "small clique" as the "sole representatives" of proletarian literature.[11] Ch'ü acknowledged that the situation had improved since 1928, but insisted that the danger of "leftism" still existed.

The views Ch'ü expressed about the romantic left in the early 1930s are interesting because they so clearly are a defense of Mao Tun and Lu Hsün. Not only did Ch'ü accept the general validity of the criticism they had leveled at the romantics in 1928, he stated categorically that the romantics had unjustly attacked Lu Hsün and others. "*Three Leisures* and Lu Hsün's other works criticizing the Creation Society reflect the clash between two different attitudes and trends in Chinese literary circles after 1927," Ch'ü asserted. "Naturally, the special feature of Lu Hsün's short essays of this period is that he uses questions concerning particular individuals to shed light on social ideas and social phenomena. But most writers of the Creation Society and other cliques . . . devoted all their attention to questions of personal behavior, age, temperament, and even drinking capacity. Here, at any rate, they revealed the cliquishness [*hsiao-chi-t'uan-chu-i*] of literary intellectuals."[12] Referring to the romantics, Ch'ü added: "Some people accused Lu Hsün of 'surrendering.' In retrospect, this petty-bourgeois vanity and self-conceit at the expense of others is ridiculously childish."[13]

9. CCPWC, 2:994; Shneider, *Tvorcheskii Put'*, pp. 137, 147-148.
10. CCPWC, 2:615.   11. CCPWC, 2:615, 994, 996.   12. CCPWC, 2:996.
13. CCPWC, 2:997. It is interesting to note that a recent Marxist study of Lu Hsün's intellectual development published in Hong Kong in the wake of the defeat of the "Gang of Four" attempts to show that Lu Hsün steadfastly opposed the ultra-leftism of the Creation and Sun societies. Although it is stated that these groups had persecuted Lu Hsün in the late 1920s, Ch'ü Ch'iu-pai's subsequent defense of Lu Hsün and his own attack on the romantic left are not even mentioned. On the contrary, it is argued that literary ultra-leftism was a manifestation in the cultural world of the ultra-leftist political line advocated by Ch'ü in 1927. Li Yung-chia, *Lu Hsün ssu-hsiang te fa-chan* [The development of Lu Hsün's thought] (Hong Kong: Ch'ao yang ch'u-pan-she, 1977), pp. 165-170.

Ch'ü's ultimate fear seems to have been that these particular "left-ist excesses," which he regarded as a manifestation of the lingering influence of bourgeois Western romanticism, could easily lead to "rightist" excesses or, in other words, a return to the individualistic and transcendental romanticism characteristic of early bourgeois cultural movements.[14] The inherent danger of romanticism, either bourgeois or socialist, was that once writers "transcended" society they ran the risk of losing touch with material reality. As a result, even leftist romantics were capable of suddenly becoming disillusioned, "dropping out" of the social movement, and reverting to a narcissistic life of self-indulgence. Romantic individualism was tolerable when it was perceived as a means to an end, but completely unacceptable when it became an end in itself. "During the high tide of revolution, they are sure to be revolutionary, but when the revolution suffers a temporary setback, some of them are sure to grow passive, turn renegade or leap about like men possessed." This assertion by Ch'ü seems harsh and unfair in view of the fact that the Marxist romantics promoted the proletarian literary movement *after* the 1927 defeat.[15] What he meant was that idealists who relied upon "intuition" instead of concrete research and practical experience when assessing the progress of the revolution tended to be overly optimistic. Then when the masses failed to live up to their high expectations, the idealists became discouraged. The line between Marxist romantics and "superfluous" intellectuals was very fine indeed.

Ch'ü undoubtedly believed that his analysis of romanticism could be applied to all the former members of the Creation and Sun groups, but he did, in fact, mention four prominent romantic leftists by name. Ch'ien Hsing-ts'un, a member of the League's first executive board, appears in a work written by Ch'ü in 1932 as a "superficial student" of Marxism and dialectical materialism whose literary shortcomings should not be "minimized."[16] More interesting was Ch'ü's brief critical reference to his old friend and student Chiang Kuang-tz'u. Writing in June 1931, Ch'ü was well aware that Chiang, a charter member of the League, was a classic case of a writer who began his career as a "bourgeois" romantic, became a Marxist romantic at a very early date, but later reverted to a more individualistic form of romanticism. Indeed, Chiang had been expelled from the Communist Party in October 1930 and denounced as a "romantic" individualist who refused to

14. What I am trying to suggest here is that, in Ch'ü's mind, although the content of individualist thought had not changed, "history" or the "stage" of the revolution had. Thus what had been relatively progressive in an earlier stage was now reactionary.
    15. CCPWC, 2:996.
    16. Ch'ü Ch'iu-pai, "Wen-i te tzu-yu ho wen-hsueh-chia te pu tzu-yu" [Artistic freedom and the writer's lack of freedom], *Hsien-tai* [Les Contemporains], 1,6 (1 October 1932); in CCPWC, 2:953.

"approach the masses."[17] Ch'ü's remarks about Chiang are interesting because, despite his analysis of the manner in which "leftist" romantics became "rightist" romantics, he refused to join in the anti-Chiang chorus. In fact, Ch'ü stressed that Chiang was a typical example of a romantic who tended to make idealist errors but who belonged to the revolutionary camp nevertheless.[18] It is likely that this was Ch'ü's way of reminding smug "leftist" romantics like Ch'ien Hsing-ts'un that the difference between "left" and "right" was not so great.

The best example of Ch'ü's criticism of literary and political romanticism is an article entitled "Revolutionary Romantic," written as an introduction to *Spring* [*Ti-ch'üan*], a novel by the well-known "proletarian" writer and League member Hua Han (Yang Han-sheng). Ch'ü's essay is important precisely because it focuses on the weaknesses rather than the strengths of a close colleague and fellow Marxist. Undoubtedly, Ch'ü approved of Hua Han's revolutionary intentions. Yet, though he recognized that *Spring* was the "product of a period of difficult times" for the proletarian cultural movement, he regarded the work as a failure caused by romantic excesses. As Ch'ü put it:

> Without question *Spring* contains new ideals [*li-hsiang*] and assumes a determination to "transform this world." But *Spring* does not even achieve the goal of commonplace realism. The extremely superficial description obviously reveals that not only is *Spring* incapable of helping to "transform the affairs of this world" but also incapable of even "understanding this world." Thus, *Spring* should be studied by the newly rising literature movement—as a model of how not to write.[19]

In Ch'ü's opinion, the language and interrelations of the characters bore little resemblance to reality, and the activities of revolutionaries portrayed in the novel were not based on any clear analysis of current conditions. The revolution advanced not by sudden change and "heroic individualism" but rather by protracted struggle of the masses—with whom the romantics had very little contact.

17. For two stimulating discussions of Chiang Kuang-tz'u, see T. A. Hsia, *The Gate of Darkness* (Seattle: University of Washington Press, 1968), pp. 55-100; and Leo Ou-fan Lee, *The Romantic Generation*, pp. 201-221.

18. CCPWC, 2:614-615. Ch'ü stated that Chiang did not have the kind of intimate knowledge of the masses that the Soviet writer Demian Bedny possessed. Bedny was, of course, the only proletarian writer truly admired by Leon Trotsky.

19. Ch'ü Ch'iu-pai, "Ko-ming te lang-man-ti-k'o—Hua Han ch'ang-p'ien hsiao-shuo *Ti-ch'üan* hsu" [Revolutionary romantic—an introduction to Hua Han's novel *Spring*] (April 22, 1932), in Ch'ü Ch'iu-pai, *Luan-t'an* [Random shots] (Shanghai: Hsia she, 1949), p. 314. This essay criticizing Yang Han-sheng, a powerful official in China after the revolutionary victory, was omitted from the 1953 Peking edition of Ch'ü's collected literary writings.

In brief, Ch'ü's introduction to Hua Han's novel is a rejection not of the romantic spirit in general but rather of the conception that romantic Chinese Marxists had of proletarian culture. "This sort of romanticism," he stated bluntly, "is an obstacle to the newly rising literature."[20] To League writers he proclaimed: "All these mistakes are worthy of research. We should take the path of dialectical-materialist realism [*wei-wu-pien-cheng-fa te hsien-shih-chu-i*], profoundly recognize objective reality, abandon all self-deceiving romanticism, and correctly reflect the great struggle; only when this occurs will we genuinely be able to help transform the affairs of the world."[21]

Less than two weeks after criticizing the idealism of Hua Han, Ch'ü turned his attention to Cheng Po-ch'i, another leading Marxist romantic. Writing on the occasion of the thirteenth anniversary of the May Fourth Incident, Ch'ü stated quite bluntly that "proletarian" writers like Cheng Po-ch'i had nothing to celebrate. Not only were Marxist romantics still the captives of bourgeois May Fourth thought, their "proletarian" literary movement was a failure. Ch'ü vigorously denied Cheng's assertion that the difficulties encountered by the proletarian literary movement were caused primarily by the failure of the masses to "comprehend our views."[22] Proletarian literature failed to reach the masses, Ch'ü explained, because leftist romantics ignored the material or organic relationship that existed between art and society. Idealists like Cheng Po-ch'i assumed incorrectly that it was possible to write proletarian literature without having intimate and direct contact with the people. Consequently not only was their literature written in a language unfamiliar to the people, it did not treat the problems they faced in daily life. "The writers are unwilling to go among the people and are unwilling to work together with the people to create a new literature and art," Ch'ü observed. "On the contrary, they call upon the people to 'prepare themselves adequately' first, so that later they might have the good fortune to be admitted into the 'Temple of Art'!"[23] Ch'ü did not question Cheng's political intentions, he simply argued that these manifestations of bourgeois idealism divided the League and retarded the growth of the revolutionary literary movement.

THE USES OF MARXISM: COUNTERING IDEALISM

A most interesting but as yet unstudied literary activity of Ch'ü Ch'iu-pai in the early 1930s was a substantial translation project de-

20. Ibid., p. 317.   21. Ibid.
22. CCPWC, 2:877. Ch'ü refers to Cheng Po-ch'i by one of his pseudonyms, Ho Ta-pai.
23. CCPWC, 2:878.

signed, among other things, to introduce a number of important Western Marxist works on literature and art still unknown in China. A few were published before his departure from Shanghai in January 1934, but most appeared after his death in an important two-volume collection compiled by Lu Hsün and entitled *Shanghai Miscellany* [Hai-shang shu-lin].[24] In view of the fact that Ch'ü had never before translated important works by Western Marxist literary thinkers, it must be assumed that he intended them to serve a specific purpose. Ch'ü never offered a systematic explanation, but it is evident that the selections he translated raise a number of theoretical questions pertaining to the "contradiction" between romanticism and realism. Ch'ü clearly believed that by reading these texts, the "idealists" who dominated the League of Left-wing Writers could learn some important lessons about the relationship between the economic base and the superstructure of society, and the role of art and artists in the transformation of society.

The most unusual piece is not a translation, strictly speaking, but rather an article entitled "A Draft Postscript on Marxist Aesthetics" in which Ch'ü discussed the significance of the famous letters written by Marx and Engels in 1859 to their socialist colleague Ferdinand Lassalle concerning the play *Franz von Sickingen*.[25] Presumably Ch'ü had no serious interest in the subject of Lassalle's play—civil conflict in sixteenth-century Germany—but he did recognize the contemporary relevance of the problems raised by Marx and Engels. Indeed, Marx and Engels do not speak in ambiguous terms in these letters: they appear instead as unwavering defenders of the materialist conception of art.[26] Hence, Ch'ü was able to use their letters to support the view that socialist idealists, like Lassalle and the Marxist romantics in China, ignore the study of objective reality and material forces and, therefore, consistently misjudge the current condition of the revolution in their literary and political work.

24. Ch'ü Ch'iu-pai, trans., Lu Hsün, ed., *Hai-shang shu-lin* [Shanghai miscellany, hereafter referred to as HSSL] (Hong Kong: San-lien shu-tien, 1950), 1:1-262. Ch'ü's translations of works by Engels, Plekhanov, and Paul Lafargue as well as the commentaries he wrote on these selections were based on the contents of *Literaturnoe Nasledstvo* (Literary heritage), 1 (1931) and 2 (1932), published in Moscow by the Institute of Literature and Art of the Communist Academy. The translations of Lenin's works were apparently included on Ch'ü's own initiative.

25. See footnote 5, above. This essay was not included in HSSL. Ch'ü was undoubtedly inspired to write it after reading the letters by Marx and Engels and an introductory essay by the young Georg Lukács in *Literaturnoe Nasledstvo*, 3 (1932). Ch'ü was probably the first Chinese Marxist to be influenced by the writings of Lukács.

26. The "ambiguity" I refer to alludes to the fact that in some writings Marx and Engels stress the relative independence of the superstructure from the economic base, while in others, including their letters to Lassalle, they emphasize the dependence of the superstructure on the economic base.

Citing Marx and Engels, Ch'ü argued that Lassalle's play failed to identify correctly the principal historical contradiction in the 1522-1523 uprising against the feudal dukes in Germany. Instead of stressing the primary contradiction between the peasant movement of Thomas Münzer and the feudal ruling class, Lassalle had emphasized a secondary contradiction which had arisen *within* the ruling class during a transitional period when the feudal system was forced to adjust to the rise of commercial capital.[27] Franz von Sickingen was the leader of a group of Swabian and Rhenish knights who sought, not to overthrow the feudal system, but to prevent the emperor and the dukes from transforming the system in order to adapt to the early stages of capitalism. Sickingen may have opposed capitalism, but in doing so he opposed the march of history. He was defeated, not because he was betrayed by his followers, but because he was representing the interests of a "perishing class." Lassalle, Ch'ü insisted, had stressed the wrong group; as Marx had put it, he had placed "the Lutheran-knightly opposition higher than the plebian Münzer one."[28] The primary contradiction had been between those who saved the feudal system by restructuring it and the peasant masses who hoped to see the *entire* feudal system abolished.

There can be little doubt that Ch'ü intended to present the letters of Marx and Engels as the authoritative Marxist critique of idealism and romanticism. Like the romantic Marxists in China, Ch'ü implied, Lassalle had not investigated the objective forces that shaped the evolution of society. Instead of introducing the "wonderfully variegated plebian social sphere of that time," as Engels had suggested, Lassalle placed the emphasis on a single "heroic individual" who did not understand the direction in which history itself was moving.[29] Sickingen was, as Marx put it, a "Don Quixote."[30] Furthermore, the play lacked realism. The characters in Lassalle's play, for example, were portrayed, not as the natural products of their social environment and class, but as "mere mouthpieces" for various ideological viewpoints. Ch'ü, like Marx and Engels, complained of excessive "Schillerism." "In *my* view of drama," Engels noted, "the realistic should not be neglected in favor of the intellectual elements, nor Shakespeare in favor of Schiller."[31]

Lassalle's "Schillerism," Ch'ü asserted, was in fact a form of romanticism. As such it constituted an "anti-realist" creative method, and

27. CCPWC, 2:1004-1005.

28. CCPWC, 2:1003-1004. The English texts of the letters by Marx and Engels are found in Lee Baxandall and Stefan Morawski, eds., *Marx and Engels on Literature and Art* (St. Louis: Telos Press, 1973), pp. 105-111, 141-143.

29. Baxandall and Morawski, p. 109.

30. Ibid., p. 106.   31. Ibid., p. 109.

produced a "muddled view of real social life." In order to devise an appropriate strategy for advancing the revolution, Ch'ü suggested, it was absolutely necessary to "recognize concrete class relations and historical conditions" by employing a "thoroughly materialist method of analysis." Any attempt to base the revolution on "heroic individuals" would result in little more than "hollow revolutionary emotionalism."[32] The Chinese proletariat had no need for this sort of romanticism, Ch'ü asserted, but it appeared on the scene nevertheless. Although it was called "proletarian literature," it was, in Ch'ü's opinion, "ten times more vulgar" than Lassalle's work.[33]

To see *Franz von Sickingen* dissected in this manner was probably not very painful for Ch'ü's readers because Lassalle was a relatively unknown figure in China. Ch'ü's decision to criticize Henrik Ibsen by translating a section of Plekhanov's "Ibsen: Petty Bourgeois Revolutionist" was a very different matter.[34] Ibsen was one of the great heroes of the May Fourth generation.

In all likelihood Ch'ü's readers focused on the content of Plekhanov's critique of Ibsen. But also important is the manner in which Ch'ü treated the problems under discussion. By selecting Plekhanov as one of his defenders of the materialist conception of art, Ch'ü was associating himself with one of the most deterministic traditions in Marxist literary thought. Known as the founder of the Russian school of Marxist literary thought, Plekhanov devoted the greatest portion of his literary efforts to establishing the absolute validity of the materialist conception of art. Scholarly and pedantic in approach, he was, above all, determined to found a "scientific," sociological, and, of course, Marxist method of accounting for the appearance of an art object at any moment in history. Unlike Marx and Engels, Plekhanov never expressed the slightest doubt about the absolute predominance of the economic substructure. In a word, Plekhanov believed that literature and art are the "mirror of social life."

In one of his most celebrated works, *Unaddressed Letters*, Plekhanov undertook anthropological research on the nature of art in various "primitive" societies. It was there, in his view, that the relationship between economic activity and artistic expression was most direct. Plekhanov brought forward an array of late-nineteenth-century ethnological studies to confirm his argument that the drawings, ornamentation, and dances of primitive peoples usually reflect the degree to which the economic system was based on hunting, fishing, or agri-

---

32. CCPWC, 2:1007-1008.   33. CCPWC, 2:1008.

34. For Ch'ü's partial translation of Plekhanov's essay, see "I-pu-sheng te ch'eng-kung" [Ibsen's achievements], HSSL, 1:84-96. For a complete English translation of Plekhanov's essay, see Angel Flores, ed., *Ibsen* (New York: Critics Group, 1937), pp. 35-93.

culture. By this simplistic and rather pseudo-scientific method, Plekhanov hoped to establish the validity of a monocausal economic explanation of the origins of artistic culture. In his view, the difference between primitive and "civilized" societies (class societies) was that the "dependence of art" on the mode of production is "direct" in primitive societies, and becomes more complicated and indirect, but no less dependent, in "civilized" societies.[35] Indeed, Plekhanov never wavered from the belief that "the art of any people has always an intimate causal connection with their economy."[36] In this rigidly deterministic formula, art trails passively in the wake of history.

In the essay on Ibsen translated by Ch'ü Ch'iu-pai, Plekhanov characterized Ibsen as a socialist who had little grasp of the materialist conception of history, and therefore saw no need to base his strategy for revolution on a detailed knowledge of objective conditions. Ibsen rejected capitalism, Plekhanov observed, and was horrified at the cultureless and philistine character of the new bourgeoisie, but his solution to the problem was to call for a "revolution of the modern spirit" among an enlightened intellectual vanguard. It was strongly implied by both Ch'ü and Plekhanov that Ibsen was "preoccupied with problems of consciousness" precisely because he believed that a revolution in the superstructure of society was a precondition for a fundamental social transformation.[37] Ibsen's concern for the liberation of the individual human spirit caused him, it was argued, to overlook the role of objective forces and ignore the need for mass political action. It will be shown later in this study that Ch'ü Ch'iu-pai was critical of Plekhanov's highly deterministic view of the relationship between art and society, but his willingness to translate this and similar works by Plekhanov, such as "French Drama and Painting of the Eighteenth Century," suggests that he believed romantic Marxists in China could benefit by exposure to theoretical works that stressed the materialist conceptions of history and art.[38]

What is especially interesting about this selection is that Ch'ü translated only a portion of Plekhanov's essay, the final section that discusses the reasons for Ibsen's worldwide popularity, particularly in "underdeveloped" areas. By stressing this theme, Ch'ü was apparently attempting to link the idealist and individualist failings of the roman-

35. Georg Plekhanov, *Art and Social Life* (London: Lawrence and Wishart Ltd., 1953), p. 48.

36. Ibid., p. 57.   37. Flores, *Ibsen*, p. 36.

38. For Ch'ü's other Plekhanov translations, see "Pieh-lin-ssu-ch'i te pai-nien chi-nien" [Centennial commemoration of Belinsky], "Fa-kuo te hsi-ch'ü wen-hsueh ho Fa-kuo te hui-hua" [French drama and painting of the 18th Century from the sociological standpoint], and "Wei-wu shih kuan te i-shu lun" [The materialist conception of art], HSSL, 1:97-134. Needless to say, each one stresses the materialist conception of art and therefore criticizes idealist outlooks.

tic left in China to the impact of "Europeanization" in the early May Fourth period. As Ibsen was virtually worshipped by romantics in the early 1920s, Ch'ü could not have chosen a better target.[39] Criticizing Ibsen was tantamount to criticizing the May Fourth generation itself. By translating Plekhanov's remarks, Ch'ü seemed to be saying that precapitalist societies, like China, tended to produce socialist intellectuals who exaggerated the role of consciousness in the transformation of society. Ibsen's "ideals," Plekhanov confirmed, "were developed in a country which had no revolutionary proletariat, and where the backward masses were petty-bourgeois to the core. These masses could not become the vanguard of the progressive ideal. That is why every forward step of necessity seemed to Ibsen to be a movement of the 'minority,' that is, of a small group of thinking individuals."[40] Plekhanov added that the situation "was quite different in countries of developed capitalist production," but in areas similar to Ibsen's Norwegian homeland, his views seemed quite relevant. The problem, Ch'ü implied, was that in places like China where capitalism was in an early and deformed stage, well-intentioned socialist intellectuals might also disregard the role of objective forces and the need to build a mass movement.

It is clear, however, that Ch'ü did not accept the determinist implications of Plekhanov's argument. Ch'ü certainly agreed that precapitalist societies like China produced idealist socialists, but he could not agree that it was impossible for socialist revolution to occur or for genuine socialist intellectuals to appear in such societies. Plekhanov was correct that socialist thought often appeared initially as an idealist and elitist "expression of the progressive strivings of the small intelligent oasis in the barren desert of philistine life."[41] But Ch'ü firmly believed that the romantics could overcome this form of "Europeanization" and participate in a new kind of socialist movement unforeseen by Plekhanov, a socialist movement in an "underdeveloped" nation where the bourgeois revolution had failed and where capitalism existed in an exceedingly distorted form. Materialist thinkers were required to study concrete social and economic conditions, but historical materialism did not dictate that each society must pass through a prolonged stage of capitalist development in order that the preconditions for socialist revolution might be created.

Psychologically speaking, Ch'ü's translation of two essays by Lenin entitled "Leo Tolstoy as the Mirror of the Russian Revolution" and "Leo Tolstoy and His Epoch" was perhaps his most dramatic effort to

39. Leo Ou-fan Lee, *The Romantic Generation*, p. 277. Lee shows that both Ibsen and Tolstoy were admired as much by romantics as by realists in the 1920s.

40. HSSL, 1:91; Flores, *Ibsen*, pp. 88-89.

41. HSSL, 1:91; Flores, *Ibsen*, p. 89.

censure the leftist romantics.[42] Indeed, it is entirely possible that by including Tolstoy among the "idealists" Ch'ü was conceding that as a young socialist intellectual he too had exaggerated the significance of subjective factors. In any case, it is clear that he intended to present Lenin's views as yet another authoritative materialist criticism of socialist romanticism. It was not easy to portray Tolstoy as a romantic, because he was regarded by many as one of the great realists of the nineteenth century. To place Tolstoy in the romantic category, therefore, Ch'ü, like Lenin, distinguished his realistic descriptive method from his idealist political views. Ch'ü could then recommend that Chinese romantics learn from Tolstoy's creative method, on the one hand, while stressing the inadequacies of Tolstoy's idealist world view, on the other.

It is, of course, this second theme that dominates Lenin's articles. In his opinion, Tolstoy was typical of early socialist intellectuals who led a "spiritual rebellion" in response to the early impact of capitalism in a relatively backward society. Thus, like Lassalle and Ibsen, Tolstoy placed excessive emphasis on the role of ideas and consciousness in history, and underestimated the role played by material or objective forces. Tolstoy was a brilliant realist in his vivid and passionate accounts of the "advance of capitalism" in the Russian countryside, but he had no understanding of "the working-class movement and its role in the struggle for socialism."[43] Like Sickingen, Tolstoy's opposition to capitalism was an expression of "the ideology of the classes that are going to be replaced by the bourgeoisie" and not a reflection of the "scientific ideology" of the class that will replace the bourgeoisie.[44] In short, Tolstoy, like idealists elsewhere, believed that the transformation of human consciousness was a precondition for the transformation of objective reality.

The materialist conception of history is defended both directly and indirectly in Lenin's writings on Tolstoy. First, it is asserted that Tolstoy failed as a revolutionary because he was unable to perceive the manner in which objective forces shape the evolution of society. But second, it is implied that the very appearance of a "false ideology" was itself a confirmation of the validity of the materialist conception. In other words, Tolstoy's work "accurately" reflected an erroneous world view that tends to be expressed only under specific historical

42. For Ch'ü's Lenin translations, see "Lieh-fu T'o-erh-ssu-t'ai hsiang i-mien O-kuo ko-ming te ching-tzu" [Leo Tolstoy as a mirror of the Russian revolution], "L.N. T'o-erh-ssu-t'ai ho t'a te shih-tai" [Leo Tolstoy and his epoch], HSSL, 1:243-256. For complete English translations of these works see V.I. Lenin, *On Literature and Art* (Moscow: Progress Publishers, 1970), pp. 28-33, 58-62.

43. HSSL, 1:245-246; Lenin, *On Literature and Art*, pp. 29-30.

44. HSSL, 1:255; Lenin, *On Literature and Art*, p. 61.

circumstances.[45] In this respect Lenin's views correspond closely to the deterministic outlook of Plekhanov. Marxist standards are employed to demonstrate the idealist failings of men like Ibsen and Tolstoy, but then it is stated that they were, after all, the products of their time. Ch'ü undoubtedly accepted these judgments because they tended to diminish the stature of Ibsen, Tolstoy, and other May Fourth models, but he could not apply this formula in its entirety to the Chinese romantics. True, the romantics failed to portray the proletariat accurately because they approached the problem of literature and revolution from an idealist point of view; and true, their mistakes were themselves the product of concrete historical conditions. But Ch'ü, unlike Plekhanov and Lenin, held out the hope that idealists of this sort could correct their mistakes by becoming more conscious of the need to study objective reality.

It can be argued that the criticisms of Lassalle, Ibsen, and Tolstoy introduced by Ch'ü in the early 1930s were distorted and unfair. Harsh as these views were, it was not Ch'ü's intention, however, to completely dismiss romanticism or deny the importance of human will. "When we say 'do not overlook the realistic element,'" he remarked in his essay on Marx and Engels, "we do not mean that all fervor, all ideals, all thought, and 'ultimate aims' should be forsaken."[46] Ch'ü recognized that the idealist approach of Ibsen and Tolstoy had a revolutionary impact during the early stages of the modern literary movement. But the activities of the "proletarian" Creation and Sun Societies had obviously convinced him that in the period following the transition from literary revolution to revolutionary literature further "rebellion of the spirit" could be counterproductive, especially when it was divorced from detailed knowledge of society and direct contact with the mass movement. Not only did Ch'ü accept the Marxist criticisms of Ibsen and Tolstoy, he believed that they could be used in China to shed light on the errors of the romantics.

It is important to point out that Ch'ü did not regard this debate as a mere intellectual or scholarly exercise. He was acutely aware that the romantics were not only writers, but political revolutionaries as well. The mistakes they made in their literary works had political implications. Ch'ü believed that from time to time history itself provided "opportunities" for qualitative revolutionary change. It was the duty of all revolutionaries, including writers, to study society and recognize moments when revolutionary change was possible. If political activities were based on unrealistic assessments of society, opportunities for advancing the revolution might be missed altogether. In fact, Ch'ü stated explicitly that Lassalle's failure to grasp the essential nature of the civil conflict in sixteenth-century Germany was no different from

45. HSSL, 1:243, 248.   46. CCPWC, 2:1008.

his failure to understand the primary contradiction of the 1848 revolution. More important, his lack of political judgment contributed to a defeat that was by no means inevitable.[47] Socialist revolution could not be advanced by "immature dreamers" like Tolstoy.[48]

The question remains of how Ch'ü's critique of romanticism relates to his general evaluation of the impact of "Europeanization" on the literary left. Should Ch'ü's criticism of Lassalle, Ibsen, and Tolstoy be understood as an essentially "nationalist" assault on the "foreign" origins of romantic thought, or as a proletarian "class" attack on the "bourgeois" nature of romantic leftism? It is, of course, difficult to separate these issues because Ch'ü himself tended in this period to identify things "bourgeois" with things "foreign." Clearly, Ch'ü was concerned with both aspects of romanticism. But because he was willing to enlist the support of "foreign" thinkers such as Marx, Engels, Plekhanov, and Lenin on this question, it would appear that he placed the emphasis on the "bourgeois" side of romantic thought. Ch'ü, it is true, had reservations about various aspects of Western Marxist literary thought, but he had no difficulty making use of what he viewed as valid fragments of this tradition to shed critical light on May Fourth idols like Ibsen and Tolstoy and their idealist followers in China.

47. CCPWC, 2:1002-1003, 1006.   48. HSSL, 1:249.

8 Realism Reconsidered

> *I must tell you from the very first that the materialist method
> is converted into its direct opposite if, instead of being used
> as a guiding thread in historical research, it is made to serve as
> a ready-cut pattern on which to tailor historical facts.*
>
> FREDERICK ENGELS, 1890[1]

Ch'ü Ch'iu-pai once observed that during his turbulent political career he sometimes "stood in the middle as a compromiser who hoped to bring both sides together."[2] This remark also describes his attitude toward the leftist literary movement in the 1930s. It is true that when he viewed the "contradiction" between the romantics and realists, and the debates on the role of the writer and the relationship between the economic base and the superstructure, Ch'ü tended to favor the realist or materialist position, but by no means did he believe the realist faction to be above criticism. On the contrary, he used the same framework to analyze realist thought that he used to analyze romantic thought. He argued that both positive and negative elements were contained in the realist tradition, and that the leftist literary movement could not be united until these ingredients were identified and understood. Ch'ü's attraction to materialist literary thought, therefore, should not be mistaken for uncritical acceptance. He believed that the realist group shared some of the responsibility for leftist factionalism. He also seems to have accepted the underlying validity of some of the charges leveled at the realists by the romantics.

Ch'ü's criticisms were taken seriously because he was perceived

1. "En-ke-ssu lun I-pu-sheng te hsin" [Engels' letter on Ibsen], HSSL, 1:55. For the complete translation of Engels' letter to Paul Ernst see Lee Baxandall and Stefan Morawski, eds., *Marx and Engels on Literature and Art* (St. Louis: Telos Press, 1973), pp. 86-89.
2. TYTH, p. 145.

by the realists (as he was perceived by the romantics) not as a hostile partisan, but as a knowledgeable "insider" intimately familiar with their intellectual predispositions. Ch'ü had been active in the Literary Research Association, had published many of his writings in the realist press, and had exceptionally good personal relationships with Lu Hsün, Mao Tun, Ting Ling, and other realist thinkers. Indeed, in 1921 he had written: "Since my childhood, I have had a strong bent for the inner strength of realism. I must carefully study reality and do things one by one. The power of reason imposes its dictatorship over me."[3] Ch'ü may have leaned toward the realist side, but what he really sought was a compromise or synthesis that would blend what he believed to be the best and most revolutionary tendencies of the two schools. To achieve this goal Ch'ü was quite willing to make a preliminary sketch of the potential pitfalls that faced realist writers. The hope of "reconciling" the two currents of romanticism and realism that Ch'ü had expressed so eloquently in his youth was obviously still very much alive in the literary thought of his later years.

Ch'ü Ch'iu-pai never wrote systematically on the subject of realism, but it is readily apparent from his miscellaneous essays and translations that his interest in realism was quite different from his interest in romanticism. Where romantics stressed the importance of the subjective realm in their writings, realists emphasized the overriding significance of matter. Where romantics celebrated the independence and creativity of the human spirit, realists insisted that individuals were, somehow, the "products" of material forces. More important, however, realists tended to assume that the human intellect was capable of understanding the objective forces or "natural laws" that determined the development of human society and history itself. In their view, the function of literature was to study society in order to comprehend the manner and direction in which society was "evolving." Thus literature was seen as one method of doing "social science" research. Unlike the early romantics, who sought to lift the individual from the abyss of society through a literature that was to transcend the brutality of society, the early realist writers accepted the materialist conception of the organic relationship between society and art. The role of literature was not to facilitate an escape from society, but rather to study and reflect objective conditions, and thus expose evil and outmoded social relationships and practices, all of which were doomed to "extinction."[4] There can be little doubt that it was this

3. CCPWC, 1:170-171.
4. For a good general discussion of early realism and naturalism, see Bonnie S. McDougall, *The Introduction of Western Literary Theories into Modern China* (Tokyo: The Centre for East Asian Cultural Studies, 1971), pp. 147-189.

materialist orientation of literary realism that drew Ch'ü's attention.

Ch'ü recognized that these general assumptions about literature and society were shared by many writers who identified with the realist school; but he distinguished between "bourgeois" and "proletarian" realism. Both, he believed, had made important contributions to the development of the revolutionary literary movement. Aside from providing modern Chinese readers with badly needed information about the horrendous condition of Chinese society, early Europeanized realist literature was inspired by a humanistic concern for the welfare of all people. Furthermore, Ch'ü had always applauded the reformist tendencies present in the thought of most realists in the early 1920s. They assumed that historical and social change was inevitable and natural, and they were constantly searching for new evidence that social evolution was in fact occurring in China. When a distinctively socialist-oriented realism emerged in the late 1920s, Ch'ü was well aware that its advocates continued to assume that there was a material relationship between art and society, and that it was the prime duty of writers to study society and master the "scientific" laws that governed its evolution. In short, materialism continued to be stressed, but the humanistic and reformist strains were rejected by many in favor of a considerably more "tendentious" realism. Inspired by the Marxist writings of Plekhanov and Trotsky, their general belief in the existence of objective historical laws was converted into a more specific faith in the laws of history described by Marx, laws that proclaimed the historical inevitability of socialism and proletarian class rule.

Ch'ü was, therefore, attracted primarily by the materialist thrust of realist theory and the willingness of realist writers to engage in detailed studies of concrete social conditions. Although he obviously welcomed the shift from bourgeois to Marxist realism, he recognized that these two schools shared the same intellectual origins. It was his hope that the materialist tradition would contribute to the leftist literary movement by convincing writers, especially the romantics, of the absolute necessity of being thoroughly familiar with real social life at all times.

In the 1930s, however, it was not Ch'ü's intention to repeat familiar refrains about the undeniable contributions made by the realist school. There were numerous observers on the scene who were more than willing to provide that service. He was much more concerned with what he regarded as the potentially nonrevolutionary political implications of certain trends in realist thought. Ch'ü suggested that Marxist realists in China who had been influenced by deterministic Western schools tended at times to place an excessive amount of emphasis on the role of objective, impersonal laws of history; that is, they exaggerated the extent to which the development of the superstructure of society, including artistic culture, is dependent upon the transformation of the economic base. Fundamental change, it was assumed, occurs first in the material base, and is "reflected" later in the art and literature of society.

Ch'ü clearly believed that there were many problems with this interpretation of the materialist conception of art. In the first place, he insisted, it was wrong to assume the existence of a single and universal "law" of historical development that could be applied mechanistically to the study of all societies. Thus he rejected the notion that theories about the relationship between the economic base and the superstructure advanced by foreign Marxists, and especially theories that minimized the significance of "cultural" revolution, were necessarily valid for conditions in China.

Ch'ü seems to have objected for two reasons to the dogmatic application of excessively mechanistic conceptions of art and society. First, in writings that ignored the role of human consciousness and will in the transformation of society, human beings might be portrayed as the passive victims of objective and highly impersonal "laws of history." If humankind is seen as being overwhelmed and consumed by material forces, Ch'ü reasoned, then the best that even a politically progressive writer could hope to do is merely reflect the human condition at a given moment in the natural evolution of society, a process above which neither human beings nor art can rise. Writers who underestimated subjective factors ran the risk of lapsing into fatalistic despair and being politically paralyzed by a sense of hopelessness, particularly at moments when the revolution suffered a defeat. This was one of the ways that those who appreciated the role of material forces in shaping society were transformed into despondent or nonrevolutionary determinists who confined themselves to writing amoral accounts of the movement of impersonal natural forces.

Second, Ch'ü was acutely aware that it was both possible and logical for Marxist writers to use highly deterministic conceptions of art to support the notion that art and partisan politics should be kept completely separate. If art "reflects" society naturally, then there is no need for artists to be conscious of their role or to be actively engaged in contemporary social movements. In fact such involvement constitutes "unnatural" interference and actually prevents artists from playing the role assigned to them by history itself.

Ch'ü's view of the dangers inherent in the materialist approach, it should be noted, was entirely compatible with his evaluation of the lingering effects of "Europeanization" on the leftist literary movement. Determinism and excessive scientism (*k'e-hsueh-chu-i*) were perceived not only as potential weaknesses in Marxist literary thought, but also as clear manifestations of bourgeois "naturalism," a deterministic variant of bourgeois realist thought that had been exceedingly popular in China at the time of the May Fourth Movement.[5] In Ch'ü's opinion, it was not at all surprising that May Fourth writers who once were interested in European realism and naturalism later found the relatively deterministic Marxist writings of Plekhanov and Trotsky to be particularly compelling.

SOME CASE STUDIES

Who did Ch'ü Ch'iu-pai have in mind when he raised these questions about the perils of excessive materialism? Although Ch'ü never made a direct reference to Lu Hsün in this regard, it is hard to avoid the conclusion that on certain issues Ch'ü might have been thinking of Lu Hsün himself. It is true, of course, that the most salient aspect of Ch'ü's major essay on Lu Hsün was his bold defense of his friend in the face of the romantic onslaught.[6] Ch'ü's criticisms of the intellectual deficiencies of the dominant romantic group were intended to confirm the essential validity of points made by Lu Hsün in the late 1920s. Ch'ü clearly believed that Lu Hsün was a great realist thinker whose writings were considerably more revolutionary than any of the works produced by the romantics. Nevertheless, Ch'ü's analysis of realism and materialism can be used to explain some of the problems encountered by Lu Hsün during his conversion to Marxism. In fact, it must have occurred to Ch'ü that, although the romantics could not supply any meaningful alternatives, at least two of the charges they leveled at Lu Hsün were similar to some of his own concerns about materialist theory: the related problems of determinism and fatalism.

Ch'ü admired Lu Hsün for accepting the materialist conception of art and urging writers to study concrete social conditions that were sometimes grim; but he undoubtedly recognized that in the period when Lu Hsün first expressed an interest in Marxist aesthetics his view of the relationship between art and society was relatively deterministic. In fact, it was well known that Lu Hsün had been influenced by precisely the schools that stressed the dependence of the superstructure on the economic base. This outlook was expressed in Lu Hsün's writings in two different ways. In the dynamic months preceeding the defeat of the revolution in 1927, it was a sense of excite-

5. Ch'ü Ch'iu-pai, "Kuan-yu Tso-la" [Concerning Zola], HSSL, 1:216. Ch'ü's remarks on Zola are based upon an essay by M. Eikhengol'ts contained in *Literaturnoe Nasledstvo*, 2 (1932): 235-248.

6. See Paul G. Pickowicz, "Lu Xun 1hrough the Eyes of Qu Qiu-bai," *Modern China*, July 1976, pp. 327-368, for a full discussion of the significance of Ch'ü's writings on Lu Hsün and the nature of their personal relationship.

ment and hope that prompted Lu Hsün to de-emphasize the role of literature. In a talk entitled "Literature of a Revolutionary Period," delivered to the cadets of the Whampoa Military Academy, Lu Hsün suggested that literature was not really needed by the revolutionary camp. In this and other works that reveal the extent of his indebtedness to Trotsky, Lu Hsün stressed the degree to which literature trails in the wake of history and "reflects" social change. Referring to those who attached more significance to the superstructure, Lu Hsün stated: "I know some people think literature has a great influence on revolution, but personally I doubt this."[7] Not only do literary "expressions of suffering and indignation have no influence on the revolution," he added, but during the peak of the revolution "literature disappears" altogether.[8]

These are, of course, the sort of deterministic views on the relationship between art and society that are contained in Trotsky's *Literature and Revolution*, a book Lu Hsün is known to have admired. "In general," Trotsky argued, "the place of art is in the rear of the historic advance,"[9] or, as he put it later in life: "Art is always carried in the baggage train of a new epoch."[10] Like Plekhanov and others who stressed the "reflective" nature of art, Trotsky attacked utopian socialists, proletarian cultural "idealists," and other moralists who "thought that mind and critical reason moved the world." "As a matter of fact," he pointed out, "all through history, mind limps after reality."[11] Art and artists do not play a significant role in the making of history; their role is to stand back and reflect the condition of society.

Lu Hsün's optimism about objective conditions gave way to pessimism following the coup, but his deterministic view of the relationship between literature and society and the role of the writer remained essentially the same. In the optimistic phase, he argued that literature was not necessary; now he argued that it could not alter the situation. Objective circumstances were now bleak and the future of the revolution was in doubt. In contrast to the romantics, who, it seems, were never deterred by unfavorable objective conditions, Lu Hsün dwelled upon the theme of "darkness"[12] and continued to insist that he had "no faith in the power of literature to move heaven and earth."[13] As late as mid-1929, still under the influence of Plekhanov's mechanistic formulae, Lu Hsün asserted: "All literature is shaped by its surround-

7. Lu Hsün, "Literature of a Revolutionary Period," SWLH, 2:333.

8. Ibid., pp. 328-329.

9. Leon Trotsky, *Literature and Revolution* (Ann Arbor: University of Michigan Press, 1964), p. 236.

10. Leon Trotsky, *On Literature and Art* (New York: Pathfinder Press, 1970), p. 209.

11. Trotsky, *Literature and Revolution*, p. 19.

12. Lu Hsün, "Two Letters," SWLH, 3:34.

13. Lu Hsün, "Literature and Revolution," SWLH, 3:21.

ings and, though devotees of art like to claim that literature can sway the course of world affairs, the truth is that politics comes first, and art changes accordingly. If you fancy art can change your environment, you are talking like an idealist."[14] If Ch'ü had written on this deterministic aspect of Lu Hsün's thought, it is highly probable that he would have agreed with the romantics: Lu Hsün consistently underestimated the importance of the superstructure and the role of the active writer.

Ch'ü did, in fact, address himself to the fatalistic consequences of such ideas. In his otherwise glowing essay on Lu Hsün written in early 1933, Ch'ü referred explicitly to the allegation that Lu Hsün had been a "pessimist." Instead of denying the charge, he acknowledged that it was an accurate characterization of Lu Hsün's outlook after the coup. "At the time," Ch'ü explained, "these early revolutionary writers who reflect the downfall of feudal society could not always free themselves at once from individualism—the tendency to doubt the masses. They see the selfishness, blindness, superstition, self-deception, and even servile submissiveness of the peasants who are small property owners; but they often fail to see the revolutionary significance behind their clumsy, conservative slogans. This fault occurs frequently in Lu Hsün's essays, and was responsible for his temporary disillusionment and despair when the revolution suffered a setback."[15] This was Ch'ü's way of saying that Lu Hsün had in fact attached too much significance to objective conditions—as Lu Hsün perceived those conditions. More important, Ch'ü's remark is interesting because it implies that the fatalistic strain in Lu Hsün's thought was less a reflection of Lu Hsün's personality than of the determinism to which materialist thinkers were especially susceptible.

Ch'ü may also have been thinking of his old companion Mao Tun when he was raising questions about materialist excesses. At any rate, he obviously realized that the cases of Lu Hsün and Mao Tun were similar in a number of respects. Both were materialist literary thinkers who temporarily dropped out of the revolution following the coup and were subsequently accused by the romantics of harboring fatalistic views about the revolution and deterministic ideas about the relationship between literature and society. Although Ch'ü had little to say about Mao Tun's views on these questions, he seems to have implied that there was a relationship between Mao Tun's fatalism and the naturalist literary theories to which he had so enthusiastically subscribed before his conversion to Marxism. In any event, it is clear that the purpose of Ch'ü's 1933 review of *Midnight* [*Tzu-yeh*], a novel that analyzes the workings of the Shanghai stock exchange, was to

14. Lu Hsün, "Some Thoughts on Our New Literature," SWLH, 3:45.
15. CCPWC, 2:995.

identify Mao Tun as a realist who ultimately avoided the dangers of the ahistorical, clinical, naturalist method. *Midnight* was neither a romantic fantasy nor a fatalistic description of "natural" forces. "This is China's first successful realist novel," Ch'ü exclaimed. "Quite obviously it bears the influence of Zola's *L'argent.* Naturally it has many shortcomings and even mistakes. But in its use of genuine social science, and in its literary expressions of China's social relations and class relations, it cannot be denied that this work represents a great accomplishment." Mao Tun, Ch'ü stressed, "is not Zola."[16]

As Ch'ü's treatment of Mao Tun suggests, his direct and indirect statements about the deterministic and fatalistic strains in the literary thought of Lu Hsün and Mao Tun were not intended as personal criticisms. On the contrary, Ch'ü regarded these cases as significant because Lu Hsün and Mao Tun had overcome the problems that often afflicted materialist thinkers. Their fatalistic view of objective forces and their tendency to minimize the importance of subjective forces, including artistic culture, were "temporary." Indeed, in the early 1930s Ch'ü looked upon Lu Hsün and Mao Tun as prime examples of revolutionary writers who successfully combined the materialist and idealist approaches, thus implying that the materialist group was in a better intellectual position to make the adjustments necessary to resolve the contradiction between the two major leftist groups. Finally, while Ch'ü conceded that Lu Hsün and Mao Tun had at one time underestimated the role of literature and writers and expressed fatalistic views about the role of objective forces, he never suggested that they had used the materialist conception of art to support the notion that art and politics should be separated.

The issue of the relationship between art and partisan politics was, of course, the focal point of the bitter polemical struggle between Ch'ü and Hu Ch'iu-yuan, one of the pillars of the ill-fated "Third Category" (*ti-san-chung jen*) literary movement launched in early 1932. Most studies of this well-known debate treat it as a classic confrontation between the Marxist and "liberal" positions on the problem of politics and art.[17] But it is quite apparent that Ch'ü himself preferred to regard Hu Ch'iu-yuan's ideas about the need to separate literature from politics as distortions of the materialist conception of art. Indeed, for Ch'ü, the significance of the Third Category movement was that Hu Ch'iu-yuan regarded himself as a Marxist literary thinker and a

16. Ch'ü Ch'iu-pai, "*Tzu-yeh* ho kuo-huo nien" [*Midnight* and the year of national products], *Tzu-yu t'an,* 3 April 1933; in CCPWC, 1:438.

17. Fu-tan ta-hsueh Chung-wen hsi, ed., *Chung-kuo hsien-tai wen-hsueh shih: 1919-1942* [A history of modern Chinese Literature: 1919-1942] (Shanghai: Shanghai wen-i ch'u-pan-she, 1959?), pp. 321-327.

faithful disciple of Plekhanov.[18] Thus the debate was important, in Ch'ü's estimation, because it brought to light the potentially "rightist" political implications of deterministic Marxist literary thought.

To understand Ch'ü's dispute with Hu Ch'iu-yuan it is necessary to consider Plekhanov's views on the role of the writer. Plekhanov categorically rejected the idealist utopian socialist belief that enlightened human beings might impose their will on material reality, and that the success or failure of the revolution in the superstructure would be decisive in the struggle to achieve socialism. Plekhanov's writings expressed no interest in artists as historical actors, but instead viewed them as products of history whose actions and words are determined by material forces.

Believing that the social role assigned to the artist by history was to reflect rather than act, Plekhanov expressed unrestrained contempt for the utilitarian and moral social roles imposed on artists by the populist critics. Indeed, in his study *Art and Social Life* Plekhanov made a spirited defense of the concept of "art for art's sake," an idea that had been repudiated time and again by the populists. Plekhanov firmly believed that his defense of artistic autonomy and art as an end in itself was entirely compatible with his materialist views. It was the utilitarians who interfered with the natural relationship between art and society by assigning artificial and unnatural political responsibilities to artists. Political engagement might contaminate the sanctity of art. Left alone, the artist would naturally (and quite often unconsciously) record the condition of society. Thus Plekhanov consistently stressed the dangers of utilitarianism. Like Engels, he was fearful that tendentious art might be robbed of its aesthetic element. In his review of *Mother*, Plekhanov accused Gorky of becoming a crude "propagandist of Marxist views."[19]

In denying that artists have any particular social or political responsibilities aside from "reflecting" life, Plekhanov was also rejecting the populist belief that writers had a duty to make direct contact with the masses in order to spread "scientific" and progressive ideas. To perform this role effectively, writers obviously would have to expand their reading audience by popularizing their writings. In Plekhanov's view, the debasement of art would result. In *Art and Social Life* he applauded Flaubert, who believed that "only second-rate writers could

18. Ch'ü's confrontation with the "Third Category" included exchanges with Hu Ch'iu-yuan and Su Wen (Tai K'e-ch'ung), a critic affiliated with the literary journal *Les Contemporaines*. I have stressed Ch'ü's remarks on Hu Ch'iu-yüan because, unlike Su Wen, Hu insisted that his views were compatible with Marxism. For a discussion of Su Wen, see Amitendranath Tagore, *Literary Debates in Modern China, 1918-1937* (Tokyo: The Centre for East Asian Cultural Studies, 1967), pp. 131-141.

19. Georg Plekhanov, *Art and Social Life* (London: Lawrence and Wishart, 1953), p. 14.

appeal to any broad reading public."[20] In other words, embracing the materialistic conception of art did not require writers to worry about their audience or its needs.

The literary views of Hu Ch'iu-yuan are, of course, well known. Like Plekhanov, he argued that precisely because there was a material or organic relationship between art and society, literature should not be used for explicitly utilitarian purposes. Just as the superstructure reflected the economic base, so too did literary works naturally reflect society. Writers need not be politically conscious to perform the role assigned to them by history. On the contrary, Hu asserted, to function properly the artist must be a detached and "objective" observer of society, not a participant in social movements. Hu thus opposed politically motivated literary movements such as the League of Left-wing Writers and the Nationalist literary organization. The "Third Category" would be composed of independent writers of neither the left nor the right.[21]

Ch'ü Ch'iu-pai's critique of Hu Ch'iu-yuan, one that had a profound influence on Lu Hsün, is in two lengthy articles entitled "The 'Free Man' Cultural Movement" and "Artistic Freedom and the Writer's Lack of Freedom." These works are significant because, beyond condemning Hu's point of view, Ch'ü attempted to account for such ideas by discussing them within the larger context of the evolution of modern literary thought, as Ch'ü understood it. It is clear that Ch'ü regarded Hu Ch'iu-yuan as a Marxist materialist who overestimated the extent to which the nature of the superstructure is determined by developments in its material base. Consequently, like other economic determinists, Hu underestimated the ability of writers to impose their consciousness upon society through their art. Stressing the fatalistic political implications of Hu's interpretation, Ch'ü observed:

> Hu Ch'iu-yuan's theory is a kind of hypocritical objectivism [*k'o-kuan-chu-i*]; he has washed away to the strong points of Plekhanov's theory and maximized Plekhanov's Menshevist development to an extreme—transforming it into a hypocritical bourgeois on-lookerism [*p'ang-kuan-chu-i*]. *In fact he refuses to recognize that art can influence social life.* . . . Of course art cannot effect a transformation of the social system, and must be regarded from beginning to end as being regulated by the mode of production and class relations. But art can also influence social life, and to a certain degree advance or block the development of class strug-

20. Ibid., p. 175.
21. Harriet C. Mills, "Lu Hsün, 1927-1936; The Years on the Left," (Ph.D. dissertation, Columbia University, 1963), pp. 178-184; Ts'ao Tzu-hsi, *Ch'ü Ch'iu-pai te wen-hsueh huo-tung* [Ch'ü Ch'iu-pai's literary activity] (Shanghai: Hsin wen-i ch'u-pan-she, 1958), pp. 80-94.

gle, changing somewhat the conditions of this struggle, and adding to or weakening the power of a given class.[22]

Aside from providing some indication of Ch'ü's own understanding of the relationship between the superstructure and the substructure, this remark is interesting because Ch'ü was accusing Hu, not of misinterpreting Marxist theory, but rather of advancing mechanistic ideas that were part of the Marxist tradition and held by Plekhanov himself. It is also significant that Ch'ü chose to make the seemingly contradictory statement that Hu's literary thought was both "bourgeois" and "Marxist." What he meant, of course, was that "Europeanized" Chinese writers tended to interpret Western Marxist literary thought on the basis of their interest in particular bourgeois schools. Indeed, there can be no question that Ch'ü (and Lu Hsün) perceived "Third Category" thought as merely the latest reincarnation of the odious and "liberal" literary theories of Liang Shih-ch'iu, Hu Shih, and other Crescent Moon leaders.[23] The difference was that in the case of the "Third Category," the separation of literature from politics was sanctioned by the highly deterministic theories of Plekhanov.

THE USES OF MARXISM: COUNTERING DETERMINISM

The key to the significance of Ch'ü's *Hai-shang shu-lin* collection of translations and commentaries on Western Marxist literary thought is its scope. To rectify the mistakes of the romantics, he selected works that stressed materialism. To criticize those who interpreted materialism in an excessively deterministic fashion, or applied Marxist theory dogmatically to China, he included works that emphasized subjective factors or the uniqueness of each historical situation.

The three selections in *Hai-shang shu-lin* that focus on the literary views expressed by Engels late in his life are rather typical in this regard. Engels' famous letter to Margaret Harkness, for example, seems to have been included because it raised questions about the tendency of some socialist materialists to exaggerate the role of objective laws of history. As a consequence, their works tended to portray the working class "as a passive mass, unable to help itself."[24] In another, more controversial letter addressed to the German critic Paul Ernst, Engels flatly rejected the idea that declarations about the

22. CCPWC, 2:954-955.

23. Ch'ü Ch'iu-pai, "'Tzu-yu jen' te wen-hua yun-tung" [The "Free Man" cultural movement], *Wen-i hsin-wen* [Literature and Art News], 23 May 1932; in CCPWC, 2:949.

24. "En-ke-ssu lun Pa-le-cha-k'e" [Engels on Balzac], HSSL, 1:25. For the complete translation of Engels' letter to Harkness, see Baxandall and Morawski, *Marx and Engels on Literature and Art*, pp. 114-116.

utter dependency of the superstructure on the economic base constituted a universal law of history. Ernst was wrong in assuming that
the ideological and cultural revolutions led by the Norwegian petty-
bourgeoisie, such as the women's liberation movement, were necessarily premature and insignificant. Under certain conditions, Engels
suggested, revolution in the superstructure could be quite important.
In contrast to Germany, Norway was a place where petty-bourgeois
individuals like Ibsen "are still possessed of character and initiative
and the capacity for independent action."[25] The materialist method of
analysis, Engels warned, cannot serve as a "ready-cut pattern on
which to tailor historical facts."[26]

Ch'ü's analysis of these letters, entitled "Engels on the Mechanistic
Conception of Literature," leaves no doubt as to his view of their
import for leftist readers in China. Far from concealing the fact that
Ernst was a Marxist intellectual, Ch'ü stressed that Ernst's tendency
to interpret the materialist conception in a highly deterministic manner was common among Marxists who once had been influenced by
bourgeois "naturalist" thought.[27] This legacy of dogmatism and
mechanistic determinism was later expressed not only in Trotsky's
writings on the relationship between the base and the superstructure,
Ch'ü added, but also in "Third Category" literary movements that
sought to separate art and politics.[28]

Neither did Ch'ü hesitate to characterize as "rightist" the political
implications of Ernst's views on cultural and intellectual revolution. It
was ludicrous and politically reckless, Ch'ü observed, to proclaim that
for objective reasons "petty-bourgeois" writers and intellectuals were
incapable of betraying their class interests to play a revolutionary
role. Western Marxist generalizations about the political character of
the European bourgeoisie in the seventeenth century could not be
applied mechanistically to the Chinese case.[29] In relatively backward
countries like Norway and China, he implied, revolutionary change in
the superstructure could be quite significant, and petty-bourgeois
writers could play an important political role.[30] But Ernst, like Hu
Ch'iu-yuan, underestimated the significance of the subjective factors
of will and consciousness. Such Marxist views constituted a "right"
deviation because they implied that human beings were the passive
objects of impersonal historical forces.

Although the issue of "proletarian" culture is raised in neither of

25. HSSL, 1:57.   26. HSSL, 1:55.

27. Ch'ü Ch'iu-pai, "En-ke-ssu ho wen-hsueh shang te chi-hsieh lun" [Engels on
the mechanistic conception of literature], HSSL, 1:52. Ch'ü's comments on Engels were
inspired, in part, by an article in *Literaturnoe Nasledstvo*, 1 (1931): 11-16, by Franz P.
Schiller.

28. HSSL, 1:37, 51.   29. HSSL, 1:39.   30. HSSL, 1:43.

the letters written by Engels, Ch'ü clearly believed that Engels was opposing a general point of view that seemed to rule out the possibility of a distinctively "proletarian" culture appearing on the historical scene well before the advent of the socialist stage or, in the Chinese case, even before the completion of the bourgeois-democratic revolution. If the superstructure of society was a mere reflection of the economic base, as the mechanistic materialists seemed to be saying, then it was inconceivable that a proletarian culture could emerge before the material prerequisites for such a culture were present. Similarly, the logic of the deterministic argument seemed to dictate that "proletarian" culture would have to be produced by the proletariat rather than by revolutionary petty-bourgeois intellectuals who had defected from their class. These familiar objections to proletarian culture, Ch'ü suggested, were based on assumptions about the relationship between the superstructure and the economic base that underestimated the extent to which the phenomenon of cultural revolution was independent of developments in the substructure. Needless to say, he did not agree with such views. But more important, the point of his essay was to demonstrate that his opposition to the literary views of Trotsky and Hu Ch'iu-yuan was based upon and related to the issues raised by Engels in his letters to Harkness and Ernst.[31]

In view of the great popularity of Plekhanov's writings on artistic culture, however, Ch'ü's lengthy article entitled "Plekhanov: Literary Theorist" must be regarded as the most provocative essay in *Hai-shang shu-lin*. Indeed, it was probably the first systematic and basically critical review of Plekhanov's aesthetic views to be published in China. Ch'ü's treatment of Plekhanov was intended to demonstrate that "Third Category" notions about the need to separate art from politics were derived, in part, from the Marxian school of aesthetics founded by Plekhanov. Although this tradition was widely regarded as the "orthodox" Marxist view of art and was upheld in postrevolutionary Russia by mechanistic materialists like Vladimir Friche, it was essentially "incorrect."[32] In fact, Ch'ü asserted, Plekhanov's literary views were a manifestation of his Menshevist political ideas. By Menshevist, Ch'ü meant Marxist explanations of historical change and the evo-

31. HSSL, 1:51-52. In some Chinese Marxist publications of the 1960s, Hu in fact is characterized as a "Trotskyite." See SWLH, 3:160.

32. Ch'ü Ch'iu-pai, "Wen-i li-lun-chia te P'u-lieh-ha-no-fu" [Plekhanov: literary theorist] (December 15, 1932), HSSL, 1:59-60. Ch'ü's remarks on Plekhanov were based upon an essay by I. Ippolit contained in *Literaturnoe Nasledstvo*, 1 (1931): 39-48. For Ch'ü's critical treatment of the Soviet critic Vladimir Friche, see Ch'ü Ch'iu-pai, "Lun Fu-li-ch'i" [On Friche], *Wen-hsueh yueh-pao*, 15 September 1932; in CCPWC, 2:564-573. Mark E. Shneider (*Tvorcheskii Put' Tsiui Tsiu-bo, 1899-1935* (Moscow: Izdatel'stvo Nauka, 1964), p. 96) asserts that this essay is based on a work by S. Dinamov.

lutionary development of the cultural superstructure that exaggerated the importance of objective or material forces.

Ch'ü disagreed with Plekhanov on two fundamental issues. Like Engels, he insisted that while material factors were important, and ultimately decisive, it was a misuse of the materialist method of analysis to assume that a single law of historical development could be applied universally. Second, he argued that Plekhanov's thesis on the relationship between superstructure and base was simply wrong. Ch'ü clearly placed more emphasis on the independence of the subjective realm, or more precisely, the interaction of subjective and material forces. Under certain circumstances, he implied, subjective forces could be exceedingly important.

Ch'ü proclaimed that Plekhanov's approach to art was not sufficiently "dialectical." He had responded to the "idealist" challenge of early proletarian cultural thinkers like Bogdanov, who alleged that art was capable of "organizing and creating life," by making artistic development totally dependent on the evolution of the economic base. Consequently, Plekhanov failed to appreciate the dialectical relationship between "spirit and reason" and between "artistic value and social value."[33] Instead he advanced what Ch'ü characterized as an "objectivist" or "biologistic" (*sheng-wu-hsueh-chu-i*) view of art.[34]

Ch'ü's article on Plekhanov is particularly interesting because he understood the logic underlying the apparent contradiction between Plekhanov's rigidly deterministic view of the relationship between artistic culture and the material base of society and his "liberal" assertion that artists must not participate in political activities or advocate utilitarian theories of art. It was precisely because Plekhanov's understanding of the relationship between art and society was so extremely mechanistic that he could argue that art would "naturally reflect real life and naturally benefit society."[35] In such a scheme, consciousness is irrelevant.

Ironically, Ch'ü reached the conclusion that in two important respects this sort of ultra-materialist conception of art was essentially "idealist" in nature. First, instead of using the materialist method of analysis as a means of understanding the peculiarities of artistic culture in each society and during each era, Plekhanov developed a single model of cultural development to which each individual case was supposed to conform. If the materialist method is made to serve as a model and if the literary historian is reduced to gathering data that seems to confirm the validity of the model, then, as Engels insisted, the materialist method has been converted into the idealist method. Second, Plekhanov's view of art was idealist because, despite its claim

33. HSSL, 1:66-67.   34. HSSL, 1:71-72.   35. HSSL, 1:66.

to account for the organic relationship between art and society, it advanced a "natural" theory of art that actually tended to divorce art from politics and sanction the existence of a "naturally" autonomous realm for the arts. Thus, the materialist conception was used by Plekhanov to deny the immediate relationship between art and society and to reject the notion that artists had any particular social or moral obligations. Like Lunacharsky before him, Ch'ü concluded his article by implying that Belinsky, a non-Marxist utopian socialist, had a much better grasp of the moral function of art than the materialist Plekhanov.[36]

In contrast to his exceedingly critical treatment of Plekhanov, Ch'ü presented the Marxist literary views of Paul Lafargue in an essentially positive light in *Hai-shang shu-lin*. In an essay entitled "Lafargue and His Literary Criticism," Ch'ü commended Lafargue's criticism of the pitfalls of bourgeois naturalism. One suspects, however, that Ch'ü's real intention was to identify the affinity between naturalism and highly deterministic Marxist theories of art. Ch'ü confined his discussion to Lafargue's comments on Émile Zola, a May Fourth hero whom Ch'ü was undoubtedly anxious to criticize; but his essay conveys the impression that his main concern was the relationship between the "naturalist" method and the pseudoscientific, mechanistic Marxist theories of Plekhanov and Hu Ch'iu-yuan. In Ch'ü's opinion, Lafargue's primary contribution to Marxist literary thought was his criticism of Zola's tendency to view the writer as an objective social scientist whose task it was to identify the natural laws governing the evolution of society in the same way that the biologist studied natural science.[37] This view of art was objectionable because it assumed that to reach valid conclusions about the laws that governed society the writer, or social scientist, was required to remain a detached and impartial observer.

To highlight the significance of Lafargue's work, Ch'ü translated a portion of his essay "Zola's *L'argent*," carefully pointing out that it was "a Marxist literary critique of naturalism" and the first of its kind to be translated into Chinese. In this work Lafargue strongly approved Zola's intention of painstakingly and scientifically "analyzing the colossal economic organisms of the modern era," and regarded this effort as an important departure from familiar European accounts of blundering romantic heroes.[38] The proletariat, Lafargue acknowledged, was actually in the best position to expose capitalism, but its cultural backwardness prevented it from articulating this critique. Thus, the task fell to well-intentioned intellectuals who did not them-

36. HSSL, 1:76-77.   37. HSSL, 1:215.
38. "Tso-la te *Chin-ch'ien*" [Zola's *L'argent*], HSSL, 1:170-171.

selves "participate in the life of the working class." But, despite his admiration for *L'argent*, a novel about the French stock exchange, Lafargue believed Zola had failed in many respects. In a comment that must have impressed Ch'ü as especially relevant to the situation among Europeanized realists and naturalists in China, Lafargue proclaimed:

> The novelists of our time, who call themselves naturalists and realists, and who pretend to follow nature, lock themselves up in their workshops and amass veritable mountains of scribbled and printed matter in which they imagine they can detect throbs of real life; they emerge from their comfortable abodes only occasionally for dilettante investigations in order to bring back from excursions the most elementary and superficial sensations. ...They claim that a writer must not only hold himself aloof from the political struggles of his time, but must even remain above human passions, in order the better to describe them.[39]

It was this idea, Ch'ü implied, that was carried on by Plekhanov and other Marxist writers who maintained that writers could play their natural role of "reflecting" society only by refraining from direct involvement in the movement for social change.

Lafargue also criticized what Ch'ü undoubtedly regarded as another important defect of naturalist writing, the tendency of clinical writers to catalog objectively every detail of social phenomena without reaching any general conclusions or moral judgments about the nature of historical change. A work like *L'argent*, Lafargue observed, "ought to express a definite conception of society. However, it does nothing of the sort."[40]

What do *Hai-shang shu-lin* and Ch'ü's other 1930s writings tell us about his understanding of the relationship between literature and society and the role of the writer? For one thing, he distinguished two poles within the Western Marxist tradition, the materialist and the idealist. Those leftists who had been influenced by bourgeois realism and naturalism during the early stages of "Europeanization" often were attracted to the materialist school, while those influenced by bourgeois romanticism were more inclined to embrace the idealist school. It is also clear that Ch'ü neither completely accepted nor totally rejected either intellectual tradition. He stressed the advantages of the materialist approach when criticizing the Marxist romantics. He emphasized the strengths of idealism when addressing the Marxist realists. Ch'ü believed that as the leader of the League of Left-wing Writers it was his task to unite the leftist literary

---

39. HSSL, 1:179. The passage quoted here is from a partial translation of Lafargue's essay that appears in *Dialectics*, 4 (1937):1-15.

40. HSSL, 1:210.

camp and thereby resolve the "contradiction" that separated the major leftist factions. This he tried by urging writers to discard the burdensome aspects of their respective schools while simultaneously synthesizing the potentially revolutionary elements of each tradition. In other words, a balance was to be struck between the subjective and objective approaches.

The materialist and idealist extremes were incompatible, and therefore caused factional strife. Also, they gave rise to undesirable political implications. Idealism, Ch'ü suggested, could produce both "rightist" transcendental individualism and "leftist" adventurism, as in the contrasting cases of Chiang Kuang-tz'u and Ch'ien Hsing-ts'un. Excessive materialism yielded "rightist" determinism and fatalism, as the case of Hu Ch'iu-yuan demonstrated. Ch'ü was quite explicit about identifying these deviations with particular Western Marxist literary thinkers: Bogdanov and the writers in Proletkult had overemphasized the role of the writer and the independence of the superstructure; Plekhanov and Trotsky had underestimated their significance.[41] For obvious political reasons, Ch'ü was in no position to include Lenin among those whose view of the relationship between the substructure and the superstructure was excessively deterministic, but it is apparent that Lenin belonged precisely in that category.[42]

Not surprisingly, Ch'ü adopted a compromise position on these important issues. His views on literature and revolution were not a return to either the idealism of his May Fourth years or the rigid determinism of 1923 when he first attempted to introduce Marxist literary thought. In rejecting these extremes, Ch'ü arrived at a position similar to the one adopted by Lunacharsky during the early postrevolutionary period when he was attempting to remind Soviet intellectuals of the significance of the literary thought of Chernyshevsky and Belinsky.

Lunacharsky occupies an unusually important position in the history of Western Marxist literary thought because, like Ch'ü, he attempted to find some middle ground between the essentially deterministic literary thought of Plekhanov and the idealist convictions of the populists and many advocates of proletarian culture. Lunacharsky's intellectual predisposition in the immediate postrevolutionary period in the Soviet Union is clearly related to a much earlier concern about the extremely mechanistic materialism of Plekhanov, who, in his opinion, had seriously neglected "the emotional and ethical side of scientific-socialist ideology."[43] Lunacharsky's intention was not to

41. CCPWC, 2:567-569.

42. In fact, in several places Ch'ü suggests that Lenin had a balanced understanding of the relationship between base and superstructure. HSSL, 1:66.

43. Sheila Fitzpatrick, *The Commissariat of Enlightenment: Soviet Organization and the Arts*

discredit the materialist conception of history, but rather to balance it by reemphasizing the "moral enthusiasm" he believed was present in original Marxism. The problem with Plekhanovism, he believed, was that while it offered a theory that explained the evolution of society, it looked upon individual human beings more as the passive objects of impersonal historical laws than as the active agents of historical change.

Even in his role as Soviet commissar of education Lunacharsky continued to be influenced by the ideas of his old friend Bogdanov, the founder of Proletkult. He did not believe that the development of artistic culture depended solely upon changes in the mode of production. On the contrary, he assumed that artistic culture can develop in advance of the economic base and even facilitate its transformation. Thus, in marked contrast to Lenin and Trotsky, Lunacharsky had no theoretical or personal objections to the proletarian cultural movement.

Lunacharsky's concern about the implications of Plekhanov's deterministic world view is also reflected in his outlook on the social role of the artist. Undoubtedly, he felt that thinkers like the populists and the futurist element in Soviet proletarian cultural circles had exaggerated the vanguard social role to be played by intellectuals, but it is apparent that Lunacharsky was not altogether hostile to "utilitarian" theories of art. He certainly did not accept the idea advanced by Plekhanov that political and moral content should only intrude unconsciously in art, nor did he agree with the view that the deliberate inclusion of tendentious content necessarily resulted in the debasement of art.

Lunacharsky's rejection of Plekhanov's interpretation of Marxist literary thought is best reflected in his sympathetic treatment of Plekhanov's principal foes, namely, Chernyshevsky and the populists. In a remarkable lecture on Chernyshevsky delivered at the Communist Academy in 1928, Lunacharsky asserted that the populists were people of great passion who sought to change the world.[44] By contrast, Plekhanov's theories were fatalistic and devoid of human emotion. His theories explained how "objective forces" shaped literature and art, but in doing so, they reduced the individual artist to observing "the progress of life," instead of exerting an "influence on the course of events." "Marxism," Lunacharsky proclaimed, "has given a correct view of the laws according to which social phenomena develop. But if we remove from Marxism the idea of consciousness, of the conscious

---

under Lunacharsky (Cambridge: Cambridge University Press, 1970), p. 2.

44. Anatoly Lunacharsky, *On Literature and Art* (Moscow: Progress Publishers, 1973), p. 51.

controlling of phenomena, of the active role we play; if we take up the standpoint that we must look upon social phenomena as processes, and discard any idea of active participation, then this would be Menshevik Marxism."[45] Chernyshevsky was not a Marxist, he pointed out, but "Marxists can accept his teaching." Looking out at an audience that undoubtedly included visiting Chinese intellectuals, Lunacharsky urged writers to "stretch out our hands to this utopian socialist who ascribed such huge significance to the power of the human reason and will. Marxism has cut these factors extremely short."

Like Lunacharsky, Ch'ü asserted that while the superstructure and artistic culture were shaped by material forces in general, the realm of the superstructure also enjoyed a certain degree of independence from the material base, and thus at times could profoundly influence developments in the economic and social realms. In his "Draft Postscript on Marxist Aesthetics," Ch'ü asserted that no one but vulgar materialists, entrapped by the myth of "bourgeois science," assumed that the only demand of the masses was a "full stomach." Genuinely realistic works demonstrated that the masses were also motivated by their visions and ideals of a just society. Those who were conscious of the "ultimate aims" of the revolution could impose their consciousness on society and thus facilitate the transformation of material reality.[46] In other words, a revolution in the superstructure can help generate change in the substructure.

Nevertheless, Ch'ü's views on these questions were somewhat ambiguous. He was no more successful than Marx and Engels in defining the extent to which, and the circumstances under which, artistic culture and the writer are independent of objective material forces. In some writings he stressed the dependency of the superstructure on the economic base; in other writings he seems to have suggested that at times when material conditions seemed especially unfavorable it was quite productive to promote a revolution in the superstructure.

45. Ibid., p. 52.   46. CCPWC, 2:1008.

9 Toward a Proletarian May Fourth

In China the laboring people are still in the Middle Ages in their cultural life.

CH'Ü CH'IU-PAI, 1932[1]

Ch'ü Ch'iu-pai responded to the "first" contradiction, the problem of factional strife within the leftist literary movement, by suggesting that the romantic and realist strains should and could be reconciled. But how did he propose to deal with the second and somewhat more complicated legacy of "Europeanization," the contradiction between all leftist writers and the Chinese people? Uniting revolutionary writers was important, but other problems remained. In his controversial criticism of the May Fourth generation of leftist writers, Ch'ü had stated explicitly that, owing to the distorted form assumed by the bourgeois-democratic cultural revolution in China, leftist writers had no first-hand knowledge of the daily life of the common people, used artistic forms imported from abroad, and wrote in a language unfamiliar to the average person. Consequently, revolutionary literary works were not read by the people, "Europeanized" writers were regarded as internal foreigners, and the leftist literary movement had a weak mass base. Of course, nonrevolutionary writers saw nothing problematic about these developments since they did not define their work in political terms or identify with social movements. But revolutionary writers hoped to use their art to effect social change, so they recognized, at least in theory, the desirability of actually reaching and

1. CCPWC, 2:885.

mobilizing the masses. A social revolution could hardly be carried out by intellectuals alone. Having identified this second problem, Ch'ü asked: How is a revolutionary literary intelligentsia that is alienated from society to make meaningful contact with the nonintellectual masses on whose behalf they presume to speak?[2]

Ch'ü addressed this question in an extraordinarily interesting and provocative series of essays that appeared in various League publications between September 1931 and July 1932. Works such as "The Real Questions of Proletarian Popular Literature and Art," "The Question of Popular Literature and Art," and "Another Discussion of Popular Literature and Art in Reply to Mao Tun" remain, even today, the most definitive Chinese Marxist treatment of the problem of the separation of revolutionary writers from the people. These writings are also significant because they represent Ch'ü's first attempt to write theoretical works. In contrast to his critical essays on idealism and materialism, which were clearly inspired by Western European and Soviet texts, Ch'ü's theoretical writings are more systematic and creative, and are related far more explicitly to the peculiarities of the Chinese revolutionary scene. Indeed, Ch'ü seems to have been well aware that the Western Marxist tradition had very little to say about the question of the relationship between revolutionary artists and the masses. Indeed, in China the conversion of modern writers to Marxism in the mid-1920s had perpetuated rather than resolved the issues related to this contradiction.

Ch'ü Ch'iu-pai believed that the various problems confronting the leftist literary movement, but especially the contradiction between revolutionary writers and the masses, could begin to be resolved by the launching of what he referred to as a "Proletarian May Fourth Movement" (*wu-ch'an-chieh-chi te wu-ssu*).[3] This was to be a two-stage

2. This is not to say that the question of the relationship between writers and the masses had not been discussed earlier or that spontaneous movements "to the people" had not included some literary figures. As early as 1902, in an essay entitled "On the Relationship between Fiction and National Sovereignty" in the first issue of *Hsin hsiao-shuo* [New fiction], Liang Ch'i-ch'ao had expressed a profound interest in popular culture as a means of promoting the growth of the "new citizenry" to save the nation. In his introduction to *Ta-chung wen-i lun-chi* [Essays on popular literature and art] (Peking: Pei-ching shih-fan ta-hsueh ch'u-pan-she, 1951), Ting I points out that during the May Fourth upheavals of 1919, the labor movement of 1925-1926, and the Northern Expedition, individual left-wing writers helped organize evening schools for workers, and participated in movements to the countryside to arouse the peasantry. The question of popular literature and art was also raised during the 1928 Shanghai debate on the nature of revolutionary literature, and was discussed in greater detail at a special conference sponsored by the League of Left-wing Writers in the Spring of 1930. In any event, Ch'ü clearly regarded all these efforts as exceedingly superficial and almost totally inadequate.

3. CCPWC, 2:886.

cultural movement in which neither the intellectuals nor the masses would act independently, and in which the bourgeois and socialist revolutions were to be linked. The first stage, led by literary intellectuals, was to begin immediately. Its goal was to complete the abortive May Fourth democratic literary revolution by bringing writers, and their literature, into direct contact with the masses for the first time.[4] The second stage was to be the unfolding of a distinctively socialist cultural revolution, one in which the participation of the masses themselves was to be steadily increased and the monopoly on the cultural arena by intellectuals thereby broken.

What is intriguing about Ch'ü's concept of a Proletarian May Fourth is his rejection of earlier movements for "proletarian literature" and "revolutionary literature" advanced by the romantics and the realists. Indeed, he stated quite frankly that the old revolutionary and proletarian literary theories of the Europeanized intellectuals were largely irrelevant to the masses of China's workers and peasants. Revolutionary and proletarian literature had failed because it was unknown to the people.[5] Had the bourgeois-democratic cultural revolution of the May Fourth period been completed, he argued, popularization of modern literature and art would have occurred. "The tendency to ignore this bourgeois-democratic task in the past," he wrote, "explains why, on the one hand, there has been so much hollow chatter in the revolutionary literary world about popular literature and art and the popularization of [elite] literature and art, while, on the other hand, there has been no effective struggle."[6] The concept of popular literature and art was, therefore, at the heart of Ch'ü's proposal. If a new movement for popular literature could be implemented, Ch'ü suggested, it would give rise to a Proletarian May Fourth, a cultural revolution that would go considerably beyond the iconoclasm and Europeanization of the original May Fourth Movement. It was to be a part-bourgeois, part-socialist cultural movement in a society where bourgeois-democratic political and cultural revolution had failed.

To understand Ch'ü's writings on this subject it is necessary to recognize that he discussed and used the term "popular literature and art" (*ta-chung wen-i*)[7] in a variety of ways. For example, he distinguished between "popularization of literature and art" (*wen-i ta-chung-hua*)[8] and "revolutionary popular literature and art" (*ko-ming te ta-chung wen-i*),[9] although both were integral parts of the Proletarian May Fourth Movement. "Popularization of literature and art" referred specifically to the sort of work that was to be done in the first stage of the Proletarian May Fourth, that is, the stage in which Europeanized revolutionary writers of the May Fourth generation were to complete

4. CCPWC, 2:886.   5. CCPWC, 2:878.   6. CCPWC, 2:887.
7. CCPWC, 2:892.   8. CCPWC, 2:878.   9. CCPWC, 2:892.

the bourgeois-democratic literary revolution by "popularizing" their work in an effort to reach as broad an audience as possible. In its unpopularized form, Ch'ü referred to this revolutionary literature somewhat sarcastically as "non-popular proletarian literature and art" (*fei-ta-chung p'u-lo wen-i*).[10]

The second term, "revolutionary popular literature and art," was meant to include popularized literary works done by intellectuals; but more important, it also referred to the necessity of beginning an altogether new, and somewhat utopian, literary movement in which the workers and poor people themselves participated—not merely an artistic movement "about" or "for" the masses, but one in which the masses themselves played an active role. This would occur in the second, and more socialist, stage of the Proletarian May Fourth. Thus the movement for revolutionary popular literature and art was to give rise to a cooperative cultural movement in which the revolutionary intellectuals and the masses would be allied in practice. Intellectuals of proletarian consciousness would have to play a leading role in the Proletarian May Fourth Movement, especially in the first stage, because the literary level of the masses was so low. Gradually, however, the participation of the masses would increase. "The workers and peasants themselves," Ch'ü explained, "will study to the point where they can make use of their own language capabilities."[11]

Another important distinction made by Ch'ü was between "literature" (*wen-hsueh*) and "literature and art" (*wen-i*). In most cases, Ch'ü used the term *wen-hsueh* to refer specifically to creative writing that generally appeared in the form of the novel or short story, and perhaps occasionally in the form of Western dramatic literature. Literature, in this narrow sense, dominated not only the nineteenth- and early twentieth-century European scene, but was also identified with the Europeanized May Fourth generation. What is noteworthy is that Ch'ü clearly believed that there were definite limitations on the ability of *wen-hsueh* to serve as the literary base for the popular revolutionary cultural movement in China. Ch'ü conceded that some of this *wen-hsueh* might be classified as "proletarian" on the basis of its content, but it was not *popular* proletarian literature.[12] It was written on behalf of the working class and peasantry yet, strangely, inaccessible to them. Given the illiteracy and semiliteracy of the people, any revolutionary artistic movement based on these Western literary forms was bound to have limited appeal.

Consequently, when discussing the new Proletarian May Fourth,

10. Ch'ü Ch'iu-pai, "P'u-lo ta-chung wen-i te hsien-shih wen-t'i" [The real questions of proletarian popular literature and art], *Wen-hsueh*, 25 April 1932; in CCPWC, 2:855–856.

11. CCPWC, 2:874.   12. CCPWC, 2:886.

Ch'ü made only occasional references to *wen-hsueh*, and then only in the context of *wen-i*. Indeed, his definition of the term *wen-i* was intentionally broad, and made use of social as well as aesthetic standards.[13] Even the most unsophisticated forms of peasant folk art were to be included within the framework of *wen-i*, despite the fact that they were not considered great or even good by serious bourgeois aesthetic standards. The point is that Ch'ü's broad definition of literature and art was designed to assault the supremacy of creative writing among radical intellectuals, and to lay the broadest possible foundation for the popular literary and artistic movement he envisioned. "Exclusive" Western literary categories were to be replaced by "inclusive" mass standards.

In promoting a movement for revolutionary or "proletarian popular literature and art," Ch'ü by no means meant to imply that China had no popular literary and artistic tradition. He was profoundly aware of the existence and powerful influence of certain popular forms. And he devoted considerable energy to criticizing his revolutionary colleagues for having rejected this popular cultural heritage at the outset, during the high tide of New Culture iconoclasm, and for failing later to take seriously the influence of popular cultural forms in the cities. The problem was that many revolutionary writers, deeply influenced by Western artistic standards, had little interest in these unpolished forms, and felt the greatest reluctance in taking them seriously as art. Consequently, Ch'ü argued, the revolutionary literary camp for years had been unable to evaluate the strength of conservative cultural forces.[14] Ch'ü's intent was to demonstrate to revolutionary intellectuals that there was indeed a popular literary and artistic life among the masses, despite the fact that it was politically conservative and ignored by Europeanized radicals.

Ch'ü was primarily interested in two general types of popular art present in China in the early 1930s: first, the massive body of traditional literature and art found in both rural and urban settings; and second, the modern, commercialized art born in the cosmopolitan coastal cities. Although Ch'ü categorized these complementary forces as "reactionary popular literature and art" (*fan-tung te ta-chung wen-i*) on the basis of their generally nonrevolutionary or apolitical content, he had an appreciation of their influence and wide appeal among the masses.[15] Leftist writers rejected traditional popular art because it was insufficiently "modern," and dismissed modern Europeanized popular art because of its poor artistic quality and because it failed to

13. Ch'ü Ch'iu-pai, "Tsai-lun ta-chung wen-i ta Chih Ching" [Another discussion on popular literature and art in reply to Mao Tun], *Wen-hsueh yueh-pao*, 15 September 1932; in CCPWC, 2:898, 900.

14. CCPWC, 2:885, 891.   15. CCPWC, 2:885, 892.

offer constructive social commentary. Furthermore, like Marx, most radical writers abhorred the commercial prostitution of the arts. Ch'ü shared these views, but was reluctant to conclude that leftist writers should simply ignore popular forms. He was unwilling, therefore, to remain silent while this particular element of Western Marxist literary thought was used by Chinese writers to rationalize their desire to disregard popular forms. Once reformed, the popular tradition would be an important foundation of the Proletarian May Fourth Movement, and the vehicle for linking literary intellectuals and the people.

The subject matter of traditional popular literature and art was quite varied: stories of ghosts and supernatural manifestations, Buddhist miracles and reincarnations, love and aspects of daily life, crimes and their detection, feats of strength and courage, and historical tales "commemorating exploits of great men or the founding and collapse of dynasties."[16] Not only did these traditional forms provide popular entertainment, Ch'ü repeatedly pointed out, but their content played an important, even crucial, role in shaping the consciousness of the illiterate or semiliterate masses.[17]

The other variety of influential "reactionary popular literature and art" discussed by Ch'ü was the slick, commercialized art forms of the treaty ports. He implied that Europeanization actually had two different effects on the arts in China; the first was the influence of serious Western bourgeois literary culture among Chinese intellectuals, and the second was the impact of popular commercialized art among the urban masses. Although modern commercialized forms of popular literature and art were obviously influenced by the traditional forms mentioned above, there were important differences. In popular urban art, the content was updated, and effective use was made of Western mass production techniques. By the 1920s and 1930s, for example, Western cinema had become a significant new form of commercialized art.[18] In the literary world, the two most important forms of commercialized art were known as "mandarin duck and butterfly" (*yüan-yang hu-tieh*) and "black screen" (*hei-mu*) literature. The content of this literature was generally quite frivolous, focusing mainly on tales of romance, detective stories, melodramatic social novels, and a certain amount of pornography.[19] In discussing the commercial concerns

16. Robert Ruhlmann, "Traditional Heroes in Chinese Popular Fiction," in Arthur F. Wright, ed., *The Confucian Persuasian* (Stanford: Stanford University Press, 1960), pp. 142-143.

17. CCPWC, 2:891.

18. See Ch'eng Chi-hua's important study *Chung-kuo tien-ying fa-chan shih* [A history of the development of Chinese cinema] (Peking: Chung-kuo tien-ying ch'u-pan-she, 1963), 1:1-168, for a history of the cinema in China from its introduction to 1931.

19. Wei Shao-ch'ang, ed., *Yüan-yang hu-tieh p'ai yen-chiu tzu-liao* [Research Materials on the Mandarin Duck and Butterfly School] (Shanghai: Wen-i ch'u-pan-she, 1962), pp. iii-v.

of such writers Perry Link has observed: "Instead of raising consciousness, most of them strove to raise only their weekly word total
which directly correlated with their pay."[20]

In formulating his theory of proletarian popular literature and art,
Ch'ü argued that the revolutionary literary movement should take
note of the popularity of these forms, and use them as weapons to
raise consciousness rather than income. By failing to do so, leftist
writers cut themselves off from an important source of mass support.
In short, Ch'ü was strongly in favor of the revolutionary literary
movement becoming active in the realm of popular art. "Reactionary
popular literature and art" could be transformed into "proletarian
popular literature and art."

THE QUESTION OF CONTENT

The first stage of Ch'ü's Proletarian May Fourth was expected to
confront many problems, including the question of why Europeanized
leftist writers were regarded as "foreigners" by the people. Part of the
reason for this phenomenon was that almost none of the revolutionary literature produced by intellectuals treated the kinds of problems
faced by the people in their daily lives. The content (*nei-jung*) of leftist
literature was too narrow and unrelated to popular concerns. The
"proletarian" literature produced by the romantics appeared to be
concerned with working-class content; but because the romantics had
very little direct knowledge of working-class life, they treated the
proletariat in an exceedingly unrealistic manner. The revolutionary
literature produced by the realists was good, in Ch'ü's opinion; but it
was largely confined to penetrating accounts of the problems encountered by the urban petty-bourgeoisie during a revolutionary period. Ch'ü fervently believed that such literature was necessary. He
personally regarded Mao Tun's *Vacillation* [*Tung-yao*] and Lu Hsün's *The
True Story of Ah Q* [*Ah Q cheng-chuan*] as his favorite fictional works,
although neither discussed the proletariat.[21] Indeed, Ch'ü defended
Mao Tun and others against the attacks of romantics like Ch'ien
Hsing-ts'un who asserted that revolutionary literature should only
portray the proletariat.[22] The fact remained, however, that the people
were not seriously interested in literature about the moral dilemmas
faced by intellectuals. Realist writers, for their part, insisted that this
was one of the few subjects with which they were genuinely familiar.

To resolve this problem, Ch'ü suggested that the new revolutionary popular literature and art would have three broad categories.

20. Perry Link, "Traditional-Style Popular Urban Fiction in the Teens and Twen-
ties," in Merle Goldman, ed., *Modern Chinese Literature in the May Fourth Era* (Cambridge:
Harvard University Press, 1977), p. 327.

21. TYTH, p. 161.   22. CCPWC, 2:891.

First, there was a need for artistic work that directly confronted and refuted the view of society and human nature contained in traditional and urban popular art. Second, the revolutionary movement required popular artistic work that analyzed and explained the roles played by *all* classes and social groups in society—works that, in effect, educated a culturally deprived public. Third, there was a need for popular art that *realistically* portrayed the various revolutionary struggles in which the people were currently engaged.[23]

Most striking about Ch'ü's early attempt to define the scope of content for revolutionary popular art was his obvious desire to be as inclusive as possible. In his opinion, hardly any subject was inappropriate for revolutionary analysis. He urged League members to write about laborers, the urban poor, peasants, soldiers, strikes, land reform, guerrilla warfare, warlordism, imperialism, the Kuomintang, and much else. Historic events such as the Boxer Rebellion, the 1911 Revolution, the May Fourth Movement, the May Thirtieth Movement and the formation of the Kiangsi Soviet Republic could provide colorful subject matter for popular tales.[24] "Content can be drawn from traditional source material, giving rise to a 'New Yueh Fei' or a 'New Water Margin.' It can be 'romantic adventures' or revolutionary struggles such as 'The Taiping Revolution,' 'The Canton Commune,' or 'Chu Teh and Mao Tse-tung Atop Chingkang Mountain.'"[25] Ch'ü also advised writers to translate more foreign revolutionary literature for Chinese readers.

It was essential to Ch'ü that art *about* and *for* working people be introduced by leftist intellectuals during the first stage of the Proletarian May Fourth. The problem of whether intellectuals were sufficiently qualified to write about the lives of the masses would not have arisen if Ch'ü had assigned no role to Europeanized writers in the movement he proposed. It is reasonable to assume that writers of genuine working-class origin would have possessed an intimate knowledge of the daily life of the masses. But owing to the low cultural level of the masses and the extreme difficulty of organizing workers' movements in Kuomintang-controlled areas, Ch'ü's revolutionary popular art movement was to be led, initially, by intellectuals. Thus the issue of their almost total unfamiliarity with the lives of workers and peasants remained a problem. As a partial solution, Ch'ü made a bold, populist-type appeal for Europeanized writers to "go to the people to learn" (*hsiang ta-chung ch'ü hsueh-hsi*).[26]

Discussion about the content of the new revolutionary popular literature and art forced this issue into the open. Leftist writers, who

23. CCPWC, 2:864-867.   24. CCPWC, 2:865.
25. CCPWC, 2:891-892.   26. CCPWC, 2:872-873, 875, 878.

at first thought that the "popularization" (*ta-chung-hua*) movement Ch'ü had in mind for the first stage was simply a matter of technique in writing, soon learned that it involved the very way in which they lived. In writing about students and the petty-bourgeoisie, the issue was perhaps only a matter of technique; but in writing about workers and peasants, the problem of content was much more complex, for it required that writers go out among them to learn about their lives. The issue became a matter of attitude. Dismissing the empty talk about "popularization" that had been heard since the May Fourth Movement, Ch'ü asserted that revolutionary intellectuals "still have not resolved to go among the ranks of the working class (*tsou-chin kung-jen chieh-chi te tui-wu*). They still view themselves as teachers of the masses, and dare not 'go to the masses to learn,' consequently in word they advocate 'popularization' but in fact they oppose and obstruct it."[27] He concluded that "popularization of the writer's life" (*tso-chia sheng-huo te ta-chung-hua*) was equally important and actually indistinguishable from "popularization of literature and art." In fact, in Ch'ü's estimation, it was "the most central question."[28]

THE QUESTION OF FORM

Because Ch'ü believed there was an intimate relationship between content and form (*hsing-shih*), he realized that literature and art that dealt with the everyday lives of the common people could do little to bridge the gap between intellectuals and the masses if it was expressed in alien forms. The masses, Ch'ü insisted time and again, had no taste for the Europeanized forms brought to China during the May Fourth literary revolution. Ch'ü condemned the content of traditional popular forms, but he believed it essential that the revolutionary cultural movement make use of "traditional forms" (*chiu te hsing-shih*) simply because they were popular among the people and relatively easy to understand. Ch'ü further explained:

> Revolutionary popular literature and art must begin by utilizing the strong points of traditional forms—things that the masses are accustomed to reading or viewing, such as fiction, lyrics, or opera—gradually adding new ingredients, and cultivating new habits among the masses, so that working together the artistic level of both writers and readers will be raised. With regard to form there are two points to be made for traditional popular literature and art: one, its relationship to the oral literary heritage, and the other, its simple and plain methods of narration

27. CCPWC, 2:875.   28. CCPWC, 2:877.

and exposition. Revolutionary popular literature and art should heed these two advantageous points. Fiction of the storytelling variety can reach the illiterate masses, and this is very important for revolutionary literature and art.[29]

In effect, Ch'ü was charging that the iconoclastic rejection of traditional forms by the Europeanized generation of leftist writers had contributed to the failure of the leftist literary movement to build a mass base. In his writings on the Proletarian May Fourth, therefore, he attempted to reacquaint leftist writers with a seemingly inexhaustible tradition of popular art, which included storytelling (*shuo-shu*), serialized picture books (*lien-huan t'u-shu*), puppet theatre (*mu-t'ou-jen hsi*), shadow plays (*ying-hsi*), poetic ballads (*ko-ch'ü*), local opera (*ko-chü*) folk music (*hsiao-tiao*), dialogue drama (*tui-hua ch'ü*), heroic tales (*ku-shih yen-i hsiao-shuo*), boatmen's songs (*t'an-huang*), and poetic Buddhist sermons (*hsuan-chüan*).[30]

Although Ch'ü probably favored these sorts of traditional popular forms (most of which he had been exposed to as a child in Kiangsu), he also recommended that writers make use of modern popular forms. For example, in "The Question of Popular Literature and Art" he made a remarkable statement about the need to imitate the despised "butterfly" form. Ch'ü proclaimed that, among other things, the new popular art could be "a new form of 'social gossip,' because if reactionary popular literature and art can make use of things such as the trial of Yen Shui-sheng, the love affair between Huang and Lu, and the Shu Ching murder trial, then revolutionary popular literature and art should also describe the family life of the laboring people and the question of love, while describing the landlord-capitalist class for everyone to see."[31] Ch'ü also mentioned the appeal of modern Western cinema and popular "cinematic peep shows" (*hsi-yang ching*), a technically crude, but inexpensive, form of street cinema in which three or four individuals peer through separate eyepieces to watch a brief "moving" picture.[32]

Although Ch'ü's warnings about the exclusivity of Western forms and his appeals for greater use of Chinese forms reflect deep-rooted nationalist concerns, it must be noted that in the tense political environment of the early 1930s he was extremely careful to avoid "nationalist" appeals of any sort. The "traditional forms" he constantly discussed were perceived, not as things belonging to the whole "nation," but rather as the cultural forms of the exploited classes. Indeed,

29. CCPWC, 2:890.

30. CCPWC, 2:856, 863, 885; and Ch'ü Ch'iu-pai, "Ta-chung wen-i ho fan-tui ti-kuo-chu-i te tou-cheng" [Popular literature and art and the anti-imperialist struggle], *Wen-hsueh tao-pao*, 28 September 1931; in CCPWC, 2:913.

31. CCPWC, 2:892.   32. CCPWC, 2:856.

Ch'ü made several attempts to place the movement for revolutionary popular literature and art in an "international" context. Once the movement is launched, Ch'ü wrote, "experience will teach us many new methods and the people themselves will be able to create new forms. To rely totally on traditional forms is to walk down the path of surrender."[33] Ch'ü did not equate internationalism and cosmopolitanism, however. Cosmopolitanism was a May Fourth concept that usually referred to familiarity with the Western bourgeois cultural world. Internationalism, on the other hand, was linked in Ch'ü's mind to the revolutionary experience of the world's oppressed people, and especially the experience of the Russian revolution. Speaking of form, not content, Ch'ü recommended that leftist writers learn from popular literary and artistic movements outside China. He mentioned specifically the "worker's correspondence movement" and "reportage literature," tested in Russian cities during the 1920s, and popularized (*ta-chung-hua*) translations of Western revolutionary literary works.[34]

But Ch'ü placed the greatest emphasis on traditional popular forms. Above all, he stressed those forms that fall into the broad category of the performing or visual arts, forms that do not require literacy on the part of either the artist or the audience. He implied that these performing, oral, and visual art forms should be of interest to revolutionaries because they are, by definition, collective art forms. He seems to have been bothered by the fact that reading and creative writing are activities carried on by a single person. Storytelling, theatre, and musical forms, on the other hand, are collective art forms for artists and audiences alike. Dramatic productions, for example, require script writers, actors, and a large audience, and thus are infinitely superior to fiction for doing educational work among people who are mostly illiterate. It is apparent, therefore, that Ch'ü's remarks on the problem of form raised serious questions about the ability of Western-style fiction to build bridges between intellectuals and the masses.

THE QUESTION OF LANGUAGE

If the "popularization" stage of Ch'ü's Proletarian May Fourth Movement was going to be successful it would also have to involve a new language (*yü-yen*) revolution. He realized that most leftist literary intellectuals of the Europeanized May Fourth generation believed that this question had been settled during the struggle between *pai-hua* and *wen-yen* during the New Culture Movement.[35] For Ch'ü, however, the question of language needed to be reopened because he rejected the notion that the May Fourth literary vernacular, which he character-

---

33. CCPWC, 2:890.   34. CCPWC, 2:883.   35. CCPWC, 2:887.

ized somewhat pejoratively as "new classical" (*hsin wen-yen*), was the language of the people or could be used as the foundation of the popular literary movement. The transition from "literary revolution" to "revolutionary literature" had been carried out, but the "continuation and final completion of the literary revolution" was neglected.[36] The "new classical" language, which Ch'ü sometimes referred to as "mule" language (*fei-lü fei-ma*), was a sterile combination of *wen-yen* and foreign languages.[37] Its grammar, syntax, and vocabulary were much more dependent upon classical, European, and Japanese norms than writers were willing to admit. Because it disregarded "the customs of spoken Chinese" it was incomprehensible to the people.[38] Ch'ü acknowledged that literary revolutions of this sort should be led by the bourgeoisie during the bourgeois-democratic stage of revolution; but, owing to the defection of the bourgeoisie in China, this task would have to be completed under proletarian political auspices. In no event could it be bypassed.

Ch'ü approached the problem of language much as he dealt with the problem of form. As far as he was concerned, a language could not be regarded as "vernacular" unless it could be understood by common people when read aloud. Using this standard, he asserted that the vernacular language of "traditional fiction," such as *Hung-lou meng*, *Shui hu chuan*, and *San-kuo yen-i*, was preferable in many ways to the semi-classical and semi-Europeanized May Fourth vernacular. By traditional vernacular, Ch'ü simply meant the language of popular fiction and theatre of the Ming and Ch'ing periods, exactly the sort of thing he enjoyed in his youth.[39] The authors of these popular works often came from gentry backgrounds, but, Ch'ü pointed out, they had been greatly influenced by the common vernacular language spoken in the streets. Consequently, the masses were still quite familiar with this tradition. Ch'ü conceded that it was not the language spoken by modern Chinese, but because it was "the speech of traditional drama" and derived from the "common speech of the Sung and Yuan dynasties" it was relatively close to the people.[40] Ch'ü noted with some irony that although Europeanized leftist writers insisted upon using the more elite form of May Fourth vernacular, writers of "reactionary popular literature and art" recognized the popularity of traditional vernacular, and used it to shape the world view of the masses.[41] It must be noted, however, that while Ch'ü advocated the use of traditional vernacular as a means of making immediate contact with the masses and competing with butterfly literature, he rejected it as a permanent foundation for the new popular cultural movement.[42]

36. CCPWC, 2:887.   37. CCPWC, 2:596.   38. CCPWC, 2:887.
39. CCPWC, 2:888.   40. CCPWC, 2:888-889.   41. CCPWC, 2:889.
42. CCPWC, 2:888-889, 907.

Ch'ü's Proletarian May Fourth was to be a "revolutionary move-ment for colloquial literature" (*su-hua wen-hsueh ko-ming yun-tung*), and its language was to be "street vernacular" (*p'u-t'ung-hua*).[43] Ch'ü stressed that *p'u-t'ung-hua* was not the "national language" (*kuo-yü*) en-dorsed by the Kuomintang, but a dynamic and entirely modern Chi-nese language that was emerging in China's large cities among the working class and urban poor. This new language, he argued, was a product of the collapse of traditional Chinese society in the period of imperialist domination of China's coastal cities, particularly Shanghai. Forced off the land in periods of dislocation, poor people migrated to the major urban centers to seek employment. Local dialects and id-ioms were brought together and influenced by the vocabulary and grammar of a variety of foreign languages. "In the major cities," Ch'ü wrote, "which have drawn people from all parts of China, and in the modern factories, the proletariat's language has already evolved, in fact, into a Chinese street vernacular."[44] Although it blended local dialects and foreign phraseology and syntax, it was—unlike its May Fourth counterpart—"placed on the foundation of the customary grammar of spoken Chinese." *P'u-t'ung-hua* was above all an urban language. Because Ch'ü's activities were urban based in the early 1930s, he thought it extremely unlikely that a modern Chinese lan-guage could be developed on a foundation provided by any particular rural dialect. The proletariat, he insisted, "cannot be compared to the rural peasantry; the language of 'rural folk' is primitive and obscure."[45]

In addition to promoting the use of street vernacular, Ch'ü also raised some provocative questions about the Chinese written script. He argued, as he had in the late 1920s, that millions of Chinese were illiterate and thus denied educational opportunities because it was extremely difficult and time-consuming to master the written script. In an attempt to focus attention on the need to reform the system of writing, Ch'ü continued to talk about the work he had done in Mos-cow between 1928 and 1930 to develop a phonetic script that would eventually replace the difficult ideograms altogether.[46]

43. CCPWC, 2:858.

44. CCPWC, 2:889. Some of Ch'ü's colleagues, including Mao Tun, were not con-vinced that "street vernacular" had already reached a high level of development. In later works Ch'ü softened his stand by stating that the "street vernacular" was in a relatively early stage of development. His central point, however, was that May Fourth vernacu-lar was virtually useless. See CCPWC, 2:895.

45. CCPWC, 2:889. Also see pp. 908-909. Ch'ü was referring to the local colloqui-alisms used by peasants and not to regional differences in pronunciation and structure. He realized that there would be a need to create special Kwangtung and Fukien liter-ature.

46. For example, see Ch'ü Ch'iu-pai, "Lo-ma-tzu te Chung-kuo-wen hai-shih jo-ma-tzu Chung-kuo-wen" [A romanized Chinese or a nauseating Chinese] (July 24, 1931), in CCPWC, 2:651-683. Also see p. 907.

THE RELATIONSHIP BETWEEN
ARTISTIC "VALUE" AND ARTISTIC "EFFECT"

It is hardly surprising that Ch'ü's suggestions concerning the best ways to generate a popular literary and artistic movement caused leftist writers to ponder their role in society and the standards for evaluating literature. Was it the primary responsibility of revolutionary writers to focus the content of literature on the lives of the people, and to "popularize" literary works of a relatively high artistic level in order to make them accessible and meaningful to the masses? Or was it their primary duty to raise the cultural and artistic standards of the masses in order to develop their appreciation of more sophisticated aesthetic standards and more varied subject matter?

Typically, Ch'ü's approach to this dilemma was to try to reach a compromise. He was sympathetic to the complaints of those who felt that "popularization" would result in the lowering of artistic standards. What alternatives, however, were open to writers who genuinely sought to make direct contact with a culturally impoverished mass populace? He agreed that the cultural level of the people had to be raised so they could enjoy good literature; but how was that going to be done if writers were not willing to "popularize" their works in the meantime? While Ch'ü was sympathetic to the general problem of maintaining standards, he knew that the "universal" standards many leftist writers had in mind were the "foreign" standards adopted by the May Fourth generation. He suspected, therefore, that some writers raised the standards question as a means of defending the accomplishments of the May Fourth literary revolution.[47] They believed that abandoning the content, form, and language of their literary revolution was too high a price to pay for making contact with the masses. In brief, some leftist writers insisted that the cultural level of the people would have to be raised first, but had little or no interest in engaging in such work themselves.

For Ch'ü, this issue was vital to the outcome of the revolution and therefore could not be avoided or ignored. It involved nothing less than the struggle to influence the consciousness of the people. If something was not done to bridge the gap between revolutionary intellectuals and the masses, the problem would simply worsen. He stated repeatedly that writers must recognize that the May Fourth literary revolution was not a success but a failure. And it was not a democratic cultural revolution. "In China," Ch'ü insisted, "the laboring people are still in the Middle Ages in their cultural life."[48] Furthermore, he pointed out, leftist intellectuals should enter the popular literary field because one of the announced goals of the revolution

47. CCPWC, 2:855.   48. CCPWC, 2:885.

was to create a society in which all people would have an opportunity to develop culturally. Thus for both tactical and utopian reasons Ch'ü recommended that the movement for "popularization" begin immediately, and he urged May Fourth writers to understand that what they perceived to be a lowering of standards was in fact a consequence of the distortions produced by the abortive bourgeois-democratic cultural revolution. Ch'ü had no illusions about the difficulties writers would face. "The struggle to create a revolutionary popular literature and art will be long and hard."[49]

Ch'ü reminded his colleagues that he was not insensitive to the question of aesthetic standards. He indicated in several essays that during the first stage of the Proletarian May Fourth, the one in which intellectuals were to play a leading role, the appearance of original or translated works directed at an educated audience would be welcomed, and he explicitly referred to the language used by Lomonosov, Pushkin, and Turgenev as a model for this sort of literature.[50] But, in his view, the most fundamental problem was not the danger of the disappearance of Europeanized literature, but rather the prospect of its continued domination of the revolutionary literary scene. The new popular movement, Ch'ü conceded, would be deficient by May Fourth artistic standards, but more important, it would afford the leftist literary movement an opportunity to place itself on a broad base for the first time. Many mistakes would be made in the beginning (just as at the outset of the May Fourth Movement), and the aesthetic level would necessarily be low by May Fourth standards (and Ch'ü lamented the low level). Nevertheless, the masses would be involved for the first time. The process of dispersing writers among the people was, in Ch'ü's opinion, a matter neither of debasing art nor of raising the cultural level of the people to a predetermined alien standard, but rather a matter of communicating with the people in order to define new and thoroughly Chinese standards of artistic excellence.[51] It was to be, not a movement in which intellectuals "enlightened" the masses, but a truly cooperative movement into fresh but uncharted waters.

In effect, Ch'ü was arguing that the conventional categories of content, form, and language were inadequate critical yardsticks for the new popular artistic movement. These categories were important, but so too was the question of artistic effect. How could a work of art be considered great if it did not have a noticeable effect on society, if it was not popular? The artistic level of revolutionary May Fourth literature was reasonably high, but its effect on the people had been miniscule.[52] What Ch'ü proposed therefore was that the effect a work of art had on society should be considered when determining its value.

49. CCPWC, 2:892. Also see p. 900.   50. CCPWC, 2:857-858, 910.
51. CCPWC, 2:874, 884.   52. CCPWC, 2:900, 909.

"Europeanized" May Fourth literature failed to meet the new standard because it was not popular. To make revolutionary literature more popular, its content, form, and language would have to be altered. This process would result in a temporary lowering of artistic standards during the transition phase. To compensate for the stress placed on "aesthetics" in the May Fourth period, "effect" would now be emphasized. Eventually, however, a balance would be established. Ch'ü saw no reason why revolutionary literature and art could not be both popular and aesthetically pleasing. Indeed, in his exchange with Mao Tun on these questions, he condemned "poster and slogan" art.[53]

The implications of Ch'ü's "new criticism" were quite radical. Europeanized writers were used to having their works appraised by other literary specialists; but on the matter of "effect" there could be only one judge, the people in the streets. Writers who sincerely wanted to reach a mass audience, Ch'ü suggested, were obligated to use whatever means possible to find out what common people thought of their work. Inevitably this would involve going out into the streets to record their suggestions and to observe their cultural life. Despite his poor health, Ch'ü himself set an example by making periodic visits to storytellers and popular theatrical productions in order to familiarize himself with the forms, content, and language to which the people were accustomed.[54]

VACANT LOTS AND BACK ALLEYS

Ch'ü Ch'iu-pai's ideas about a Proletarian May Fourth Movement are of additional interest because a significant part of his time after 1931 was devoted to transforming theory into practice, or as he put it, bringing experimental popular art to the "tea houses, vacant lots, factories, back alleys, and street corners."[55] Considering the lack of enthusiasm among many leftist writers and Kuomintang suppression of revolutionary activities, it is remarkable that attempts to implement these practical programs were made at all. Nevertheless, in the three-year period from 1931 to the end of 1933 a number of leftist artists attempted to popularize their works by using traditional and modern popular forms, and showed a willingness to help build a truly proletarian literary and artistic movement by assisting potential working-class artists.

At the end of his essay "The Real Questions of Proletarian Popular Literature and Art," Ch'ü addressed himself to the first of the prob-

53. CCPWC, 2:900.

54. Mark E. Shneider, *Tvorcheskii Put' Tsiui Tsiu-bo, 1899-1935* (Moscow: Izdatel'stvo Nauka, 1964), p. 185.

55. CCPWC, 2:873.

lems: how could Europeanized literary intellectuals begin the task of popularizing their artistic work? Ch'ü responded by calling for the organization of a "Street Literary Movement" (*chieh-t'ou wen-hsueh yun-tung*) that would enable leftist writers to conclude the abortive bourgeois-democratic literary revolution. Ch'ü saw two aspects in the Street Literary Movement. First, literary intellectuals would popularize their work by writing in the "street vernacular" and by employing a variety of traditional and modern popular forms. Second, artists would bring these works directly to the people in the streets, factories, slums, tea houses, and bookstalls. This would enable them to make personal contact with the people, learn about their daily lives, and be exposed to their criticisms. "It is not that the people should serve the writers," Ch'ü proclaimed, "on the contrary, it is the writers who should serve the people (*kei ch'ün-chung fu-wu*)." "It is not enough," he added, "to simply have proletarian consciousness, it is also necessary to perceive things in the same way as the proletariat."[56]

In the League of Left-wing Writers there were a number of activities for young writers who were interested in the Street Literary Movement. One, for example, was referred to by Ch'ü as "reportage literature" (*pao-kao wen-hsueh*), a form used widely both in the Soviet Union in the late 1920s and in the United States (in leftist literary magazines such as *New Masses*) throughout the 1930s.[57] Ting Yi, a student of Chinese reportage literature, has observed:

> The main characteristic of reportage is that it gives quick information on current events. It is highly journalistic in nature but is different from the news items of newspapers. A piece of reportage is more or less a feature article. It gives vivid word pictures of people and scenes which convey to the reader almost a visual picture of the event and enables him to understand the message the writer wants to put across. The chief aim of reportage is to give timely reflection as well as keen analysis of the constantly changing political and social scene.[58]

In the early 1930s, the content of Chinese reportage literature dealt mainly with the Japanese threat and the failure of the Kuomintang government to resist its advance.

Ch'ü was also responsible for encouraging leftist writers to break into the flourishing cinema industry, long dominated by foreign interests and a relatively small number of Chinese capitalist enterprises. Cinema was, of course, a logical choice for inclusion in Ch'ü's movement for popular art. Immensely popular among the inhabitants of

---

56. CCPWC, 2:872-873.   57. CCPWC, 2:899.

58. Ting Yi, *A Short History of Modern Chinese Literature* (Peking: Foreign Languages Press, 1959), p. 211.

China's coastal cities, Chinese films and foreign films (mostly American) shown in China were intended, from the time of their introduction around 1915, to provide escapist entertainment that focused on crime detection, love stories, and heroic traditional tales.[59] Although the popularity and influence of the cinema was undeniable, the leftist literary movement had made no effort to employ this modern form until 1931.

In the "Program of Action" of the League of Left-wing Dramatists adopted in September 1931, some emphasis was placed on the desirability of bringing the cultural revolution to the film industry. League members, it was recommended, "must produce scripts for the film-makers; join in the film production of the various companies; organize a society for film research and bring together progressive actors and technicians to form a base for China's left-wing film movement; and we must criticize and analyze the present state of the Chinese cinema."[60] The problem was that film making required elaborate equipment and extensive resources, neither of which the League possessed. But after the Japanese bombing attack on Shanghai in January 1932 in which a number of film companies and almost half the film theatres were destroyed, a few Shanghai film companies, especially Star (Ming-hsing), expressed interest in cooperating with leftist dramatists for the purpose of making patriotic films.[61] Recalling the debate within the League on this question, Hsia Yen, a prominent League member, has written that he, Ch'ien Hsing-ts'un, and Cheng Po-ch'i were asked to submit scenarios for consideration. They discussed the matter with Ch'ü, who was apparently the advisor to the League's film group, and decided to go ahead with the arrangements.[62] According to Jay Leyda, the success of this experiment "went beyond the hopes" of Ch'ü and his colleagues.[63] Others who cooperated with the Ming Hsing, I Hua, and Lien Hua film studios include Hung Shen, Ting Ling, Hua Han, and Ou-yang Yü-ch'ien. In June 1932, however, the Kuomintang concluded an agreement with Japan that called for the suppression of all anti-Japanese cultural activities. On the morning of November 12 a contingent of the Kuomintang's Blue Shirt organization, a fascist so-

59. Commenting on the impact of foreign films, Lu Hsün noted: "European and U.S. imperialists dispose of their old guns to give us war and unrest, then they use old films to astound and stupefy us. After the films and guns get even older, they will be sent to the interior of China, to enlarge their potency of making people foolish." Jay Leyda, *Dianying: Electric Shadows: An Account of Film and Film Audience in China* (Cambridge: M.I.T. Press, 1972), p. 61.

60. Leyda, *Dianying*, p. 74.   61. Ibid., pp. 72–73.

62. Hsia Yen, "Kuan-nien Ch'ü Ch'iu-pai t'ung-chih" [In memory of comrade Ch'ü Ch'iu-pai], *Wen-i pao*, 30 June 1955. Also see Hsia Yen, "History of Filmmaking in China and Party Leadership," *Jen-min jih-pao*, 16 November 1957; in *Survey of China Mainland Press*, no. 1695, pp. 28–29.

ciety modeled on the European black and brown shirts, raided and completely destroyed the I Hua studio in an effort to "cleanse the cultural world."[64] Eventually, leftist film activity was forced entirely underground.

Much less is known about other attempts made by literary intellectuals to popularize their work. Some sources indicate that the members of the League of Left-wing Dramatists supported the anti-Japanese troops of General Ts'ai T'ing-k'ai in February 1932 by going to the front lines to stage dramatic performances among the troops.[65] It is also known that following the organization of the League of Left-wing Artists in the winter of 1931, dozens of artists concentrated on turning out woodblock prints, an art form promoted by both Ch'ü and Lu Hsün.[66] Finally, the League magazine, *Crossroads*, carried a substantial number of ballads and folk tunes written by leftist intellectuals. One of Ch'ü's many contributions was a lengthy song entitled "Japanese Troops on the March," which was apparently quite popular in Shanghai after the January 28 Incident.[67]

It is important to recognize, however, that the new movement for popular art involved more than the popularization of works done by literary intellectuals. At the end of "The Real Questions of Proletarian Popular Literature and Art," Ch'ü touched upon the problem of creating effective cooperative programs aimed at increasing the participation of the nonintellectual masses in the revolutionary cultural movement. The Proletarian May Fourth was to bring about not only the popularization of intellectual artistic works in the final stages of the bourgeois-democratic literary revolution, but also the beginning of a truly popular and more socialist revolution in which the masses were to participate directly. Ch'ü discussed all these possibilities under the general heading of a "Workers', Peasants' and Soldiers' Correspondence Movement" (*kung-nung-ping-shih te t'ung-hsin yun-tung*). Ch'ü urged young intellectuals who had succeeded in making contact with workers to build an effective network of communications among the factories and working-class neighborhoods. Such a correspondence movement, he thought, might be built around a popular newspaper that contained not only popular journalism, but also comic strips, popular tunes based on current events, and film reviews. Ch'ü believed that commentaries written by workers would be the founda-

63. Leyda, *Dianying*, p. 77.   64. Ibid., p. 88.

65. Nym Wales, *Red Dust: Autobiographies of Chinese Communists* (Stanford: Stanford University Press, 1942), p. 188.

66. Ibid., p. 187.

67. Ch'ü Ch'iu-pai, "Tung-yang jen ch'u ping" [Japanese troops on the march], *Wen-hsueh tao-pao*, 28 September 1931; in CCPWC, 1:364-389.

68. CCPWC, 2:873-874.

tion of a genuinely proletarian literary movement.[68] Young literary intellectuals should "foster working-class writers (*p'ei-yang kung-jen tso-chia*).[69] "Literature and art consultation groups" (*wen-i ku-wen hui*) should be organized for the dual purpose of educating literary intellectuals about the realities of working-class life while encouraging them to provide patient assistance to semiliterate workers interested in the arts.[70]

Virtually all of these programs were undertaken by the League during the three years after January 1931. In fact, a Workers' and Peasants' Correspondence Movement Committee was established under the leadership of Hu Yeh-p'in, one of the League writers executed in February 1931. A number of literary and cultural groups were formed in Shanghai factories, and emphasis was placed on an array of popular forms including storytelling, folk songs, wall newspapers, dramatic skits, and poetry. The League of Left-wing Dramatists organized a well-known mobile drama group called the "Blue Denim Troupe" (*Lan-shan t'uan*). One young participant recalled: "In the factory districts we also organized *Lan-pu* or 'Blue Denim' dramatic groups, named for the heavy blue working clothes of the factories. We had four groups in several factories, all made up of local factory workers. First we started evening schools, and then the dramatic groups developed from these."[71] Although most of this popular cultural activity seems to have collapsed by 1934 because of increasing Kuomintang pressure, these early cooperative ventures won significant popular support in the period after the formation of the League.

THE SIGNIFICANCE OF THE
PROLETARIAN MAY FOURTH MOVEMENT

The importance of Ch'ü Ch'iu-pai's writings on revolutionary popular literature and art is not that they resulted in any elaborate practical program in the hostile environment of Shanghai but that they discuss, in an unusually frank and perceptive manner, the condition of the leftist literary movement in the early 1930s. Ch'ü's appeals for a popular literary movement can be fully appreciated and properly understood only in the context of his review of the history of the modern literary revolution and his controversial criticism of the May

69. CCPWC, 2:877.   70. CCPWC, 2:903.

71. See Nym Wales, *Red Dust*, pp. 187-188. According to Shneider, *Tvorcheskii Put'*, p. 156, each of the four drama groups had between twenty and forty members. He also mentions the existence of twelve working-class "literary groups" with a total membership of two hundred. In twelve Shanghai factories wall posters were put up by these groups two or three times a week. Wall posters reportedly played a significant role in promoting the objectives of the 1932 Shanghai bus strike.

Fourth generation of leftist writers. The theory of popular literature and art was Ch'ü's formula for resolving what he believed to be one of the central contradictions of the revolutionary literary movement after 1928—that is, the contradiction between Europeanized leftist intellectuals and the masses. Furthermore, by engaging in such a movement, the writers themselves were to be united, thus easing a second contradiction, the divisiveness between contending factions within the leftist literary movement.

Ch'ü's ideas on popular culture are interesting precisely because they stood in diametrical opposition to the May Fourth literary values accepted by most Europeanized revolutionary writers. For example, Ch'ü repeatedly recommended that they immediately abandon their overriding commitment to European forms of creative writing such as the novel and short story in favor of a variety of traditional and modern popular forms that had been ignored by most writers. Ch'ü encouraged them to pay much less attention to their urban intellectual audience and more to a vast audience composed mainly of illiterate and semiliterate workers and urban unemployed. Having redefined and broadened standards for judging the value of a work of art, he suggested that popularization ultimately would "raise" not "lower" artistic standards. He insisted that literary intellectuals would have to go out among the masses of poor people to "learn from them." Ch'ü stressed both the need for literary intellectuals to bring their work directly to the people in the street, and the priority of spending long hours training writers and artists from among the masses. Furthermore, he confronted them with the prospect of a revolutionary literary movement no longer monopolized exclusively by intellectuals, particularly in the second and more socialist phase of the "Proletarian May Fourth." Considering that the issues raised by Ch'ü continue even today to be important problems confronting the Chinese cultural world, it is not at all surprising to find that there was considerable resistance to these notions among leftist writers in the early 1930s. His views were undoubtedly perceived by most radical literary intellectuals as a serious challenge to the validity of virtually every literary concept valued by the Europeanized May Fourth generation. Many artists, particularly those in the film and drama fields, made an effort to respond to all or some of these challenges, and continued to do so for years thereafter; others were unable even to begin.

10 An Interpretation of Marxist Theory

The method of popularization must be used to introduce [foreign] revolutionary proletarian literary theory as well as international literature and art into China. . . . But naturally it is also necessary to conduct systematic research on the many old views of literature and art found among the masses of Chinese people, in order to understand and criticize such views. This means applying Marxism-Leninism in a practical way to study literary phenomena in China, especially the literary life of the common people.

CH'Ü CH'IU-PAI, 1932[1]

Ch'ü Ch'iu-pai made no serious attempts to place his literary thought in a Western socialist context by comparing his ideas to the views on literature and society held by Marx, Engels, the Russian populists, Plekhanov, the early proletarian cultural thinkers, Trotsky, Lenin, Lunacharsky, or others whose works were known in China in the early 1930s. Aside from the fact that he devoted most of his time to more immediate problems, it is undoubtedly true that it would not have been politically prudent to suggest that he differed from the writings of Marx, Engels, or Lenin. On the contrary, Ch'ü often implied that his ideas were entirely consistent with those expressed earlier by these leading figures. Neither did Ch'ü organize his views under the exact headings mentioned in the introduction to this study: the relationship between base and superstructure, the social role of the writer, the impact of capitalism on the arts, the correct method of regarding the artistic heritage of the past, and the problem of art

1. CCPWC, 2:883.

during the transition to socialism. Nevertheless, it is possible to identify Ch'ü's position on these fundamental issues by referring not only to his writings on the contradiction between the idealist and materialist factions within the League, but especially to his numerous essays on popular art. Indeed, Ch'ü had much to say about the basic problems under consideration in this study, although he did not always do so in an explicit manner.

Ch'ü's position on the nature of art—or, more specifically, the relationship between the economic base and the cultural superstructure—is an interesting case in point. It has already been shown that Ch'ü's essays on the intellectual weaknesses and undesirable political implications of the idealist and mechanistic extremes on this matter suggest that he, like Lunacharsky, attempted to balance the two poles by stressing the *interaction* between base and superstructure. But Ch'ü's formula, as expressed in these particular works, did not assign *equal* weight to base and superstructure. Changes occur first in the economic base, then cause changes in the superstructure, including artistic culture. The superstructure, once transformed, is then able to react upon and influence material life. Thus, compared with Plekhanov, he provided for a fair measure of independence for the superstructure; but he argued that material factors are ultimately decisive. These statements are significant for two reasons: they show that Ch'ü was desperately seeking to reconcile the romantic and realist currents, and they indicate a shift in his own thinking. Though he had been inclined in 1923 to stress the deterministic strain present in the writings of Marx and Engels on base and superstructure, he now emphasized the strain that underscored the relative independence of artistic culture.

It is crucial to understand, however, that Ch'ü's writings on popular literature, which are more original and thus a good deal more revealing than his works on idealism and materialism, appear to say something noticeably different about the relationship between base and superstructure. Indeed, one is struck by the emphasis Ch'ü placed on the role of the superstructure in contemporary Chinese society. Although objective factors were by no means ignored, Ch'ü time and again characterized popular artistic culture as an enormously powerful realm almost entirely responsible for shaping the consciousness and world view of the masses.

Strictly speaking, this outlook does not contradict the materialist conception of art. One could argue, as Ch'ü did, that this elaborate superstructure was nothing but the "product" of the prevailing economic base. But Ch'ü, like the populists, turned materialist doctrine on its head when he looked to the future. He argued that because the superstructure is so important in China, it must be altered before the economic base can be transformed.

Ch'ü left the clear impression, therefore, that the future of the revolution will depend to a large extent upon the ability of intellectuals to help bring about a revolution in popular consciousness. He was suggesting that, in the Chinese case, the cultural revolution had primary importance. Revolution was not a matter of waiting for objective conditions to become more favorable. On the contrary, one suspects, Ch'ü's faith in objective forces and the historical inevitability of socialism had waned during the period of revolutionary ebb tide so that he began to believe that objective factors were really not so important. In his "Draft Postscript on Marxist Aesthetics," Ch'ü strongly implied that revolution is a two-way street and not simply a matter of the inexorable flow of history. The speed and direction of social change are determined, to a significant degree, by the ideas that prevail in society. The introduction of new ideas, including "lofty ideals" about the good society of the future, can result in an acceleration of the revolutionary process. Similarly, either the failure of revolutionary forces to engage in the cultural and ideological revolution, or the perpetuation of the "consciousness of a previous age," can serve to retard the revolution or even erase revolutionary victories already won.[2] In all his writings on popular art and mass consciousness, Ch'ü suggested that conditions in China were such that a revolutionary breakthrough might occur first in the realm of the superstructure and only later in the social and economic spheres. Ch'ü, like the populists and early proletarian cultural theorists, asserted that in some cases revolution in the superstructure is a precondition for revolution in the base of society.

Ch'ü's stand on the issues of the social role of the writer followed logically from his view of the relationship between base and superstructure. He believed that intellectuals in general and artists in particular had an exceedingly important, even indispensable, role in the transformation of society because they occupied a strategic position in the superstructure. Their gentry or petty-bourgeois class backgrounds would not prevent them from playing a revolutionary role if they succeeded in transforming their own consciousness. Intellectuals who had been "proletarianized" not only were qualified to lead the masses, they had a moral obligation to do so by using their art to transform the consciousness of the people. What is interesting about Ch'ü's position on intellectuals, however, is his belief that it is somehow easier for those, like himself, who were raised as gentry intellectuals to become "proletarianized" and play an active role than those who

2. CCPWC, 2:1008-1009.

had already become "bourgeois" intellectuals. It is not that Ch'ü believed there was anything inherently revolutionary about gentry thought (although he did at times suggest that the gentry was relatively close to the masses), but rather that the gentry, as a precapitalist social class, was relatively uncontaminated by bourgeois thought; thus, its political progress could be faster. To become leaders and contributors to society, writers would have to avoid or cut short the "bourgeois stage" in their own intellectual development.

Ch'ü, of course, believed that his positions on these two issues were Marxist. They were based upon his own Marxist analysis of conditions in China, which he clearly thought were quite different from conditions in Europe. He stated repeatedly, in his criticisms of Plekhanov, that Marxist theory could not be applied mechanistically to the study of non-European or noncapitalist societies. Instead Marxism was a method of analyzing the unique phenomena of each society. But how should the conclusions he reached about the relationship between the economic base and artistic culture, and the social role of the writer, be characterized? It is possible to say that Ch'ü, like Lunacharsky, was developing a line of thought actually present in original Marxism. This may be correct: but what is truly striking about his views is the extent to which they break with the writings of Plekhanov, Trotsky, and Lenin. Indeed, it appears that Ch'ü accepted many of the assumptions held by the populists and the various early-twentieth-century proletarian cultural groups active in Russia. However, he never acknowledged this.

On the effect of capitalism on artistic culture, Ch'ü, like the utopian socialists, was in agreement with the basic perspectives contained in the Marxist classics. For example, he believed that the early impact of capitalism had given rise to greater professional specialization and division of labor, and that artistic life became increasingly commercialized in capitalist society. As a result, the cultural condition of the masses was extraordinarily poor. With the loss of distinctively human artistic sensibilities, which include the capacity to create and appreciate art, people are only able to achieve a crippled development. But while Ch'ü agreed that these were the consequences of capitalism and were already features of modern Chinese cultural life, he by no means believed that a full development of the capitalist cultural stage was unavoidable or historically necessary for China. On the contrary, it was his fervent hope that this odious stage, in both its cultural and economic forms, could be bypassed. Ch'ü was able to take such a position precisely because he placed so much emphasis on the importance of cultural revolution and revolution in the superstructure. If the capitalist economic stage was not a precondition for socialist revolution, then the undesirable consequences of the capitalist cultural stage need not be accepted either. And, because Ch'ü did not accept the crippled cultural condition of the masses as an inevitable consequence of the development of capitalist productive forces, he did not believe that their cultural liberation would have to be postponed until the appropriate material conditions for such a mass cultural revolution existed.

It is true, of course that virtually all of Ch'ü's writings of the 1930s insisted upon the completion of the "bourgeois-democratic" cultural revolution. But he was able to uphold this concept only because he radically redefined it. Ch'ü's references to the bourgeois-democratic stage must be understood in the light of his more significant statements about the "abnormal form of capitalism in China."[3] In the early 1920s Ch'ü may have believed that some sort of capitalist revolution could occur in China; but he had obviously abandoned that belief by the early 1930s. The bourgeois-democratic revolution had failed in China and had no chance of being completed by the bourgeoisie in the future. The bourgeois-democratic cultural revolution that Ch'ü called for was intended not as a means of promoting bourgeois culture, but rather as a way of securing a victory in the struggle against "feudal" culture. In fact, Ch'ü made it quite clear that, aside from combating feudalism, the purpose of the bourgeois-democratic cultural revolution was to move away from rather than toward the bourgeois cultural stage.[4] This cultural revolution was to be led by the representatives of the proletariat, not the bourgeoisie, and would be linked to the upsurge of a new and truly socialist cultural revolution. Thus, while Ch'ü may have accepted basic Marxist assumptions about the effect of capitalism on artistic culture, he attempted to persuade his sometimes reluctant colleagues that such conditions were by no means inevitable or historically necessary and that the liberation of human "artistic sensibilities" need not be postponed.

Even more interesting is Ch'ü's position on the manner in which socialist revolutionaries should regard the artistic heritage of the past, especially the bourgeois past. All his writings indicate quite clearly that he did not agree that the Chinese proletariat and its intellectual representatives had an obligation to inherit and digest the bourgeois cultural tradition. On the contrary, he believed that such a process would actually retard the development of the revolution. He urged writers to reject the bourgeois heritage. But one must realize that to Ch'ü "bourgeois" culture meant "foreign" culture—or more specifi-

3. CCPWC, 2:995.
4. Mao Tse-tung's treatment of the "bourgeois-democratic stage" in his writings of the 1940s was quite similar. See Maurice J. Meisner, "Utopian Socialist Themes in Maoism," in John W. Lewis, ed., *Peasant Rebellion and Communist Revolution in Asia* (Stanford: Stanford University Press, 1974), p. 238.

cally, the "Europeanized" culture that dominated the modern literary scene in the post-May Fourth era. In short, Ch'ü tended to view this issue through nationalist lenses. Tolstoy and other utopian socialists rejected bourgeois cultured because it was "unnatural": Ch'ü rejected it because it was "European." To embrace "bourgeois" culture, from Ch'ü's point of view, was to embrace the culture of the imperialist nations that exploited China. He bitterly denounced "pseudo-nihilists" who rejected their own culture in favor of the alien culture of the enemy.[5] In "Long Live the Literary Warlords" he stated quite directly that some "national traitors" still had not been exposed twelve years after the May Fourth Movement.[6] The Europeanized culture of the May Fourth generation was quite literally "foreign" to the people, he proclaimed, and its acceptance by Chinese intellectuals had prevented the completion of a more democratic cultural revolution in China.

It is clear, however, that Ch'ü did not reject the Marxist *principle* of maintaining cultural continuity during periods of great cultural discontinuity. What he objected to was the idea that China's cultural salvation necessitated the "Europeanization" of Chinese society.[7] This may or may not have been what Marx had in mind, but Ch'ü strongly rejected anything that suggested this. He therefore disapproved of leftist writers who believed that Western Marxist statements about the need for the European proletariat to "inherit" European bourgeois culture meant that the Chinese proletariat must therefore inherit *European* bourgeois culture. To Ch'ü this was only an attempt to justify on Marxist grounds the fundamentally European orientation of the May Fourth generation of leftist writers. In this regard, he indicated, Western Marxist theory had played a conservative role in China.

It would be misleading to suggest that Ch'ü's position on the Western bourgeois heritage was xenophobic. He undoubtedly was pleased that modern Chinese writers were a good deal more cosmopolitan than their European counterparts, who knew little or nothing about the Asian cultural tradition. And despite his abrasive statements, he believed that Chinese intellectuals should remain receptive to foreign culture. Ch'ü himself was reading the works of Hugo, Pushkin, and Chekov in the early 1930s. The danger was not that Western literature would cease to be influential, but rather that leftist writers would continue to ignore their own literary heritage.

Ch'ü's view of the "bourgeois heritage," therefore, should not be confused with the position of the futurist proletarians active in Russia

---

5. CCPWC, 2:998.   6. CCPWC, 2:595.

7. It has been suggested, with good cause, that Marx believed that economic and cultural Europeanization would be required of all nations forced to or hoping to modernize. See H. Carrère d'Encausse and Stuart Schram, eds., *Marxism and Asia* (London: Allen Lane, 1969), p. 116.

at the turn of the century, who asserted that *all* artistic traditions of the past were contaminated and irrelevant to the new age of proletarian creativity. For Ch'ü, the "bourgeois" heritage was to be rejected primarily because it was foreign, and not from rejection of the "building block" theory of cultural continuity per se. But, like the proletarian cultural theorists, Ch'ü was not preoccupied with the fact that the masses did not have access to what Marx and Engels regarded as the universally valid bourgeois classics. For Ch'ü, the cultural liberation of the masses need not involve the assimilation of the Western bourgeois heritage.

Ch'ü's attitude toward Western culture is especially interesting in that he was one of the very few Chinese Marxist thinkers who shared at least some common ground with the most traditionalistic and reactionary elements in society. Of course, it was not his intention to revive, much less celebrate, traditional Confucian culture; but neither did he believe that leftist intellectuals should adopt a nihilistic attitude toward their national cultural heritage, or uncritically accept the culture of the modern West. Such an approach was humiliating, psychologically devastating, and therefore unacceptable. In a remarkable letter to Lu Hsün entitled "On the Question of Revising the History of Chinese Literature," written in June 1932, Ch'ü stated that literary specialists should give much more attention to the history of Chinese literature and art. He made no attempt to deny that Western literature had profoundly influenced the development of modern Chinese literature, but he rejected the notion that Chinese literature had not developed prior to the introduction of Western culture.[8] Ch'ü had no time to engage in such scholarship himself, but, he suggested, if Chinese scholars used a materialist method of analysis they would be able to determine the interaction between economic development and cultural development in each historical period. Ch'ü recommended that writers study the elite literature of each period in order to learn about the class structure of society, judge the extent to which elite literature was influenced by the literature of the common people, and assess the means by which the gentry used literature to shape the thought of the people.[9] In his opinion, the increasing commercialization of society during the Sung, Yuan, Ming and Ch'ing periods was accompanied by the development of an "urban people's literature" (*shih-min wen-hsueh*) which was highlighted by the activities of storytellers and the-

8. The question of pre-May Fourth origins of modern Chinese literature is discussed by Milena Doleželová-Velingerová, "The Origins of Modern Chinese Literature," in Merle Goldman, ed., *Modern Chinese Literature in the May Fourth Era* (Cambridge: Harvard University Press, 1977), pp. 17-35.

9. Ch'ü Ch'iu-pai, "Kuan-yü cheng-li Chung-kuo wen-hsueh shih te wen-t'i" [On the question of revising the history of Chinese literature] (June 10, 1932); in CCPWC, 2:974.

atrical troupes. This, Ch'ü held, was the indigenous origin of bourgeois culture in China.[10]

Ch'ü conceded that the bourgeoisie and its new culture did not develop normally in China. As a partial explanation he pointed to the great resilience of the gentry as a social class, and its ability to control the new class and influence its culture.[11] Ch'ü said nothing about the fate of this new popular art in the period following the introduction of the foreign bourgeois cultural revolution during the May Fourth period; we can assume, however, that he saw it as existing in the form of urban traditional popular literature and art and continuing to have an impact on popular thought. Thus in Ch'ü's view, both the internal and external bourgeois cultural revolutions failed: one because it was infected with "feudalism," and the other because it was alien. Of the two, however, Ch'ü seemed to be more interested in the post-Sung bourgeois literary tradition because it was thoroughly Chinese and could more readily provide the healthy rootstock for his Proletarian May Fourth Movement. Though far from modern, its language and forms were more familiar to the people. In a sense, then, Ch'ü was doing precisely what Marx insisted was necessary. He was telling writers that they could not simply cut themselves off from the past: they must study the national past, identify its unique course, and critically inherit its cultural legacy. In the Chinese case, however, this would necessarily involve a rejection of the Western bourgeois stage so admired by Western Marxists. There could be no separate bourgeois cultural stage for China.

Finally, Ch'ü's writings of the early 1930s reflect quite clearly his position on the issue of the relationship between art and socialist revolution. Differing from Plekhanov, Trotsky, and Lenin, Ch'ü believed that it was possible and necessary to build a distinctively "proletarian culture." Furthermore, in contrast to at least some of the early Russian proletarian cultural theorists, he felt it was possible to have such a cultural movement not only before capitalist society passed from the historical scene but even before a *capitalist* revolution had been fully achieved. Ch'ü consistently referred to the "Proletarian May Fourth" as the beginning of an essentially socialist cultural movement in a precapitalist society. Despite his insistence that the movement would witness the completion of the bourgeois-democratic cultural revolution, its basic aim was to challenge the influence of traditional "feudal" culture and "bourgeois" foreign culture.[12] This does not mean that Ch'ü believed there were no material prerequisites for

10. CCPWC, 2:976.   11. CCPWC, 2:976.

12. This was Ch'ü's way of saying that China was a "semifeudal" and "semicolonial" society, a formulation developed in greater detail by Mao Tse-tung in the late 1930s and 1940s.

the development of proletarian culture, but it does show that, in his judgment, the existence of a fully developed capitalist system was not one of the prerequisites.

A socialist cultural movement could begin before state power was seized by socialist revolutionaries: the utopian goals of the socialist cultural revolution could also be addressed in the present. Ch'ü's remarks about the importance of the "people's own literary revolution" suggest that he did not believe that attempts to resolve the problems of the alienation of artistic sensibilities and the cultural backwardness of the masses had to be postponed to a time when objective conditions were more favorable.[13] On the contrary, Ch'ü implied that precisely because material conditions were so unfavorable it was necessary to devote more attention to the cultural revolution. By calling for the immediate enrichment of the cultural lives of the people, by insisting upon their direct participation in the new cultural movement, and by stressing the need to make people conscious of the utopian or ultimate goals of the socialist revolution, he was implying that the lofty *ends* of the socialist promise could be converted into a practical *means* of achieving a revolutionary victory. Thus Ch'ü was motivated by considerably more than purely strategic considerations. He viewed the spread of culture as an important strategic means to a more grandiose revolutionary end; but Ch'ü looked upon the release of the latent but inherent creative and artistic impulse of the "several hundreds of millions" as a legitimate revolutionary end in its own right.[14] Ch'ü hoped that what Marx referred to as the "richness of the subjective human sensibility"[15] might be awakened during the act of revolution itself.

Ch'ü's position on the role to be played by intellectual cultural experts also differed from the formula spelled out by Trotsky and Lenin. He assigned an important leadership role to literary intellectuals and hoped that they would transmit the knowledge they possessed. However, they were to act not as "bourgeois" experts, but rather as "proletarianized" intellectuals. Before they could serve, they would have to merge with the people and transform their lives. Indeed, their task was to create conditions that would permit the masses to produce their own intellectuals, and thus end their dependence on proletarianized specialists. Ch'ü's outline of the Proletarian May Fourth makes it quite clear that although intellectuals are to play a leading role in the first stage (because of the cultural poverty of the people), they will gradually be replaced during the second or a later socialist stage, and eventually disappear as a social group.

13. CCPWC, 2:881.   14. CCPWC, 2:889-900, 909.
15. Quoted in Georg Lukács, *Writer and Critic and Other Essays* (New York: Grosset and Dunlap, 1971), p. 65.

Ch'ü's position on the need for intellectuals to popularize their work and take into account the response of the common people did not really refute Plekhanov's assertion that art would be debased if writers felt they were obligated to address a mass audience. It would be misleading to say that Ch'ü disagreed with this view. He realized that by any—including bourgeois—standards, the quality of the new arts would not be high at the outset, but he believed that such a step was unavoidable if a mass cultural revolution was going to be carried out. If revolutionary artists failed to act, they would be partly responsible for the perpetuation of the cultural poverty of the people. Ch'ü believed that this somewhat utopian plan would sacrifice aesthetic quality only temporarily—and even then not completely, because he saw no reason why works intended for an intellectual audience should be entirely suspended. In the long run, however, he looked forward to a time when socialist literature would be both popular and aesthetically pleasing.

One question Ch'ü did not address was the relationship between the proletarian cultural movement and the proletarian political party, that is, the Chinese Communist Party. On the surface, it would appear that Ch'ü agreed with the view expressed by many European Marxists before Stalin that the party was not required to play the leading role or make decisions in the cultural and literary realm. Ch'ü did not raise this question, nor did he so much as mention the party in his literary writings of the 1930s. In some places he made vague references to the leading role of the "proletariat" in the revolutionary literary movement, but one can argue that he meant nothing more than the "content" of the current stage of the cultural movement or the leading role to be played by "proletarianized" elements.[16] His failure to talk about the issue does not necessarily mean that he was opposed in principle to the party having some degree of control over the arts, although it is hard to believe he would have approved of the almost total dictatorship over the arts imposed by Stalin in the Soviet Union after 1934. Actually, the relationship between the party and the arts was not a burning issue in China in the 1930s, partly because the party had no coherent policy toward the arts and did not attempt to impose policy decisions on the League of Left-wing Writers during the period in which it was led by Ch'ü.[17] It is also likely that Ch'ü failed to raise the issue because, personally, he had very little respect for the Wang Ming leadership group. He could probably think of nothing worse than having to take orders from Wang Ming on the direction of the cultural movement.

16. CCPWC, 2:885.

17. Leo Ou-fan Lee, "Literature on the Eve of Revolution: Reflections on Lu Xun's Leftist Years, 1927-1936," *Modern China*, July 1976, p. 300.

Ch'ü's attitude toward the role of the party was somewhat ambiguous. He never spoke in favor of party control, but he never made a specific statement against such control. On one hand, he referred specifically to Engels' remark to Margaret Harkness about the desirability of literary "tendentiousness"; but this could be interpreted, as Engels intended, to mean that writers should inject their *individual* political views into their writings, but only in a natural and subtle way.[18] On the other hand, he referred to the concept of literary "partinost" on one or two occasions, a term that could be interpreted as meaning that revolutionary literature should reflect the political positions of the party to which the writer belongs.[19]

THE SOVIET MODEL REVISITED

One of Ch'ü Ch'iu-pai's loudest complaints about the "European-ized" May Fourth generation, including its left wing, was that it tended to accept and imitate foreign theories of literature in an uncritical way. Not enough attention was given to the question of whether foreign theories were suited to distinctively Chinese problems. Most of them, he felt, were not. Ch'ü himself, it has been shown, had introduced Western Marxist literary thought into China in a dogmatic fashion in 1923. Then in 1931, when he reentered the leftist cultural world and began to criticize the shortcomings of Europeanization, one of his goals was to apply Marxist literary theory to Chinese cultural problems in a more creative manner. Although he regarded himself as a Marxist, the views he expressed on the major issues raised in European and Soviet Marxist literary circles were in fact often quite different from the opinions expressed by Marx, Engels, Plekhanov, Trotsky, Lenin, and Lunacharsky. But what was the relationship between Ch'ü's literary thought of the 1930s and Soviet literary thought of the same period, and especially Stalinist literary thought? What did Ch'ü know about contemporary Soviet literary life, and how did it influence his writing? His ideas may have departed from those contained in the Marxist classics, but did they represent nothing but an uncritical acceptance of the new Stalinist orthodoxy?

To begin, it is necessary to say something about Soviet literary life in the late 1920s and early 1930s. Without question, one of the most significant changes was the formation of the Russian Association of Proletarian Writers in April 1928. The Association was the first large-scale national literary organization to receive the official blessing of the Communist Party. Even Lunacharsky, who in the early 1920s had spoken against party endorsement of any particular literary group,

18. HSSL, 1:5, 20-21, 26.
19. HSSL, 1:72. Also see CCPWC, 2:1010 for a vague reference to the party.

proclaimed that the Association should represent the party in the cultural realm.[20] This change in the party's attitude toward the arts, which had been discussed by party members as early as 1926, was related to the general shift in the economic realm from the liberal policies of the New Economic Plan to the launching of the socialist First Five Year Plan in 1928. Following the defeat of Trotsky, a vocal opponent of proletarian cultural movements, many party members began to accept the idea not only that proletarian culture was possible, but that it could be used to promote the transition to socialism contemplated by the architects of the Five Year Plan. Literature and art were to become a part of the enormous machine that was being assembled for the purpose of modernizing the nation.

This was a highly important development in the history of Marxist literary thought. Among other things, it represented radical redefinitions of the role of the writer, the nature of proletarian art, and the role of art in socialist society. Indeed, what one finds here are several of the elements that distinguish Stalinist literary thought from the numerous and vastly dissimilar schools of Marxist literary thought that preceded it. First, Stalin's cultural theoreticians spoke with unprecedented clarity on the issue of the relationship between the party and the realm of artistic culture. Indeed, the hallmark of the Stalinist approach to art is the notion that the development of artistic culture is subordinate to and controlled by the Communist Party. It is the party's responsibility to define social and economic priorities in each stage of the transition to socialism; it is the duty of artistic workers to promote such goals in ways approved by the party, and publicize any progress. What the Stalinist approach demands, therefore, is a highly integrated society. Literary activity is not simply regulated by the party, it becomes part of what is presumed to be a finely tuned state apparatus. Organized into large bureaucratic literary unions, writers in effect work for the state. A second characteristic of the Stalinist approach to art is its insistence upon literature that paints a positive picture of socialist society and confines itself to glorifying the heroes of the revolution. In literary terms this tended to mean considerably less emphasis on realism, and more attention to a form of romanticism or idealism that stresses "vanguard" developments and "advanced" individuals rather than typical or backward phenomena. Finally, in many respects the most characteristic feature of literary Stalinism was the imposition of the personal dictatorship of Stalin himself. Stalin's unparalleled dominance of postrevolutionary Soviet society created a political and psychological environment never before experienced by Western Marxist literary thinkers. Every writer had to

20. Edward J. Brown, *The Proletarian Episode in Russian Literature, 1928-1932* (New York: Columbia University Press, 1953), pp. 54-55.

confront the fact that this one person, Stalin, was the final arbiter on all cultural and aesthetic matters. Consequently, all writers were obligated to show, in one way or another, that their work was consistent with Stalin's own pronouncements on the nation's economic and social priorities.

But, aside from the content of Stalinist literary thought, it is also necessary to know when the Stalinist program for art began to be fully implemented in the Soviet Union. As Edward Brown has pointed out, it would be misleading to assume that a distinctively Stalinist literary policy dominated the Soviet scene from the moment the Russian Association of Proletarian Writers was founded in 1928.[21] On the contrary, misunderstanding rather than accord characterized the relationship between the party and the Association. The leaders of the Association sought the support of the party in order to advance their power within the literary world, but they quite obviously did not want the organization to become merely another propaganda arm of the party. In the first two years of its existence, 1928 to 1930, the Association made numerous attempts to assert its independence by resisting overt party control. The party policy of praising the heroes of the Five Year Plan soon clashed with the Association's advocacy of realistic socialist literary works that "tear off the masks" of those who oppress the people. From 1930 to 1932, at a time when Stalin had succeeded in consolidating his political power, increasing pressure was brought to bear on the Association. Several ideological campaigns were launched in an effort to force the Association to accept the party view of the role of literature and writers during the transition to socialism.[22] Failing in this task, the party Central Committee, on Stalin's personal order, abolished the Association of Proletarian Writers in April 1932 because its members insisted upon a significant degree of autonomy from the state and party, wrote in a relatively realistic manner, and proved unwilling to implement party directives. As Herman Ermolaev has suggested, it was not until 1932 that the Stalinist conception of art was able to prevail, and not until the first congress of the new Union of Soviet Writers was held in August 1934 that an effective organizational network was established.[23] By contrast, the transitional period between 1928 and 1932 was one in which a surprisingly wide range of Marxist views on art and society were advanced and debated.

How much did Ch'ü Ch'iu-pai know about these developments, and what was his attitude toward Stalinist literary thought? It is

21. Ibid., p. 86.

22. Herman Ermolaev, *Soviet Literary Theory: 1917-1934* (Berkeley and Los Angeles: University of California Press, 1963), pp. 89-118.

23. Ibid., pp. 4, 161-168.

difficult to provide a complete answer because some time before Stalinist literary organization became a fact of Soviet life, Ch'ü had left Shanghai to assist Mao Tse-tung at the rural base area in remote Kiangsi. In fact, he does not seem to have been aware that the Association of Proletarian Writers was dissolved in 1932.[24] But, while it is impossible to say how Ch'ü would have reacted to the Stalinization of Soviet literary life, it is probably true that Ch'ü knew more than anyone in China about literary developments in Russia just prior to the dissolution of the Association, that is, in the period between 1928 and 1932. Ch'ü had, of course, lived in the Soviet Union between June 1928 and August 1930, during the two most interesting years in the history of the Association, and continued to correspond with students and friends in Moscow and receive Soviet books and periodicals following his return to China.[25] Nevertheless, it is still quite difficult to assess his views because, while he undoubtedly knew a great deal about Soviet literary trends, he wrote almost nothing about them. As far as original essays are concerned, Ch'ü's total output consisted of three pieces, two of which he never bothered to publish, and all of which were written in a six-week period in December 1931 and January 1932.

The first of the three articles, entitled "Stalin and Literature," says absolutely nothing about Stalin's views on literature. Instead, it simply asserts that to avoid the problem of the economic base advancing faster than the superstructure, writers obviously would have to give greater attention to the new and revolutionary developments associated with the Five Year Plan. Written in the style of a news report, the essay offers no real evaluation of Soviet cultural trends and makes no attempt to explain their significance for China. Ch'ü simply stated at the end that China should learn from developments in the Soviet Union.[26] In view of the fact that Stalin was on the verge of dissolving the Association when Ch'ü was writing his article, it is ironic that Ch'ü's remarks about the organization were essentially positive. He made vague references to unresolved problems, but was extremely optimistic about the future of the organization. As one might expect, Ch'ü was enthusiastic about the anti-bourgeois thrust of the new movement, and applauded the determination of Soviet proletarian writers to investigate the new social and economic phenomena in a

24. Ch'ü certainly had enough time to learn of this new development. The Association was dissolved eight months before he left Shanghai. Nevertheless, he stopped writing about Soviet literary trends in January 1932.

25. See Ts'ao Ching-hua, *Hua* [Flowers] (Peking: Tso-chia ch'u-pan-she, 1962), pp. 42-47.

26. Ch'ü Ch'iu-pai, "Ssu-ta-lin ho wen-hsueh" [Stalin and literature] (December 6, 1931); in CCPWC, 2:563.

realistic and concrete manner and to "expose" all evil practices. He also was interested in the efforts made by the Association to recruit writers from among the working class by sending literary "shock brigades" (*wen-hsueh t'u-chi-tui*) to the factories.[27] Such direct contact with the masses would not only produce proletarian intellectuals, he suggested, it would also enable writers to portray better the heroes of the Five Year Plan. But in general, this article is quite uninformative and fails to shed any light on the tension between Stalin and the proletarian writers over the relationship between the party and the Association and the place of realistic literature in socialist society.

Ch'ü's second article, entitled "On Friche," appears, on the surface, to be a highly theoretical and somewhat abstract discussion about the excessively deterministic literary views of the well-known Soviet critic Vladimir Friche. Indeed, as I have already suggested, Ch'ü wrote this article for the purpose of showing materialist literary thinkers in China the dangers of the mechanistic approach to art taken by Friche and his mentor, Plekhanov. But this article also says something about Ch'ü's knowledge of Soviet literary polemics in the period before the dissolution of the Association of Proletarian Writers. Although Ch'ü nowhere mentions the Association or its leaders, it is quite clear that his view of Friche is almost identical to the view expressed earlier by the eminent Soviet novelist Alexander Fadeyev, a man who played a leading role in the Association and was much respected by Ch'ü, Lu Hsün, and others in China. Ch'ü's article on Friche shows that he was familiar with and accepted a number of the positions adopted by the Association before its clash with Stalin. Like Fadeyev, Ch'ü identified irrationalism and rationalism as the most counterproductive trends in modern literary thought.[28] As Herman Ermolaev has pointed out, the "irrational" school referred to Freudians and semi-Freudians such as Alexander Voronsky who stressed the dominance of the subconscious over the conscious, and thus advocated a literature that explores the manner in which subconscious forces shape human development. The "rational" school, on the other hand, referred to theorists like Plekhanov and Friche who exaggerated the conscious and thus disregarded the role of subconscious factors.[29]

Like his unpublished essay "Stalin and Literature," Ch'ü's piece on Friche is disappointing because it does not allude to or take a stand on the issue of party control of artistic activity, but it does indicate that Ch'ü interpreted Fadeyev's call for a "dialectical-materialist" approach to literature as meaning that a realistic literature should maintain a dialectical unity between conscious and subconscious forces. As Leo Ou-fan Lee has shown, Chinese writers like Lu Hsün and Ch'ü Ch'iu-

27. CCPWC, 2:561.   28. CCPWC, 2:567-569.
29. Ermolaev, *Soviet Literary Theory*, pp. 72-73.

pai were strongly attracted to works of "psychological realism," such as Fadeyev's own masterpiece *The Rout*, that offer a realistic treatment of the "inner conflicts and psychic tensions" confronting all revolutionaries.[30] In sharp contrast to the idealized and positive "heroes" of the Five Year Plan demanded by Stalin, Fadeyev and other leaders of the Association of Proletarian Writers called upon writers to "tear off masks" and portray the "living man." Virtually everything Ch'ü wrote in the early 1930s suggests that he agreed with Fadeyev.[31]

By far the most interesting and informative of the three essays is a long, yet unpublished, work entitled "The New Stage in Soviet Literature." In contrast to his shorter articles, it provides more detail about Ch'ü's knowledge of Soviet literary trends in the 1928-1931 period and suggests much more clearly the developments to which he was personally attracted. Ch'ü began by suggesting that, generally speaking, postrevolutionary Soviet literary trends reflected socioeconomic developments. The first stage coincided with the period of "War Communism" from 1917 to 1921. Ch'ü had lived in the Soviet Union for part of this period and was well aware that it was characterized in the literary realm by the exciting work carried on by Bogdanov and others associated with Proletkult. Ch'ü acknowledged that their work was revolutionary insofar as it promoted proletarian culture and sought to develop distinctively working-class forms of art; but, he now concluded, they were ineffective because their work was confined, for the most part, to the interests of a small group of revolutionary intellectuals and tended to ignore the needs of the common people.[32] The second stage coincided with the life of the New Economic Plan of 1921-1927. Where the first period was marked by "leftism" in literary development, the second period was seen as essentially "rightist." Not only were concessions made to capitalism in economic life, in the literary realm there was a veritable restoration of bourgeois literary theories and a refusal to recognize the need for proletarian culture.[33]

The new, third stage, which was the topic of Ch'ü's essay, corresponded with the unfolding of the First Five Year Plan in the period between 1928 and late 1931. At first, Ch'ü observed, literary leaders either resisted the idea of further cultural transformation or were slow to raise the question of the role of art during the transition to socialism. In this sense, the superstructure was lagging behind. Never-

---

30. Leo Ou-fan Lee, "Literature on the Eve of Revolution," p. 311.

31. For example, see CCPWC, 2:891, for one of Ch'ü's many references to the need for Chinese writers to "tear off all masks."

32. Ch'ü Ch'iu-pai, "Su-lien wen-hsüeh te hsin chieh-tuan" [The new stage in Soviet literature], (January 16, 1932); in CCPWC, 2:574.

33. CCPWC, 2:574-575.

theless, Ch'ü asserted, developments at the Fourth Congress of the Association of Proletarian Writers held in September 1931 indicated that problems were being solved and the future was bright.[34]

The third stage "problem" to which Ch'ü directed most of his attention was the fate of the literary "fellow travelers" (*t'ung-lu jen*) during the transition to the new order. By "fellow travelers" Ch'ü meant the noncommunist, bourgeois intellectuals who tended to sympathize with the revolution and who were willing to participate in a literary "united front" (*t'ung-meng chün*) with the working class. Although Ch'ü said nothing about China in this regard, it is likely that his essentially hopeful and optimistic handling of the "fellow travelers" question in the Soviet Union reflected his concern for the same issue in China. During the New Economic Plan, Ch'ü conceded, the petty-bourgeois fellow travelers dominated the literary scene and were in a position to promote the restoration of the capitalist superstructure. But the launching of the Five Year Plan forced them to make a difficult choice. They could continue to develop and defend the bourgeois superstructure, or they could join the proletariat in a literary united front.[35]

It is clear from his remarks that Ch'ü believed the literary fellow travelers to be an indispensable ally of the socialist revolution. The question of their future role was of crucial importance. Simply ignoring or isolating the literary intellectuals, he indicated, was no solution. Proletarian literature eventually would have to be the product of working-class pens, but the assistance of the revolutionary fellow travelers in the united front was absolutely necessary. To make the united front succeed, it would be the responsibility of the proletariat to accept the advice and leadership of the intellectuals on technical and artistic matters. At the same time it would be the responsibility of the intellectuals to transform and proletarianize their political thought through their direct contact with the working class.

Ch'ü firmly believed that the Association of Proletarian Writers was best qualified to serve as the organizational vehicle for the proposed cultural transformation.[36] He seems to have had no inkling whatsoever that the Association would be dissolved less than three months following the writing of his article. To be sure, Ch'ü looked forward to a time when bourgeois cultural ideology would be an insignificant factor in Soviet life and when literary activity would no longer be dominated by specialists, but he clearly believed that the Soviet Union was in a transitional stage. Under such circumstances, he declared, the Association was completely justified in criticizing "leftists"

34. CCPWC, 2:575.   35. CCPWC, 2:578.

who indiscriminately condemned all petty-bourgeois fellow travelers as class enemies.[37]

In the second part of the article Ch'ü simply described two movements discussed at the September 1931 meeting of Association members: the literary "shock brigades," and the campaign to represent the "heroes of the Five Year Plan." Ch'ü seems to have been interested in both efforts because he believed they would serve to bridge the gap between petty-bourgeois fellow travelers and the people, speed up the ideological transformation of the intellectuals, and help raise the cultural level of the masses.[38] Ch'ü's claim that the Association's membership rose from 1,800 to 10,000 just after the program was begun in September 1930, a development that raised proletarian participation to 80 percent, is confirmed by Harriet Borland's research on Soviet literature during the Five Year Plan.[39] Among other things, the two programs involved going to the factories to recruit new writers, opening evening schools, and encouraging workers to participate in "correspondence" movements. Ch'ü was attracted to what seemed to be the utopian goals of the new efforts. Indeed, he stated explicitly that, although the literature produced in this manner would be immature at first, an important and necessary step had been taken toward abolishing the distinction between mental and manual labor. The writers of the future socialist society would, at the same time, be workers whose art was inspired by their intimate knowledge of the life of the common people.

What conclusions can be reached, then, about these articles and their influence upon Ch'ü's creative work? Although it is apparent that he had a reasonably good command of Soviet literary trends of the 1928-1931 period, one is struck by how little time he actually devoted to familiarizing his colleagues with such matters. He wrote three articles and published only one. It is also likely that these articles are actually little more than paraphrases or summarizations of items that had appeared in the Soviet press.[40] Thus, like the articles he wrote on Soviet literature in 1923, they read like descriptive news reports, contain no real personal analysis of the Soviet cultural scene, and make virtually no reference to the significance of such trends for China.

36. CCPWC, 2:581.   37. CCPWC, 2:582.   38. CCPWC, 2:589-590.

39. CPPWC, 2:586; Harriet Borland, *Soviet Literary Theory and Practice During the First Five Year Plan, 1928-32* (New York: King's Crown Press, 1950), pp. 56-62.

40. According to Mark E. Shneider [*Tvorcheskii Put' Tsiui Tsiu-bo, 1899-1935* (Moscow: Izdatel'stvo Nauka, 1964), p. 190], Ch'ü's essay "The New Stage in Soviet Literature" simply paraphrased points of view expressed at an Association of Proletarian Writers meeting held in August and September 1931.

Furthermore, while Ch'ü's articles contain considerable detail on Soviet developments, the information appears to be quite superficial. There is no evidence whatsoever that Ch'ü had any understanding of what was taking place backstage between Stalin and the Association of Proletarian Writers. Nowhere does Ch'ü discuss the issue of party control of the arts, or the clash between the realistic approach advocated by writers like Fadeyev and the idealistic approach promoted by Stalin. This may mean that Ch'ü had little idea of what was really occurring. On the other hand, it is possible to interpret his brief writings in another way. The three essays discussed above, including the one entitled "Stalin and Literature," are interesting because without exception they represent a subtle defense of the interests and perspectives of the Association of Proletarian Writers at a time when the organization was feeling the weight of pressure exerted by the party. Indeed, one can argue that Ch'ü, a man who had direct and bitter experience with the Stalinist mode of political operation, intentionally chose to summarize works written by Association members for the purpose of defending the organization. In each piece, lip service is paid to Stalinist slogans about the supporting role of literature in the drive to industrialize the Soviet Union, but in each selection the Association's commitment to independence and realism is upheld. If it is true that Ch'ü was sympathetic to the plight of the Association, then it would come as no surprise that he failed to support the decision to abolish it.

MAXIM GORKY:
VARIATIONS ON OLD THEMES

Ch'ü's interest in Soviet literary life reached well beyond his concern about the role played by the Association of Proletarian Writers. Indeed, Ch'ü's hastily prepared essays on Soviet trends are insignificant when compared with his translations of Soviet literary works, which include selections by Lunacharsky, Alexander Serafimovich, Fedor Gladkov, and Demyan Bedney.[41] Above all, however, Ch'ü's attention was focused on a single towering figure, Maxim Gorky. In addition to translating a number of his individual short stories and essays, Ch'ü edited and translated two complete volumes of works by Gorky entitled *An Anthology of Essays by Gorky* and *An Anthology of Creative*

---

41. The most important translations were the second and third acts of Lunacharsky's play *Don Quixote Liberated*, Gladkov's "New Land," Serafimovich's "A Day's Work" and "Robbers," and Bedny's long poem "No Time to Spit on and Revile." For publication details, see Ting Ching-t'ang and Wen Ts'ao, eds., *Ch'ü Ch'iu-pai chu i hsi-nien mu-lu* [A chronological bibliography of Ch'ü Ch'iu-pai's writings and translations] (Shanghai: Jen-min ch'u-pan-she, 1959), pp. 50-57.

Works by Gorky, both of which were completed by the end of 1932.[42] Why did Ch'ü place so much emphasis on Gorky, and what does this emphasis reveal about the nature of Ch'ü's interest in Soviet literary affairs of the 1930s?

Some of the works selected by Ch'ü for translation are inferior both artistically and politically. With the exception of some of the short stories written at an earlier stage of his career, the works collected by Ch'ü are not representative of Gorky's best efforts. This is especially noticeable in the volume devoted to essays (*lun-wen*), most of which were written in the period between 1928 and 1931. Despite Ch'ü's assertion that these works reminded him of Lu Hsün's *tsa-wen* essays, Gorky appears in them as a crude apologist for the Communist Party and the Soviet state.[43] One wonders, therefore, why Ch'ü even bothered to translate such material.

Of course, there is no question that Ch'ü, like leftist intellectuals throughout the world during the depression years, was quite willing to defend the Soviet system against what was perceived to be the unfair and menacing criticisms of those in the troubled capitalist world who hoped to conceal their own failures. But this fact alone does not fully explain why Ch'ü spent so much time translating Gorky. In Ch'ü's own writings the theme of "defending the Soviet Union" was given very little space indeed. His failure to write anything of substance on this topic may be related in part to his own bitter experiences with Soviet politics and Comintern meddling in the Chinese revolution; but it seems more likely that Ch'ü was simply too preoccupied with China and its problems to show much enthusiasm for "defending" the Soviet Union. It would appear, therefore, that Ch'ü translated these works for other reasons. He was not primarily interested in their pro-Soviet propaganda value. Neither was it his intention to pass along information about Soviet literary life, because these works say very little on that subject.

A close reading of essays by Gorky such as "To the Humanitarians," "Reply to an Intellectual," "On Cynicism," and "To the Mechanical

---

42. The volume entitled *An Anthology of Creative Works by Gorky* [Kao-erh-chi ch'uang-tso hsuan-chi], CCPWC, 3:1479-1699, was published first by the Moscow State Publishing House in 1930; Ch'ü's translation was published in October 1933 by Shanghai's Sheng-huo shu-tien and again in the second volume of Ch'ü's *Hai-shang shu-lin*, edited by Lu Hsun. The volume entitled *An Anthology of Essays by Gorky* [Kao-erh-chi lun-wen hsuan-chi], CCPWC, 4:1719-1972, was published first in Moscow in 1931; the Chinese edition prepared by Ch'ü appeared first in *Hai-shang shu-lin*, vol. 1. See Ting Ching-t'ang and Wen Ts'ao, eds., *Hsi-nien mu-lu*, pp. 57-58. Ch'ü also translated the following miscellaneous works by Gorky: "Twenty-six Men and a Girl," "Malva," the first chapter of *The Life of Klim Samgin*, "Ode to a Philistine," and "Indifference." See Ting Ching-t'ang and Wen Ts'ao, eds., *Hsi-nien mu-lu*, pp. 55-64, for publication details.

43. See Ch'ü's preface to *An Anthology of Essays by Gorky* in CCPWC, 4:1719.

Citizens of the U.S.S.R." suggests other motives for translating these works.[44] Indeed, the themes that are repeated again and again by Gorky are themes already thoroughly familiar to Ch'ü. In fact, they are themes that absorbed Ch'ü during the May Fourth period, well before his conversion to Marxism.

The complete corruption of bourgeois culture is, for example, one of the subjects underscored in virtually all of the works Ch'ü translated. "Class states," Gorky asserted, "are built after the fashion of zoological gardens where all the animals are imprisoned in iron cages. In class states these cages, constructed with varying degrees of skill, serve to prolong those ideas which divide humanity, and prevent the development of an awareness in man of his own interests as well as the birth of a genuine culture embracing all humanity."[45] Bourgeois culture is portrayed by Gorky, as it was in the utopian socialist texts Ch'ü read as a youth, as an unnatural phenomenon that alienates humankind from its true aesthetic sensibilities, produces "deformities of thought," and "stunts the growth" of intellectual forces.[46] Above all, the bourgeois cultural world is, for Gorky, a "philistine" world of culturelessness and extreme "individualism."[47]

Gorky's remarks about philistine culture tended to confirm beliefs Ch'ü had held since his youth. For one thing, Gorky stated quite explicitly in several places that the homeland of the culture that imprisons the "human spirit" is Western Europe. In his "Reply to an Intellectual," Gorky suggested that while European intellectuals might proclaim the "universal significance" of bourgeois culture, the "inhuman and cynical policies" pursued by the European powers in Asia were "creating a host of enemies of European culture." "Hindus, Chinese and Annamites bow their heads before your cannon," he added, "but that does not in the least mean that they venerate European culture."[48] Thus, while Gorky did not say so explicitly, his accounts of the degenerate and aggressive nature of European bourgeois culture leave his readers with the definite impression that every step should

---

44. For Ch'ü's translations of these Gorky essays, see "Kei Su-lien te ĉhi-hsieh te kung-min'" [To the "mechanical citizens" of the U.S.S.R.], CCPWC, 4:1723-1736; "Tsai lun chi-hsieh te kung-min" [More about mechanical citizens], pp. 1736-1746; "Ta-fu chih-shih-fen-tzu" [Reply to an intellectual], pp. 1918-1935; "Kei jen-tao-chu-i-che" [To the humanitarians], pp. 1851-1863; "Wu-ch'ih-chu-i" [On cynicism], pp. 1893-1904. The English translations of passages from these five articles are based on Maxim Gorky, *On Guard for the Soviet Union* (New York: International Publishers, 1933), pp. 54-66, 67-77, 80-99, 107-114, 122-132. For the sixth essay referred to here, see "Ju-kuo ti-jen pu t'ou-hsiang—nei chiu-shih yao hsiao-mieh t'a" [If the enemy does not surrender he must be destroyed], CCPWC, 4:1847-1851. The translations of extracts used here are based on Maxim Gorky, *Creative Labor and Culture* (Sydney: Current Book Distributors, 1945), pp. 59-60.

45. CCPWC, 4:1924-1925.   46. CCPWC, 4:1919, 1926.

47. CCPWC, 4:1902.   48. CCPWC, 4:1920.

be taken to avoid this particular cultural stage. That is to say, bourgeois culture is neither inevitable nor a prerequisite for the development of socialist culture.

A second, and related, Gorky theme is the problem of the "superfluous" intellectual. In all his articles Gorky portrayed petty-bourgeois intellectuals as a group whose fate is hanging in the balance. It is particularly interesting that Gorky considered this problem to be of unusual importance. His grotesque caricatures of "bourgeois philistines" were undoubtedly intended to focus attention on the utterly horrible "spiritual death" that awaited all those who failed to rise above the abyss.[49] Conceding that he himself had passed through an agonizing superfluous stage at the time of the Bolshevik Revolution, Gorky attempted to describe the psychological tensions that weighed upon petty-bourgeois intellectuals in revolutionary historical settings.[50] He spoke in dramatic terms about "imprisoned thoughts" that cause the intellectual "to place the burden of his own conditions of life on the whole world" and to formulate subjective conceptions that "give rise to philosophical pessimism, scepticism, and other deformities of thought."[51] In some selections, it is fair to say, Gorky seemed obsessed with the possibility that many well-intentioned intellectuals will become superfluous by retreating to the mysterious and "secluded" realm of the "microscopic ego."[52] It is significant that in the context of this sort of discussion Gorky, the Marxist, would make a surprisingly favorable reference to the old populist intellectuals. He noted that during his youth he had become acquainted with "revolutionaries of populist tendencies." "This was fortunate for me," he pointed out, "for it was the first time I met people whose interests in life were beyond their own satisfaction, beyond the goal of a personally secure life. These people, who knew intimately and thoroughly the burdensome life of the toiling people, spoke of the imperative necessity of changing this life. And they not only talked, they acted."[53] By contrast, superfluous intellectuals were precisely those people who stood paralyzed between self and society, those people who were tortured, psychologically speaking, because they knew what had to be done but were unable to act.

Finally, and what is perhaps most important, one is struck by the number of utopian cultural themes developed by Gorky in these works. He spoke in almost mystical language about the "spiritual regeneration" and release of "creative powers" in the Soviet Union.[54] The process of revolution is conceived in strikingly cultural terms. "Reality is created by the inexhaustible and intelligent will of man," he proclaimed, "and its development will never be arrested."[55] Elsewhere

49. CCPWC, 4:1724.   50. CCPWC, 4:1730.   51. CCPWC, 4:1926.
52. CCPWC, 4:1742.   53. CCPWC, 4:1731.   54. CCPWC, 4:1848, 1894.
55. CCPWC, 4:1927-1928.

Gorky saw the revolution as a "struggle for culture and for the creative potentialities of culture," a struggle that is highlighted by the imposition of the "rationally organized will" of the masses on objective reality.[56] Bourgeois, philistine culture is guilty of no greater crime than retarding the development of distinctively human "creative powers" and "consciousness of self."[57] It follows, then, that Gorky—like Ch'ü—would see the cultural revolution as the key link in the struggle for socialism. The "people," Gorky insisted, "are an inexhaustible source of energy and can transform all the possible into the necessary, all dreams into reality."[58] But before such energy could be released, it would be necessary to discredit the cultural "rubbish" propagated by the philistines.

Gorky not only announced that the liberation of the "human spirit" is a goal of the revolution, he stated quite categorically that, to a significant degree, this utopian aim has already been realized in the Soviet Union. Once the obstacles that "hinder the growth of consciousness" have been eliminated, the way will be clear to develop rapidly "the gifts and abilities of the whole people and of each individual," and to create conditions that permit each individual to "reach a level to which, so far, only the exceptional, the so-called 'great' people, have been able to attain."[59] Gorky recognized that a certain level of material development was necessary to generate such a cultural revolution, but it is surprising how little he required. In 1931 he wrote that Saint-Simon, Fourier, and others dreamed of utopia "at a time when the industrial technique necessary for the realization of this dream was as yet nonexistent. Now all requisite conditions exist. The dream of the utopians has found a firm foundation in science, and the work of realizing this dream is being carried on by millions."[60] Gorky spoke at great length of the movements to eradicate illiteracy and to recruit large numbers of amateur artists and writers from among the ranks of the people. "The difficulties are tremendous," he noted, "but when one really desires, one can achieve!"[61] "Has it ever been, and can it ever be," Gorky asked rhetorically, "the aim of a bourgeois state to draw all the millions of its working people into cultural activities?"[62]

This last remark is, I think, the key to understanding Ch'ü's interest in Maxim Gorky. The material translated by Ch'ü does not indicate in any way that Ch'ü was exploring new problems in the cultural field. On the contrary, these translations are significant because they dwell upon themes that had attracted Ch'ü's attention from the moment he entered the New Culture Movement in 1919. Like Tolstoy, Ch'ü's

56. CCPWC, 4:1918, 1934.   57. CCPWC, 4:1894.
58. CCPWC, 4:1894.   59. CCPWC, 4:1848.   60. CCPWC, 4:1923.
61. CCPWC, 4:1849.   62. CCPWC, 4:1924.

May Fourth hero, Gorky assaulted what he perceived to be the unnatural and dehumanizing nature of bourgeois culture, celebrated the creativity of the human intellect, and proclaimed that the cultural utopia described in socialist and Marxist texts was at hand. It is hard to know if Gorky meant to imply that the pernicious bourgeois cultural stage could be bypassed, but it is fairly evident that Ch'ü adopted this interpretation. And, like Turgenev, Gorky seemed preoccupied with the fate of intellectuals who were still floundering in a sea of powerful psychological crosscurrents. One might even say that Gorky's somewhat mystical descriptions of the powerful but intangible "creative forces" that arose from the Russian people are reminiscent of Ch'ü's use of Buddhist terminology in *A Journey to the Land of Hunger* to account for the unusual vitality of the Russian revolution. At the very least, Ch'ü seems to have selected works for translation that were compatible with his own work on the problems of culture and revolution in China. He used Gorky, just as he had used the works of other foreign Marxist writers, on a selective basis in order to support the nationalist, anti-bourgeois, and relatively idealist thrust of his own literary thought.

Ch'ü Ch'iu-pai, it seems fair to say, was not a thinker who was merely parroting Soviet or Stalinist literary theories. Instead, he should be recognized as the first Chinese to apply Western Marxist literary thought to uniquely Chinese conditions. He was the first to "sinify" Marxist literary thought. Of course, Ch'ü was influenced by contemporary Soviet literary theory, but he was obviously influenced by much more than that. No one in China was more familiar with, or therefore more influenced by, the entire Western tradition of socialist and Marxist literary thought. This tradition included not only the works of Soviet and Russian thinkers, but also the works of Marx, Engels, Lafargue, and other non-Russian figures. While one can detect the influence of these various schools on Ch'ü's thinking, it is equally apparent that his ideas do not conform to those of any particular school. Furthermore, when Ch'ü wrote about developments abroad or translated a foreign text, he normally did so because he believed such things were related to or similar to problems he was confronting in China.

Ch'ü's standing as an original Marxist literary thinker rests, more than anything else, on his voluminous writings about cultural problems in China itself. Ch'ü's analysis of the stages through which the modern literary movement had passed since May Fourth days, his discussion of the failings of the May Fourth generation, his writings on the consequences of "Europeanization," and his views on popular literature were not borrowed from foreign textbooks. They were born of a thorough knowledge of the problems of Chinese society.

11 Kiangsi: To the People

A bookworm [shu-sheng] cannot really understand realities; he only succeeds in making himself a personal embodiment of all his hodgepodge ideas. . . . The same thing can be said about intellectuals who do not have any knowledge about practical matters. They might be able to discourse on "the most important problems confronting the nation" in the abstract, but they would be at a complete loss if asked to repair an automobile, fill a medical prescription, manage a cooperative, serve as a purchasing agent, audit a balance sheet, or run a school. In short, they have no confidence in themselves as far as practical matters are concerned.

CHÜ CH'IU-PAI, 1935[1]

Ch'ü Ch'iu-pai's final months in Shanghai were extremely difficult, although he continued to write and translate prolifically. Shortly after the appearance in early July 1933 of *The Selected Essays of Lu Hsün*, a book compiled by Ch'ü for the purpose of elevating Lu Hsün's standing in leftist literary circles, Ch'ü and his family were forced for a third time to take refuge in Lu Hsün's home. They returned to their apartment on North Szechuan Road at the end of the month, but were compelled to abandon it once and for all in November. Anxious not to endanger friends, they wandered from place to place in the following weeks seeking temporary asylum. Suddenly one night in late December Ch'ü received a telegram requesting him to come to the Kiangsi Soviet to serve as Mao Tse-tung's Commissar of Education.[2]

1. TYTH, pp. 153-154.
2. Yang Chih-hua, "I Ch'iu-pai" [Recollections of Ch'iu-pai], *Hung-ch'i p'iao-p'iao,* 8:47-48; Yang Chih-hua, "Ch'iu-pai ho Lu Hsün" [Ch'ü Ch'iu-pai and Lu Hsün], *Jen-min jih-pao,* 18 June 1949; Hsu Kuang-p'ing, "Ch'iu-pai t'ung-chih ho Lu Hsün hsiang-ch'ü te shih-hou" [The period during which comrade Ch'iu-pai and Lu Hsün resided together], *Yü-wen hsueh-hsi* [Language study], 6 (June 1959):2.

Ch'ü spent the evening of January 4, 1934, one of his last nights in Shanghai, with Lu Hsün at his Ta-lu Villa home. He had stopped in only to say goodbye, but the two friends talked until late. Finally Lu Hsün insisted that he and his wife, Hsu Kuang-p'ing, give over their bed to Ch'ü "so that he could have a good night's sleep, saying that he himself would spread a pallet on the floor."[3] Although they may have suspected as much, neither could have known for certain that their morning farewell would be their final one.

Shortly thereafter, Ch'ü bade farewell to his wife and daughter, and set out on a long journey that would take him from cosmopolitan Shanghai to the remote and relatively backward communist base area in south Kiangsi. Never again would he return to his native Kiangsu or set his eyes on the city whose very name was synonymous with twentieth-century Chinese radicalism, a city in which he had spent almost a decade as an active revolutionary. Ch'ü later noted: "In January 1934, when it became clear that Shanghai was no longer a safe place for me to recuperate from my illness, I left that city for Juichin and arrived at my destination on February 5."[4]

Needless to say, conditions in Kiangsi contrasted sharply with those in the areas controlled by the Kuomintang. The central difference was, of course, that for the first time since the mid-1920s Chinese communists were able to work openly. Despite systematic and massive Kuomintang "encirclement and annihilation campaigns," the revolutionary base area was able to survive for several years. Among other things, this essentially favorable environment provided intellectuals, who had been cut off from meaningful contact with the proletariat since 1927, with another opportunity to organize the people, in this case the peasantry.

In terms of revolutionary theory, the Kiangsi experiment constituted an attempt to carve out a small revolutionary "state" within the larger "semifeudal, semicolonial" state during a distinctively prerevolutionary and precapitalist historical stage. It was assumed by some communist leaders that a revolutionary victory in China would be won, not by a swift military coup d'état, but rather by effecting meaningful economic and social reforms in remote base areas controlled by revolutionary forces. By mobilizing popular support in this manner, the "liberated" zones would expand and eventually overwhelm the opponents of the revolution. This strategy dictated that at least some of the social and economic goals of the revolution would have to be achieved even before state power was seized nationwide. If land re-

3. Hsu Kuang-p'ing, *Lu Hsün hui-i lu* [Reminiscences of Lu Hsün] (Peking: Tso-chia ch'u-pan-she, 1961), p. 130.
4. TYTH, p. 147.

form could be carried out and if the political power of the gentry could be broken, some suggested, a revolutionary cultural movement could also be advanced.[5]

But new opportunities brought unanticipated problems. To be sure, writers like Ch'ü who had lived underground for years welcomed this change in working conditions. At least they enjoyed some measure of personal security. But most of the literary intellectuals who left the cities did so out of necessity, not out of choice. In their eyes, nothing could have been further removed from the literary world of Shanghai than the isolated villages of Kiangsi. The writers from the urban areas would no longer be working with the urban proletariat or with other intellectuals, but with peasants instead. How were they going to adjust to the rural environment? How were the literary concerns of the intellectuals related to the immediate cultural problems confronting the peasantry? How would writers cope with having to discontinue the kind of work they normally did because there was no audience for it? The experiments carried out in the Kiangsi Soviet Republic are interesting because, whether intended or not, the locus of the revolutionary literary movement was beginning to shift from the metropolitan to the rural areas. To be sure, there was now an unusual opportunity to place the movement on a mass base. But what would be the cost? Ch'ü Ch'iu-pai's lonely trip from Shanghai to Juichin symbolized the new and unfamiliar course being taken by the leftist literary movement.

The land tenure system and landlord political domination were the central economic and social problems facing the peasantry. Massive educational deprivation and illiteracy would have to be the primary concern of those interested in the cultural mobilization of the people. It has been estimated that in China during the period from 1929 to 1931 nearly 70 percent of male peasants and nearly 99 percent of female peasants were functionally illiterate. Of the men, only 45 percent had attended any school: among peasant women, the figure was only 2.3 percent.[6] A rich tradition of folk art would, under normal circumstances, have been accessible to the peasantry and a factor in the formation of their world view. But the combination of ceaseless civil conflict, natural disasters, and foreign incursion disrupted rural life in many parts of China in the 1920s and 1930s and had a devastating effect on the cultural development of the people. Ch'ü and other

5. For two important studies of this period, see Ilpyong J. Kim, *The Politics of Chinese Communism: Kiangsi Under the Soviets* (Berkeley and Los Angeles: University of California Press, 1973), and John E. Rue, *Mao Tse-tung in Opposition, 1927-1935* (Stanford: Stanford University Press, 1966).

6. Irene B. Taeuber, "The Families of Chinese Farmers," in Maurice Freedman, ed., *Family and Kinship in Chinese Society* (Stanford: Stanford University Press, 1968), pp. 105-109.

cultural revolutionaries believed that the peasants had a right to receive an education and become literate, and would support steps taken by the government to provide them with an opportunity to do so. They also assumed that any progress toward achieving this socialist cultural goal would also facilitate the revolutionary mobilization of the people. Education and literacy were not simply utopian goals whose realization would have to await the construction of a modern economic base in the postrevolutionary period.

Although he did not arrive in Kiangsi until early February 1934, Ch'ü's name figured prominently among the leaders of the mass cultural movement from the day the Chinese Soviet Republic was proclaimed on November 7, 1931, at the First All-China Congress of Soviets held in Juichin. The Constitution of the Soviet Government called for the Central Executive Committee of the Soviets to appoint a number of people's ministers who would coordinate government programs.[7] Despite the glaring fact that Ch'ü had been expelled from the party's Central Committee and Politburo by the Wang Ming leadership in Shanghai in January 1931, he was elected in absentia as minister of education at the First Congress of Soviets held nine months later.[8] While Ch'ü was in Shanghai his post was filled by Mao Tse-tung's former teacher, Hsu T'e-li.[9] At the same conference Mao was selected as Chairman of the Soviet, Hsiang Ying as Vice-Chairman, and Chu Teh as Commander-in-Chief of the Red Army. It is difficult to determine how much influence Ch'ü had in the formulation of educational and cultural programs prior to his arrival in February 1934, but it is evident that a number of efforts, particularly in the organization of drama activities, were compatible with his ideas about popular art and his general vision of a Proletarian May Fourth Movement. There is no reason to doubt that Ch'ü's writings were regarded as the theoretical cornerstone of the Kiangsi cultural revolution. There was, of course, considerable correspondence and travel between Shanghai and Juichin after 1931. Educational and cultural programs developed by the League of Left-wing Writers were known to intellectuals in Kiangsi, some of whom were recent arrivals from Shanghai.

At the Second All-China Congress of Soviets, which opened on January 21, 1934, Ch'ü was reelected minister of education. His official title was People's Commissar of Culture and Education (Wen-hua chiao-yü jen-min wei-yuan). Ch'ü was also appointed head of the

7. Conrad Brandt, Benjamin Schwartz, and John K. Fairbank, eds., *A Documentary History of Chinese Communism* (New York: Atheneum, 1966), p. 221.

8. Chang Ching-lu, ed., *Chung-kuo hsien-tai ch'u-pan shih-liao* [Documentary sources on publications of contemporary China] (Peking: Chung-hua shu-chü, 1954-1957), 3:350.

9. Ts'ai Hsiao-kan, *Chiang-hsi Su-ch'ü, Hung-chün hsi-ts'uan hui-i* [Memoirs on the Kiangsi soviet and the westward flight of the Red Army] (Hong Kong: Ta Chung-hua ch'u-pan-she, 1970), pp. 138-144.

Soviet Art Bureau and on April 1 was named president of Shen Tse-min University. Ch'ü was also elected to the Central Executive Committee of the central soviet government at the Second Congress.[10] It is unlikely, however, that Ch'ü had any real political power. His election to the Central Executive Committee reflects Mao Tse-tung's desire to surround himself with those who were known to be hostile to Wang Ming and his followers, most of whom had arrived on the scene by 1934. Nevertheless, Ch'ü did not play a very active role in the intense struggle that was taking place between Mao and the Comintern-supported Wang Ming leadership. Ch'ü was a relatively late arrival, and, owing to his extremely poor health, his work was necessarily confined to cultural matters. Ch'ü's activities in Kiangsi are important, not because he was a key figure in the political struggle, but because the cultural and artistic experiments carried on in the soviet base area represent the first serious attempt made by Chinese Marxists to implement programs consistent with Ch'ü's theoretical writings.

POPULAR EDUCATION

The most striking feature of Kiangsi cultural life was the absence of the sort of spirited debates among sophisticated Marxist literary thinkers that occupied so much of Ch'ü's time in Shanghai. In Kiangsi the problem was much more basic: how to provide the peasant population with fundamental educational and cultural opportunities. The revolutionary government had committed itself to pursuing these goals in its constitution. The people's government "shall guarantee to all workers, peasants, and the toiling masses the right to education" and give young people "every opportunity of participating in the political and cultural revolutionary life with a view to developing new social forces."[11] But initiating popular educational and cultural work was exceedingly difficult during the early years. Even if one assumes that most leftist intellectuals were willing to participate in popular cultural work on at least a temporary basis, their numbers were small, their resources were limited, and they had almost no experience administering the sort of concrete, practical programs that were required. Furthermore, the size of the soviet area was overwhelming. At its peak of development, the Kiangsi Soviet may have included as many as a hundred counties (*hsien*) with a population of twelve million.[12]

10. Chang Ching-lu, *Ch'u-pan shih-liao*, 3:532; Ts'ao Tzu-hsi, Ch'ü Ch'iu-pai te wen-hsueh huo-tung [Ch'ü Ch'iu-pai's literary activity] (Shanghai: Hsin wen-i ch'u-pan-she, 1958), p. 20.

11. Brandt, Schwartz, and Fairbank, eds., *Documentary History*, p. 223.

12. Kim, *Politics of Chinese Communism*, pp. 31-32.

Just after Ch'ü assumed personal control of the cultural apparatus, a survey by soviet authorities on the growth of popular education indicated that the program was remarkably successful. At the time the base area embraced 2,932 hamlets (hsiang) and a population of nine million in Kiangsi, Fukien, and Kwangtung.[13] The basic educational system included 3,052 Lenin primary schools (*Lieh-ning hsiao-hsueh*) with an enrollment of 89,000; 6,462 supplementary schools (*pu-hsi hsueh-hsiao*) with 94,517 adults enrolled in evening sessions; and 32,388 literacy groups (*shih-tzu tsu*) with 155,371 members.[14] In addition to these formal and informal educational programs, there were a variety of cultural organizations, including 1,656 clubs (*chü-lo-pu*) with an active membership of 49,668.[15] Elementary instruction was free of charge, but as Mao Tse-tung pointed out, students were obliged to supply their own equipment and school materials.[16]

Ch'ü Ch'iu-pai was directly involved in the administration of the soviet educational system in a number of central counties, such as Hsing-kuo, a county generally regarded as the model for the others.[17] For example, of the 20,969 children of elementary school age in Hsing-kuo county in 1934, 12,806, or 60 percent, actually attended elementary school. According to the 1934 report, the number of children who attended primary school during the preceding period of Kuomintang rule never exceeded 10 percent of school-age children.[18]

In Hsing-kuo, as elsewhere, massive illiteracy was the foremost problem confronting those who led the various adult education programs. Special efforts were made to offer educational opportunities to women, among whom illiteracy was particularly prevalent. In Hsing-kuo county, for example, of the 15,740 people in evening supplementary schools, 10,752 or 69 percent were women. Of the 22,519 people who participated in Hsing-kuo's literacy groups, 13,519 or 60 percent were women.[19] Aside from these evening schools and the home-study literacy groups, a third option, "roadside literary study" (*shih-tzu p'ai*), was available to peasants who wanted to begin the long process of attaining literacy. Like the various "street literary movements" Ch'ü proposed in Shanghai, roadside literacy study in Kiangsi was designed to meet the needs of people who had no opportunity to participate in more formal study groups. Cultural workers were instructed to take various teaching materials, including language flash cards, directly to

13. Kung Yung-kang, "The Revolutionary Bases in the Countryside in 1928-1933," *People's China*, 16 April 1957, p. 36.

14. Chang Ching-lu, *Ch'u-pan shih-liao*, 2:22.   15. Ibid.

16. Mao Tse-tung, "Ch'ang-kang hsiang tiao-ch'a" [A survey of Ch'ang-kang hamlet] (December 15, 1933), in *Mao Tse-tung chi* [The collected works of Mao Tse-tung] (Tokyo: Hokubosha, 1970-1973), 4:157.

17. TYTH, p. 154. Ch'ü also worked in Juichin and Ningtu counties.

18. Chang Ching-lu, *Ch'u-pan shih-liao*, 2:22.   19. Ibid., p. 23.

the peasants during work breaks.[20] In Hsing-kuo there were 130 hamlet literacy committees, 561 village (*ts'un*) subcommittees, and a total of 3,387 literacy groups in which 22,519 people were active.[21]

Surveys conducted by Mao Tse-tung himself in December 1933 give a fairly clear picture of cultural conditions at the grass roots level. For example, during his visit to Hsia-ts'ai-ch'i hamlet, Shang-hang county, Fukien Province, Mao learned that the hamlet had four villages, and a population of 2,610 people living in 503 families. Regarding elementary education, he observed that the hamlet had 5 day schools, 5 administrators, 5 teachers, and 150 regular students. An additional 60 students attended a district (*ch'ü*) school outside the hamlet. As far as adult education was concerned, the hamlet had 8 night schools, 8 teachers (the 5 day-school teachers among them), and 240 students. Furthermore, he noted the existence of 26 literacy groups attended by 260 people, as well as 5 roadside literacy stations. The hamlet also had one club whose activities were carried on by fifty cultural activists, and one "newspaper reading troupe" (*tu pao t'uan*) that traveled among the villages reading newspapers aloud for the benefit of interested peasants. Finally, the hamlet had 5 "bulletin boards" (*ch'iang-pao*) for the display of posters and artwork.[22]

This information is fascinating for two reasons. It illustrates the extent to which leaders, who were faced with staggering economic, military, and political problems, were willing to promote the mass education movement. It also indicates that under the circumstances, very little attention could be devoted to the problems of higher education, aesthetics, and the fine points of Marxist literary thought. Aside from Marx University, Soviet Political University, and Lenin Normal University (institutions about which very little is known), the most prominent centers of higher education were Shen Tse-min University headed by Ch'ü, the Gorky Drama School organized and named by Ch'ü but headed by his associate Li Po-chao, and the Red Army University administered by Generals Yeh Chien-ying and Liu Po-ch'eng.[23] Although these institutions were obviously very simple enterprises, they are interesting nevertheless. Red Army University, known at the time as Hung-ta, was an early experimental version of the famous and highly publicized Resist Japan University (K'ang-ta) of the Yenan period. Similarly, the Gorky Drama School was an important model for Yenan's Lu Hsün Academy of Arts.

20. Ibid.

21. Ibid. The model Hsing-kuo County Entertainment Club was led by Liu Chin-tung.

22. Mao Tse-tung, "Ts'ai-ch'i hsiang tiao-ch'a" [*A survey of Ts'ai-ch'i hamlet*] (1933), in *Mao Tse-tung chi*, 4:175, 195-196. Also see *Mao Tse-tung chi*, 4:126-127, 156-160.

23. Ting Yi, *A Short History of Modern Chinese Literature* (Peking: Foreign Languages Press, 1959), p. 46: Kung Yung-kang, "Revolutionary Bases in the Countryside," p. 36.

In view of the high rate of illiteracy, it is not surprising that relatively few books were published in the base area. Other factors that contributed to this situation include constant warfare, lack of publishing facilities, and the relatively small number of intellectuals present in the Soviet. The list of titles reportedly published between 1930 and 1934 gives some indication of the type of publication leaders considered most valuable. Among the ninety-seven known titles were books to aid in language teaching, school texts for physical science and mathematics, and books designed to introduce a variety of political topics. Virtually all the books in these categories were published by the Ministry of Education. The list also shows that leaders published a number of popular literary and art books, such as *Soviet Cultural Education, Revolutionary Songs and Dances, A Collection of New Songs of the Soviet,* and *New Tunes of the Soviet Area.*[24] No novels or collections of poems and short stories were printed. Aside from the books, a number of newspapers and periodicals were published. A contemporary source puts the number of periodical publications for the 1931-1934 period at thirty-four. These included *Red China* [*Hung-se Chung-hua*] with a circulation estimated as high as 50,000 copies; *Truth for Youth* [*Ch'ing-nien shih-hua*] with 28,000 copies; *Struggle* [*Tou-cheng*] with a circulation of 27,000 in Kiangsi Province alone; and *Red Star* [*Hung hsing*] with a circulation of 17,300.[25]

Ch'ü himself made very little use of the press. Most of the information about his activities is in memoirs written by Li Po-chao, Chao P'in-san and others who worked closely with Ch'ü, and in the general accounts and social surveys that treat the subject of cultural conditions in the base area. Ch'ü's single article, an essay entitled "Education During Class Warfare," is, nevertheless, a rather interesting piece of work. Written in the stiff and "official" political language Ch'ü used in the 1920s and reflecting the tense atmosphere created by the Kuomintang's fifth and final encirclement campaign, this essay also indicates that Ch'ü was still emphasizing several of the cultural themes he had first articulated in Shanghai. For example, Ch'ü continued to stress the importance of the revolution in the superstructure and in popular consciousness. At a time when Kuomintang military and economic pressure was beginning to strangle the base area, Ch'ü insisted that the cultural revolution was more important than ever. "None of us should forget that education is also a weapon in class struggle, and only when Soviet education is under the leadership of the proletariat will it be able genuinely to assist the revolutionary war. If this class leadership and the worker-peasant democratic dictatorship are even slightly weakened, the landlord and rich peasant

24. Chang Ching-lu, *Ch'u-pan shih-liao*, 2:24-31.   25. Ibid., pp. 24, 31.

elements will be able to use our educational system to carry out their 'class work': that is, to destroy the Soviet educational system, propagate reactionary traditional thought, and even openly engage in counterrevolutionary activities."[26] Thus, once again, Ch'ü presented cultural transformation as a two-way street. If the revolutionary camp takes the initiative in this area, the revolution will advance more quickly; if the nonrevolutionary group establishes its dominance, the growth of the revolution will be retarded.

A second familiar theme, the role of intellectuals, is also discussed once again by Ch'ü. His concern about the worsening political and military situation led him to cite a number of cases in which intellectuals who once held positions of leadership in the Soviet educational system later collaborated with the Kuomintang. To consolidate revolutionary control over the cultural realm, it would be necessary to identify those engaged in counterrevolutionary educational activities. Nevertheless, Ch'ü continued to insist, as he had all his life, that not all gentry intellectuals and experts were counterrevolutionaries. Intensifying class struggle in the cultural world did not mean suppressing all intellectuals. Local intellectuals who supported the revolution should be encouraged to continue their work. "We oppose the doctrine of 'consuming intellectuals.' We must continue to oppose this variety of left-wing opportunism." But, he added, "we must also oppose right-wing opportunism that divorces itself from the class line."[27] Thus, even in his last days, Ch'ü was attempting to balance extremes.

Finally, it is clear from his article that Ch'ü continued in Kiangsi to believe it was necessary to promote the direct participation of the people in cultural and educational affairs in order to reduce their dependency on gentry or bourgeois intellectuals. Ch'ü pointed out that intellectuals who held teaching and administrative positions tended to select the sons of landlords and rich peasants for special education or training programs for future cadres, despite the fact that they were often as illiterate as middle and poor peasants. New cadres should be trained from among "worker and peasant lads and laboring women" and then assume the responsibility of educating the "unknowledgeable rich peasants and landlords."[28] During his own tours of inspection in rural areas, Ch'ü encouraged young men and women of worker and peasant origin to become involved in "eradication-of-illiteracy associations" and the "worker and peasant drama societies."

---

26. Ch'ü Ch'iu-pai, "Chieh-chi chan-cheng chung te chiao-yü" [Education during class warfare], *Tou-cheng* [Struggle], 62 (1934): 15. By his use of the phrase "under the leadership of the proletariat," Ch'ü could only have meant the Communist Party and the government of the soviet region because there was no working class to speak of in the base area.

27. Ibid., p. 17.   28. Ibid.

As in Shanghai, Ch'ü held that many of the cultural problems of the Chinese revolution could be addressed only when the people themselves became involved. And few could deny that, despite the gravity of the military situation, revolutionary cultural programs, such as the Soviet drama movement, were easier to organize in the base areas than they had been in Kuomintang-controlled cities.

THE SOVIET DRAMA MOVEMENT

Without question, the most interesting "cultural organization" (*wen-hua t'uan-t'i*) under Ch'ü's direction was the Soviet drama movement. The history of its development can be traced to the founding of the base area itself. Chao P'in-san, one of the earliest Soviet cultural leaders, has identified a number of phases through which the movement passed. Initiated largely for the purpose of entertaining the troops, the Soviet drama movement began in the Red Army as early as 1929 and 1930. Gradually, informal army drama teams, composed of both officers and ordinary soldiers, realized that drama also "was an important form for arousing the masses." Consequently, following each of the early military victories, the soldiers called the local peasants together for an evening meeting during which several dramatic skits were performed.[29] In Chao's view, these efforts were unusually effective in mobilizing peasant support for land revolution and expansion of the Red Army. In the winter of 1930, just prior to the formal proclamation of the Chinese Soviet Republic, the Workers' and Peasants' Red Army School was opened in Juichin. "Because the cultural level of the students was so low," Chao observed, "the school's educational program not only included formal military and political instruction, but also placed considerable emphasis on extracurricular cultural and recreational activities."[30] Within the school a number of "entertainment clubs" were established to coordinate dramatic work. Eventually, a Drama Administration Committee (*hsi-chü kuan-li wei-yuan-hui*) including Chao P'in-san, Li Po-chao, and Wei Kung-chih was formed. "There was a time," Chao recalled, "when each week there would be an evening gathering and dramatic productions. Most dramas were performed under the stars, therefore whenever the Red Army School had an evening gathering not only did the school members participate, but the masses came from all directions to participate. . . . The Entertainment Club of the Red Army School was known at the time as the 'cultural center.'"[31] Owing to the success of this early informal drama

29. Chao P'in-san, "Kuan-yü chung-yang ko-ming ken-chü-ti hua-chü kung-tso te hui-i" [Reminiscences concerning drama work in the central revolutionary base area]; in TKTL, 1:578.

30. Ibid., p. 579.   31. Ibid., p. 580.

work, the first formal Soviet drama troupe was founded in late 1931. Known as the "August First Dramatic Troupe" (Pa-i chü-t'uan), its leading members included Chao P'in-san, Li Po-chao, Wei Kung-chih, Ts'ai Jen-hsiang, Huang Huo-ch'ing, Wu Hsiu-ch'uan and others. It was the first Soviet drama troupe to travel widely to bring art and culture to the outlying areas.[32]

Under Ch'ü's direction the drama movement continued to expand at both the central and local levels. In Juichin it had two centers: for the military, the movement continued to be based in the old Entertainment Club of the Red Army School (renamed Red Army University); for the civilian population, the Workers' and Peasants' Drama Society (Kung-nung chü she) was established under the leadership of Chang Hsin, a former member of the August First Dramatic troupe. The Worker's and Peasant's Drama Society in Juichin administered the newly formed Gorky Drama School as well as the Blue Denim Troupe, the civilian equivalent of the August First Dramatic Troupe.[33] In the villages, the drama movement was advanced by the various decentralized workers' and peasants' drama groups, the 1,656 local entertainment clubs, and the nearly 50,000 grass roots cultural activists.[34]

One of the interesting aspects of the drama program is that it took into consideration the different needs of the central and local levels. The various central organizations were responsible for recruiting mobile drama troupes who would bring cultural programs to the villages and to the troops at the front. Their primary task was to present current news and government programs and policies in dramatic form, but Ch'ü advised them to maintain close contact with local people by studying their cultural traditions and by considering the problems they faced in daily life as source material for dramatic productions. Commenting on his discussions with Wei Kung-chih about the Kiangsi program, Edgar Snow reported that "the peasants, always grateful for any diversion in their culture-starved lives, voluntarily arranged all transport, food and housing for these visits."[35] Ch'ü also encouraged central units to assume the responsibility for recruiting new cultural activists from among the peasant population itself. He suggested that these young people come to Juichin under the auspices of the central Drama Society to study for six months, and then, upon graduation, return to the hamlets and villages to organize new and decentralized "drama groups" (chü-t'uan).[36] Commenting on the success of this pro-

33. Ibid.   32. Ibid., p. 581.

34. Chang Ching-lu, *Ch'u-pan shih-liao*, 2:22.

35. Edgar Snow, *Red Star over China* (New York: Grove Press, 1961), p. 114.

36. Liu Shou-sung, *Chung-kuo hsin wen-hsueh shih ch'u-kao* [A preliminary draft on the history of modern Chinese literature] (Peking: Tso-chia ch'u-pan-she, 1957), 1:308.

gram, Chao P'in-san, who served as a liaison between military and civilian drama groups, proclaimed: "Everywhere the flowers of the drama movement bloomed."[37]

The Gorky Drama School was created in 1934 specifically to organize mobile drama troupes and recruit cultural leaders from among the people. At its peak the school had one thousand peasant students and sixty mobile theatrical troupes. According to Edgar Snow: "Every troupe had long waiting lists of requests from village Soviets."[38] Li Po-chao, Ch'ü's close associate and director of the school, reported that 90 percent of the students were members of the Communist Youth League, and virtually all were young, illiterate peasants who had participated in the Soviet land reform movement. Not only did the dramatic workers have no artistic background, their training took place without benefit of teaching materials or stage equipment, props, and elaborate costumes. As a consequence, soviet cultural workers became masters of improvisation and pantomime. Because drama teachers were also scarce, Ch'ü approved of the decision to permit several Kuomintang prisoners of war who had experience in the theater to teach in the Gorky Drama School.[39]

Li Po-chao's Central Blue Denim Troupe (Chung-yang lan-pu t'uan), the best-known drama group associated with the Gorky School, was already in existence when Ch'ü arrived in 1934. Renamed the Blue Denim Drama Troupe (Lan-pu chü-t'uan), this group performed during the First and Second Soviet Congresses in 1931 and 1934 as part of a joint effort by the Workers' and Peasants' Drama Society and Red Army University Entertainment Club.[40] The Blue Denim Drama Troupe was, of course, named after the drama group organized in Shanghai by the League of Left-wing Writers to bring Ch'ü's Proletarian May Fourth Movement to the people in the teashops and back streets. Like the Gorky School, the Blue Denim Troupe had few drama experts among its members.

The work style of the central groups and local groups, such as the Hsing-kuo County Entertainment Club, was essentially the same. A fundamental feature of the drama work of both was its collective nature. After selection and discussion of themes appropriate for dramatic treatment, the work of researching the subject was divided among group members, and talks were held to determine the best methods of producing the play. Literate troupe members were assigned the task of script writing, and criticisms were offered and revi-

37. Chao P'in-san, "Hua-chü kung-tso," TKTL, p. 582.

38. Snow, *Red Star*, p. 114.

39. Li Po-chao, "Hui-i Ch'ü Ch'iu-pai t'ung-chih" [Reminiscences of comrade Ch'ü Ch'iu-pai], *Jen-min jih-pao*, 18 June 1950.

sions made following rehearsals. The final product was often sub-
mitted to interested government officials such as Ch'ü for a final
assessment.[41] After the first public performance, criticism and revision continued. It is clear that Ch'ü used many of the same standards
to evaluate Kiangsi drama that he had used in Shanghai. Ch'ü advised
troupe members to use the language of "living people," language that
could be "understood when read aloud."[42] One also gets the impression that in terms of form, Ch'ü believed that nothing was better
suited to conditions and problems in Kiangsi than drama. Its collective
nature required the direct participation of a relatively large artistic
team and assured a large audience. Its oral and visual characteristics
guaranteed that even those peasants who were completely illiterate
could take an active part in artistic activity, or at least be part of the
audience. Moreover, the flexibility of the dramatic form meant that
the Soviet movement was able to make use of traditional forms familiar to the people while, at the same time, introducing foreign forms.[43]

Dramas were produced at two levels, and the Ministry of Culture
and Education was the central organization most responsible for making available a number of relatively polished productions for general
distribution.[44] Often, however, the general themes of the central
drama were outdated or simply failed to treat rapidly changing circumstances in local areas. In such cases local drama groups or especially
creative mobile troupes carried the burden of addressing local problems. Among the sixty "guerrilla theatre" troupes of the Gorky Drama
School, the concept of "living newspaper drama" (huo pao chü) became
quite popular. Like other productions, the dialogues and music were
written by troupe members, but the content was subject to rapid
revision based on the latest news developments. These dramatic performances were designed to educate the peasant population about
current political, economic, social, and military problems by using an
artistic form that would captivate a preliterate audience. During the
period of land reform, emphasis was placed on the traditional land
tenure system and peasant resistance; later, more attention was given
to the activities of the Red Army and the Japanese threat.[45] Regret-
tably, none of the scripts for the central dramas or the local living
newspaper productions survived the collapse of the base area in 1934,
although at a later date Chao P'in-san and others recorded the titles
and summarized the stories of some plays.[46]

It is apparent, however, that cultural workers were guided by many

40. Liu Shou-sung, Hsin wen-hsueh shih, 1:311.
41. Ibid., 1:312-313.　　42. Li Po-chao, "Hui-i Ch'ü Ch'iu-pai."
43. Liu Shou-sung, Hsin wen-hsueh shih, 1:310-311.
44. Ibid., 1:312.　　45. Ibid., 1:310-311.
46. Chao P'in-san, "Hua-chü kung-tso," TKTL, pp. 582-583.

of the principles of popular art Ch'ü had spelled out in Shanghai. To collect new and realistic source material, actors and writers were urged to visit and interview peasants in their homes to record the story of their lives and to determine topics of interest to them. Troupe members were also encouraged to ask peasants who had seen some of the new productions to evaluate their effectiveness. These policies were, of course, entirely compatible with Ch'ü's earlier writings about the value of "going to the people to learn."

The soviet drama movement also accepted Ch'ü's belief that the problems of form and language were somewhat more important than the problem of content. Cultural activists could agree upon the most appropriate content for revolutionary artistic works, but often ignored or failed to resolve the question of form. But in Kiangsi, where there was a rather small audience for modern fiction and even fewer literary intellectuals who were interested in producing such works, cultural leaders agreed that the emphasis should be placed on traditional forms such as *ch'ü* drama and other performing arts already familiar to and welcomed by the people. The idea was that, although the content of traditional drama often reflected a nonrevolutionary world view, new and revolutionary content could be injected into the old forms without much difficulty. The conservative, traditional theater would thus be transformed into a vehicle for social mobilization.[47]

The same approach was employed in the treatment of folk music, an art form that received almost as much attention at the Kiangsi Soviet as drama. Ch'ü Ch'iu-pai was particularly enthusiatic about this form. As in the case of drama, he advocated the retention of traditional folk tunes and the introduction, where appropriate, of new lyrics that reflected the contemporary social scene. "The words of a popular song are of great educational value to the people," Ch'ü remarked. "If you have no one who can compose a song, then write out the words and sing them to the tune of a folk song that is familiar to the audience, pleasant to hear, and easy to sing."[48] He urged cultural leaders to go out among the people and begin, for the first time in the history of the leftist literary movement, to systematically collect and transcribe traditional folk tunes.[49] Many of these survived the Long March.[50]

Though a far cry from the complex and sophisticated Shanghai world of letters, the Kiangsi drama program by all accounts was enormously popular among the peasants. Some would travel for miles with their families and sit spellbound for hours in the cold night air to

47. Liu Shou-sung, *Hsin wen-hsueh shih*, 1:311.
48. Li Po-chao, "Hui-i Ch'ü Ch'iu-pai."
49. Liu Shou-sung, *Hsin wen-hsueh shih*, 1:314.
50. See ibid., 1:314-317; and TKTL, 1:590-606.

witness the agonies of the past and the hopes of the future acted out before their eyes.[51] Foreign and other observers have written numerous reports of similar peasant responses to outdoor drama staged during the Yenan period.

The Kiangsi experiments in popular education and drama are important, not because Ch'ü led these movements from the beginning (for it is clear that he did not), or because Ch'ü was on the scene for an extended period of time (although his presence for over one year should not be underestimated), but rather because the Kiangsi popular cultural program represented the first systematic effort made by Chinese revolutionaries to implement the type of popular movement Ch'ü advocated so ardently in his critical and theoretical writings, and because, embryonic as the Kiangsi cultural movement was, it clearly served as the model for the better-known Yenan cultural program of the 1936-1946 period. The continuity between the Kiangsi and Yenan programs was guaranteed, in part, by the leading role played in Yenan by former Kiangsi cultural leaders like Li Po-chao, Wei Kung-chih, and Chao P'in-san.[52] The point is that the Kiangsi popular culture movement is important because it was notably successful and was thus regarded as an attractive model. Indeed, it seems fair to say that Ch'ü and his colleagues were more successful than their Yenan successors.[53]

Although Ch'ü obviously did not have a rural environment in mind when he mapped out his hopes for a Proletarian May Fourth, the Kiangsi cultural program was consistent with his theoretical formulations in many regards. The class composition of the soviet artistic movement indicated that a viable alliance between revolutionary intellectuals and the masses could in fact be forged during a "popular" literary movement. A relatively small number of revolutionary intellectuals played a leading role at every level and accepted the responsibility of advancing what Ch'ü had always regarded as the "bourgeois-democratic" cultural revolution. Yet, on the other hand, the soviet cultural program was also very much a movement of the people themselves, rather than a "proletarian" literary movement led exclusively by revolutionary intellectuals on behalf of the masses. Of course, in Kiangsi the overwhelming majority of mass participants were not workers, but peasants. It is interesting that the general absence of proletarian participation did not prevent Ch'ü from regarding this popular activity as essentially socialist in character. He clearly believed that a distinctively "proletarian" cultural movement could exist in

51. Chao P'in-san, "Hua-chü kung-tso," TKTL, p. 580.

52. Nym Wales, *Red Dust* (Stanford: Stanford University Press, 1942), p. 183; and Snow, *Red Star*, p. 113.

53. Snow, *Red Star*, p. 254.

these miniature revolutionary states or liberated zones even before state power was seized nationwide. Thus in Kiangsi, the abortive bourgeois-democratic cultural revolution was revived and advanced in conjunction with the initial stages of a new socialist cultural revolution that was highlighted by the direct participation of the people.

The stress on dramatic forms was compatible with all Ch'ü's ideas about the requirements of a popular literary movement that would be able to resolve distinctively Chinese problems. The oral and visual characteristics of the performing arts were especially well suited to a situation in which massive illiteracy existed. Further, the collective nature of the performing arts, from the perspective of both the participants and the observers, helped to create an environment favorable to the spread of modern culture. Drama, the dominant art form of the Kiangsi Soviet, was accessible to all citizens. Peasants with a low cultural level were encouraged to become active participants in the drama movement at all levels. The self-reliant and collective nature of dramatic work also boosted morale and mutual cooperation among the cultural activists. They were responsible for script writing, directing, costume making, acting, and scheduling, all of which required close contact with the people. For their part, the peasants accepted the responsibility of housing, feeding, and assisting the drama troupes.

Another important feature of Ch'ü's theory of popular art was its emphasis on traditional popular forms. The drama movement at Kiangsi used a wide variety of traditional forms including opera, storytelling, folk ballads, and dancing. Peasants, it was learned, were more receptive to new content when it was presented in familiar forms, and the use of such forms was psychologically satisfying to nationalists like Ch'ü. Nevertheless, he called for the gradual introduction of modern and foreign forms, and once again drama proved to be the form most adaptable to Chinese needs. Western drama, ballet, and the living-newspaper plays were all components of Kiangsi cultural life and were often combined with traditional Chinese forms.

The Kiangsi popular culture movement is also interesting because it was slowly becoming clear to those intellectuals on the scene that a price would have to be paid for the undeniable success of the movement. It would be wrong to suggest that intellectuals in Kiangsi made any systematic attempt to raise such questions, or complained about the work they were doing; but it must have occurred to at least some of them that there was a conflict between the urban orientation of the old leftist literary movement and the new rural movement. One of the reasons that this question was not raised in Kiangsi, and a fact that may in part explain the relative success of the popular movement, was that not many urban intellectuals were actually on hand. Of the well-known Shanghai writers, only Feng Hsueh-feng, Ch'eng Fang-wu, and a few others appeared in Juichin. As Ch'ü had pointed out in his Shanghai writings, Europeanized leftist intellectuals were likely to be the least enthusiastic about promoting a popular cultural movement. Although many urban intellectuals recognized in theory the need for such a program, they were likely to find the transition from "Europeanized" leftist literary culture to a popular culture difficult in practice, especially when the arena of such work was in the backward villages.

There were other problems on the horizon. Although no one seems to have raised the question, it is fairly apparent that the creation of a small revolutionary "state" in south China was accompanied by an attempt to reintegrate art and society in China. From the time of the New Culture Movement, the revolutionary literary movement of the Europeanized intellectuals had based itself on the premise that the writer, including the socially conscious writer, should be independent from the state in order to permit criticism of the state and society. In general, the role of the writer during the May Fourth period was to criticize those in the family, or at the summit of political life, who had power. Very little May Fourth writing was intended to support government programs or praise political parties. Whether Ch'ü was aware of it or not, in Kiangsi the first practical steps were taken to reverse this course. The locus of the modern literary movement had shifted from the city to the countryside. The fashion had changed from sophisticated literary activities to basic and simplistic popular works. And now art and the artist were being reintegrated into the new society planned for the future.

Ch'ü Ch'iu-pai wrote nothing about such problems while he was serving in Kiangsi. It is likely, however, that he was aware of these issues. Following the collapse of the soviet base area and the retreat of communist main forces, Ch'ü had several opportunities to reflect on what had taken place in Kiangsi. Although his remarks were random in nature and unusually pessimistic in tone, they show Ch'ü torn between a desire to assist in the cultural liberation of the masses and his commitment to advanced literary work. He stated quite directly that he too was one of those intellectuals who "only knows concepts and ideas and the kind of rhetoric to make them sound attractive." If one asks such an intellectual about details, "he becomes confused and will not be able to answer your question. Like a man who looks at a flower through a dense fog, he is unable to see life as it really is."[54] Ch'ü stated further that, although he was in charge of the popular cultural program in Kiangsi: "I had no special knowledge of problems pertaining to juvenile education; nor had I any idea of how the work-

54. TYTH, p. 153.

ing masses should be educated during a period of civil war. As far as being an educator was concerned, I was worse than an amateur."[55] Ch'ü's physical condition may have had something to do with his difficulty in adjusting to rural life. His tuberculosis worsened and his bouts with insomnia started up again. Ch'ü tried to make contact with and learn from the peasants, and was probably more successful than his final statements indicate. But his frank admission of the problems he encountered indicates that Chinese intellectuals were standing on the threshold of a difficult future. "After three or four years of land revolution in the Central Soviet Region, I wished to find out how the peasants felt about it and in what way their lives had changed because of it. Twice I embarked upon an inspection tour, but my findings amounted to very little. There was no common language between me and the peasants."[56]

55. TYTH, p. 154.　　56. TYTH, p. 154.

12 Superfluous Words

Waking from a Dream
A drizzling rain cools the mountain town's spring.
Shivering cold seized a lonely man from his dreaming,
While all things are sinking into quietude.
Why should a dangling fantasy still be haunting?
                                    CH'Ü CH'IU-PAI, 1935[1]

In October 1933, four months before Ch'ü's arrival in the Soviet area, the Kuomintang's fifth (and final) encirclement campaign was launched with 900,000 troops mobilized against the Chinese Soviet Republic. Stalled briefly by the revolt of its Nineteenth Route Army in Fukien, the campaign was renewed after January 1934. After the Second All-China Congress of Soviets, according to Mao Tse-tung, planning began to evacuate the base area. The frontiers of the Soviet Republic were shrinking, and the Red Army numbered only 126,000 in September 1934. This, of course, was hardly the time for Ch'ü to ask whether the Kiangsi popular cultural movement was what he had in mind when he sketched out his vision of a Proletarian May Fourth. On October 15, 1934, 100,000 men and 35 women assembled in the Juichin area to prepare for the epic Long March. Of the departing forces, 80,000 were army regulars and 20,000 were government officials and party cadres.[2]

Many remained behind, including 26,000 Red Army soldiers who

1. Ssu-ma Lu, *Ch'ü Ch'iu-pai chuan* [A biography of Ch'ü Ch'iu-pai] (Hong Kong: Tzu-lien ch'u-pan-she, 1962), p. 105. The translation used here is from Warren Kuo, "Tsunyi Conference: Part II," *Issues and Studies*, 5 (February 1968):55.

2. John E. Rue, *Mao Tse-tung in Opposition, 1927-1935* (Stanford: Stanford University Press, 1966), pp. 266-267.

were to slow the advance of Kuomintang troops, and with the exception of 35 wives, all other women and all children.[3] Ch'ü Ch'iu-pai was among those leaders who did not join the Long March. Ironically, it was assumed that those who stayed behind stood a greater chance of surviving than those who were marching out into the unknown. "At first I did not know, but they decided to leave me behind," Ch'ü subsequently recalled; "Hsiang Ying later told me of the decision. Since I thought my illness would prevent me from enduring the hardships of a long journey, I consented. Hsiang Ying stayed behind with his men for two purposes: first, to lead the 24th Division and the Eighth and Ninth Regiments to pin down the pursuing Nationalist troops, and second, to carry on certain activities in the Soviet area. It was decided to abandon all cities and scatter their troops in order to concentrate on the remote villages."[4] According to Ch'ü, he and Hsiang Ying had the responsibility of forming "a rear office of the Party Central Committee at Chiu-pao, Juichin." His official posts were Head of the Propaganda Department of the Central Bureau and Chief of Affairs of the Southeast Area.[5] Other leaders left behind included Teng Tzu-hui (head of the Fukien Soviet), Ho Shu-heng (Hunanese delegate to the first congress of the Communist Party in 1921), and Chang Liang (wife of Hsiang Ying, Vice-Chairman of the Soviet Republic).[6] According to Chao P'in-san, Ch'ü continued to organize drama activities after the departure of the Long March.[7]

Although details are scanty and often contradictory, it appears that sometime in February 1935 Ch'ü and several others decided to leave the central area and travel across the provincial border to Sheng-su, Fukien Province. "At Sheng-su," he wrote, "a local unit was dispatched to escort us to Yung-ting, Fukien, where we would proceed to Hong Kong or Shanghai."[8] But Ch'ü's contingent never reached Yung-ting. Around March 20, Ch'ü, Chang Liang, and Chou Yueh-lin (wife of Liang Pai-t'ai) were apprehended at a village called Shui-k'ou near the town of Wu-p'ing, Fukien, by a unit of the Kuomintang's Security Corps under the command of Chung Ch'ao-kuei.[9] At first Ch'ü's

3. Ibid.

4. Li K'e-ch'ang, "Ch'ü Ch'iu-pai fang-wen chi" [An interview with Ch'ü Ch'iu-pai], *Kuo-wen chou-pao* [National news weekly], 8 July 1935, pp. 1-7.

5. Ts'ao Tzu-hsi, *Ch'ü Ch'iu-pai te wen-hsueh huo-tung* [Ch'ü Ch'iu-pai's literary activity] (Shanghai: Hsin wen-i ch'u-pan-she, 1958), p. 20.

6. Li K'e-ch'ang, "Fang-wen chi," p. 3.

7. Chao P'in-san, "Kuan-yü chung-yang ko-ming ken-chü-ti te hua-chü kung-tso te hui-i" [Reminiscences concerning drama work in the central revolutionary base area], in TKTL, p. 586.

8. Li K'e-ch'ang, "Fang-wen chi," p. 3.

9. Ibid., p. 1; TYTH, p. 17; and Chang Ching-lu, ed., *Chung-kuo hsien-tai ch'u-pan shih-*

identity was unknown to his captors. He asserted that he was a physician by the name of Lin Ch'i-hsiang who had been pressured by communist officials to work as a doctor in the Red Army. Ch'ü was then taken to Shang-hang, Fukien, and detained for about a month in barracks quartering raw military recruits. During this period his health declined rapidly.[10] Apparently he had been coughing blood and suffering from acute insomnia for some time. In early May, Ch'ü was transferred to Ting-chou Prison in Ch'ang-t'ing, Fukien, following speculation that important revolutionary leaders had been captured.[11] At this point, Ch'ü made a final and desperate attempt to conceal his identity and seek release by using his assumed name to write to Lu Hsün, who he hoped would be able to intervene on his behalf. But almost immediately after his internment in Ting-chou Prison, located at the headquarters of the Kuomintang's 36th Division in Ch'ang-t'ing, Ch'ü was identified by a captured cook who had served in the Soviet area.[12] Apparently, the identities of Chang Liang and Chou Yueh-lin, who were imprisoned in Lung-yen, Fukien, were revealed at about the same time.[13]

There can be no question that Ch'ü became deeply depressed in the days following the discovery of his identity. Sitting alone in a damp cell day after day, he had plenty of time to think about the past: the bitter tragedies of his youth, the spiritual exhilaration of his May Fourth experience, his odyssey to the Land of Hunger, his disastrous political career, and especially his love of literature and companions like Lu Hsün, Kuo Mo-jo, Ting Ling, and Mao Tun. In Ting-chou Prison he was alone with these thoughts. His friends in Shanghai, and those who were struggling for survival on the Long March, were not even aware that he had been captured. Ch'ü, for his part, knew nothing about the fate of his family and friends. He had not received any letters from his wife since June 1934.[14] At age thirty-six it must have been difficult for Ch'ü to accept the fact that soon he would be dead. The photographs of Ch'ü in his final days, and eyewitness reports, indicate that he was dying of tuberculosis. He also knew that if the disease that had haunted him since his Peking days did not claim his life, he would probably be executed by the Kuomintang.

It was under these circumstances that Ch'ü Ch'iu-pai spent the six days from May 17 to May 22 writing an extraordinary final testament entitled "Superfluous Words" (To-yü te hua). Ch'ü divided his long, melancholy essay into seven parts. Although each section has a dif-

---

liao [Documentary sources on publications of contemporary China] (Peking: Chung-hua shu-chü, 1954-1957), 3:532. Reports of the time of arrest vary: February 23, "middle of March," March 20, "beginning of April."

10. Li K'e-ch'ang, "Fang-wen chi," p. 1.   11. TYTH, p. 19.
12. Li K'e-ch'ang, "Fang-wen chi," p. 1.   13. Ibid.   14. Ibid., p. 3.

ferent theme, the whole work is characterized primarily by the constant repetition of certain points: his physical and spiritual exhaustion, his impending doom, and his startling assertion that he was precisely one of those "superfluous intellectuals" he had been writing about for years. Considering Ch'ü's lifelong intellectual concerns, he could have thought of no harsher self-condemnation.

The opening section is a brief and sad introduction. Aside from setting the mood for the entire piece, it gives some indication of Ch'ü's state of mind at the time: "My life is quickly marching toward its end; its continuance will be measured in days rather than years. Whatever I have in mind, it really matters little whether I should or should not express it in words."[15] Ch'ü insisted that he had no wish to be regarded as a revolutionary hero, and urged the "younger generation" not to waste their time indulging in "such idle speculation as to what ideology my past writings really represent." Now that he was alone, he wished for nothing else but an opportunity to analyze his emotions, "a luxury that all bourgeois intellectuals truly enjoy."

The second portion, entitled "Historical Misunderstanding," presented a relatively factual account of his life from 1916 to 1931, but insisted that his life had been marked by one accidental entanglement after another that led gradually to even deeper political involvements for a man who was basically apolitical. For example, he observed:

> I often said to myself that a man of my temperament, ability, or learning, to be a communist leader was in fact an "historical misunderstanding." Deep in my heart I knew that I was nothing but a carefree, unconventional, and easygoing "man of letters." Even today I still feel the same way. My interest in politics began to decline as early as 1927, and for the last year, the year I was in Juichin, it virtually ceased to exist. As far as political work was concerned, all that I was interested in was not to commit too many errors, and I was too indifferent to be concerned with the overall political situation in China. This indifference stemmed partly from my physical condition (I tired easily when I engaged in concentrated work) and partly from my desire not to "rock the boat." For more than ten years I did some political as well as translation work more out of inertia than out of interest; this kind of work was in fact contrary to my own nature or character. All these years I was involved in an "historical misunderstanding" or, perhaps more correctly, a nightmare. . . . I do not intend to seek forgiveness by indulging in sentimentalities. I am interested only in describing the situation as I see it before my impending death. How else could one describe it except as an

15. TYTH, p. 126.

"historical error" that an ordinary man of letters like me was a "great" political leader of the Chinese Communist Party for more than ten years?[16]

It is hard to know what to make of this statement. It is true, of course, that Ch'ü was essentially a cultural figure who, under normal circumstances, would have been most content doing literary work. Yet he lived in an exceedingly abnormal period and was by no means the only literary personality who felt compelled to participate in political activities. Although it is difficult to say precisely why Ch'ü chose to summarize his political life in the manner that he did, it is impossible to avoid the conclusion that in his final days Ch'ü overemphasized the role played by coincidence and accident in his political development and exaggerated his own lack of enthusiasm.

The third part, entitled "A Weak Dual Personality," is of greater interest than Ch'ü's summary of his early political activities because it discusses the role of intellectuals in proletarian revolutions, a matter that absorbed much of his intellectual energy in previous years. Ch'ü certainly did not rule out the possibility that intellectuals might participate in such revolutions, but he now regarded his own attempt as something of a farce. Although it is impossible to take seriously Ch'ü's contention that "only emptiness has occupied my mind ever since the Fourth Congress of the Chinese Communist Party expelled me from the Political Bureau in January 1931,"[17] his fear of becoming an ineffective gentry intellectual probably weighed heavily upon him throughout his career. But "Superfluous Words" was not an attempt to resolve this nagging problem; instead it was Ch'ü's way of acknowledging that he had never really succeeded in transforming his consciousness. Ch'ü probably would have agreed that all revolutionary intellectuals had a "dual personality," but that to be an effective revolutionary the "proletarian" personality would have to dominate the gentry personality. In his own case, he was now insisting, the proletarian face was a facade. In essence he remained a gentry intellectual. His emotional and physical weakness resulted from the tension between his "gentry subconsciousness" and his acceptance of Marxism and the proletarian revolution. "A man's attitude toward life is his ideology, his road of thought. Once the Marxist road is taken, few have been able to leave it and take another road. What is Marxism? It is an attitude toward life and a concept of the universe from the proletariat's point of view, which is in direct contrast to my hidden gentry subconsciousness—the traditional subconsciousness of the Chinese intelligentsia."[18] Ch'ü had always said that those gentry intellectuals who failed to proletarianize ran the risk of becoming petty-

16. Ibid., pp. 132-133.   17. Ibid., p. 134.   18. Ibid., p. 136.

bourgeois philistines. Now, he confessed, he could recognize the manifestations of vulgar philistine subconsciousness in his own thought. "I am far from being an old man," he commented, "but the toil of ten years, however unworthy it was, has reduced me to a physical as well as emotional cripple. What a weakling I really am! How little I can stand hardship!"[19]

Ch'ü's encounter with Marxism, the subject of the fourth section of his memoir, is consistent with the themes that run throughout the whole work. On one hand, he asserted that his introduction to Marxism was accidental, and, on the other hand, insisted that his understanding of Marxism had always been superficial. Thus, it was his interest in Russian literature and language that left him "no choice but to join China's first Marxist society," while later, as an interpreter in Moscow, he was "compelled by necessity to go over Marxist ideology."[20] As a result of this imperfect grasp of Marxism, Ch'ü concluded that his theoretical political writings were of little use to the party. "The kind of Marxism I have learned is really common sense, acquired at random by reading articles in newspapers and magazines and also several of Lenin's pamphlets."[21] Of course, this critical self-evaluation is equally applicable to the majority of early Chinese Marxists. In any case, despite Ch'ü's protestations to the contrary, his knowledge of Marxist theory surpassed the level attained by most prominent Chinese Marxists. It is to be noted, however, that nowhere in this final essay did Ch'ü renounce Marxism or the Chinese Communist Party. On the contrary: "To say that I have abandoned Marxism is definitely not true. If people insist on discussing political problems with me, I shall have no choice except to discuss them in the context of my superficial understanding of the word Marxism. . . . During my younger days, my thinking led me to the road of Marxism which I have not been able to change."[22]

The section entitled "Adventurism and the Li Li-san Line" is the only portion of the essay that presented a detailed discussion of substantive political issues in the history of the Chinese Communist Party. Although Ch'ü insisted that it was "incorrect" to say that the policies he pursued as leader of the party from August 1927 to the spring of 1928 were "adventurist," and that he sometimes "failed to comprehend the reasoning" of the twenty-eight Bolsheviks, his bitterness toward the Comintern and the Wang Ming group is not expressed.[23] Instead, in his assessment of party history from 1927 to 1931, Ch'ü repeatedly drew attention to his practical and theoretical errors and stressed his failure to recognize the shortcomings of the Li Li-san leadership. "I may even go further by saying that the Li Li-san

19. Ibid., p. 135.   20. Ibid., pp. 137 and 138.   21. Ibid., p. 139.
22. Ibid., p. 142.   23. Ibid., pp. 141 and 143.

line (which some people called the 'theory of Ch'ü Ch'iu-pai') was actually the logical development of my own conceptual errors. . . . I was as much responsible for the Li Li-san line as he was."[24]

The longest, and perhaps most morbid and masochistic, section of "Superfluous Words" is called "Literary Intellectuals." It is, in part, a merciless indictment of traditionalistic Chinese intellectuals. As such, it does not differ in essence from his earlier attacks on "superfluous" figures like Hu Shih, Liang Shih-ch'iu, and Hsu Chih-mo. Now, however, Ch'ü placed himself squarely in their category. Carefully excluding leftist writers and critics, Ch'ü charged that "the so-called intellectuals are in fact the most useless creatures on earth. By 'intellectuals' we do not mean men of letters, writers, or literary critics in the modern sense, we mean the traditional scholars with an eccentric bent who 'sing with the wind and play with the moon.' In short they are highbrow loafers who know a little about everything but not much about anything."[25] At least physicians, chemists, and engineers do practical work, but "the literary intellectual, on the other hand, is a hopeless case; often he himself does not even know what he is doing. . . . Unfortunately I am one of these intellectuals."[26] Ch'ü noted with some irony that he had a reputation as a "communist chieftain" who specialized in "murder and arson." "The fact is," he wrote, "I am a bookworm, cowardly and 'womanly,' who does not even dare to kill a mouse." His lack of self-confidence and his "tendency to drift with the crowd" were, in his opinion, "natural characteristics of all of China's literary intellectuals."[27]

In the final section, Ch'ü bid a sentimental and somewhat pathetic farewell to his friends and former colleagues. He told them that he had no right to take credit for the tasks that were accomplished in the post-May Fourth period, and that they should not regard him as a revolutionary martyr. In 1932, when rumors of Ch'ü's death began to spread, Ch'ü recalled, memorial services were held in many places. He was upset by the knowledge that friends were eulogizing him:

> Now that I have been imprisoned and lost my freedom, I could easily pretend to have possessed all the virtues of a true martyr and play the role of a great tragic hero before his impending death. But I do not dare to do this; nor do I wish to do this. We cannot and should not deceive future historians. I do not want historians to record me in a way I do not deserve; I shall feel very guilty indeed if my comrades mistake a traitor like me for a martyr. Die I shall and must, but I will not die a hypocrite![28]

---

24. Ibid., p. 146.   25. Ibid., pp. 148-149.
26. Ibid., p. 149.   27. Ibid., pp. 150-151.   28. Ibid., pp. 157-158.

Yet despite his personal despair, Ch'ü raised himself from the depths of depression long enough to offer some encouraging words to his friends: "You, dear comrades, are marching forward, constantly and indomitably. I envy you and pray for your success, but I cannot follow you any more. Though feeling badly, I nevertheless do not have any regret."[29] In the final paragraphs of his testament, Ch'ü restated his enthusiasm for the literary works of Lu Hsün, Mao Tun, Ts'ao Hsueh-ch'in (*Dream of the Red Chamber*), Tolstoy, Turgenev, and Gorky, and indicated a willingness to donate his body to a medical laboratory in hopes that something new might be learned about tuberculosis.

Of course Ch'ü did have some regrets. He hated the thought of leaving behind "the children of the world, including my own daughter" who were young, courageous, and "marching forward." Above all, he regretted that he would no longer be able to enjoy the companionship of his "true love," Yang Chih-hua. In his last days he wrote a touching classical poem entitled "To My Wife from Imprisonment":[30]

A night-long nostalgia reminds me of old-time pleasures;
The living shall be dead with a posthumous world unknown.
The man on the road need not inquire into events past;
The seagull flies and you shall stand alone.

One can only speculate about Ch'ü's motives for writing such an essay. It is reasonable to assume that a man like Ch'ü would take advantage of an opportunity to write some final reflections on his life; and there is no longer much doubt that the essay is authentic. One must explain, therefore, the numerous and obvious distortions. One possibility is that in a final moment of reflection a deeply depressed Ch'ü actually believed what he was saying: that he had been wearing a "mask" for over fifteen years, that his involvement in the revolution was a misunderstanding, and that he had accomplished nothing in his short life. It is also possible that Ch'ü was making a final (though half-hearted) plea for life by suggesting that he was never really interested in politics, that his political errors only made him a burden on the party, and that he no longer had the vitality or interest to be active in any aspect of the revolutionary movement. Aware that he would soon die of tuberculosis in any case, Ch'ü may have simply wanted the luxury of dying naturally outside prison walls. To build a credible case, Ch'ü thus made it known that if he obtained his freedom he could not again become an active communist.[31]

Yet it would be a mistake to dwell only upon the distortions con-

29. Ibid., p. 156.

30. Ssu-ma Lu, *Ch'ü Ch'iu-pai chuan*, p. 106. The translation used here is from Warren Kuo, "Tsunyi Conference," p. 55.

31. TYTH, p. 157.

tained in this remarkable and rather sensitive work. The verdict Ch'ü pronounced on himself may have been excessively harsh, but he did so within the context of intellectual and cultural themes he had been pondering since 1916. "Superfluous Words" is revealing because it shows how seriously Ch'ü regarded the intellectual problems that captured his imagination when he was being introduced to utopian socialist thought. It is extraordinary how many references he made in this final work to the "anarchist ideal" of a "classless and stateless" society where "peace and love dominate the world."[32] The key was transformation of consciousness, which included ferreting out the "degenerate elements" contained in "gentry subconsciousness." The point of "Superfluous Words," therefore, was not to denounce his comrades or the revolution, but to simply state that he had failed to live up to their expectations.

Finally, "Superfluous Words" is interesting for what it does not say. Despite the fact that Ch'ü's most enduring contribution to Chinese Marxist thought, and to the revolution itself, was in the area of literary criticism and theory, he said absolutely nothing about such matters in his final testament. Since Ch'ü was indulging in such unsparing self-evaluation, it is remarkable that he avoided any mention of his cultural activities in Shanghai during the 1931-1934 period. One gets the impression that Ch'ü was not sure how much his captors knew about these activities. Ch'ü had, after all, lived underground during this period and used scores of pseudonyms to publish his writings. Ch'ü obviously preferred that they remain ignorant, and thus made no effort to evaluate his writings on Marxist literary thought. At one point he stated that he wanted to do some useful literary work after he was expelled from the Politburo in 1931 but "became seriously ill and wasted three more years."[33]

Although Ch'ü wrote nothing about his literary views and activities, it is clear that he was thinking about his most intimate literary associates. Just as he had tried to balance realism and romanticism in his writings of the early 1930s, so too was his letter of early May to Lu Hsün followed by a gentle and sentimental letter of May 28 to Kuo Mo-jo, who was residing in Tokyo.[34] And later, on the morning of June 4 during an interview with Li K'e-ch'ang, a reporter for the *National News Weekly*, Ch'ü did what he could to protect some old literary companions. When questioned about the relations Lu Hsün, Kuo Mo-jo, and Ting Ling had with the Communist Party, Ch'ü replied that Lu Hsün was merely a fellow traveler, that Kuo Mo-jo had already withdrawn from the party, and that Ting Ling was essentially a harmless "romantic." The League of Left-wing Writers, Ch'ü in-

32. Ibid., p. 138.   33. Ibid., p. 147.
34. For the full text of the letter, see Ssu-ma Lu, *Ch'ü Ch'iu-pai chuan*, pp. 102-104.

sisted, had "no more than four to five communists among its members."[35]

Ch'ü spent much of his time in early June engaged in the sort of spare-time activities he had enjoyed during his youth in Changchow. He wrote several elegant poems in the classical style, which he hung on the walls of his cell, and carved a number of stone seals. Meanwhile, Kuomintang officials were meeting in Nanking to decide his fate. Not surprisingly, it was Tai Chi-t'ao, the Kuomintang ideologist Ch'ü had attacked with such vigor in the mid-1920s, who argued that Ch'ü should be executed. Among those who participated in the discussion, only Ts'ai Yuan-p'ei, one of Ch'ü's New Culture heroes, spoke against the death penalty. Chiang Kai-shek personally signed the execution order that, among other things, instructed local authorities to shoot Ch'ü immediately, photograph his body, and publish the picture in a prominent newspaper. The message was received in Ch'ang-t'ing on June 17.[36]

On the morning of June 18, 1935, Ch'ü was sitting in his cell writing a classical poem. He included a short preface:

> The night of June 17, 1935, I dreamed I was walking on a mountain path. The setting sun was glorious but was sometimes hidden, and a cold stream was moaning nearby. It was like a fairy land. The next morning as I was reading the T'ang poets, I came upon the line, "Setting sun, in ragged ridges, now bright, now dim." So I wrote an impromptu poem, a composite of these four lines:
>
> Setting sun, in ragged ridges, now bright, now dim;
> Falling leaves and cold stream, in two tunes sing requiem.
> A solitary ten years have I endured,
> Ties all dissolved, my heart clinging to half a hymn.[37]

At approximately 10 A.M., as Ch'ü was completing these lines, his momentary tranquility was broken by prison officials who informed him of the arrival of the Nanking decision and ordered him to accompany a unit of riflemen to the execution grounds. The Ch'ang-t'ing correspondent of the Kuomintang-affiliated newspaper Tientsin *Ta Kung Pao* seems to have been the only eyewitness to report the details:

> This morning news came that he was to be executed. Your correspondent, doubting the truth of this, went out of curiosity to

35. Li K'e-ch'ang, "Fang-wen chi," p. 4.

36. Ssu-ma Lu, *Ch'ü Ch'iu-pai chuan*, p. 100; Mark E. Shneider, *Tvorcheskii Put' Tsiui Tsiu-bo, 1899-1935* (Moscow: Izdatel'stvo Nauka, 1964), p. 214.

37. T. A. Hsia, *The Gate of Darkness* (Seattle: University of Washington Press, 1968), p. 54.

visit the prisoner. When I entered his room he was writing his last words. As soon as he had finished, he went to Chungshan Park. The whole place was utterly silent, for even the birds had stopped chirping. He made his way leisurely to the pavilion where four dishes and a jug of good wine were ready. He talked and smiled as usual, as if nothing were amiss. After a few drinks he said, "The greatest happiness a man can have is to die for the revolution. The philosophy of us communists is to devote our lives to serving mankind—until our dying day." Then, as loud as he could, he sang the Internationale, breaking the silence of the air. After the wine was finished, he walked with dignity to the execution grounds, escorted by guards in front and behind. It was a most solemn moment. At one street corner his eyes fell on a blind beggar, and he looked back as if touched by the sight. When he reached the place of execution, a volley was fired and Ch'ü left the world forever.[38]

Ch'ü Ch'iu-pai's execution took place at Pan-lung Hill at the foot of Lo-han Mountain outside the west gate of Ch'ang-t'ing slightly less than five months after his thirty-sixth birthday.

SHANGHAI POSTSCRIPT

Sometime in mid-July 1935, Lu Hsün received the letter Ch'ü had written from prison in early May before his identity had been revealed. By the time the letter was in Lu Hsün's hands, Ch'ü was already dead. Unaware of Ch'ü's fate, Lu Hsün began to raise funds to purchase Ch'ü's release. The July 30 entry in Lu Hsün's diary reveals that he immediately contacted his editor to request an advance on a translation of P.A. Pavlenko's article "On Lermontov's Stories," a piece actually translated by Ch'ü himself. "I am in urgent need of money," he pleaded.[39] On August 9, he sent another urgent note to his editor requesting "money in a hurry."[40] In her own memoirs, Lu Hsün's wife, Hsu Kuang-p'ing, recalls: "Lu Hsün was extremely miserable for a long time after Ch'ü Ch'iu-pai's death. He could not even bring himself to do any writing. It seemed to him that this was the first and only time he had been unable to help his dear comrade-in-arms."[41] In a letter to Ts'ao Ching-hua, a former student of Ch'ü's, Lu

38. Quoted in Wu Wen-tao, "A Visit to the Old Soviet Areas," *Chinese Literature*, February 1959, p. 111.

39. Ting Ching-t'ang, *Hsüeh-hsi Lu Hsün ho Ch'ü Ch'iu-pai tso-p'in te cha-chi* [Learn from the message of Lu Hsün's and Ch'ü Ch'iu-pai's works] (Shanghai: Shanghai wen-i ch'u-pan-she, 1961), p. 25.

40. Hsu Kuang-p'ing, *Lu Hsün hui-i lu* [Reminiscences of Lu Hsün] (Peking: Tso-chia ch'u-pan-she, 1961), p. 131.

41. Ibid.

Hsün put it more simply: "The news is correct. I received confirmation of it last month. Nothing more can be done. The loss to our cultural work is incalculable."[42] In a letter dated October 15 he lamented: "'Realist' essays . . . were always 'difficult to understand.' There is not a person in China who can translate them as well as Ch'ü did."[43]

The last sentence of the October 22, 1935 entry in Lu Hsün's diary is short but significant: "Afternoon, the editing of Ch'ü's *Shu-lin* begins."[44] Mortally ill, Lu Hsün was to use much of the remaining year of his life to pay final tribute to Ch'ü Ch'iu-pai. This final literary project of Lu Hsün's involved the editing of a massive collection of translations and commentaries that Ch'ü had left in Lu Hsün's hands as he departed from Shanghai. The collection consisted of writings on Marxist aesthetics by Engels, Lenin, Plekhanov, Lafargue, and Gorky, as well as creative writings by Gorky, Lunacharsky, and others, altogether nearly eight hundred thousand words translated by Ch'ü in the early 1930s.

Lu Hsün insisted upon doing all the work himself. He financed the printing from his own savings and with money he raised. He personally edited and proofread the material, designed the cover, arranged the layout, chose the title, managed the advertising, bought the paper, and sent the manuscript to the printer in Japan.[45] It was, of course, the famous two-volume collection entitled *Hai-shang shu-lin*. The title page indicated that the publisher was the "Chu-hsia hsüan Shuang" firm, an archaic, almost coded, way of saying "China mourns Ch'ü." Owing to Kuomintang censorship, Lu Hsün could not give Ch'ü credit for the translations and commentaries, but on the binding of each volume are the letters STR: an abbreviation of Strakov, Ch'ü's Russian pseudonym. At the beginning of October 1936, Lu Hsün received the first printed copies of volume one from the printer. While waiting for volume two he wrote: "I am publishing his writings as an act of commemoration, and as a protest, a demonstration. . . . They have killed the man, but they cannot kill his writings, these will never die."[46] Refusing to rest, his weight fell below eighty-five pounds. He caught a cold on October 17 and died on October 19, 1936, without having seen a printed copy of *Hai-shang shu-lin*, volume two.[47]

42. Ibid.   43. Ibid., p. 132.

44. Lu Hsün, *Lu Hsün jih-chi* [Lu Hsün's diary] (Shanghai: Shanghai ch'u-pan-she kung-ssu, 1951), 13:1042.

45. Hsu Kuang-p'ing, *Lu Hsün hui-i-lu*, p. 132.

46. Wen Chi-che, "Ch'ü Ch'iu-pai t'ung-chih chan tou te i-sheng" [Comrade Ch'ü Ch'iu-pai's battling life], *Hung-ch'i p'iao-p'iao*, 5:79-107.

47. Ting Ching-t'ang, *Hsüeh-hsi Lu Hsün ho Ch'ü Ch'iu-pai*, p. 23.

13 Yenan and Beyond

*The art of the various nations of the world each has its own
peculiar national form and national style. Some people do not
understand this point. They reject their own national characteristics and blindly worship the West, thinking that the West
is better in every respect. They even go so far as to advocate
"complete Westernization." This is wrong. . . . Chinese art,
Chinese music, painting, drama, song and dance, and literature
have each had their own historical development. In rejecting
Chinese things, the people who advocate complete Westernization
say that Chinese things do not have their own laws, and so they
are unwilling to study or develop them. This is adopting an
attitude of national nihilism towards Chinese art.*

MAO TSE-TUNG, 1956[1]

Ch'ü Ch'iu-pai was one of the first of the unique May Fourth generation of leftist literary thinkers to pass from the scene. Most of his
colleagues—including Mao Tun, Ting Ling, Pa Chin, Yeh Sheng-t'ao,
Kuo Mo-jo, Hsia Yen, Yang Han-sheng, Cheng Po-ch'i, and Ch'ien
Hsing-ts'un—remained active during the bitter revolutionary struggle, and went on to important leadership posts in the People's Republic after 1949. Indeed, most of his companions were still very much in
the limelight when the Proletarian Cultural Revolution erupted in
1966. The obvious question presents itself: what, in the decades since
his execution, has been the influence of Ch'ü's writings about this
generation of writers and the problems of China's leftist literary movement? Is there, for example, a relationship between Ch'ü's works and
Mao Tse-tung's highly celebrated writings on literature and art?

1. Stuart Schram, ed., *Chairman Mao Talks to the People* (New York: Pantheon Books,
1974), p. 85.

THE YENAN SETTING

In many respects, the Kiangsi experiment was regarded as a model by the communist leaders as they sought to revive the revolutionary movement following the defeat in the south and the arduous Long March. Compared with Kiangsi, the people were poorer, the land more barren, and the cultural level lower in northern Shensi where the first contingents of the Red Army arrived in 1936; but the revolutionary strategy employed was essentially the same. It was still assumed that revolutionary forces could win genuine popular support by creating a revolutionary "state" or a series of "liberated zones" in which social, economic, and political reforms beneficial to the majority of peasants could be introduced. That is to say, some of the fundamental socio-economic ends of the movement would be achieved in the present and thus become the means by which state power would be achieved nationwide. The development of a popular cultural movement was seen, therefore, as both an important goal in its own right and an important means to a more comprehensive revolutionary end.

The Yenan literary and cultural movement was modeled on the program Ch'ü led in Kiangsi. Li Po-chao, Wei Kung-chih, and others who played a leading role in Kiangsi survived the Long March and became active once again. Chao P'in-san, a pioneer in the rural drama movement, arrived in Yenan in February 1937 with four hundred of his students and several drama troupes.[2] Hsu T'e-li, Ch'ü's former assistant, was made commissioner of education in Yenan. Wei Kung-chih informed Edgar Snow that "most of our experienced players from the south have now become instructors."[3] Not surprisingly, the Lu Hsün Academy of Arts and the Resist Japan University (K'ang-ta) were modeled on the Gorky Drama School and Red Army University, respectively.

Like its Kiangsi predecessor, the Yenan popular culture movement operated at both the central and local levels. Cultural activists were recruited from among the peasants to undergo two years of training in the central area, and then returned to the various local units to organize grass roots cultural movements.[4] As in Kiangsi, the central drama societies dispatched mobile drama troupes to tour the countryside and the military front. Describing a six-week drama tour, Nym Wales reported: "They had marched on foot everyday, they told me, and had played thirty-one times in seven hsien. The purpose of the tour was to put on open-air plays explaining the new policies of the

2. Nym Wales, *Red Dust* (Stanford: Stanford University Press, 1942), p. 184.
3. Edgar Snow, *Red Star Over China* (New York: Grove Press, 1961), p. 114.
4. Harrison Forman, *Report from Red China* (New York: Henry Holt and Co., 1945), p. 87.

Yenan government to the Shensi people and to encourage participation in the elections which were to begin July 15 of that year."[5]

Contemporary reports also indicate that the theoretical principles upon which the Yenan movement was based were consistent with many of the ideas outlined by Ch'ü in Shanghai and put into practice in Kiangsi. Because the literacy rate was only 5 percent, the popular culture movement emphasized the performing arts such as music, drama, and dance rather than literary forms.[6] Amateur activity was stressed, to encourage the active participation of the people. The content of Yenan art continued to focus on contemporary social and political problems, and the forms were mainly traditional, and thus popular among the peasants. A close relationship between the peasants and the cultural workers was regarded as essential, and considerable stress was placed on the use of the simple, straightforward language of the people.

There were, however, some notable differences between the Yenan and Kiangsi settings, differences that affected developments in the cultural realm. First, and most important, the bitter civil and class conflict that characterized the Kiangsi years changed in late 1936 to a new Communist-Kuomintang United Front to resist the Japanese invasion of China. The communist leadership now stressed the need for the Chinese people of all social classes to unite in the face of the alien foe. Regardless of class background, all who were genuinely willing to participate in the resistance movement led by the Communist Party were welcomed in Yenan. To attract patriotic Chinese who had earlier been categorized as class enemies of the peasantry and proletariat, revolutionary social and economic programs were modified, although by no means abandoned.

A second major difference between the Kiangsi and Yenan environments was the presence in Yenan of large numbers of urban, Europeanized writers, many of whom came to Yenan because they believed the communists were more willing and better able to resist the Japanese advance. Commenting on the problems encountered by these writers from Shanghai, Harrison Forman observed: "The Westernized, highly sophisticated art and literature of Shanghai were as far from the peasant folk lore of hinterland China as James Joyce is from Confucius. Under war conditions, away from Shanghai, the literati resembled fish out of water. It was almost impossible for them not to look down upon the ignorant peasants, workers and soldiers, who retorted by rejecting them."[7] A significant number of urban writers made an effort to adjust to the new conditions and contribute to the popular cultural movement; others showed little interest, and con-

5. Wales, *Red Dust*, p. 194.　　6. Snow, *Red Star*, p. 253.

7. Forman, *Report from Red China*, p. 88.

tinued to do the type of work they had pursued in the cities. Thus in contrast to Kiangsi, there was more modern literary activity but not all was integrated with the popular movement. There were, in effect, two artistic trends: a popular mass-oriented movement, and a Europeanized literary movement serving the displaced urban intellectuals. There was a tension between these two trends, but the United Front policy dictated that the petty-bourgeois urban intellectuals were a valuable asset and should be welcomed rather than isolated. Nevertheless, the policy of class cooperation and unity conflicted with the revolutionary government's clear desire to reintegrate art and society. The May Fourth generation writers did not disapprove of utilitarian art, but they were inclined to reject the notion that art should be a cog in the machine of state. While this issue may have been in the background in Kiangsi, it was brought to center stage in Yenan.

It was during the Yenan period that Mao Tse-tung expressed most of his highly publicized views on literature and art. The student of Mao's literary thought is, however, faced with several problems. Mao, like Marx, Engels, and Lenin, was not in fact a literary specialist and had relatively little to say about artistic culture. Furthermore, his most celebrated works, such as "Talks at the Yenan Forum on Literature and Art," were written under rather specific historical circumstances. Nevertheless, Mao's followers have tended to lift essays such as "Talks at Yenan" from their historical context in order to proclaim their universal utility. As a result, Mao's writings on art have been viewed in China and elsewhere as the most important and brilliant statements on literature and art ever made by a Marxist, despite the fact that they discuss a limited number of carefully selected problems arising from the Yenan United Front environment. Indeed, the impression is often left that Chinese Marxist literary thought was developed by Mao himself. It is true that no one has had a greater impact than Mao on the Chinese literary world in recent decades, but it by no means follows that he was not influenced by the works of other Chinese Marxist literary thinkers who had been writing about China's literary and cultural problems since the early 1920s. A careful look at Mao's "Talks at Yenan" supports two generalizations about the relationship between Mao's views and those expressed ten years earlier by Ch'ü Ch'iu-pai. First, while the ideas of Mao and Ch'ü are by no means identical, Mao said very little that had not been said already by Ch'ü. Second, and perhaps more significant, where their views differ, Ch'ü seems to have adopted the more radical position.

Mao's outlook on the general and theoretical issues raised throughout this study are not very different from Ch'ü's. On the relationship between economic base and superstructure, Mao—like Ch'ü—acknowledged from time to time that "a given culture is the ideological reflection of the politics and economics of a given society."[8] But only in a formal sense did Mao accept this conventional and rather deterministic formula. Elsewhere, Mao insisted that not only can the superstructure influence the substructure, but under certain conditions cultural and ideological movements can play the decisive role in advancing the revolution. "When the superstructure (politics, culture, etc.) obstructs the development of the economic base," Mao argued in 1937, "political and cultural change become principal and decisive."[9] One gets the impression that Mao, like Ch'ü, tended to interpret the Chinese revolution as an exceptional case of prolonged cultural and ideological obstruction.

Thus it comes as no surprise that Mao, like Ch'ü, placed a good deal of emphasis on the revolutionary role of writers and the utilitarian function of art. In commemorating the twentieth anniversary of the May Fourth Movement, Mao asserted: "In the Chinese democratic revolutionary movement it was the intellectuals who were the first to awaken."[10] To him, the role of the writer was not limited to passively reflecting social and economic changes brought about by objective and impersonal historical laws; it was to "awaken the masses, fire them with enthusiasm and impel them to unite and struggle to transform their environment."[11] For Mao, culture is a "powerful revolutionary weapon" that "prepares the ground ideologically before the revolution comes and is an important, indeed *essential*, fighting front in the general revolutionary front during the revolution."[12]

Mao's voluntaristic interpretation of the relationship between art and society is also apparent in his treatment of questions concerning the class character of literature. On the one hand, Mao seemed to be affirming the materialist conception of art when he wrote: "In the world today all culture, all literature and art belong to definite classes and are geared to definite political lines. There is in fact no such thing as art for art's sake, art that stands above classes or art that is detached from or independent of politics."[13] But, like Ch'ü, Mao was inclined to use subjective standards when evaluating the class affiliation of writers and intellectuals. Intellectuals of gentry origin, for example, were not limited in any objective sense to the production of feudal or bourgeois art. If their consciousness was transformed, he

8. Mao Tse-tung, *On Literature and Art* (Peking: Foreign Languages Press, 1967), p. 58.

9. Quoted in Jan Myrdal and Gun Kessle, *China: The Revolution Continued* (New York: Vintage Books, 1972), p. 189.

10. Mao Tse-tung, *On Literature and Art*, p. 54.

11. Ibid., p. 19. The original text of Mao's "Yenan Talks" is in *Mao Tse-tung chi* [The collected works of Mao Tse-tung] (Tokyo: Hokubosha, 1970-1973), 8:111-148.

12. Mao Tse-tung, *On Literature and Art*, p. 76 (emphasis added).

13. Ibid., p. 25.

suggested, they might even be able to write "truly proletarian literature."[14]

Mao adopted a similar approach to the problem of how Marxist revolutionaries should regard the culture of the past. He accepted the idea that even following periods of qualitative revolutionary change there are cultural links between past and present. "We are Marxist historicists," Mao proclaimed in 1938, "we must not mutilate history. From Confucius to Sun Yat-sen we must sum it up critically, and we must constitute ourselves the heirs of all that is precious in this past."[15] But, like Ch'ü, Mao used this standard conception to underscore his profoundly nationalistic cultural concerns. To be sure, he allowed for the possibility of foreign cultural influence; but he rejected the idea that this formula should be used to rationalize the dominant position of European models in the modern literary movement. Like Ch'ü, Mao accepted the "cultural inheritance" theory as a principle, but insisted that it be applied to China's own cultural past. Mao, of course, gave no concrete guidelines as to how one determines what should be inherited by the proletariat and what should be discarded; but it is clear that he believed Chinese culture, like Chinese history itself, was unique and could not be expected to conform to foreign patterns of development. Instead, Marxism should be used as a method by which the peculiarities of Chinese development might be understood. And, like Lenin and Trotsky, Mao recognized that intellectuals were the repositories of traditional culture and thus were in the best position to provide continuity between past and present.[16]

Regarding the question of the impact of capitalism on artistic culture, there is no reason to doubt that Mao accepted the basic Marxist premise that the highly developed division of labor in capitalist society causes individual aesthetic sensibilities to become alienated so that the masses experience only a crippled cultural development. But, like Ch'ü, he refused to accept the idea that material abundance and advanced industrial development are preconditions for the cultural liberation of the common people. On the contrary, Mao assumed that, in the Chinese case, the transformation of the economic substructure presupposed a cultural revolution. Indeed, Mao, like Ch'ü, saw no reason why a distinctively "proletarian" cultural movement could not be launched in an essentially precapitalist society.[17]

14. Ibid., p. 14.

15. *Selected Works of Mao Tse-tung* (Peking: Foreign Languages Press, 1965), 2:209; quoted in Stuart Schram, ed., *The Political Thought of Mao Tse-tung* (New York: Frederick Praeger, 1969), p. 72.

16. Mao Tse-tung, *On Literature and Art*, p. 23.

17. Ibid., p. 25.

In two important respects, however, Mao's definition of proletarian literature departed from Ch'ü's. First, Mao firmly believed that literature should be integrated completely into the new society being created in Yenan. "The purpose of our meeting," Mao explained to the Yenan Forum on Literature and Art, "is precisely to ensure that literature and art fit well into the whole revolutionary machine as a component part."[18] Although he presumably realized that the vitality of the modern literary movement was a product of its autonomy from the state, Mao implied that the continued autonomy of the leftist literary movement would be damaging to the interests of the revolutionary political movement. In effect, Mao was calling quite explicitly for the reintegration of art and society in China. Second, when Mao spoke of proletarian literature as a "part of the whole proletarian revolutionary cause," he made it quite clear that its development would of necessity be guided by the vanguard political party.[19] Mao spoke repeatedly of the absolute necessity of a close relationship between the revolutionary literary movement and the Communist Party. "Party work in literature and art occupies a definite and assigned position in Party revolutionary work as a whole, and is subordinated to the revolutionary tasks set by the party in a given revolutionary period."[20] On the troublesome issues of the relationship between literature and the state and the role of the party in directing literary life, Mao therefore departed from Marx, Engels, Plekhanov, Trotsky, and Lenin, and stood squarely on Stalinist terrain.

Despite these important differences, Mao's conception of the present "New Democratic" stage of the modern cultural movement bore a striking resemblance to Ch'ü's understanding of the "Proletarian May Fourth" stage. Both men recognized that the bourgeois-democratic (or capitalist) cultural movement had failed in China and had no prospect of succeeding in the future as a separate movement led by the bourgeoisie. Both argued that the "anti-feudal" historical tasks of the bourgeois cultural movement must be completed, even if the bourgeoisie was incapable of doing so. Yet while both acknowledged the need to complete the required bourgeois cultural "stage," they radically redefined this stage by indicating that the goal of the contemporary revolutionary cultural movement was not to promote bourgeois culture but to advance beyond it. Thus Ch'ü's "Proletarian May Fourth" and Mao's "New Democratic" stage were conceived as unique cultural movements that relate to the problems of a society that is neither capitalist nor socialist. As Mao put it: the culture of New Democracy was neither the "cultural despotism of the bourgeoisie" nor the "socialism of the proletariat," but rather an anti-feudal and

18. Ibid., p. 2.   19. Ibid., p. 25.   20. Ibid.

anti-imperalist cultural movement.[21] Like Ch'ü's Proletarian May Fourth, it sought to integrate the last phase of the abortive bourgeois cultural revolution with the beginning of a more socialist mass cultural movement, all of which was to take place under proletarian political auspices.

Mao's general beliefs about literature and society are sketched out rather clearly in his Yenan writings, but how did he propose to put his New Democratic cultural movement into operation? What problems would have to be solved? In a very real sense, Mao, like Ch'ü, believed that the cultural revolution he had in mind could not be carried out without the active support of writers and intellectuals; yet he also understood that many of the problems the movement would encounter were rooted in the May Fourth intellectual predispositions of these same intellectuals. The question arises, therefore, of Mao's views regarding the May Fourth generation of leftist writers. Although Mao made no mention of Ch'ü Ch'iu-pai in his cultural writings, the similarity of their critique of the May Fourth generation is striking.

Above all, it is a preoccupation with the phenomenon of "Europeanization" that characterizes Mao's concerns about the May Fourth generation. In "On New Democracy," Mao stated rather bluntly: "To advocate 'wholesale Westernization' is wrong. China has suffered a great deal from the mechanical absorption of foreign material."[22] "For several decades," Mao observed in 1941, "many of the returned students from abroad have suffered from this malady. Coming home from Europe, America or Japan, they can only parrot things foreign. They become gramophones and forget their duty to understand and create new things. This malady has also infected the Communist Party."[23] Because of the extreme iconoclasm of the Europeanized intellectuals, modern writers knew too little about the popular culture of the people. The masses, for their part, regarded the writers as internal foreigners.

Like Ch'ü, Mao seems to have believed that Europeanization had two major effects on the leftist literary movement. Mao's analysis of the problem of factional disputes within the left, which reduced its unity and effectiveness, was not nearly as elaborate or complex as Ch'ü's; but he seems to have recognized that one legacy of Europeanization was that Chinese writers tended to accept Western Marxist literary theories uncritically and in ways consistent with their earlier interest in Western bourgeois literary theories. To accept Western Marxist notions uncritically would be to repeat the mistake of "wholesale Westernization." Rather, Western Marxist theory should be integrated "with the concrete practice of the Chinese revolution," and

21. Ibid., p. 73.   22. Ibid., p. 74.   23. Ibid., p. 84.

"combined with specific national characteristics and acquire a definite national form if it is to be useful, and in no circumstances can it be applied subjectively as a mere formula."[24] Unlike Ch'ü, Mao did not distinguish between the mechanistic and idealist schools in Western Marxist theory, but his brief remarks on the influence of Trotsky were essentially a restatement of Ch'ü's critique of Plekhanov.

Similarly, Mao did not refer specifically to the romantic and realist traditions and their role in China, but he did speak of the relationship between certain political tendencies and their manifestations in literary works. His reference to "right capitulationism and tailism," which leave the writer and literature on the sidelines of history, was not unlike Ch'ü's argument about the fatalistic implications of naturalism and clinical objectivism. Mao also referred to "left" exclusivism and sectarianism, which isolate writers and their work in the "vanguard" of the revolution.[25] Whether Mao had in mind the various "proletarian" groups active in the late 1920s is problematic, but his reference to the elitist leadership styles of some literary cliques was similar to Ch'ü's assessment of the romantic left. On one point, however, they were in complete agreement: Lu Hsün was the greatest writer of the modern period. Picking up on themes Ch'ü had set forth nearly a decade before, Mao proclaimed: "On the cultural front he was the bravest and the most correct, the firmest, the most loyal and the most ardent national hero, a hero without parallel in our history."[26] One gets the impression that Ch'ü and Mao admired Lu Hsün for the same reason: he had not been a victim of superficial Europeanization.

Like Ch'ü, Mao believed that Europeanization had also had the effect of separating leftist writers and the revolutionary literary movement from the common people. The "proletarian" literary movement of the intellectuals was unknown to the proletariat. In "Talks at Yenan," Mao asserted that the Europeanized writers present in the base area were still unclear about whom the revolutionary literary movement was supposed to be serving. Consequently, "their sentiments, their works, their actions and their views on the guiding principles for literature and art have inevitably been more or less at variance with the needs of the masses."[27] Using the sort of language Ch'ü had used ten years before, Mao stated that even well-intentioned leftist writers "seldom come into contact with the masses of workers, peasants and soldiers, do not understand or study them, do not have intimate friends among them and are not good at portraying them."[28] With regard to the problem of the language used by May Fourth writers, Mao observed: "Since many artists and writers stand aloof from the masses and lead empty lives, naturally they are unfamiliar with the language

24. Ibid., p. 74.   25. Ibid., p. 27.   26. Ibid., p. 62.
27. Ibid., p. 10.   28. Ibid., p. 13.

of the people. Accordingly their works are not only insipid in language but often contain nondescript expressions of their own coining which run counter to popular usage."[29] Thus, while the leftist literary movement appeared to be quite formidable, it had failed in practice to forge the link between intellectuals and the people. It therefore obstructed the development of a New Democratic culture.

Not only was Mao's evaluation of the failings of the Europeanized generation of leftists similar to Ch'ü's, his ideas about resolving these problems bore a striking resemblance to Ch'ü's. Both men placed the burden of transformation on the shoulders of the intellectuals. The long process of changing one's thought and life began with rigorous self-examination and ended with a "change from one class to another." To resolve the contradiction between the "proletarian literary movement" and the people, Mao, like Ch'ü, called upon writers to "go among the masses" and "learn about the people," because "the writers and artists do not have a good knowledge either of those whom they describe or of their audience."[30] For gentry and bourgeois intellectuals to "become proletarian," it would be necessary for them to live and work among the masses and identify with them, and to "go into the heat of the struggle, go to the only source, the broadest and richest source, in order to observe, experience, study and analyze all the different kinds of people, all the classes, all the masses, all the vivid patterns of life and struggle, all the raw materials of literature and art."[31] A populist-type movement of this sort would have three beneficial effects: the content of revolutionary literature would become more diverse and more directly related to the daily lives of the people; writers would be exposed to the colloquial language spoken by the people; and intellectuals would be in a position to study the popular artistic forms familiar to the people. Mao, like Ch'ü, was acutely aware of the nagging tension between cultural iconoclasm and revolutionary nationalism in the thought of Europeanized leftist writers. They both assumed that the modern cultural movement could not be placed on a mass base until the intellectuals who led the movement focused more of their attention on Chinese forms. In the anti-Kuomintang and anti-imperialist settings of Shanghai and Kiangsi, Ch'ü referred to these models as "traditional popular forms"; Mao, in the United Front setting of Yenan, was in a position to call them "national forms" (*min-tsu hsing-shih*). The meaning was the same, however. The stress on popular and folk art was meant as a criticism of the iconoclastic, Europeanized May Fourth writers. The anti-imperialist culture of New Democracy, Mao explained, was explicitly national.

It is also clear that Mao, like Ch'ü, also recognized that there were

29. Ibid., p. 6.   30. Ibid., pp. 5-6.   31. Ibid., p. 19.

two basic, but somewhat contradictory, approaches to the problem of bridging the cultural gap between intellectuals and the masses. Some critics stressed the need for writers to "popularize" their Europeanized works so that the people could understand them; others argued that the emphasis should be placed on raising the cultural level of the people so that they could appreciate more sophisticated literary works. Mao agreed that both approaches were valid, but suggested that Europeanized leftist writers "to a certain or even serious extent, belittled and neglected popularization and laid undue stress on raising standards."[32] Furthermore, Mao insisted, many writers had interpreted "raising standards" as meaning raising the cultural standards of the masses to a predetermined bourgeois or foreign level. Using precisely the same language as Ch'ü, Mao asserted that it was not the masses who were to be "elevated," but rather literature and art itself. In short, Mao thought that popularization and redefining what constitutes artistic excellence were part of the same process.

The new standard Mao proposed stressed the unity of "motive" and "effect." Using the idealist-determinist dichotomy employed so often by Ch'ü, Mao noted that "idealists stress motive and ignore effect, while mechanical materialists stress effect and ignore motive." "The motive of serving the masses is inseparably linked with the effect of winning their approval," he insisted.[33] The problem with May Fourth literature, including revolutionary works, was that it had no "effect" on the people. To meet the "new" standards, writers would have to be attentive to the response of the people to their works. Mao agreed with Ch'ü that it was the writers and not the masses who represented the central problem. Popularization, not raising standards, was the first order of business.

On the whole, Mao's critique of the May Fourth generation was not as thorough as Ch'ü's, but he clearly believed that the contradictions he discussed could become antagonistic if they were not attended to by writers in Yenan. He did not use the term "superfluous intellectual," but he warned that the tendency of Europeanized leftists to "look down upon the workers, peasants and soldiers"[34] might lead them down the path taken by nonrevolutionary figures like Liang Shih-ch'iu.

Despite these important similarities of Ch'ü's and Mao's views on the problems of the leftist literary movement, Ch'ü's recommendations were more radical in some respects than Mao's. It is the issue of the United Front that distinguishes Mao's proposal for a New Democratic culture from Ch'ü's earlier call for a Proletarian May Fourth. Mao wholeheartedly accepted the need for "proletarian literature and

32. Ibid., p. 16.   33. Ibid., p. 28.   34. Ibid., p. 15.

art," but—unlike Ch'ü—he did not discuss the important, indeed crucial, issue of the direct participation of the masses in this movement. Rather, it is assumed in "Talks at Yenan" and other works that the masses will be *provided with* "proletarian literature" by intellectuals who have transformed and "proletarianized" their consciousness. When Mao referred to "truly proletarian literature" he spoke only of a literature *for* workers, peasants, and soldiers, but not *by* them.[35] In sharp contrast to Ch'ü's works, Mao's writings of the Yenan period are confined almost exclusively to the problem of defining the role to be played by intellectuals in the new multiclass mass movement.

Unconcerned with the imperatives of United Front strategy, Ch'ü's conception of the proletarian cultural movement was different. Of course, Ch'ü spoke of the need for both intellectual leadership and intellectual political transformation, but it was usually in the context of the first stage of the "Proletarian May Fourth," the stage during which the bourgeois-democratic cultural movement was to be concluded. Unlike Mao, Ch'ü repeatedly referred to the beginning of a cultural stage in which the masses would participate directly, and alluded to a time when the people would no longer have to be dependent upon gentry or bourgeois intellectuals. Mao, on the other hand, gave no guidelines whatsoever as to how and when the age-old division of labor will break down and permit the release of the latent, creative cultural energies of the masses.

It must be acknowledged, however, that Mao's failure to discuss the utopian themes that distinguish Ch'ü's work stems more from political constraints imposed by the wartime environment than from any lack of enthusiasm on Mao's part for the cultural liberation of the people. There is no reason to believe, for example, that Mao's failure to write anything about the direct participation of the people in the New Democratic culture meant that he did not fully support the Kiangsi-type popular cultural programs organized by Hsu T'e-li and others in Yenan. Such programs were entirely consistent with Mao's approach to revolution and his interpretation of Marxism.

Despite the differences in emphasis arising from contrasting political environments, it is the similarities, then, that characterize Mao's and Ch'ü's views on the cultural problems of the Chinese revolution. How should we account for these similarities? It is certainly possible that Mao had read Ch'ü's works and was influenced by them, although nowhere does he acknowledge such influence, or so much as mention Ch'ü's name. Hence, it is impossible to prove that Ch'ü's writings were the source of Mao's literary thought. Much more significant and interesting than whether Mao was "influenced" by Ch'ü is the con-

35. Ibid., p. 22.

sideration whether certain concrete historical situations are likely to result in thinkers separately coming to similar conclusions about history, revolution, and culture. Ch'ü's fields of inquiry were much more limited than Mao's, but his writings on artistic culture indicate that he shared many of Mao's general assumptions about the nature of the Chinese revolution. With regard to cultural questions, Ch'ü's approach was characteristically "Maoist."

Nowhere is the affinity between Ch'ü's and Mao's general approach to revolution more apparent than in their attitude toward capitalism as a stage of history. Although Ch'ü was primarily concerned with the cultural implications of the capitalist stage, he shared with Mao a profound hostility toward capitalism in any form. In contrast to Marx, neither Mao nor Ch'ü believed that capitalism was a necessary and inevitable stage of historical development. For them, capitalism, and bourgeois culture in particular, was thoroughly identified with the aggressive and alien forces of Western imperialism. Both men indicated repeatedly in their writings that, although a Chinese form of capitalism might have developed naturally, the intrusion of imperialism—an essentially alien form of capitalism—caused unusual distortions and perversions in China's historical development. The goal of the Chinese revolution, in their view, was not to promote a bourgeois revolution, but to use every means to avoid and bypass the alien capitalist stage and move directly to socialism. It is Mao's and Ch'ü's attitude toward imperialism, therefore, that is at the heart of their critique of the Europeanized May Fourth generation of leftist writers. By identifying with foreign culture, they stressed, this generation had neglected their own national culture and isolated themselves from the people. They were, in effect, internal foreigners.

This distinctively Chinese approach to Marxism and history itself is also reflected in the attitude of Ch'ü and Mao toward cultural revolution. Precisely because they placed relatively little faith in the ability of objective and impersonal laws of history to propel China through the various Marxist-defined stages of historical development, they, like the populists, stressed the ability of conscious human beings to impose their rational will on history. Specifically, they believed that unfavorable objective conditions can be combatted more effectively if a cultural and ideological revolution can be carried out. In a sense, for Mao and Ch'ü, revolutionary breakthroughs may occur first in the cultural realm, although there is nothing inevitable about such breakthroughs. The progress of the revolution can be accelerated if the struggle against feudal and bourgeois culture is advanced vigorously, but it will be severely retarded if the cultural base of feudal and foreign rule is not assaulted. It was for this reason that both Ch'ü and Mao placed so much emphasis on the role of intellectuals, the group that occupies the most strategic position in the superstructure. And it was for this reason that they placed so much emphasis on the need for intellectuals first to transform or "proletarianize" their thinking.

THE PEOPLE'S REPUBLIC

Although Ch'ü Ch'iu-pai's literary thought obviously remained relevant in the decades following his execution, his personal reputation has been the source of considerable controversy, most of which centers upon his final essay, "Superfluous Words." Initially, the revolutionary camp regarded this text as a "forgery" designed to smear Ch'ü's reputation and undermine the revolution.[36] Ch'ü's wife, Yang Chih-hua, acknowledged that Ch'ü wrote an essay entitled "Superfluous Words," but insisted that the version that appeared in March 1937 had been altered by the Kuomintang.[37] Eventually, Chinese Marxist commentators chose simply to ignore the text, focusing instead on Ch'ü's martyrdom.

A survey of Chinese newspapers, journals, and literary histories published since the proclamation of the People's Republic shows that in the period from the early 1940s to the early 1960s the homage paid to Ch'ü Ch'iu-pai placed him second only to Lu Hsün as the greatest cultural revolutionary of twentieth-century China. Hundreds of articles praised Ch'ü's numerous contributions to the development of Chinese Marxist literary thought. There were even some flattering remarks about Ch'ü's disastrous political career. The kindest of these references to Ch'ü's undistinguished tenure as party leader were based on a statement by Mao Tse-tung: "Comrade Ch'ü Ch'iu-pai, who was alleged to have committed 'the error of the line of conciliation,' was then a Party leader of prestige, and after he was attacked, he continued to do much useful work (mainly in the cultural field) and died heroically in June 1935 at the hands of the enemy executioners."[38] Although their political thought was quite different, especially on the role of the peasantry, Mao presumably appreciated Ch'ü's attacks on both the Ch'en Tu-hsiu and Wang Ming leadership groups. More typical, however, are the scores of articles on party history that completely ignore Ch'ü's involvement in party affairs or simply refer to the 1927-1928 party leadership as "ultra leftist," or "adventurist" without singling out Ch'ü for special criticism.[39] Other discussions of

36. T.A. Hsia, *The Gate of Darkness* (Seattle: University of Washington Press, 1968), pp. 46-47.

37. Ibid., p. 47.

38. *Selected Works of Mao Tse-tung*, 3:188.

39. Ho Kan-chih, *A History of the Modern Chinese Revolution* (Peking: Foreign Languages Press, 1959), pp. 186-187.

the period skip from criticism of Ch'en Tu-hsiu to attacks on Li Li-san and Wang Ming without even mentioning Ch'ü's name.[40] In this sense, Chinese treatment of Ch'ü as a former party leader was unique. Until the Cultural Revolution, Ch'ü was the only one of Mao's predecessors who had not been identified as a major political renegade.

Virtually all the articles and books on Ch'ü that appeared after 1949 focused on two aspects of his life: his revolutionary literary activities, and his martyrdom. Feng Hsueh-feng wrote that Ch'ü "laid the first firm foundation of Marxist literary criticism in China."[41] Ch'ü's May Fourth activities, his introduction of Western Marxist literary thought, his criticism of Europeanized leftist writers, his theory of popular literature, and his close friendship with Lu Hsün were singled out for special attention. "All these efforts," wrote Wen Chi-che, "were of great significance in laying the foundation of Marxist and Leninist literary criticism in China."[42] Although most studies attempted to balance the roles played by Ch'ü and Lu Hsün in the 1930s, on occasion it was conceded that it was Ch'ü who "helped the great writer to a better understanding of the Communist Party and strengthened his resolve to identify himself with the masses of workers and peasants."[43] Furthermore, Ch'ü, not Mao, was credited with making the "first correct and comprehensive analysis of Lu Hsün's mental growth and the place of his essays in modern Chinese literature."[44]

Ch'ü's martyrdom was also the subject of countless articles, although the precise details of capture, imprisonment, and execution varied considerably. Typical romantic accounts of Ch'ü's death suggest that he was "subjected to torture" but "remained loyal to his principles to the end."[45] Virtually all accounts mention that he "walked calmly to the execution ground," and sang the Internationale just before he was shot. "His deathless contribution to the cause of the Chinese revolution," Wen Chi-che wrote, "will be remembered by the Chinese people forever."[46] After 1949 Ch'ü's name was inscribed in gold letters on the monument to the martyrs of the revolution in T'ien-an-men Square in Peking, a memorial museum was erected in Changchow, and in 1955 his remains were interred in the Martyrs'

40. See Snow, *Red Star*, pp. 158-175, for Mao's own account of the period.
41. Feng Hsueh-feng, "The Works of Ch'ü Ch'iu-pai," *People's China*, 1 February 1954, p. 41.
42. Wen Chi-che, "Ch'ü Ch'iu-pai: Revolutionary and Man of Letters," *People's China*, 1 July 1955, p. 20.
43. Ibid.
44. Hu Yu, "The Collected Works of Ch'ü Ch'iu-pai," *Chinese Literature*, September 1963, p. 109.
45. Wen Chi-che, "Ch'ü Ch'iu-pai: Revolutionary and Man of Letters," p. 25.
46. Ibid.

Cemetery at Pa-pao-shan, Peking, in a ceremony attended by Chou En-lai and other political leaders.[47]

By 1964, Ch'ü's hitherto untarnished image was beginning to change. The reassessment was related almost wholly to a reopening of the controversy surrounding "Superfluous Words." Chou En-lai is reported to have raised the issue at a work conference of the Politburo in 1964, but he did not make a public statement on the matter until August 30, 1966, in a speech to the Academy of Sciences at the beginning of the Cultural Revolution. "Ch'ü Ch'iu-pai," he charged, "who was of big bureaucrat bourgeois origin, wrote 'Superfluous Words' in his later life. I delivered a report at a meeting of the Politburo, but before it was published it came to the knowledge of the Red Guards who rushed to Pa-pao-shan Cemetery and smashed the stone tablet."[48] On March 21, 1967, Chou proclaimed that "'Superfluous Words' written by Ch'ü Ch'iu-pai before his death was a statement of confession by a renegade. . . . It has been discovered recently that before his execution Ch'ü Ch'iu-pai wrote a letter to the authorities begging for mercy. He was a renegade."[49]

The language of the Red Guards was much stronger, and their coverage of the issue more extensive, although in the perspective of countless criticisms of personalities living and dead made at the time of the Cultural Revolution it was a small matter indeed. In fact, the major Red Guard paper responsible for criticizing Ch'ü, *Denounce Ch'ü Combat Bulletin*, published jointly by the Political Science and Law Commune of the Peking Institute of Political Science and Law, and the Red Revolutionary Rebel Headquarters of the Peking People's Municipal Court, printed only nine issues. Aside from offering brief derogatory accounts of Ch'ü's life, this Red Guard paper devoted itself almost exclusively to a thorough repudiation of "Superfluous Words." "To put it bluntly," they stated, "it was the impulse of a coward who was afraid of death and it was the need for kneeling down before the butcher's knife in order to save his life. It was the dirty language of a renegade."[50] As for Ch'ü's prison conduct, his critics wrote: "For the sake of staying alive Ch'ü Ch'iu-pai won favors by engraving seals not only for Kuomintang army doctors and reactionary reporters, but also for high ranking Kuomintang generals whose hands were smeared with the blood of the people. . . . [He] smugly drank and fraternized with Kuomintang secret agents."[51] Quite obviously, the posthumous attack on Ch'ü was related to Red Guard criticism of high officials who previously had honored Ch'ü. "At the suggestion of Liu Shao-

47. Warren Kuo, "Tsunyi Conference: Part II," *Issues and Studies*, 5(February 1968):45; *Survey of China Mainland Press*, No. 1073, June 21, 1955, pp. 3-4.

48. *T'ao Ch'ü chan pao* [Denounce Ch'ü Combat News], 6 May 1967.

49. Ibid.   50. Ibid.   51. Ibid.

ch'i, Lu Ting-yi, and his like," it was said, "this corpse was brought out each year, gilded and dressed up with no efforts spared to eulogize it."[52]

Denounce Ch'ü Combat Bulletin is also interesting for what it failed to discuss. First, the Red Guards offered no new analysis of Ch'ü's activities as a party leader from 1927 to 1931 but simply repeated the familiar charges of "ultra-leftism" and "adventurism," a charge that would later be made against the Red Guards themselves. Second, and more significant, no review or interpretation was offered of Ch'ü's leadership of the leftist literary movement, his friendship with Lu Hsün, or his voluminous critical and theoretical writings of the 1931-1934 period. The most obvious explanation for the deficiency in Red Guard publications is that Ch'ü's literary thought was not only similar to Mao's but was consistent with the Cultural Revolution critique of literary trends in China since 1949.

The revolutionary victory of 1949 by no means automatically resolved the problems and contradictions that had characterized leftist literary life since the 1920s. It was precisely the same group of Europeanized May Fourth writers discussed by Ch'ü in the early 1930s and again by Mao in the 1940s who emerged after 1949 as leaders of the new postrevolutionary literary and cultural organizations. As such, they were partly responsible for the institutionalization of the revolution that occurred in the early years of the new People's Republic. In the cultural world, the popular movement that had thrived in the rural base areas gradually gave way to an urban and more bureaucratic literary movement led by intellectuals who had always felt more comfortable in the cities.[53]

The return to power of the Europeanized generation of cultural leaders led to three decades of recurring tension between the literary intellectuals and the advocates of popular artistic activity. Neither faction ever really succeeded in totally dominating the other. The assault on the literary establishment during the utopian Great Leap Forward of 1958 raised many of the problems discussed by Ch'ü in the 1930s. Europeanized writers were criticized for holding "bourgeois" and "elitist" ideas about the nature of art, and accused of detaching themselves from the lives of the people. Great stress was suddenly placed on the revolution in the superstructure. Renewed emphasis was given to reviving Kiangsi and Yenan types of popular cultural movements. Writers were dispatched in large numbers to the factories and communes to live with and learn from the people. The masses themselves were encouraged to become active participants in

52. Ibid.
53. Paul G. Pickowicz, "Modern China's Artistic and Cultural Life," *Holy Cross Quarterly*, 7 (1975): 109-116.

national amateur artistic campaigns. Such a movement, some thought, would serve to reduce the distinction between mental and physical labor, end the cultural alienation of the masses, and thus release the creative energies of the people. Many literary intellectuals opposed the Great Leap cultural policy, just as they had opposed Ch'ü's proposal for a Proletarian May Fourth, because it threatened their prestige and political power and negated most of their May Fourth literary values. The failure of Great Leap economic and social programs provided many of Ch'ü's former Shanghai colleagues with an opportunity to regain control of the organizational machinery of the cultural movement. Consequently, in the early 1960s there was, once again, a turn away from popular cultural activities ushering in a period of "Thermidorian reaction" to Great Leap radicalism and utopianism. Mao Tun, Kuo Mo-jo, Hsia Yen, T'ien Han, Yang Han-sheng, and others active in leftist literary circles in the 1930s triumphantly returned to power in the early 1960s.

Perhaps the most spectacular episode in the cyclical drama was the Great Proletarian Cultural Revolution of the mid-1960s. This is not the place to review the details of the Cultural Revolution, the sometimes brutal manner in which it was carried out, and its impact on the arts; but it is quite clear that the major literary issues were strikingly similar to those raised in the early 1930s. It is remarkable that despite the accomplishments and stability of the People's Republic, none of the basic contradictions that had haunted the leftist literary movement throughout its history had been resolved by the time the Cultural Revolution erupted. Referring to the failures of the literary leadership in 1964, Mao repeated old, familiar charges: "They have acted as high and mighty bureaucrats, have not gone to the workers, peasants and soldiers and have not reflected the socialist revolution and socialist construction."[54]

Ch'ü probably would not have approved of the manner in which the Cultural Revolution was waged in the literary world. But there is a striking resemblance between Ch'ü's recommendations for introducing a popular literary movement and the policies promoted by advocates of popular art during the Cultural Revolution. On one hand, literary intellectuals were criticized for "worshiping the bourgeois culture" of the West and neglecting the cultural needs of the semi-educated masses; and were instructed to "go among the people" for reeducation. On the other hand, enormous emphasis was placed on a massive popular artistic movement that stressed the performing and visual arts, traditional "national" forms, and widespread amateur participation. Professional artists whose thinking had been reformed

54. Mao Tse-tung, *Five Documents on Literature and Art* (Peking: Foreign Languages Press, 1967), p. 11.

were required to participate in frequent tours of the rural areas in order to facilitate the "decentralization" of the cultural movement and to train amateur cultural activists from among the peasants. The theme of self-reliance of the people was promoted in all fields. The language of the Cultural Revolution was not as utopian as that used in the Great Leap Forward, but the goal of bridging the gap between mental and manual labor by breaking down the division of labor was a major underlying theme of the cultural program. In 1966, for example, it was proclaimed: "In the Great Proletarian Cultural Revolution the only method is for the masses to liberate themselves, and any method of doing things on their behalf must not be used."[55] Cultural leaders of the May Fourth generation were simply removed from positions of authority.

It is also significant that throughout most of the postrevolutionary period "romanticism" and "realism" have remained important—although by no means exhaustive—conceptual categories. For essentially nationalist reasons the Soviet concept of "socialist realism" was abandoned by the Chinese in the mid-1950s. Shortly thereafter, cultural leaders began to assert that the object of Chinese art was to combine "revolutionary realism and revolutionary romanticism." It is likely that, in theory, this formulation represented an attempt to work out the sort of ideological compromise Ch'ü Ch'iu-pai had in mind in the 1930s. On the questions of the relationship between art and society and the role of the writer, the deterministic and idealist extremes were to be rejected and replaced by a conception that balanced a respect for the role of objective forces in the evolution of society with a respect for the role played by subjective factors such as human will and determination. In fact, however, the "revolutionary realism and revolutionary romanticism" formula never really succeeded in creating a balance. Generalization may be risky. However, the romantic or voluntaristic view of the relationship between culture and society (and between superstructure and base) seems to have prevailed in periods—such as the Great Leap and the Cultural Revolution—when stress was put on popular cultural programs. Similarly, during periods when the May Fourth literary establishment was firmly in charge, less emphasis was placed on the vanguard function of cultural revolution and more emphasis was given to art as reflecting the economic foundation. One is also tempted to conclude that there has been a relationship between the type of policy pursued and the aesthetic merits of art. During periods when the materialist conception of art was emphasized, party and state control of artistic life was reduced (though by no means eliminated), cultural life was depoliticized some-

55. Quoted in *China Quarterly*, October-December 1966, p. 160.

what, and artistic standards were relatively high. But at times when cultural revolution was being stressed, the artistic realm became more important politically, party and state control was expanded, and artistic quality declined, partly as a result of increased mass participation.

As much as the promethean element may have dominated the cultural scene in the late 1960s, even the Cultural Revolution was not successful in resolving the major tensions and conflicts that have characterized the revolutionary literary movement since the New Culture Movement was launched in 1915. Events of the late 1970s indicate that the remarkably resilient May Fourth generation was able once again to rally and launch a broadly successful counteroffensive against the Cultural Revolution policies. The tensions between the professional and the amateur, between city and countryside, between raising cultural standards and popularizing art, and between nationalism and cosmopolitanism persist in China, just as they do in other parts of what has come to be known as the "Third World."

In March 1980 the Chinese Communist Party officially announced that the charges leveled against Ch'ü during the Cultural Revolution were without foundation and constituted an irresponsible defamation of character. Ch'ü was, after all, an "outstanding" theoretician and man of letters.[56] Nevertheless, articles that detail the circumstances surrounding Ch'ü's "rehabilitation" (*p'ing-fan*) give very little indication of how his complex literary views are likely to be regarded in the future. Marxist writers in China will continue to discuss the relationship between economic base and superstructure, the moral and political responsibilities of the writer, the manner in which foreign and Chinese artistic traditions should be regarded, the impact of capitalism on artistic culture, and the prerequisites for the cultural and aesthetic liberation of humankind. The conclusions they reach on these issues will depend, in large part, upon their interpretation of Marxist theory. Those who stress the deterministic and mechanistic theories of Plekhanov will be inclined to view Ch'ü Ch'iu-pai as a figure who departed from Marxism in a variety of fundamental ways. Those who point to the ambiguities present in the writings of Marx himself, and emphasize the nondeterministic and activist elements, will look upon Ch'ü as a Marxist who sought to develop themes already present in the works of Marx, Engels, Lunacharsky, and the Russian proletarian cultural thinkers. Others will see that Ch'ü was at once a product and a critic of the May Fourth intellectual revolution. He used Marxist conceptual categories to analyze the modern literary movement; but, more important, he did not hesitate to redefine the Marxist vocabulary to suit a distinctively non-European historical en-

56. *Ming pao* (Hong Kong), 7 March 1980; *Beijing Review*, 16 (21 April 1980): 6.

vironment. Ch'ü was a Marxist, but one cannot resist the temptation to suggest that his interpretation of Western Marxist literary thought and his radical critique of the May Fourth generation were inspired, perhaps more than he would have been willing to admit, by the exciting utopian socialist or Tolstoyan beliefs he held as a youthful May Fourth literary activist in Peking.

Bibliographical Note

Like other intellectual biographers, my research began with questions about precisely what works Ch'ü Ch'iu-pai had written and where they could be found. I also needed to know what those scholars and commentators who came before me had to say about these writings. In both cases my task was made considerably easier by the efforts of dedicated Shanghai-based scholars who compiled two extraordinarily useful bibliographies on the life and works of Ch'ü Ch'iu-pai. The most important of these is *Ch'ü Ch'iu-pai chu i hsi-nien mu-lu* (Shanghai: Jen-min ch'u-pan-she, 1959), compiled by Ting Ching-t'ang and Wen Ts'ao. Aside from listing in chronological order the titles and publication details of well over five hundred works written by Ch'ü in the period from 1919 to 1934, it mentions dozens of handy, book-length anthologies of these writings, and lists over fifty pseudonyms used by Ch'ü, which is very helpful to scholars who want to locate the original text of articles published by Ch'ü in relatively obscure or short-lived journals. A second indispensable book, *Hsueh-hsi Lu Hsün he Ch'ü Ch'iu-pai tso-p'in te cha-chi* (Shanghai: Shanghai wen-i ch'u-pan-she, 1961), also compiled by the tireless Ting Ching-t'ang, provides a chronological listing and full publication details on over two hundred articles about Ch'ü and his life written by literary figures in China in the period from 1931 to 1959. Both works contain a few errors and some insignificant omissions—except, of course, Ting and Wen's failure to list Ch'ü's "To-yü te hua," an omission that cannot be considered insignificant.

The existence of two major anthologies of Ch'ü's writings, a four-volume collection entitled *Ch'ü Ch'iu-pai wen-chi* (Peking: Jen-min wen-hsueh ch'u-pan-she, 1953-54) [abbreviated as CCPWC] and a two-volume collection entitled *Hai-shang shu-lin* (Hong Kong: San-lien shu-tien, 1950) [abbreviated as HSSL], saved me the trouble of tracking down the original text of many of his works. These anthologies stress Ch'ü's cultural writings, including critical essays, theoretical works, original fiction and poetry, *tsa-wen* essays, and literary translations. By no means does the *Ch'ü Ch'iu-pai wen-chi* contain all of Ch'ü's literary writings, but it has most of the important ones and a high percentage of the total. Most important, it includes a number of extremely valuable, but previously unpublished, manuscripts completed by Ch'ü in the 1930s. From time to time, colleagues ask me about the reliability and authenticity of texts contained in *Ch'ü Ch'iu-pai wen-chi*. To date I have failed to detect a case in which the text of a work in the Peking edition departs from the original. It must be noted, however, that a number of important works, including some that are critical of literary figures who later held powerful political positions in China after the formation of the People's Republic in 1949, were simply not included in *Ch'ü Ch'iu-pai wen-chi*. Some unofficial anthologies, such as *Luan t'an* (Shanghai: Hsia she, 1949), that were meant for distribution in Hong Kong, do not always remain faithful to the original text and must, therefore, be used with great care.

The secondary scholarly literature on Ch'ü Ch'iu-pai is both deep and diverse. The most significant book-length studies by Chinese Marxist scholars are Shang-kuan Ai-ming, *Ch'ü Ch'iu-pai yü wen-hsueh* (Nan-ching: Chiang-su wen-i ch'u-pan-she, 1959), Ting Ching-t'ang, *Hsueh-hsi Lu Hsün he Ch'ü Ch'iu-pai tso-p'in te cha-chi* (mentioned above), and Ts'ao Tzu-hsi, *Ch'ü Ch'iu-pai te wen-hsueh huo-tung* (Shanghai: Hsin wen-i ch'u-pan-she, 1958), all by scholars based in Ch'ü's home province of Kiangsu. Not surprisingly, Ting Ching-t'ang's work is the most thorough and original; but ironically, each of these books fails to grasp the radical implications of Ch'ü's literary thought. The tendency of these writers is to distinguish between "heterodox" and "orthodox" traditions of Western Marxist literary thought and then identify Ch'ü with the "orthodox" tradition of Marx, Engels, and Lenin. Unable to divorce itself from present-day ideological imperatives, this approach misrepresents Western Marxist literary thought and obscures Ch'ü's most creative departures from "orthodoxy."

Eastern European scholarship on Ch'ü goes in different directions. Prior to the appearance of my own study, the only book-length publication on Ch'ü done in the West was by the Soviet scholar Mark Shneider. Aside from suffering from some of the same problems that plague Chinese Marxist studies, Shneider's *Tvorcheskii Put' Tsiui Tsiu-bo, 1899-1935* (Moscow: Izdatel'stvo Nauka, 1964) tends, quite naturally, to exaggerate Ch'ü's indebtedness to Soviet literary theory. Ch'ü is important, in Shneider's estimation, because he had the good sense, in contrast to other unnamed figures, to carry the Soviet torch into China. Thus Ch'ü appears more as a faithful disciple than as an independent critic. Needless to say, Ch'ü's bitter encounter with the Comintern is not discussed in this book. The work of the noted Czech scholar Marián Gálik is highly sophisticated and always stimulating. Gálik, a product of Jaroslav Průšek's Prague school of Chinese studies, has no ideological ax to grind. His short essay entitled "Studies in Modern Chinese Intellectual History: II. Young Ch'ü Ch'iu-pai (1915-1922)," *Asian and African Studies*, 12 (1976): 85-121, which discusses the manner in which Ch'ü used Buddhist vocabulary to interpret Marxist theory and the Russian revolution in the early 1920s, has profoundly influenced my own thinking on the immediate post-May Fourth period of Ch'ü's intellectual development.

Apart from the present study and several of my articles, such as "Lu Xun Through the Eyes of Qu Qiu-bai," *Modern China*, 2,3 (July 1976): 327-368, that treat topics peripheral to the book, American scholars have produced a number of articles on specific aspects of Ch'ü's life and thought. Ellen Widmer's nicely written "Qu Qiubai and Russian Literature," which is contained in Merle Goldman, ed., *Modern Chinese Literature in the May Fourth Era* (Cambridge: Harvard University Press, 1977), pp. 103-125, argues that Ch'ü's May Fourth interest in nineteenth-century Russian literature underwent surprisingly little transformation following his acceptance of proletarian literary theories. T.A. Hsia's provocative essay "Ch'ü Ch'iu-po: The Making and Destruction of a Tenderhearted Communist," in his book *The Gate of Darkness* (Seattle: University of Washington Press, 1968), pp. 3-54, makes fascinating use of psychoanalytical techniques to account for a variety of emotional and intellectual dilemmas that he feels inevitably confront cultured intellectuals who embrace Marxism. Although Hsia was a literary historian, his article does not discuss Ch'ü's literary thought. Instead it examines his May Fourth autobiographical works and his final autobiographical essay written days before his execution, and concludes that Ch'ü was not really the communist type. In certain respects Hsia, an influential literary figure in Taiwan, developed a theme that was already present in a book by the Hong Kong writer Ssu-ma Lu entitled *Ch'ü Ch'iu-pai chuan* (Hong Kong: Tzu-lien ch'u-pan-she, 1962). Another extremely useful study, though it does not deal with Ch'ü's literary life, is Bernadette Yu-ning Li's Ph.D. dissertation, "A Biography of Ch'ü Ch'iu-pai: From Youth to Party Leadership (1899-1928)," Columbia University, New York, 1967. This thoroughly researched dissertation includes many important details concerning Ch'ü's early years, but focuses on his political activities in the 1923-1928 period. But as a study of politics, Li's work does not, in my opinion, improve upon Benjamin Schwartz's classic work *Chinese Communism and the Rise of Mao* (New York: Harper Torchbooks, 1967).

Other important and surprisingly useful secondary sources include the many memoirs written by those who knew Ch'ü Ch'iu-pai. Written for the most part more than twenty years after Ch'ü's execution, most works of this genre have rather little to say about Ch'ü's intellectual development, but tell us a great deal about his personality and provide fascinating biographical tidbits. Ch'ü's wife, Yang Chih-hua, wrote an exceedingly interesting memoir entitled "I Ch'iu-pai," which was published in *Hung-ch'i p'iao-p'iao*, 8:24-56, as part of a famous multivolume collection of reminiscences written by old revolutionaries. Lu Hsün's wife, Hsu Kuang-p'ing, included an intriguing chapter on the friendship between Ch'ü and Lu Hsün in her book *Lu Hsün hui-i lu* (Peking: Tso-chia ch'u-pan-she, 1961). The noted writer Ts'ao Ching-hua, one of Ch'ü's former students, included an emotional account of his relationship with Ch'ü in his book *Hua* (Peking: Tso-chia ch'u-pan-she, 1962). Much of what is known about Ch'ü's activities in Kiangsi is based upon the memoirs of people like Chao P'in-san, who wrote "Kuan-yü chung-yang ko-ming ken-chü-ti hua-chü kung-tso te hui-i," which is contained in *Chung-kuo hsien-tai wen-hsueh shih ts'an-k'ao tzu-liao*, 1:577-590, a well-known documentary collection that will be discussed below. Ch'ü's May Fourth activities are discussed by his famous friend Cheng Chen-to in "Ch'ü Ch'iu-pai t'ung-chih tsao-nien erh-san shih," *Hsin kuan-ch'a*, 12 (June 16, 1955): 26-28. Another interesting general memoir is Wen Chi-che's "Ch'ü Ch'iu-pai t'ung-chih chan-tou te i-sheng," *Hung-ch'i p'iao-p'iao* 5:79-107. Other, less useful essays by noted figures such as Mao Tun and Hsia Yen are listed in the bibliography contained in Ting Ching-t'ang's book *Hsueh-hsi Lu Hsün he Ch'ü Ch'iu-pai tso-p'in te cha-chi* mentioned above.

To understand the significance of Ch'ü Ch'iu-pai's literary thought, and especially his critique of "Europeanization" and the May Fourth generation of leftist writers, it is also necessary to familiarize oneself with the history of the modern literary movement in China, particularly the twenty-year period from 1915 to 1935. A number of important studies have been published in China. Three of my personal favorites are Fu-tan ta-hsueh Chung-wen hsi, ed., *Chung-kuo hsien-tai wen-hsueh shih* (Shanghai: Shanghai wen-i ch'u-pan-she, 1959?), Liu Shou-sung's two-volume work *Chung-kuo hsin wen-hsueh shih ch'u-kao* (Peking: Tso-chia ch'u-pan-she, 1957), and Wang Yao's well-known two-volume study *Chung-kuo hsin wen-hsueh shih-kao* (Shanghai: Hsin wen-i ch'u-pan-she, 1953). Each of these works is better than Ting I's *Chung-kuo hsien-tai wen-hsueh shih-lueh* (Peking: Tso-chia ch'u-pan-she, 1955); but they tend, nevertheless, to stress the unity of the May Fourth generation in the face of its political enemies, while minimizing or neglecting the significance of intellectual conflicts that divided the leftist literary world itself.

There are a number of useful Western studies of China's modern literary movement, but four deserve special mention. Bonnie McDougall's thorough study *The Introduction of Western Literary Theories Into Modern China, 1919-1925* (Tokyo: The Centre for East Asian Cultural Studies, 1971) is the best survey of the impact of Western literary thought in China, even though it has rather little to say about early Chinese interest in Marxist literary ideas. Leo Ou-fan Lee's outstanding book *The Romantic Generation of Modern Chinese Writers* (Cambridge: Harvard University Press, 1973) brilliantly analyzes the impact of Western romantic thought on a number of important non-Marxist and Marxist cultural figures. Marián Gálik's stimulating book *Mao Tun and Modern Chinese Literary Criticism* (Wiesbaden: Franz Steiner Verlag Gmblt, 1969) is a good introduction to the influence of Western realist and materialist literary thought. The most significant recent study is Merle Goldman's *Modern Chinese Literature in the May Fourth Era* mentioned above. It is a collection of outstanding essays by young scholars such as Perry Link and John Berninghausen who are playing a leading role in developing the exciting literature-and-society field.

Of course, it is also necessary to get beyond the various secondary studies by analyzing the critical and theoretical texts written by Ch'ü Ch'iu-pai's contemporaries. Two of the best collections of literary texts are Chang Ching-lu's four-volume *Chung-kuo hsien-tai ch'u-pan shih-liao* (Peking: Chung-hua shu-chu, 1954-1957) and the indispensable *Chung-kuo hsien-tai wen-hsueh shih ts'an-k'ao tzu-liao* (Peking: Kao-teng chiao-yü ch'u-pan-she, 1959-1960), a three-volume collection [abbreviated as TKTL]. There are also a number of specialized anthologies that treat specific literary debates. For example Li Ho-lin's well-known volume *Chung-kuo wen-i lun-chan* (Peking: Hua-hsia ch'u-pan-she, 1930) covers the 1928 debate on the nature of revolutionary literature very well; Ting I's *Ta-chung wen-i lun-chi* (Peking: Pei-ching shih-fan ta-hsueh ch'u-pan-she, 1955) contains most of the essential documents related to the 1930 debate on popular literature and art.

The other important context for understanding Ch'ü's literary thought and the debates held in leftist literary circles in China is Western Marxist literary thought itself. The best place to begin any study of this intellectual tradition is Lee Baxandall, ed., *Marxism and Aesthetics: A Selective Annotated Bibliography* (New York: Humanities Press, 1968). This is an excellent list of Marxist theoretical and critical essays on art and literature available in English. Baxandall's bibliography should be used together with Donald Egbert's massive *Social Radicalism and the Arts* (New York: Alfred A. Knopf, 1970), a stimulating general study of art and radical social change in the West between the French Revolution and the late 1960s. For those who want to know precisely what Marxist texts on literature and society were available in China in the 1920s and 1930s, Mark Shneider's article "Perevody Trudovpo

Markistskoy Estetike v Kitaye v 20-30ye Gody," *Norody Azii i Afriki*, 5 (May 1961): 188-193, is essential. The work of the nineteenth-century Russian populists can be found in a number of handy editions: V.G. Belinsky, *Selected Philosophical Works* (Moscow: Foreign Languages Publishing House, 1948); N.G. Chernyshevsky, *Selected Philosophical Essays* (Moscow: Foreign Languages Publishing House, 1953); Alexander Herzen, *Selected Philosophical Works* (Moscow: Foreign Languages Publishing House, 1956); and Ralph E. Matlaw, ed., *Belinsky, Chernyshevsky, and Dobrolyubov: Selected Criticism* (New York: E.P. Dutton and Co., 1962). There are many editions of Marxist works, but the most useful and reliable are Lee Baxandall and Stefan Morawski, eds., *Marx and Engels on Literature and Art: A Selection of Writings* (St. Louis: Telos Press, 1973); V.I. Lenin, *On Literature and Art* (Moscow: Progress Publishers, 1970); Leon Trotsky, *Literature and Revolution* (Ann Arbor: University of Michigan Press, 1966); Anatoly Lunacharsky, *On Literature and Art* (Moscow: Progress Publishers, 1973); and two editions of Georg Plekhanov's works, *Unaddressed Letters and Art and Social Life* (Moscow: Foreign Languages Publishing House, 1957), and *Art and Social Life* (London: Lawrence and Wishart Ltd., 1953). There are, of course, many fine studies of Western and Soviet Marxist literary thought. Here I will mention only the two books that most influenced my thinking. Peter Demetz's impressive study *Marx, Engels, and the Poets: Origins of Marxist Literary Criticism* (Chicago: University of Chicago Press, 1967) is essential reading, even though the author tends to minimize the importance of the tension between the deterministic and idealist traditions in Western Marxist literary thought, preferring instead to emphasize the deterministic element. Herman Ermolaev's *Soviet Literary Theory: 1917-1934* (Berkeley: University of California Press, 1963), is a relatively unknown but brilliant study of Soviet literary life in the period prior to the complete Stalinization of the artistic realm.

Index